Global Financial Turmoil and Reform:

A United Nations Perspective

EDITED BY A TEAM FROM THE UNITED NATIONS DEPARTMENT OF ECONOMIC AND SOCIAL AFFAIRS

BARRY HERMAN
Supervising Editor

United Nations

United Nations University Press

TOKYO • NEW YORK • PARIS

The views expressed in this publication are those of the authors and do not necessarily reflect the views of the United Nations University.

United Nations University Press
The United Nations University, 53-70, Jingumae 5-chome
Shibuya-ku, Tokyo, 150-8925, Japan
Tel: +81-3-3499-2811 Fax: +81-3-3406-7345
E-mail: sales@hq.unu.edu
http://www.unu.edu

United Nations University Office in North America
2 United Nations Plaza, Room DC2-1462-70, New York, NY 10017, USA
Tel: +1-212-963-6387 Fax: +1-212-371-9454
E-mail: unuona@igc.apc.org

United Nations University Press is the publishing division of the United Nations University.

Cover design by Joyce C. Weston

Printed in the United States of America

UNUP-1032

Library of Congress Cataloging-in-Publication Data

Global financial turmoil and reform : a United Nations perspective / edited by a team from the United Nations Department of Economic and Social Affairs ; Barry Herman, supervising editor.

p. cm.

Includes bibliographical references and index.

ISBN 9280810324 (pbk.)

1. International finance. 2. Financial crises—East Asia.
3. Developing countries—Economic conditions.
4. Economic history—1990-

I. Herman, Barry. II. United Nations. Dept. of Economic and Social Affairs.

HG3881.G57535 1999

332'.042—dc21 99-6223

CIP

CONTENTS

CONTENTS

CONTENTS

FOREWORD

Dear Reader,

The Asian financial and economic crisis which broke out in July 1997 with the collapse of the Thai currency triggered an intense debate within the international community. This dialogue has focused primarily on ways and means to strengthen the capacity of developing and transition economies to cope with international financial volatility and, more generally, on the institutional mechanisms which might help reduce the risks posed by the globalization of financial markets. It is still unfolding within the United Nations.

Against this background, the Secretary-General submitted last year a number of proposals and recommendations to the General Assembly which grew out of an expert group meeting held in New York in July 1998 under the auspices of the UN Secretariat on the broad economic and political implications of the Asian crisis. The present volume fully documents this process of policy reflection, analysis and prescription. It is the second in a series which seeks to bring to a wider audience timely expert information and policy insights on critical global issues of concern to the United Nations. As such, it augments and supplements its companion volume which the UNU Press published last year under the title of *International Finance and Developing Countries in a Year of Crisis.*

It is my hope that in publishing this book, the United Nations University will help nurture the necessary dialogue that must underpin our current search for cooperative responses to global problems and concerns.

Hans van Ginkel
Rector
The United Nations University

PREFACE

On behalf of the chief United Nations officials in the economic, social and related fields, I had occasion in October 1998 to express to the Interim and Development Committees of the Bretton Woods institutions our grave concern regarding the global economic and financial situation and the damage it was doing to economic and social development. From the offices that we head in Asia, Latin America, Africa and the Middle East, as well as in our headquarters in Geneva and New York, we saw fear substituting for hope in one country after another. We wished to bring to the international discussion of financial reform the sense of urgency that we ourselves felt from witnessing the tragedies in country after country and from observing the distress and frustration that heads of State and senior government officials brought to the meeting halls of the United Nations. The present publication, which grew out of our joint consideration of the crisis at an expert group meeting in July 1998, is offered as a further contribution to that discussion.

This publication is part of a larger, ongoing effort of the United Nations to address the economic and social dimensions of the global financial turmoil. That effort includes studies of the situation in the annual *World Economic and Social Survey*, which is prepared by the Department of Economic and Social Affairs of the United Nations Secretariat, and the *Trade and Development Report*, which is prepared by the United Nations Conference on Trade and Development, as well as in publications of the regional commissions, and studies by the United Nations University, in particular at the World Institute for Development Economics Research (WIDER).

The aforementioned effort also embraces intergovernmental discussions in the General Assembly and its subsidiary bodies. In 1999, these discussions begin a new phase, as the Assembly has established an ad hoc open-ended working group that is charged with recommending the "form, scope and agenda of an appropriate high-level international intergovernmental forum on financing for development", to be convened by the year 2001. I hope this volume will contribute to the discussions on financing for development.

Nitin Desai
Under-Secretary-General
for Economic and Social Affairs

Part One

Overview

Edited by

Barry Herman

1

Introduction

Barry Herman*
United Nations Department of Economic and Social Affairs

Soon after the Thai baht collapsed at the beginning of July 1997, Barbara Stallings in Santiago, Chile, at the Economic Commission for Latin America and the Caribbean (ECLAC), contacted Azizul Islam in Bangkok, Thailand, at the Economic and Social Commission for Asia and the Pacific (ESCAP), and myself at United Nations Headquarters in New York in the Department of Economic and Social Affairs (DESA). Something important had begun to happen, she believed, and in response to queries from national officials in her region, she was seeking information on the evolving situation. These contacts continued as the crisis deepened in Asia and spread to other regions. There seemed to be much that UN staff in the various regional offices could learn from each other. As a result, one year later, on 21-23 July 1998, DESA held an expert group meeting in New York in cooperation with the regional commissions to try to deepen our joint understanding of a situation that was increasingly taking on the dimensions of a global crisis.

That meeting provided the occasion for an intensive exchange of views among United Nations economists and guests who were invited from other international organizations, the private sector and academia. The exchange helped the Secretariat prepare a report for the General Assembly on the policy

* Chief, International Economic Relations Branch. The views expressed herein are those of the author and not necessarily the views of the United Nations.

lessons of the financial crisis in emerging market economies, as seen in early September 1998 (see chap. 3). It also led to preparation of the present volume, which contains revised and updated versions of papers presented at the July meeting and comments of the discussants. To set the stage for these discussions, Barbara Stallings and I prepared an overview essay that seeks to take stock as at the beginning of 1999 of the financial reforms that have been set in motion by the crisis and suggest, in our personal capacity, some further reforms that might be considered by the international community (see chap. 2).

Keynote panel of senior officials

The meeting began with a keynote panel discussion by the Executive Secretaries in charge of each of the regional commissions, chaired by Mr. Nitin Desai, Under-Secretary-General for Economic and Social Affairs. The aim was to offer overall assessments, raise questions and set the tone for the ensuing meetings of staff experts.

Mr. Adrianus Mooy, Executive Secretary of ESCAP, began by underlining how the severity of the crisis in East Asia surprised all, how a currency crisis became a financial crisis, which turned into an economic and social crisis, and in some countries a political crisis. The crisis had roots, in his view, in the productive sectors of the affected countries, as well as in the more discussed institutional weaknesses in finance, governance and macroeconomic policy. He therefore drew implications for industrial sector policy, as well as lessons about sound macroeconomic management, strengthening the financial sector and developing an effective social safety net. He stressed that it was necessary to raise overall competitiveness and productivity in the crisis countries. The increased competition in manufacturing from relatively poorer countries required the crisis countries to accelerate the transition, however difficult, into relatively more sophisticated production capacities.

Mr. José Antonio Ocampo, Executive Secretary of ECLAC, saw the impact of the Asian crisis in his region mainly in terms of a much greater volatility in the availability of credit, the greater risk premia charged on foreign borrowing , and in adverse trade effects, especially collapsing international commodity prices (although not due exclusively to the Asian crisis). He also saw a contractionary bias in the macroeconomic policy responses in the region. The latter was reflected in steps policy makers took both to maintain confidence of international financial markets and to continue the strong and successful anti-inflationary thrust of policy, through maintaining the value of their nominal exchange rates. The main lesson is that policy makers have very little room to manoeuvre once a crisis starts and thus the best strategy is to reduce the probability of crisis by better managing boom periods of high capital inflows, including the restriction of short-term capital movements. At the same time, he emphasized that developing countries cannot do it all on their own and that better international oversight of financial markets and flows, on the one hand, and a stronger International Monetary Fund (IMF), on the other hand, are also essential.

Mr. Yves Berthelot, Executive Secretary of the Economic Commission for Europe, focused on the economies in transition from central planning to market systems. These are a very diverse group of countries, including some that will need to reach fully liberalized capital accounts in a matter of years, as part of their goal of joining the European Union. Mr. Berthelot emphasized the role of credibility in policy at both the national and international levels. He characterized the credibility that a government or international institution has with the financial markets as a function of its past record, pointing to the case of Hungary, where Government commitment to a comprehensive adjustment programme in 1996 was credible because of Hungary's policy history. He also suggested that credibility could be built over time by setting medium-term goals for a set of indicators (for example, the current-account deficit as a percentage of gross domestic output, or the ratio of official reserves to domestic money or credit), monitoring them, and using macroeconomic policy to maintain the indicators within pre-established zones. As an example of the obverse, he expressed concern about the risks that IMF took with its credibility in the July adjustment and financing package for the Russian Federation. He feared that were IMF to come to make loans for political reasons, it could undermine the credibility of the institution in other circumstances. Financial markets look to IMF as a guarantor of the credibility of emerging-market economies.

Mr. Hazem El-Beblawi, Executive Secretary of the Economic and Social Commission for Western Asia, spoke mainly as an observer of the international situation, since the crisis had not impacted his region very heavily, except for the contribution of the fall in Asian demand to the weakening of oil prices and some significant losses on portfolio investments of West Asian investors. The most striking aspect of the crisis, in his view, was the widely shared surprise at how events unfolded in 1997 and 1998. This suggested an unexpected degree of ignorance on the part of analysts of how economic and financial forces work today. He wondered whether IMF, as a key lending agency with an important assistance function in crisis situations, might have difficulty in standing back sufficiently from daily engagement to be able to see the underlying picture adequately. He suggested that precisely because the United Nations is not a financial institution, it might be able to contribute in this regard to international analysis and overall monitoring and perhaps as a result better alert the public when difficulties begin to emerge.

Finally, Mr. K.Y. Amoako, Executive Secretary of the Economic Commission for Africa, saw important lessons for Africa from the Asian crisis. While the commodity price effect has had an impact in many countries, South Africa also directly experienced the financial contagion. It was especially noteworthy since macroeconomic management in South Africa could hardly be faulted, the banking system is regarded as quite sound, and the central bank is one of the most independent in the world. And yet the financial markets lost confidence in the rand in mid-1998. He believed the reason lay in the deep social difficulties—such as very high unemployment—embodied in South Africa's transition from *apartheid* and the limitations this places on the actions of the monetary authorities.

For the rest of Africa, Mr. Amoako concluded that the limited impact of the Asian crisis reflected the lack of integration into the global system. He saw the need to hasten that integration, but indicated that it is important to learn from the Asian mistakes and integrate through an appropriate sequence of actions. Considerable progress has already been made in many African countries in macroeconomic stabilization and economic growth is increasing. However, it is indicative of the distance still to be travelled that wealthy Africans keep some 30 per cent of their resources abroad, a much higher percentage than in other developing country regions. Developing a robust, transparent and appropriately supervised domestic financial sector is paramount if this is to change. Development and strengthening of the domestic financial sector is thus a particularly urgent priority.

Drawing overall conclusions from these statements and from the points raised during the subsequent floor discussion, Mr. Desai emphasized three points. The first was to recall that the official governance structures for international monetary and financial relations were designed after the end of the Second World War and were based on a set of experiences and theoretical understandings that developed during the Great Depression. It is now half a century later and the world of international money and finance has changed dramatically; however, our understanding of how it works has not kept pace with the changes. This led to his second major point: there would be no return to the *status quo ante*. We are entering a period of deep thinking about reform of international systems and development of new theories of international economic relationships. For example, while we have thought of balance-of-payments adjustment for 50 years in terms of the current account, we now must increasingly think of adjustment in terms of the capital account.[1]

Mr. Desai's third point was perhaps the most fundamental one from the perspective of the United Nations: we should be sure to remind ourselves, as we think about reform of the international monetary and financial system, that there are major political dimensions to economic adjustment and international policy reform. Echoing a point made by Mr. Ocampo, Mr. Desai stressed that financial crises impose losses on economies and these have to be allocated within the society in one way or another to one group of individuals or another and how this comes about reflects domestic power relations. Moreover, making matters more complicated, he suggested, power in international finance is more concentrated than it is in international trade. Some industries producing tradable goods or services might be highly concentrated globally, but others are highly competitive. In the financial sector, despite all the competition and innovation, a relatively small number of financial institutions and central banks still play a central role in mediating the bulk of the financial flows. A similar concentration of influence determines the principles for overseeing the system. This could be a source of difficulty. As in international affairs generally, it is important for international comity that all countries develop a sense of participation and ownership and perceive that they too can help shape international policy.

Implications for applied research

While most of the discussion in the expert group meeting concerned the urgent policy matters that are the focus of this book, Mr. Desai also stimulated thinking about methodological issues for the study of current international financial relations. There was substantial agreement among participants that both data collection and research on the rapidly changing international economy need to be rethought. Indeed, an informal discussion was scheduled following the formal meetings on implications of the exercise for research and analysis activities in the United Nations and elsewhere. The discussion was led by Professor Lance Taylor, Director of the Centre for Economic Policy Analysis at the New School for Social Research.

Among the various topics touched upon, one set of issues stood out as fundamental. The analysis of macroeconomic relations typically focuses on "flow variables", such as total income earned in an economy in a period, output produced, exports shipped and changes in prices of goods and services purchased.

1 The sizes of the current-account and capital-account balance are, of course, simultaneously determined, as one is equal to the other with its sign reversed. However, it matters a great deal whether current-account or capital-account activities are driving changes in the balance.

The problems brought to the surface by the Asian crisis, however, have much to do with "stock variables", such as the total amount of foreign debt owed by residents of a country, the portfolio of assets held at home and abroad, the balance sheets of companies and banks and so on. As the kinds of data that are collected by national statistical authorities reflect the analytical questions put by policy researchers, it is increasingly clear that a new analytical focus on stock variables will require a new emphasis on gathering data about stocks.

A good illustration, initially noted by Mr. Mooy in his comments in the senior officials' panel, was that the foreign debt of firms had been grossly underestimated early in the Indonesian crisis. The total foreign debt of enterprises had not figured prominently in thinking about national balance-of-payments problems in Indonesia or elsewhere; thus, inadequate data were collected on the net asset position of the enterprise sector or on its net foreign liquidity position (for example, amount of the debt falling due within one year).

In the past, developing country enterprises did not borrow abroad extensively other than for the financing of international trade, and most of that was mediated by and appeared on the books of the better-monitored banking sector. Indeed, enterprises in developing countries typically needed government approval to borrow abroad and access to foreign borrowing had been limited as part of policy controls on capital movements. The liberalization of international capital movements may have reduced the limitation on this type of borrowing in many countries, but it certainly did not reduce the need to monitor how much firms were borrowing.

Saying that it was important to monitor the net foreign asset position of firms, however, was not the same as being able to do it easily. In the case of international trade, data usually originate in customs declarations as goods cross international boundaries. In the case of international finance, not only was official clearance no longer required in many cases, eliminating the obvious point at which to collect data, but it has become possible for enterprises and banks to borrow in foreign currency using financial derivative contracts without any outright cross-border transfer of funds taking place.[2] Data collection would thus have to rely on direct reporting of financial positions by enterprises, which imposes a cost on them and tends to be less accurate.

Thus, one consequence of the global financial turmoil of recent years is a new set of research questions that range from how to model balance-of-payments and

2 For example, a firm that has local debt in one country can swap the repayment obligations with a firm or bank in another country that has debt of equal size but denominated in the currency of that country. The swap raises the foreign debt-servicing obligations of the first country as much as if the company had directly borrowed overseas.

exchange-rate movements when the driving forces are adjustments to enterprise stock variables, to questions of statistical methodology in collecting appropriate data. In short, there is a full agenda of work for international institutions and their academic partners.[3]

Organization of the meeting and acknowledgements

The participation of six senior United Nations officials in a substantive discussion to inaugurate an expert group meeting is quite unusual. It underlined how seriously the evolving international financial situation was being viewed by the United Nations Secretariat. This sentiment was echoed by national delegates to the United Nations, several of whom also participated in the meetings. In particular, each of the working sessions of the expert group meeting—reflected in the six following parts of this book—was chaired by a national representative at the United Nations.

First among them was the Chairman of the Second Committee (Economic and Financial Questions) of the Fifty-second Session of the General Assembly, Ambassador Oscar R. de Rojas of Venezuela, who chaired the session on Latin America. The two Vice Chairmen of the Committee also participated in the meeting. Mr. Adel Abdellatif, at the time Counsellor in the Permanent Mission of the Arab Republic of Egypt, chaired the session on Africa and Mr. Hans-Peter Glanzer, Counsellor in the Permanent Mission of Austria, chaired the session on foreign direct investment. The Rapporteur of the Second Committee, Mr. Rae-kwon Chung, Counsellor in the Permanent Mission of the Republic of Korea, chaired the session on financial markets. Two other active delegates to the Second Committee chaired the remaining sessions. Ms. Nandhini Iyer Krishna, Counsellor in the Permanent Mission of India, chaired the discussion of Asia and Mr. Sorin Mihail Tanasescu, First Secretary in the Permanent Mission of Romania, chaired the session on the economies in transition.

In addition to these individuals, the support and encouragement of other representatives at the United Nations are gratefully acknowledged, in particular that of Mr. Alfredo Sfeir-Younis, Special Representative of the World Bank to the United Nations, and Mr. Justin B. Zulu, IMF Special Representative to the United Nations. The assistance of Mr. Zulu must especially be noted. At a time when IMF has come in for criticism from many quarters, Mr. Zulu has consistently and frequently gone the extra mile on a personal

3 Indeed, some of the work is well under way in the international system; for example, the Inter-Agency Task Force on Finance Statistics, which is chaired by IMF, has recently focused on identifying gaps in data needed to analyse the external debt and liquidity positions of countries and how to close the gaps.

basis to promote informal, frank and very useful exchanges of views between the staffs of the UN Secretariat and IMF. He has been an important resource to the United Nations.

Just as the initial inspiration for the expert group meeting and for this book came from the regional commissions, so, too, the assistance of the New York Office of the Regional Commissions and its Chief, Ms. Sulafa al Bassam, was important in mobilizing the participation and self-financing of regional commission attendance, which made the experience a collective effort in more sense than one.

The support of the Development Policy Analysis Division of DESA and its Director, Mr. Ian Kinniburgh, is also warmly acknowledged. Readers will judge for themselves the results of the efforts of the DESA authors and editors whose work appears in this volume and of the support staff, but I can attest to the long hours over several months that many people devoted to this volume. Thanks to you all and a special thank you on behalf of myself and my co-editors to our chief copy editors, Béatrice Frankard-Little and Alice Villarama, and to Valerian Monteiro, who designed and typeset the book, as well as to Rose Arago, Remedios Catolico, Judith Goss, Diane Horton and Ramachandra Kurup.

Finally, I would like to express my sincerest appreciation to Mr. Manfred Boemeke, Director of the United Nations University Press in Tokyo, and to Mr. Jacques Fomerand, Director of the United Nations University Office in North America, for their interest in publishing this volume and bringing the results of the expert group meeting to a wider audience.

2

International Finance and the Developing Countries: Liberalization, Crisis and the Reform Agenda

BARRY HERMAN
United Nations Department of Economic and Social Affairs

and

BARBARA STALLINGS*
United Nations Economic Commission for Latin America and the Caribbean

The international crisis began in mid-1997 as a series of national financial crises in emerging market economies: first in Thailand, soon followed by Malaysia, Indonesia and the Philippines, and by the end of the year the Republic of Korea. In 1998, it deepened and spread to the extent that one could fairly say the world had entered a period of global financial turmoil. While the ensuing chapters of this book examine various dimensions of the crisis and its impact on developing and transition economies, this chapter seeks to provide a broad overview of the policy

---

* Chief, International Economic Relations Branch, DESA, and Director, Economic Development Division, ECLAC, respectively. The views expressed herein are those of the authors and not necessarily the views of the United Nations. Parts of an earlier version of this paper were presented at an expert group meeting organized by ECLAC in Santiago, Chile on 26 and 27 November 1998 and the policy conclusions herein were stimulated by discussions at that meeting. The authors would like to thank Ricardo Ffrench-Davis and Ian Kinniburgh for comments on earlier drafts of the paper.

reforms that preceded the crisis, followed it, and at the beginning of 1999 seemed to warrant further attention by the international community.

In fact, events in the third quarter of 1998 brought the world close to a global financial meltdown. The currency and financial crisis and the collapse of economic activity spread to the Russian Federation in August. Shortly thereafter, Latin America and Africa—in particular, Brazil and South Africa—were confronted by speculative attacks on their currencies, even though there had been no significant change in their domestic economic circumstances. Unemployment and poverty levels surged, especially in Asia but also in Latin America. Here was a human catastrophe, one that arose not from war or disease or the ravages of violent storms, but from the operation and governance of the global economic system.

Adding to the global turmoil, developed countries also experienced major economic problems. Japan was again in recession in 1998, while its banking system was in crisis and unable to supply the liquidity needed to get the economy moving again. Politically difficult decisions had to be taken to close insolvent banks and rescue the banks that could be salvaged, employing large-scale public assistance to do so. There was also a financial scare in the United States in September.The fragility of the US financial system was exposed when officials of the Federal Reserve Bank of New York organized an emergency infusion of funds and a take-over by some of its creditors of Long Term Capital Management (LTCM), a well-known hedge fund. No one wanted to discover how the financial markets, let alone several of the world's major financial institutions, would absorb the closure of LTCM.

After the collapse of the Russian rouble and the hedge-fund scare in New York, world financial markets went into a panic. During the course of a single day, the Japanese yen rose 15 per cent against the dollar, an unprecedented move in the exchange rate between the currencies of the two largest economies in the world. Stock markets plunged and the risk premiums for financial market lending to corporations jumped, reflecting investors' "flight to quality" (in particular, to cash and US Government bonds). A credit crunch seemed to be threatening the United States in addition to the one that already existed in Japan.

By November, however, the panic eased. Interest rates had been reduced in the world's major financial markets as part of a policy initiative of the Group of Seven major industrialized countries (G-7), which also committed itself to make quick progress on several pending international financial reform proposals. Nonetheless, analysts in the markets knew that improved market psychology aside, vulnerability to massive volatility lay just below the surface. Policy makers still had a lot of work to do.

Build-up to the crisis

The current crisis, with all its devastating implications for the development process, did not occur in a historical vacuum. To make sensible recommendations for policy improvement, it is essential to understand how we arrived at the present situation. Indeed, world history is full of financial crises, domestic and international, and it is well known that financial markets are extraordinarily volatile. One of the best-known analyses of economic history, Kindleberger's *Manias, Panics and Crashes* (1978), studies financial crises over time and presents a five-stage model that is still relevant today: exogenous shock, euphoria, financial distress, financial crisis and (in the absence of a lender of last resort) financial revulsion.

Partly as a result of the especially severe crisis in the 1930s, the post-Second World War years did not begin with an open financial system. Such openness as currently exists is the result of several decades of changes in the international capital markets and in the policies of industrialized and developing countries alike. In the 1950s and 1960s, most European currencies were not convertible and even the United States had controls on capital movements. It was the emergence of the unregulated Euromarkets in the 1960s that began the financial liberalization process that ultimately led to the current crisis. Initially, these new international markets were separated from domestic capital markets in the industrialized nations. Gradually, however, the wall began to fall as industrialized country Governments liberalized access and the major markets became integrated.

First was the dismantling of policy barriers to cross-border financial flows. This involved the elimination of taxes, exchange controls, and various types of restrictions on access to domestic markets. Second, as a result of the new access, banks began to set up branches or buy other banks in industrialized countries. Once branches were established, they increased lending. Third, many new financial instruments were developed, which also speeded up the growth of capital markets. In general, securities became more important at the expense of bank loans; bank loans were packaged into tradable securities and sold in the market; and futures and options gained popularity. Swaps were added in the 1980s. Pension funds and other traditional institutional investors increasingly sought to diversify their portfolios internationally and new mutual funds brought individual investors into the international market. Together with improvements in communication technology, these developments led to a very significant increase in the volume of finance crossing international borders.

The financial policies of developing countries lagged behind those of the industrialized nations. Although they were the recipients of large quantities of aid and direct investment in the 1950s and 1960s, and of loans from the Euromarkets in the 1970s, most still maintained non-convertible currencies and controls on capital outflows. For Latin American countries, the debt crisis of the 1980s temporarily suspended access to international capital, and the region made net transfers of financial resources abroad during the "lost decade". Partially as a consequence of that experience, Latin American Governments undertook a major change in economic policy as of the mid-1980s, moving quickly in the direction of economic liberalization.

A convenient, shorthand expression for this new economic model, which replaced the old government-dominated closed-economy stance of the post-war period, is the phrase "Washington Consensus", coined by British economist John Williamson (1990). Washington is in the name in part because it is the seat of the International Monetary Fund (IMF) and the World Bank, which negotiate with developing and transition economy Governments and financially support the reform programmes they adopt. But Washington is also in the name because of the policy leadership on adjustment issues that emanated from the United States in the 1980s, spearheaded by US President Ronald Reagan.[1]

The Washington Consensus was a list of ten reforms focused on macroeconomic stability, domestic financial liberalization, privatization and trade liberalization. Interestingly, it did not include international financial liberalization. Indeed, Williamson noted that he saw "relatively little support for the notion that liberalization of international capital flows is a priority objective for a country that should be a capital importer and ought to be retaining its own savings for domestic investment" (ibid., p. 19).

Accurately forecasting policy changes to come later, Stanley Fischer, then Chief Economist of the World Bank and currently First Deputy Managing Director of IMF, observed in his comment on Williamson's paper that he doubted "that Washington regards the freeing up of capital flows as less urgent than the freeing up of goods flows...[rather, he feared] that much of Washington does believe strongly that financial capital flows should not be constrained, but that it simply has not yet focused on the problem" (ibid., p. 26).

The policy debate was soon overtaken by events. By the early 1990s, a new surge of foreign capital was beginning to gather steam, partly because of low interest rates in some of the industrialized countries and partly because of policy changes in the developing world. The latter included the new economic model

1 Policy leadership was, of course, shared (indeed, initiated) by the British Government under Mrs. Thatcher.

in Latin America, some similar changes in the highly successful East Asian economies, and the political and economic transition in the former centrally planned economies in Central and Eastern Europe and the former Soviet Union. As a consequence, the international bond markets opened on a large scale to developing countries for the first time since the 1920s, and American and global depository receipts provided their companies with a means to float equity issues on industrialized countries' stock markets. In addition, stock markets in developing countries themselves took on new importance, as foreign-access restrictions were relaxed and foreign investors rushed to take advantage of attractive opportunities.

Capital account liberalization was already under way when IMF, in particular, sought to reinforce this policy change. In 1993, the Fund produced an important study on capital account liberalization (Mathieson and Rojas-Suárez, 1993). While broadly supportive of the liberalization of capital flows, the study highlighted various caveats about capital account liberalization in developing countries and identified several preconditions for establishing capital account convertibility (ibid., pp. 30-33). The following year, the Executive Board of IMF discussed capital account convertibility, revealing a split among the Executive Directors on the issue.

Then, in October 1994 in Madrid, IMF celebrated its fiftieth anniversary and the ministerial-level Interim Committee adopted a special Madrid Declaration. The second paragraph began by celebrating the planned entry into force of the Uruguay Round trade agreements and the trade liberalization it would further. It went on to welcome "the growing trend toward currency convertibility", and it encouraged "member countries to remove impediments to the free flow of capital" (IMF, 1994, p. 320).

The same day that the Interim Committee issued its Declaration, the Finance Ministers and Central Bank Governors of the Group of 10 countries (G-10) issued a communiqué that would prove prophetic. The G-10, sensitive to changes taking place in international financial markets, "...welcomed efforts to enhance awareness of the risks involved in the use of new or highly leveraged financial products [and] supported efforts to ensure that financial entities of all types have capital adequate for the full range of risks to which they are exposed" (ibid., p. 324). The concerns expressed in the communiqué, however, were not carried over to the Declaration.

The year ended with the eruption of the peso crisis in Mexico, followed in early 1995 with the US$50 billion bailout package, a contagion crisis in Argentina and a second bailout package. There was a growing awareness that the capital flows that had recently been surging into a number of developing countries were a mixed blessing, since those funds could exit even more quickly than they arrived. In response, IMF adopted measures to facilitate the rapid provision of large amounts of resources to combat future financial panics of the sort that Mexico and Argentina had experienced. It also sought to restore the confidence of the international financial markets in placing funds in emerging market economies, with such recommendations as the provision of more information to the financial public.

In addition, the Interim Committee updated its Madrid Declaration at its meeting in September 1996. In effect, it also updated the Washington Consensus. In a list of 11 propositions, the sixth was "Encouraging current account convertibility and careful progress toward increased freedom of capital movements through efforts to promote stability and financial soundness" (IMF, 1996, p. 327). The eleventh and last was "Ensuring the soundness of banking systems through strong, prudential regulation and supervision, improved co-ordination, better assessment of credit risk, stringent capital requirements, timely disclosure of banks' financial conditions, action to prevent money laundering, and improved management of banks" (ibid.). With hindsight, the former—at least the capital movements part—should have been made explicitly contingent on the latter.

The warnings that even the advocates of capital-account liberalization had made in the early 1990s were widely ignored in the quick, inappropriately sequenced liberalization policies pursued by the countries that are now in crisis. It appears they were forgotten in the giddy rush of investors to provide funds and of borrowers to tap them.

Investor confidence in the emerging markets reached new highs by 1996, especially in East Asia because of its history of sustained, rapid economic growth, but also in Latin America. The quick and effective policy response in Mexico and Argentina in 1995 convinced investors that a different breed of national policy maker was in control in Latin America, one that was committed to "sound" policy design. Indeed, the Latin American adjustments of the 1980s had paid off in low inflation, sharply curtailed fiscal deficits, and (following resolution of the debt crisis with the Brady Plan) a more sustainable foreign exchange situation. Also, the transition first of Central and Eastern Europe and then of the former Soviet Union towards market economies attracted investor interest, and the end of apartheid made South Africa again a legitimate destination for financial investors.

Today, the bursting of the bubble of financial exuberance has once again made the issue of financial volatility a high concern. The catastrophic experience of the past two years may keep investor fear of emerging markets salient for some time to come. In addition, the financial sectors of the industrialized economies have been exposed to more risk than they understood, and it is increasingly realized that the global financial system of the late 1990s also poses dangers for them. In response, the industrialized country Governments have proposed reforms to deal with the new risks.

The new programme of international reform

Less than a month after their regular 1998 fall meeting, the Finance Ministers and Central Bank Governors of the G-7 met again on 30 October and issued a major policy declaration on financial reform (Group of 7, 1998). At the same time, the Heads of State and Government of the G-7 issued a statement supporting the declaration and asking their Ministers and Central Bank Governors to "consult with other key countries, including emerging market economies" to work up detailed reform proposals to be agreed at the next G-7 summit in June 1999 (Group of 7, 1998a). The same day, the Executive Directors of the G-7 at IMF sent a joint memorandum to the Managing Director and the other members of the Executive Board to propose priorities "as we develop the work programme of the Executive Board to address these issues" (Group of 7, 1998b). The memo presented in more detail the IMF-related proposals of the Finance Ministers and Central Bank Governors.

All of the proposals had been voiced before with varying degrees of specificity and commitment. Several were working their way through the intergovernmental machinery of IMF. What was new was the G-7 "agreement on a number of follow-up steps...which [they] will be implementing as rapidly as possible". It was, in other words, a firm statement of purpose and resolve addressed to a nervous and uncertain global financial audience, one that had seen the G-7 performance at the IMF meetings in early October as less than decisive or united.

The sobering events in September and October in developed country financial markets had undoubtedly focused the attention of G-7 policy makers. The G-7 agreement was, in fact, one of several steps by these Governments to bolster the sagging confidence of the financial markets, including a sequence of interest rate reductions (albeit in small steps) in several developed countries, the passage of a more credible bank rescue plan in Japan, and US Congressional approval of the IMF funding request. In this context, urgent and serious international economic reform was also placed squarely on the table.

Policy for pending crises

A major part of the initiative was agreement on a set of measures to mobilize substantial foreign exchange resources so as to discourage and, if necessary, counter currency panics, such as was then threatening Brazil. A keystone of the proposal was to establish contingent short-term lines of credit in IMF for countries pursuing strong, IMF-approved policies (a proposal along these lines had been made several weeks earlier by the President of the United States). Although the funds to be drawn upon would come from the regular resources of IMF, use of the credit line would be more expensive than usual (the Executive Directors specified a 3 percentage point interest rate surcharge) and the drawings would have to be repaid rapidly (within 1 to 2½ years, compared with 5 years in standard drawings). The G-7 thus built into the proposal an incentive for an early return to private market financing (tough terms such as these had been requested by the US Congress in legislation adopted in October that endorsed US participation in the pending IMF quota increase).

The G-7 also called for "appropriate private sector involvement" in such operations, which seemed to mean that bank creditors would have to participate in concerted refinancing of short-term claims during currency crises. In this way, the special IMF loans would not serve merely to finance the withdrawal of the private bank creditors. Moreover, provision was made to complement use of the new facility with "bilateral contingent financing", determined by what individual Governments might wish to provide in any particular case.

Reform of the international financial system

Beyond crisis-management proposals, the G-7 promised to seek specific reforms of the international financial "architecture". They aimed, on the one hand, to reduce uncertainty about countries and financial markets through greater transparency and more complete and quicker provision of relevant information, with the intention to increase stable, long-term flows. On the other hand, they sought to shift more of the risk of lending to emerging market economies to the creditors, so as to discourage excessive and speculative flows. Argumentation and details for many of the proposals were already put forward in the October 1998 reports of the ad hoc Group of 22 and in work already under way in IMF, such as on codes of conduct in macroeconomic policy.[2] In addition, the G-7 addressed governance of

2 The "Group of 22" comprised the Finance Ministers and Central Bank Governors of 21 countries that had been invited to join with the United States in an ad hoc forum to explore the implications of the financial situation in Asia and how to respond. The Group met in February 1998 at the Willard Hotel in Washington (hence, also called the Willard Group) and again in April, when it established three working groups that reported to a final meeting in October (see Group of 22, 1998, 1998a, 1998b). For a description of work under way in IMF, see IMF (1998a).

IMF itself in terms that went beyond previous general statements, as had been made in the Interim Committee communiqué in early October.

Transparency would be fostered by adoption of codes of good practices for fiscal and monetary policy, principles of sound corporate governance and accounting, and new standards of disclosure and transparency of internationally active financial institutions in developed and developing countries. The G-7 also called upon IMF to monitor compliance and publish regular "transparency reports" on individual countries.

In addition, the G-7 called for establishing a process for international surveillance and peer review of national financial sectors and their regulatory and supervisory regimes. The process would involve national and international regulatory and supervisory expertise. The G-7 also agreed to "bring together the key international institutions and key national authorities involved in financial sector stability" to cooperate on policies to reduce systemic risk. More precisely, the G-7 Ministers committed themselves to focus on the risk exposure of their own financial institutions, including hedge funds, and to seek to involve offshore financial centres and other countries in new regulatory exercises they might undertake. These proposals appear to reflect the Canadian suggestion in April 1998 to establish a collaborative inter-agency secretariat of international supervisory agencies and bodies (Martin 1998), as well as the proposal of the United Kingdom in October to set up a "standing committee for global financial regulation", with IMF at the centre of the framework (Brown 1998).

In addressing the "moral hazard" problem—wherein foreign private creditors were said to assume that they would be bailed out and so took excessive risk in lending to emerging market economies—the G-7 appeared to accept the thrust of the 1996 recommendations of the Deputies of the Group of 10 to shift more of the risk of lending to the creditors (see Group of 10, 1996). Currently, in the event of an extreme situation warranting rescheduling of official debt, it is very difficult to include holders of government bonds in the exercise, owing to the contractual terms typical of such securities. Knowing this, government bondholders assume they face less risk of interrupted debt servicing than bank creditors of governments. However, unlike the situation in the 1980s, foreign debt is increasingly in the form of bonds. Thus the G-7 "called upon the private sector to facilitate [including] 'collective action clauses' for more orderly debt workouts" in bond contracts. This would put bondholders more on a par with bank creditors of governments in renegotiating debt servicing and make bonds a little less "risk-free". Finally, in this regard, the G-7 voiced approval of the recently reaffirmed IMF policy of "lending into arrears" (that is to say, lending to a Government in a currency crisis even if it did not yet have an accepted plan for a sovereign debt workout). This was aimed to pressure the creditors to come to an agreement with the debtor, implicitly accepting a bigger share of the losses than otherwise.

The G-7 also called on the private sector to proffer "market-based contingent financing mechanisms...which might provide greater payments flexibility or the assurance of new financing in the event of adverse market developments".[3] In addition, reflecting the increasing amount of foreign lending directly to the private sector in emerging economies, the G-7 asked the World Bank to take the lead in assisting countries to implement effective insolvency and debtor-creditor regimes (that is to say, legal frameworks for handling enterprise insolvency and collecting debt). One aspect of the idea is to make the possibility of bankruptcy—and thus possible loss to creditors—more routine and thereby reduce the pressure on governments to take extraordinary measures to bail out insolvent firms in order to avoid disruptive and confused legal proceedings.

Regarding governance of IMF, the G-7 sought to improve the transparency and accountability of the institution through a policy to limit IMF confidentiality. The presumption would now be to release all information to the public except for clearly stated exceptions, albeit with a possible delay of up to three months in selected classes of situations (the need for specific restrictions would be reviewed periodically). The G-7 also agreed to seek development of a "formal mechanism for systematic evaluation [of IMF], involving external input". This seemed to respond to charges of insularity of IMF and to provide a mechanism for external input in consideration of its reform.

Additional issues for a reform agenda

The measures announced by the G-7 speak to serious concerns repeatedly expressed by Governments and by investors in the financial markets about the fragility of the international financial situation and the extreme disruption of normal economic activity in Asia and elsewhere that has been related to it. What remains is for all concerned to assess the proposed architecture of the global financial system and possibly suggest modifications.

---

3 One such mechanism would be a kind of insurance provision in a loan or bond that automatically refinances debt-servicing obligations falling due (or triggers an option to refinance) if some pre-defined extreme situation takes place. Another mechanism would be a free-standing credit commitment (for example, a group of foreign lenders agreed in 1996 to allow Argentina to borrow on demand up to US$7.3 billion in the form of a "repurchase agreement" at an interest rate of LIBOR plus 205 basis points; Argentina would pledge its own outstanding dollar bonds as collateral (at 125 per cent of the loan amount) and if the market price of the bonds fell past specified benchmarks, the Government would put up more collateral).

There are two related concerns about the G-7 proposals. First is whether they will be fully and promptly implemented, since other promising proposals in the past have not been. Second is whether the proposals, even if fully implemented, will be sufficient to resolve the pending problems. While looking forward to the implementation of the G-7 programme, a number of additional measures may be suggested for consideration that would extend the G-7 agenda and, in our view, strengthen it. They are grouped below around the issues of crisis prevention, crisis management and democratization of international financial discussions.

Crisis prevention

The ideal situation is to prevent future crises of the sort that followed the Thai devaluation of July 1997. While total prevention is impossible, given the inherent volatility of the financial markets, some steps could lessen the number of episodes and moderate the virulence of future international financial turbulence. These should include steps at the international, regional and national levels.

Stronger global financial supervision and regulation

The scope of the existing regulation of international capital flows is insufficient, as the G-7 itself emphasizes. One reason is the lack of transparency in the capital markets, which parallels the lack of transparency of borrowers on which most international attention has focused. Planned improvements in global market data will help, for example, on derivative contracts. But another concern is the strategy adopted by the Basle Committee on Banking Supervision in its recent amendments to the Basle Accord on capital adequacy standards for banking regulation. The Committee recommends that national regulators allow banks to measure and monitor their exposure to various types of risk using complex "value-at-risk" models and to base capital requirements on the model results. Many financial institutions used such models during the 1998 episodes and their experiences are being evaluated. It may be that some additional approach to containing the risk is needed, such as dividing banks into different classes and specifying the kinds of activities in which each class could engage.[4] In addition, the regulation of non-bank financial institutions (for example, hedge funds, mutual funds and other institutional investors) would also need to be on the agenda, since they account

4 A parallel requirement might be that domestic lender-of-last-resort protection would only be available to banks engaging in the most limited range of activities.

for a substantial and increasing share of international capital flows.[5]

Strengthening of incentives for prudent lending

Beyond regulation, a new set of incentives must be built into the system so that the lenders will be more cautious about their activities. The G-7 programme contains a number of steps in this vein, as noted above. A complementary step would be to reach an explicit international understanding on when a "debt standstill" would be warranted, in effect, to define what is meant by "absence of reasonable alternatives" (the term is from Group of 22, 1998b, p. 41).[6] Once standstill conditions obtained, courts would not enforce debt-servicing obligations on covered loans and securities, pending the cooperative resolution of the debt crisis. Such an understanding should prompt investors before crises occur to pay close attention to the risks they are assuming, which thus might deter some investments of a speculative nature. It would also lay the groundwork for a key step in the process for managing crises once they occur (see below).

Regional surveillance and peer review

While additional control over the supply of finance circulating around the globe is a central element in a crisis prevention package, the maintenance of sound macroeconomic and financial policies within countries is the other side of the issue. While IMF Article IV surveillance will continue, and the amount of data that Governments provide will increase, a complementary process could be especially useful in the context of increasing regional integration, namely, surveillance and peer review by regional partners. Given the tendency of crises to have a regional scope, and given the increased volume of trade and finance, it is in the interest of countries to limit the ability of their neighbours to follow policies that could put all at risk.

---

5 Currently, non-bank financial institutions are regulated by a variety of authorities that differ across countries, and some of the institutions are not regulated at all. The agenda is thus quite a challenging one.

6 The Group of 10 Deputies had considered the temporary suspension of debt payments by the debtor to sometimes be unavoidable, but sought to make it "part of a process of cooperative and non-confrontational debt renegotiation". It noted that if a debtor declared a unilateral moratorium, it could soon be "accorded tacit agreement by the creditors", which would make it a "standstill". Also, if private-sector obligations were at issue, the government might have to impose the moratorium through "formal or informal exchange controls" (Group of 10, 1996, paras. 84-88).

Rethinking convertibility of the capital account of the balance of payments

One lesson of the 1997-1998 crisis is that sound macroeconomic policy in fully open economies is insufficient to prevent financial crises from striking. In response, international advocacy of the complete opening of the capital account has already moderated, but it can go further. In the light of recent events, full capital-account liberalization should be a long-term goal at best. For those countries wanting to pursue such an opening, the issue of sequencing is crucial, both with respect to opening the current account and to opening for different types of foreign capital (direct investment, other long-term capital, short-term capital). There should be no international pressure against those countries wanting to maintain capital controls or to institute a stand-by policy to use them in times of crisis.

Crisis management

Since crises will undoubtedly occur, regardless of the best preventative measures, it is important to agree in advance on ways to manage them so as to minimize damage to countries involved, especially to avoid large declines in output and employment. Beginning with Mexico in 1995 and following with the three Asian cases, the Russian Federation and now Brazil, the basic formula has been a multi-billion dollar bailout package, coordinated by IMF and conditioned on a programme of both macroeconomic and structural reform. The political resistance in developed countries to providing the funding to continue these programmes makes it likely that the Brazilian package will be the last. Thus, it is necessary to find a viable alternative approach. At the theoretical level, an international lender of last resort might seem to be the solution, but this option is even less viable politically than the bailout packages. The following three elements may constitute the kernel of a more feasible approach under current international circumstances.

Temporary capital controls on outflows

To buy time in a crisis to work out an agreement among creditors, it is essential to limit the short-term loss of reserves. Temporary controls on the outflow of capital—even with all their negative effects, including the certainty of leakage—offer the best emergency instrument. They would be eliminated once a more generalized solution is negotiated.

Low-conditionality, quick-disbursing finance to maintain import capacity

If a large-scale decline in output is to be avoided in a currency crisis, it is crucial for a country to maintain the capacity to import. Several sources of funds could be used in this context to provide semi-automatic credits to Governments that are steering their economies within the limits of sound policy, as evidenced by their Article IV consultations.[7]

That is, after demonstrating need for balance-of-payments assistance and after affirming that it is making "reasonable efforts" to overcome its balance-of-payments difficulties and that it will cooperate with IMF in this regard as necessary, the Government should be able to draw on such financing. Governments already have access under such terms to the first IMF "credit tranche" (the first 25 per cent of a country's borrowing quota). In addition, funds of the Compensatory and Contingency Financing Facility (CCFF) were formerly disbursed under "low-conditionality", albeit only for a limited number of reasons.[8] The international community agreed in the 1970s to add substantial low-conditionality credit lines when concern rose about coping with international economic volatility.[9] Today, it could begin by redefining access to the CCFF.

In addition, regional funds (such as the Latin American Reserve Fund or the fund of the Andean Development Corporation or the proposed Asian Fund) could provide trade credits. All would be relatively small amounts compared to the big bailout packages, but the important point is that they be disbursed quickly and with few strings attached.

Orderly debt workout procedures and official financing

A key aspect of any international strategy for crisis management should be to apply orderly workout procedures for excessive indebtedness. Such procedures would begin, as noted above, with the warranted invocation of a temporary standstill on debt servicing. It would be followed by an orderly sequence of collective agreements between creditors and the Government of the debtor

---

7 The G-7 proposal for short-term IMF lending noted above is partly in the spirit of the proposal here, except the potential beneficiaries of the G-7 proposal are a smaller set of countries that could potentially afford the terms of the lending.

8 The facility may help finance temporary shortfalls in commodity export earnings or temporarily high costs of food imports; for countries under IMF-supported adjustment programmes, the facility can also be used to cover increases in international interest rates or shocks to receipts from tourism or workers' remittances (IMF, 1998, p. 17).

9 The funds in question were the Oil Facility, created in 1974 and the IMF Trust Fund, created in 1977 for low-income countries using part of the proceeds from IMF gold sales.

country on servicing of debts owed by the public sector and sometimes by the private sector as well (the latter to the degree that national foreign exchange limitations have been a source of difficulty). The agreements would aim to prevent conflicts among creditors and avoid disruption of economic activities to the degree possible; for example, it would ensure that the low-conditionality emergency funds discussed above, which might be drawn from IMF, would be used for imports rather than debt servicing.

It is likely that any such orderly workout procedures would be carried out under the auspices of the Bretton Woods institutions. They should be accompanied by extensive consultation with appropriate domestic interests and organizations of civil society, as well as the Government. At the same time, the stopgap low-conditionality flows would begin to be supplemented and replaced by traditional IMF credits; and these would be extended once stand-by agreements were reached, whether or not the country had also reached agreement with its foreign private creditors (the process of IMF lending into arrears, as has been previously mentioned). The issue of timing is crucial. Agreed-upon procedures should be made available immediately after a crisis so as not to prolong the negative effects on production and income.

Democratizing international financial discussions

If the procedures outlined above—or any other set of measures to prevent and manage crises—are to have legitimacy with the various participants, all must have some say in their design and adoption. One shortcoming with the current system is that decisions are effectively taken by a small group of Governments within the international monetary and financial organizations and in the G-7 and G-10 processes. While discussions within the formal IMF machinery provide a forum for international consultation and while formal votes are rarely taken, decisions are made which are binding on all. There are thus deep political issues of governance of the international financial system to consider, as well as social and development questions of first importance.

Some modest steps to open up the process have been taken recently. It is important that while the G-7 has reasserted active leadership in international monetary and financial policy affairs, they have also made an effort to consult with other countries, as reflected in the work of the Group of 22 (developed and developing countries). Moreover, the G-7 pledged in its October statements noted above to continue to consult, "particularly with emerging market and other industrial countries to build a broad consensus in support of [its] declaration...." The appropriate institutionalization of this principle is extremely important, since any new architecture should have greater democratization built in from the beginning.

It is equally important, however, that discussions also go forward in other forums, not least within the machinery of IMF itself and other multilateral venues, but also outside official circles, in academia, among concerned non-governmental organizations and in the press. The matters at issue are vital, regardless of their technical nature, and they have important political and developmental dimensions that informed citizens of the world need to consider.

References

Brown, Gordon (1998). "Steering a course for stability", Statement by the Right Honourable Gordon Brown, MP, Governor of the Fund for the United Kingdom, at the Annual Meetings of the Boards of Governors of the International Monetary Fund and the World Bank, Washington, D.C., 6-8 October.

Group of 7 (1998). "Declaration of G-7 Finance Ministers and Central Bank Governors", available on the Internet at www.imf.org/external/np/g7/103098dc.htm (30 October).

______ (1998a). "G-7 Leaders' statement on the world economy", available on the Internet at www.imf.org/external/np/g7/103098ld.htm (30 October).

______ (1998b). "Work programme on strengthening the architecture of the international monetary system" (Office Memorandum to the Managing Director of IMF), available on the Internet at www.imf.org/external/np/g7/103098ed.htm (30 October).

Group of 10 (1996). *The Resolution of Sovereign Liquidity Crises: A Report to the Ministers and Governors prepared under the auspices of the Deputies.* Basle: Bank for International Settlements and Washington, D.C.: IMF (May).

Group of 22 (1998). "Report of the working group on transparency and accountability", available on the Internet at www.ustreas.gov/press/releases/ docs/g22-wg1.htm (October).

______ (1998a). "Report of the working group on strengthening financial systems", available on the Internet at www.ustreas.gov/press/releases/docs/g22-wg2.htm (October).

______ (1998b). "Report of the working group on international financial crises", available on the Internet at www.ustreas.gov/press/releases/docs/g22-wg3.htm (October).

IMF (1994). *IMF Survey,* 17 October.

______ (1995). *Annual Report, 1995.* Washington, D.C.: International Monetary Fund.

______ (1996). *IMF Survey,* 14 October.

______ (1998). *IMF Survey,* Supplement, September.

______ (1998a). "Report of the Managing Director to the Interim Committee on strengthening the architecture of the international monetary system", available on the Internet at www.imf.org/external/np/omd/100198.htm (1 October).

Kindleberger, Charles (1978). *Manias, Panics and Crashes.* New York: Basic Books.

Martin, Paul (1998). "Statement prepared for the Interim Committee of the International Monetary Fund [by] the Honourable Paul Martin, Minister of Finance for Canada", Washington, D.C., available on the Internet at www.fin.gc.ca/newse98/98-043e.html (16 April).

Mathieson, Donald J. and Liliana Rojas-Suárez (1993). "Liberalization of the capital account: experiences and issues", IMF Occasional Paper, No. 103 (March).

Williamson, John, ed. (1990). *Latin American Adjustment: How Much Has Happened?* Washington, D.C.: Institute for International Economics (April).

______, ed. (1994). *The Political Economy of Policy Reform.* Washington, D.C.: Institute for International Economics (January).

3

Global Financial Flows and their Impact on Developing Countries: Addressing the Matter of Volatility

Report of the United Nations Secretary-General[1]

A number of developing countries, mainly in Asia and Latin America, became increasingly successful in the early 1990s in accessing international financial markets...By the summer of 1995, [however,] Mexico and Argentina [had passed through currency crises and] were in deep adjustment recessions and the international community began to formulate policy measures to deal with a new class of crises, ones in which increasingly open developing and transition economies suddenly found themselves having to cope with large movements of financial flows (see United Nations, 1996 and 1997a).

In the light of these experiences, the General Assembly [has held] a series of discussions on development and global financial integration.[2] As reflected in those [discussions], the international community updated its strategy for dealing with economic and financial crises in developing countries, for example, through improved standards of information flow to the public on emerging market economies and establishment of an emergency financing mechanism at

---

1 Report to the General Assembly, Fifty-third session, under agenda item 91(b) Macroeconomic policy questions: financing of development, including net transfer of resources between developed and developing countries (document A/53/398, 16 September 1998). [The text has been slightly shortened and edited — *Editor's note.*]

2 These discussions led to the adoption of Assembly resolutions 50/91, 51/166, 52/180 and 53/172 in 1995, 1996, 1997 and 1998, respectively.

the International Monetary Fund (IMF). In addition, the Latin American crisis countries entered into recovery paths. Concern remained, however, about the degree of exposure to potential financial volatility.

Indeed, in July 1997 [after] economic crisis erupted in South-East Asia...the updated international strategy for dealing with such situations was applied in assisting Thailand, the Philippines and then Indonesia (Malaysia was also heavily affected, but did not arrange an internationally supported adjustment programme). Beginning in October 1997, [however,] the nervousness spawned by the South-East Asian situation spilled over into financial and currency market volatility in Hong Kong (China), Brazil, South Africa, the Russian Federation and elsewhere. Even the New York Stock Exchange was affected for a time. The year ended with the Republic of Korea engulfed in a major financial crisis and a growing international chorus [as at the General Assembly (see Herman and Sharma, 1998)] that questioned whether the new strategy was working....

1. Towards a new consensus

...Under this wave of criticism and the unrelenting economic decline in the Asian crisis countries, internationally advocated policies slowly changed [in 1998]. Fiscal and monetary policy conditions [were] eased in the more recent adjustment agreements that crisis countries struck with IMF, and the time-frame for reaching the goal of complete capital account liberalization [was] repeatedly lengthened [until it stretched] to upward of 50 years, at least for some countries.[3] Moreover, in April 1998, the Institute of International Finance (IIF), which reflects the views of the major international commercial banks that are its members, sent a letter to the Interim Committee of IMF, *inter alia*, expressing reservations about amending the IMF's Articles of Agreement to make capital account liberalization a main goal of the Fund.[4]

---

3 The Managing Director of IMF, in his remarks to the special high-level meeting of the Economic and Social Council of the United Nations with the Bretton Woods institutions held on 18 April 1998, noted that IMF had been working towards full current-account liberalization for over 50 years and had not yet reached that goal for all countries and that presumably it would take a like period for capital account liberalization (see E/1998/SR.4).

4 The letter from Charles Dallara, Managing Director, IIF, to Philip Maystadt, Chairman of the Interim Committee of IMF, dated 8 April 1998, says that the "private financial community supports the prudent and progressive liberalization of capital account transactions, but it is clear now that liberalization should be approached with care and complemented by steps to strengthen domestic financial systems. The Fund has a central role in furthering capital account liberalization. However, the case has not been made that an amendment of the IMF Articles is necessary" (see http://www.iif.com/PublicPDF/icdc0498.pdf on the Internet).

One strength of the multilateral institutions over the past 50 years has been their capacity to learn and adapt, which [in 1998] required a period of reflection and study.[5] Indeed, thinkers from all corners of the world [had] been analysing and discussing recent developments for over one year. It thus seemed timely [in mid-1998] to see if a new consensus was emerging on policy for macroeconomic management and growth and for effective integration into the global financial system. A meeting to take stock was therefore held in July[6] comprising individuals from many parts of the United Nations, IMF, the World Bank, other international institutions, the private sector and academia, who have grappled with these policy concerns. The coalescing of views that seemed to emerge from this meeting was less a break with the Washington consensus than a pragmatic modification, in the light of recent experience, of some aspects of it.

The political art of policy-making

The first element of the new consensus may set the tone for the discussion to follow. It entails the awareness that policy-making is carried out in a political context, and policy prescriptions must be politically viable. Thus, policy formulas developed for one set of national institutions do not automatically work well in others; institutions developed for one period can become inappropriate in later ones. The art of policy-making consists in recognizing when change is necessary in policies and/or institutions, when change is possible, and how change can be brought about effectively.

The choice of policies and measures involves a wide range of considerations and frequently will not be optimal from a purely technical point of view, even in those circumstances where there is agreement on what is optimal. Moreover, there is a fine line between policies that are suboptimal but tolerable and policies that are unsustainable. To the degree that a country is open to international financial movements—and no country is completely closed—incomplete (or even erroneous) "news" about the economy can move perceptions across the line and turn what is seen as a policy flaw into a policy disaster.

Therefore, institutions need to be sufficiently robust to withstand the consequences of perceptions of policy shortcomings; in particular, loss of confidence

5 In this regard, at the end of June 1998, the Executive Board of IMF initiated an external evaluation of its surveillance role, which will complement the external evaluation, completed in March 1998, of economic policy programmes under the Enhanced Structural Adjustment Facility (the Fund's concessional lending arm). For text and discussion of the latter, see http://www.imf.org/external/pubs/ft/distill/index.htm.

6 The meeting on which this book is based — *Editor*

of short-term investors should not threaten economic collapse. Institutions must also be in place before they can be drawn upon; for example, the time to weave a social safety net is before there is a crisis. In addition, sometimes the appearance of institutional change will exceed what is actually achieved; for example, privatizing state enterprises need not by itself produce the expected economic restructuring or competition. Continued monitoring is essential, and this requires provision and dissemination of reliable and appropriate data, and vigorous public discussion of policy and institutional concerns.

The new consensus, moreover, is well aware that the international institutions that stand behind their policy advisers may offer "carrots" or "sticks" to prod policy reform, but that in the end it is only the Government that implements any policy decision. International observers should not expect more from a policy dialogue between a Government and an international institution than is realistic.

This notwithstanding, there is widespread recognition that international policy advisers can take on unusually powerful roles during economic crises. At such times, they need to be particularly sensitive to local conditions. For example, in a country emerging from years of civil conflict, priorities normally accorded to fiscal adjustment have to be weighed against programmes to build confidence in government and development. This could affect the assessment of the government's debt-servicing capacity and foreign assistance requirements. Or, to take another example, potentially viable firms may easily be lost in the middle of a financial crisis. As their reconstitution may be far from automatic or quick, the economic and social consequences can be long-lasting. Debt workouts in such cases might be considered part of the policy dialogue. In such situations in particular, international policy advisers act on behalf of the broadest interests of the international community and need to be particularly sensitive to social and structural fragility.

Macroeconomic policy in capital-importing countries

Macroeconomic policy-making—always difficult—is made even more complex when capital markets are open and financial flows are volatile. As a practical matter, macro-policy should thus aim to attain medium-term goals and incorporate automatic stabilizers to help absorb short-term fluctuations (for example, stabilization funds can even out the tax revenues from unstable earnings on commodity exports).

As a general rule, in order to smooth the growth of aggregate demand, fiscal policy should tend to offset private spending booms that may accompany strong financial inflows, and vice versa during outflows. Medium-term budgeting with built-in plans to accelerate or slow certain outlays as needed might mitigate the political difficulty of cutting discretionary spending during periods of strong growth when there is no crisis to be seen. Operationally, the budgetary policy target should be the "structural" balance, which takes account of the impact of cyclical developments on the budgetary outcome, rather than the nominal balance.[7]

The ability to use monetary policy for domestic stabilization purposes is inseparable from the choice of exchange-rate regime. Typically, monetary policy is one of the policy tools for managing the balance of payments. For example, increases in domestic interest rates may be called upon to stem an unwanted financial outflow. This may be effective, but it is a dangerous policy choice when the domestic financial sector is weak and the level of debt in the economy is high. An increase in domestic interest rates has a psychological effect as well as a financial impact on firms and financial institutions and so must be a credible signal of government commitment to a tight policy stance. If the economy cannot withstand the shock (as was the case in certain Asian economies in 1997), the signal is unlikely to have the desired impact and may even have the obverse one.

Financial outflows from a country may reflect a loss of confidence in the local economy. Sometimes they can be triggered by unrelated developments elsewhere. Certain macroeconomic indicators, such as an increasing difference between domestic and foreign interest rates, a falling ratio of official foreign reserves to the money supply, a high share of short-term financing in external capital inflows, or a rising ratio of current-account deficit to gross domestic product (GDP), may be monitored for signs of an approaching unsustainable situation. However, there are no universally applicable rules or "standards" regarding the critical level of such indicators. Confidence may be lost at different values of the indicators for different countries or at different times for a single country. Decisions of the private sector to move money in or out of a currency are matters of judgement in an uncertain situation subject to dramatic changes.

One such dramatic change occurs when a "pegged" or fixed exchange rate becomes unsustainable and has to undergo a discrete adjustment. An alternative is to allow some flexibility in the exchange rate so that smaller, daily changes prevent the build-up of pressure for a large change. The problem is that the inherent volatility of financial flows may make the daily changes excessively large. For such reasons, some form of controlled flexibility can be attractive. For example, a thoughtfully designed "crawling peg" can stop the real

7 For a review of budgetary targets, see United Nations (1997), chap. V; see also Economic Commission for Latin America and the Caribbean (1998).

exchange rate from appreciating, the trade balance from widening and the expectation of a significant devaluation from growing.[8]

The crucial issue is to avoid creating a situation of "one-way bets" for speculators in which a Government endeavours to maintain an exchange rate that is widely perceived to be overvalued. Under such circumstances, currency traders will usually be able to mobilize more financial resources than the Government and will force a devaluation by selling more local currency than the Government can buy.[9] While controls on short-term capital movements can limit such possibilities, controls become harder to enforce as the profit expected from evading them rises. The expected profits can be held down by allowing exchange rates to be changed before speculative pressures build. On the other hand, flexible exchange rates call for the development of forward markets or markets in futures securities that enable firms to reduce their exchange-rate risks. In any event, the fact that forward and futures markets for the currencies of most developing countries are likely to be relatively thin reduces the attractiveness of freely floating exchange rates.

A common compromise is to allow flexibility within a band around a given exchange-rate peg. For this to work, however, the authorities must keep the exchange rate well within the band; if the value of the currency approaches the edge of the band, speculative pressures can build, as in the case of a strictly fixed exchange rate. A more sophisticated approach would be a combination of periodic changes in the central rate to compensate for differences in inflation with trading partners, combined with intermittent and irregular central-bank intervention in the market to raise uncertainty about the size and direction of short-term movements in the exchange rate (that is to say, "vigorous dirty floating"). If this strategy exceeds the resources and capabilities of the central bank, the authorities may have to choose between accepting vulnerability to

8 Another option—followed, for example, by countries employing "currency board" systems—is to announce a permanent peg and commit to defending the peg no matter how great the disruption of the economy that is required. If confidence is maintained, the durability of the system need not be tested. Once confidence is lost, however, a deep economic contraction and high unemployment may have to be withstood before confidence in the peg is restored. The attraction of the peg, particularly in the currency board variant, is that it can be a potent tool for fighting high inflation, in which case it can be seen as an alternative to discredited central-bank currency management. Given the possibility of policy-induced economic contraction, however, it is a policy with some risk.

9 A currency speculator should be thought of not as belonging among the limited number of "hedge fund" managers who operate internationally, but as being potentially any financial or non-financial enterprise or individual with access to credit who perceives the low-risk, high expected return of a bet against a central bank with limited foreign exchange reserves that is trying to defend an overvalued exchange rate.

potentially sharp fluctuations in the exchange rate and using some controls on capital movements to strengthen the hand of the central bank.

Speed and sequencing of financial liberalization

Relaxation of policy limitations on a domestic financial sector should not be carried to the point of complete laissez-faire. That financial institutions are inherently prone to excess and vulnerable to crisis warrants appropriate supervision and prudential regulation. By the same token, liberalizing international capital flows opens an economy not only to important opportunities, but also to additional volatility which could present dangerous challenges, especially for small economies in which the external financial flows might grow to a significant share of GDP.

It thus seems generally preferable to develop and locally deregulate the different elements of domestic financial markets before opening them externally.[10] The top priority should be to build a robust banking system. The development of stock exchanges has also been given priority in many countries, but next to the banking system and the potential benefits of domestic bond markets, stock markets are of relatively marginal importance for development, especially for the development of small and low-income economies in the early stages of financial development.

Foreign direct investment (FDI) can be an especially fruitful form of financial inflow, which is why it is often encouraged as one of the first components of capital inflow to be liberalized. Although it is typical to think of the benefits that can be brought by large multinational corporations, small and medium-sized companies can also offer important opportunities in transborder investing.

However, FDI is not a panacea and total flows should be monitored; for example, a surge in FDI inflows can overvalue a currency's exchange rate as much as any other type of international finance. Also given the physical presence of direct investors from foreign countries, there is a possibility of broad resentment and political backlash. This could be the case, for example, if it were deemed that substantial amounts of local corporate assets had been acquired by foreign firms at distress-sale prices owing to a crisis. More generally, as FDI is not an undifferentiated financial flow but investment in a sector-specific activity, policy makers have to ensure its consistency with national development

10 The point here is not to prevent foreign direct investors from operating in a local financial sector, but to limit foreign financial inflows (for example, direct investment might be permitted in local brokerage houses, while foreign purchases on the local stock exchange might not be allowed).

strategies and social and environmental priorities.

The most difficult issue in financial liberalization is choosing which flows to deregulate and which to control at any point in time. Much of the blame for the Asian financial crisis is commonly attributed to the untimely and poorly sequenced liberalization of financial movements. In light of the above discussion on exchange rate management, some form of impediment to volatile financial flows seems warranted in most developing countries. However, it is not a simple matter to separate volatile flows from the long-run investments that should be encouraged; as an example, even funds brought into a country by a direct investor can be used to take a speculative position in a currency.

In this regard, there has been considerable interest in policy experiments that use broad, market-based measures rather than selective administrative restrictions to discourage financial volatility. The Chilean effort to limit vulnerability to speculative outflows by limiting speculative inflows is the best known in this class of policy measures. In the context of its highly open economy, Chile adopted a combination of financial and quantitative controls on external flows. Most attention has focused on the requirement that financial investors sequester a fraction of their capital inflow with the central bank at no interest for one year, even if the funds are removed in less than one year (see Agosin and Ffrench-Davis, 1999). While this technique appears to have limited speculative inflows initially, it was increasingly evaded. In 1996, when international demand for Chilean investments was especially strong, the sequestering requirement appeared to serve in effect as the willingly paid price of entry into the Chilean stock market. Moreover, in 1998, with Chile's stock market and currency heavily impacted by the economic fallout of the Asian crisis, the policy was substantially eased so as to be less of a barrier to capital inflows.

The lesson of the Chilean experience—like the lesson of countries with stringent administrative controls—is that controls can be evaded and are more likely to be evaded the greater the financial incentives for such evasion. On the one hand, this means that the exchange rate should not be allowed to become clearly unsustainable because the incentive to evade the controls is thereby increased. On the other hand, it means that the instruments of control need to be strengthened as weaknesses and loopholes appear. In addition, the degree of restrictiveness of the controls needs to be relaxed when conditions warrant, in other words, controls should be a flexible instrument of policy. Moreover, non-discretionary and semi-automatic instruments will be less susceptible to corruption and evasion. All in all, countries that seek to manage their foreign exchange market should have a battery of policy instruments available, rather than try to rely on a single policy tool.

Quality of regulation in capital-importing countries

As a matter of accounting, external imbalances have internal counterparts. However, to trace these adequately requires more information, and on a more timely basis, on aggregated domestic stocks as well as flows (for example, levels of debt in corporate as well as banking sectors, private liquidity ratios and debt/equity ratios, as well as borrowing flows). It is essential for the authorities to monitor the financial state of the domestic economy in order to identify and address unsustainable situations as they arise, and for this they may need new types of information.[11]

In many cases, this also means that the government should take measures to improve accounting and reporting by domestic businesses; such a step is important especially in countries seeking to develop domestic securities markets. Regarding banking per se, a compendium of supervisory documents has been produced by the Basle Committee on Banking Supervision, particularly the 1997 core principles for effective banking supervision.[12] This is only a step, however, as the integrated nature of finance requires a comprehensive supervisory framework that can provide a perspective on the financial sector as a whole, covering, in particular, banks, non-bank financial institutions, securities and insurance firms.

While inadequate regulation is a concern, weak enforcement of regulations is especially costly. One crucial issue here is how to manage what are called "non-performing assets", not only the overall level but also the distribution by size of loan. In some cases—most dramatically, but not exclusively, in transition economies—lending officers in financial institutions, supervisors and regulators will need training to function adequately in a new environment of enterprise-bank relations and accountability. Local authorities must have the necessary resources and autonomy to carry out their responsibilities in this regard.

Policy in developed countries

Developing-country policy makers have to cope as best they can with the external economic environment as they find it. However, that environment is

11 Little national data on stocks (as opposed to flows) of financial assets and liabilities are collected even by countries with sophisticated statistical systems, although the conceptual framework for detailed balance-sheet data is already part of national income accounting (see Commission of the European Communities *et al.*, 1993).

12 See Basle Committee... (1997). The Basle Committee has also formed liaison and consultation groups with a number of countries (joined by IMF, the World Bank and the European Commission in informal capacities) in order to assist in implementation.

very much influenced by the policies and measures of developed countries, particularly the major-currency countries, both individual and collective. In mid-1998, for example, it was generally considered essential for the Government of Japan to address more effectively the problems besetting its economy, particularly its banking situation and need for a credible economic stimulus package, since this had been adversely affecting other countries, particularly other countries in crisis in the region.

In general, however, macroeconomic policy coordination among the world's major economies has proved difficult, otherwise than in the occasional joint intervention in foreign exchange markets when policy makers together signal that they believe exchange-rate changes have become excessive. One reason for limited coordination is that different Governments have not always shared the same view of the essential driving forces in their economies or the same policy priorities.

The difference of views has been especially sharp in the case of the Japanese economy in recent years and can be seen in the efforts of partner countries to encourage policy changes in Japan. This experience suggests that a useful instrument for international coordination is vigorous international public debate on policy questions of global importance as a means to build a consensus on policy.

One area in which thinking in different official circles has been along relatively similar lines is that of the principles of financial market regulation and oversight. The financial volatility seen in Asian and other emerging-market economies in 1997 and 1998, however, suggests that some regulatory gaps remain in developed economies. A number of financial institutions in developed economies took excessively risky positions by accumulating large holdings of poor quality and poorly diversified foreign assets. Thus, in these countries, as well as in the emerging-market economies, regulatory systems and early warning mechanisms need to be strengthened.

The oversight begins at the level of the financial firm, where it is in the nature of the industry for individual loan officers and portfolio managers to have incentives to take risky, albeit potentially profitable positions. Financial firms thus need strong internal risk measurement and control systems to ensure that the sum of the activities of their managers individually does not expose the firm as a whole to excessive risk. Equally, risk managers should have the authority to override senior management if necessary in order to cut excessive exposures.

It might be assumed that financial enterprises would act on such principles independently, but regulatory authorities have instead found themselves pushing firms in this direction. Indeed, at the urging of some of the banks that developed sophisticated internal risk management systems, this has become the broad thrust of new banking regulation.[13] Among the questions begging for answers, however, is, How well or poorly did these systems work during the Asian crisis?[14] There is also a question whether the established capital standards themselves are sufficiently strict and comparable for bank and non-bank financial institutions and for financial conglomerates that combine various categories of activities and may operate in several countries.[15]

International reform

The main avenues for international cooperation in the financial arena are IMF and the Bank for International Settlements (BIS). Forty-five central banks, several of which are independent institutions, are members of BIS, which is the locus of decision-making in the international coordination of financial regulation. BIS services a group of committees, including the Basle Committee, that are concerned with different aspects of international banking and that work increasingly closely with unaffiliated international associations concerned with non-bank components of the financial sector. These are ad hoc arrangements that arose in response to perceived needs, but they have been carried out at a high level of professional competence.

IMF undertakes a periodic review of global capital markets, and principles adopted in the BIS committees may be included by IMF in its surveillance of the financial sectors of individual developed and developing countries. This gives a degree of international oversight regarding implementation of the BIS regulations. Nevertheless, there are concerns whether this combination of

13 The Basle Committee, in particular, adopted the approach in its 1996 amendment to the Basle Capital Accord. The Accord was the 1988 agreement that established common capital backing ratios for banks to protect against credit risk, which arises from the possibility of non-payment of principal or interest by borrowers. The 1996 amendment standardized protection against market risk (arising from possible changes in the prices of financial instruments in which a bank has an exposure) and in doing so allowed banks to use internal risk models to figure the required capital backing; it also put regulators in the position of assessing risk management models.

14 Indeed, in July 1998, the Institute of International Finance (IIF) established several working groups of private sector financial executives to learn from the Asian crisis, including by assessing the performance of risk management models and processes during the crisis (IIF press release, 7 July 1998).

15 These questions, *inter alia*, are being considered by the Joint Forum on Conglomerates, comprising the Basle Committee, the International Organization of Securities Commissions and the International Association of Insurance Supervisors, which in February 1998 released a set of consultative papers for discussion (see www.bis.org/press/index.htm, release of 19 February 1998).

technical work in BIS committees and implementation oversight by IMF is an adequate mechanism for global cooperation in financial sector supervision. Bringing new regulatory questions under international discussion, for example, depends on acceptance of the issue by one of the existing committees or establishment of a new ad hoc arrangement. Also, IMF surveillance of implementation is necessarily less intense than a peer review mechanism of regulators, such as might be undertaken among BIS-member banking authorities. In addition, the World Bank and regional development banks provide financial support and technical cooperation for financial sector reform (with capacity in the case of the World Bank recently bolstered by the creation of its Special Financial Operations Unit in February 1998).

Proposals to pull these various threads together more effectively range from establishing a new institution to enhancing the responsibilities of one or more of the existing institutions... There have also been proposals to supplement the overall surveillance role of IMF in macroeconomic and financial policy with surveillance at the regional level, most actively in Asia. Although originally conceived in the context of a proposed Asian Fund, a new cooperative surveillance arrangement has been established by the member countries of the Association of South-East Asian Nations (ASEAN). Modelled on "the G-7 format with a distinct ASEAN character", the group envisages regular informal meetings of central bank and finance officials at deputy and ministerial level in which they would evaluate "potential economic and financial risks of Member Countries ... (and encourage) early action to minimize such risks" (ASEAN 1997, para. 12). The initiative is being assisted by the Asian Development Bank.

Peer review and surveillance at the regional level are likely to be more sensitive to local conditions and requirements and, by bringing a plurality of views into discussions of appropriate conditionality, enhance their political effectiveness. There was also a financial dimension to the ASEAN plan: a "cooperative financing arrangement" of mutually supplied funds would potentially supplement the resources of IMF and other international financial institutions in the adjustment programme of a member country. Quick disbursement of funds for financial crisis situations was also made part of the arrangement, in this case through the agreement to maintain an existing ASEAN swap arrangement. However, the extremely difficult situation into which most ASEAN nations have fallen since adopting this plan has rendered the financial cooperation dimensions almost moot for the moment. It has also meant that the absence of the Asian Fund is felt more strongly.

As a result, IMF remains the only institution with the mandate to deal with international financial crises...This notwithstanding, the [volume of] resources that IMF needs to deploy in any specific crisis [depends] in part on how the claims of private foreign lenders are treated. In the case of the Republic of Korea, it became most clear that a considerable portion of the international official resources channelled to the Republic of Korea at the end of 1997 was helping to finance the retreat of foreign bank lenders. Even though international commercial banks are the arteries for monetary and payment systems and thus warrant special treatment, it was widely felt that they should have been required to roll over maturing loans and replace short-term credits with longer-term maturities; indeed, by early 1998, this was the approach adopted (see United Nations, 1998).

There is considerable sentiment, especially among experts, in favour of international adoption of stronger proposals in the same vein. Conditions would be established under which debtor countries in balance-of-payments crisis would not be penalized for undertaking a "debt standstill", that is to say, a moratorium on debt servicing having at least implicit approval of the creditors (see Group of 10, 1996, para. 84). The availability of such a mechanism could be made manifest before a crisis struck by writing into loan contracts that some potential event—perhaps validated by an international assessment of need—might trigger a warranted standstill. Knowledge that such a standstill might be declared would increase the perception of riskiness of bank lending to emerging-market economies, and this in turn could discourage excessive inflows. It would also probably slightly raise the cost of credit, as banks would bear more risk. Above all, however it would perforce "bail in" the private creditors that accepted being exposed to such situations: they would have every incentive to accept a "voluntary" debt restructuring should an emergency arise, rather than write off their loans.

A complementary proposal would further encourage creditor cooperation in restructuring the debt due in such circumstances. This proposal has come to be called "IMF lending into arrears". It would entail an IMF policy decision to permit agreement to a Fund-supported economic adjustment programme with a member country under certain circumstances even if arrears were continuing to accumulate on outstanding debt. If the debt standstill and "lending into arrears" were deployed together, these two options could make the difference in terms of maintaining adequate liquidity and avoiding the kind of credit crunch that seized up the financial systems of the Asian crisis countries.

Conclusion

This report is submitted while we are still in the midst of the storm that has hit the global financial system. Hence, the outlines of the consensus on national and international policies for macroeconomic and financial management presented above must be considered an interim exercise. If the storm blows over soon, a widespread recession is avoided and the most affected economies resume the path of growth relatively quickly, then the new consensus presented above may be sufficient to reduce the risks of a similar episode in the future. If, however, the storm worsens, then the changes suggested by the new consensus may not be sufficient and the policy paradigm for development in a globalized market economy may need to be revised.

References

Agosin, Manuel and Ricardo Ffrench-Davis (1999). "Managing capital flows in Chile". This volume.

ASEAN (1997). Joint Ministerial Statement, Special ASEAN Finance Ministers Meeting, Kuala Lumpur, 1 December 1997.

Basle Committee on Banking Supervision (1997). "Core principles for effective banking supervision." Available on the Web site of the Bank for International Settlements (www.bis.org/press/index.htm), release of 22 September.

Commission of the European Communities, IMF, Organisation for Economic Cooperation and Development, United Nations and World Bank (1993). *System of National Accounts, 1993.* United Nations publication (Sales No. E.94.XVII.4).

Economic Commission for Latin America and the Caribbean (1998). *The Fiscal Covenant: Strengths, Weaknesses, Challenges.* United Nations document LC/G.1997(SES.27/3).

Group of Ten (1996). *The Resolution of Sovereign Liquidity Crises*, a report to the Ministers and Governors prepared under the auspices of the Deputies. Basle: Bank for International Settlements.

Herman, Barry and Krishnan Sharma, eds. (1998). *International Finance and the Developing Countries in a Year in Crisis: 1997 Discussions at the United Nations.* Tokyo: United Nations University Press.

United Nations (1996). "Global financial integration: challenges and opportunities." Report of the Secretary-General (A/51/388).

______ (1997). *World Economic and Social Survey, 1997.* United Nations publication (Sales No. E.97.II.C.1 and corrigenda).

______ (1997a). "Global financial integration: an update." Report of the Secretary-General (A/52/406).

______ (1998). "Enhancing international cooperation towards a durable solution to the external debt problem of developing countries." Report of the Secretary-General (A/53/373).

Part Two

ASIA

Edited by

Wenyan Yang

4

Introduction – Asia

WENYAN YANG*
United Nations Department of Economic and Social Affairs

It has been more than one year since Thailand gave up defending the pegged exchange rate between its currency, the baht, and the United States dollar, which set off the chain of events that came to be known as the East Asian crisis. During this period, the international community and governments have taken measures to deal with the fallout from the crisis, while many analyses of the causes of the crisis and evaluations of government actions have been published. Looking back, many observers were surprised by the severe consequences of what started out as a currency crisis in a region that had been widely known for its "economic miracle" and sound macroeconomic fundamentals.[1]

The severity of the crisis in East Asia can be underscored by the following social and economic indicators. Net foreign capital inflows to the five Asian countries directly hit by the crisis, which had reached $95 billion in 1996, reversed and became a net outflow of about $12 billion during 1997, implying a swing in capital flows in a very short period of time equivalent to about 11 per cent of these countries' combined GDP in 1996. Fiscal tightening and higher interest rates aggravated contractions in demand in crisis countries.

---

* Economic Affairs Officer, Developing Economies Section. The views expressed herein are those of the author and not necessarily the views of the United Nations.

1 See, for example, papers by Islam and Azis in this section for macroeconomic indicators in these countries prior to the crisis.

Although policies were relaxed during the year, the net result was declines in output ranging from 6 to 15 per cent in 1998, compared with growth of 5.5-8.2 per cent in 1996[2]. As a result of economic difficulties, the rate of unemployment went up sharply and continues to increase, averaging, for example, 15 per cent in Indonesia and 10 per cent in Thailand for 1998, compared with 5 per cent and 4.5 per cent respectively in 1997. Even in Hong Kong (China), an economy not directly hit by the crisis, the rate of unemployment had reached 5.5 per cent in November 1998, more than doubling the 1997 rate of 2.4 per cent. The impact of the crisis in the social area has been profound, reversing trends in poverty reduction and improvements in education and basic health care (Lee, 1998).

By 1998, a consensus of sorts had emerged regarding the causes of the Asian crisis. Several factors were identified as "fundamental weaknesses" in these economies that together almost inevitably led to the crisis: widening current-account deficits, increasing short-term capital inflows, financial sector liberalization, fixed exchange rate regime, weak domestic financial institutions, crony capitalism that prevented governments from taking action in time etc. While recognizing these weaknesses in the Asian economies prior to the crisis, however, authors in this section point out that some of these are long-existing conditions and are shared by countries that were not struck by the crisis. Rather, Islam argues that the key causes of the crisis rest with the improper timing of financial liberalization when financial institutions were still weak. Lee and Orr then illustrate the argument for the case of the Republic of Korea. The trigger in the Republic of Korea and elsewhere was the sudden drop in export earnings due to the collapse of the market for key exports such as electronics, and to the loss of competitiveness resulted from rising domestic labour costs. However, it was crucial that by the time the trigger was pulled, external debt had become unsustainable.

As Islam and Azis argued in their respective papers, the economic fundamentals of the crisis countries were still reasonably strong prior to the crisis and the weak financial sector and so-called "crony capitalism" existed even during the "miracle" years of economic growth. The role of psychology, or market behaviour was seen by the authors and other speakers to be very important in bringing on the crisis. The proper balance between stocks and flows (such as capital inflows) was also deemed important. It should not be overlooked during periods of strong capital inflow into countries of high economic growth. Massive capital inflow should be recognized, speakers pointed out, as a shock to the domestic

2 The Philippines is the only crisis economy that grew in 1998, if only by 1 per cent, or four percentage points lower than its growth rate in 1997.

economy, and thus, should be managed appropriately.

Authors and discussants in this section tried to evaluate government and international policy reactions to the crisis, which they present as lessons from the crisis and the effort to recover from it. The most significant lesson, a common theme in all the papers that follow, is the need for careful timing and sequencing of liberalization measures. Institution-building should be an integral part of any financial reform and liberalization programme. Moreover, attention to the impact of policy measures on aggregate demand is called for by authors and discussants alike.

Based on an appreciation of the intensifying interdependence of financial markets in a globalizing world economy, proposals were also made to reduce the frequency and to better manage future financial crises. Islam and Wade supported creating an Asian fund to pool regional resources for additional balance-of-payments assistance during crises. Another proposal pertains to redefining the role of IMF. One commentator suggested that the Fund should cease to advise member countries in matters of macroeconomic policy and institutions. Instead, the Fund should focus on formulating "rules of the game", namely, standards and acceptable practices consistent with IMF goals. The general discussions also underscored the importance of international cooperation in financial markets. Several speakers advocated establishing a world financial organization to regulate international financial flows, similar in structure and function to the World Trade Organization (WTO) in formulating and enforcing international trade rules. Another point raised during discussions, however, was that repeated financial crisis took place in countries with strong regulatory institutions such as the United Kingdom of Great Britain and Northern Ireland and the United States of America. Consequently, we may need to shift attention away from regulating the financial market to insulating the rest of the economy from it.

As of late 1998, the short-term economic outlook for Asia is still quite uncertain. However, a somewhat more optimistic view of the Asian economic outlook is warranted than was envisioned in July, when the United Nations Expert Group Meeting was held. Major industrial countries lowered their interest rates and this has facilitated interest rate reductions in Asian countries that had been under a credit crunch. Governments in Asia also implemented policy measures, such as recapitalization of banks (Thailand), mergers and/or nationalization of weak financial institutions (Indonesia) and lowering reserve ratios (Malaysia) to encourage bank lending. Fiscal policy was also relaxed in several countries. Currency markets stabilized, with some of the Asian currencies that had suffered the greatest depreciation in 1997 appreciating, some markedly. Financial and corporate restructuring continues, as the corporate debt problem is being addressed, especially in the Republic of Korea and Thailand. On the other hand, the Government of Malaysia had introduced capital controls while others intervened to bolster the equity and property markets. These measures were received negatively by the financial market, but the financial situation appears to have nonetheless stabilized for the time being. All in all, we might not be seeing the light at the end of the tunnel yet, but we seem to be approaching the corner that will turn us towards the light.

Finally, the Asian crisis also illuminated the different roles an economic process such as regional economic integration could play under changing circumstances. Close investment and trade links had served as an important source of economic growth in Asia in the recent past, even when other regions of the world experienced slowing growth. However, they became the primary channel of contagion, especially in countries with inadequate domestic financial institutions, once the crisis was set in motion. This point should be appreciated by decision makers in developing countries pursuing strategies of economic development that aim to take advantage of opportunities afforded by the globalizing international economy. The importance of strengthening domestic institutional capacity while liberalizing national economies cannot be overemphasized.

Reference

Lee, Eddy (1998). *The Asian Financial Crisis—The Challenge for Social Policy*. Geneva: International Labour Organization.

5

The Dynamics of Asian Economic Crisis and Selected Policy Implications

AZIZUL ISLAM*
United Nations Economic Commission for Asia and the Pacific

1. Introduction

For many years East and South-East Asian countries received universal acclaim as the fastest growing economies in the world. Their remarkable achievement in sustaining a high rate of economic growth over a long period was significantly fostered by their active participation in the globalization process. This enabled them to take advantage of the increasing opportunities for using trade as an engine of growth and for accessing external capital and technology. However, enhanced participation in the globalization process brings with it certain risks. Unless adequate precautionary measures are taken, these risks can have an unexpected debilitating impact on a national economy. During the second half of 1997, several East and South-East Asian economies fell victim to some of the pitfalls associated with closer integration into the international economy. The most seriously affected, albeit with varying degrees of severity, were Indonesia, Malaysia, the Philippines, the

* Director, Development Research and Policy Analysis Division. The views expressed herein are those of the author and not necessarily the views of the United Nations. The author gratefully acknowledges valuable research support from Mr. Abul Hashem, Mrs. Janet Farooq and Mr. Prabowo.

Republic of Korea and Thailand. Three of them (Indonesia, the Republic of Korea and Thailand) were forced to seek emergency assistance from the International Monetary Fund (IMF).

The objective of this paper is to contribute to an understanding of the essential causes underlying the upheaval that gripped the above-mentioned five economies more or less simultaneously and to raise some policy issues that merit serious consideration at national, regional and international levels in order to minimize the likelihood of the recurrence of such upheavals in the future. Section 1 analyses the dynamics leading to the crisis. Section 2 explains the persistence of the crisis. Section 3 highlights selected domestic policy issues which arise in the context of liberalization of the financial sector, particularly liberalization of the capital account of the balance of payments. Section 4 provides some thoughts for regional and international cooperation. The paper ends with some concluding observations.

2. The dynamics leading to the crisis

The immediate trigger to the crisis was the sharp depreciation of Thai currency, the baht, following the country's decision to float its currency on 2 July 1997. The decision was forced by major speculative attacks on the baht in February and May 1997 which caused a large depletion of foreign exchange reserves as the country attempted to defend its exchange rate by selling official reserves. The crisis soon spread like a wild fire engulfing a number of other countries. Its dynamics were rooted in a number of factors.

(a) An inventory of causes

Financial sector liberalization

An important policy-related factor was the swift liberalization of the financial sector. The process was intensified during the 1990s. The various elements of liberalization can be grouped into several major areas: reduction of barriers to entry for banks and non-bank financial institutions, deregulation of interest rates, relaxation of directed credit requirements, promotion of new financial markets and instruments, and liberalization of the external dimension of the financial sector. The focus here is on the last aspect. With some variation among countries, liberalization in this area permitted local citizens and non-resident foreign entities to open accounts with commercial banks either in national or foreign currencies; banks to extend credit in foreign currencies in the domestic markets, non-bank private sector corporations, as well as financial institutions to borrow abroad; foreigners to own shares listed by national companies on domestic stock exchanges; the sale of securities on international stock and bond markets by national companies; the sale of domestic monetary instruments such as central bank bills and treasury bills to non-residents; and establishment of off-shore banks, which were also allowed, in some cases, to borrow abroad and lend domestically.

The rising current account deficit

One of the major causes that triggered the crisis was the large deficit in the current account of the balance of payments in all the affected countries (table 1). The magnitudes of the deficit differed, ranging from 3.5 per cent of gross domestic product (GDP) in Indonesia to 8 per cent in Thailand by the end of 1996. But the deficit increased in all cases in that year with the exception of Malaysia where the deficit during 1993-1995 was much higher than in the previous three-year period. The most rapid deterioration took place in the Republic of Korea, where the deficit averaged less than 1 per cent during the period 1993-1995, but reached 5 per cent in 1996.

The deterioration in the current-account balance was caused mainly by the slowdown in export growth, which was particularly sharp in 1996 (see table 1) and persisted in many cases through 1997. A slackening in demand for some major exports from the region, such as electronic goods, was partly responsible for the sharp export slowdown in 1996. To some extent, it reflected the deceleration in global trade. An important reason, however, was the gradual erosion of the competitiveness of the region's export industries as a result of rising domestic costs, especially wage costs, against the backdrop of the industrialization process which was not very effective in shifting from labour-intensive

Table 1. Changes in dollar value of exports and current-account balances

	Annual percentage change in dollar value of exports			*Current-account balance as percentage of GDP*	
	1993-1995	*1996*	*1997*[a]	*1993-1995*	*1996*
Indonesia	10.2	9.7	8.9	-2.2	-3.5
Malaysia	21.9	6.2	3.2	-6.5	-4.9
Philippines	21.7	16.7	24.0	-4.2	-4.7
Republic of Korea	18.1	4.2	0.3	-0.8	-5.0
Thailand	20.1	-1.2	2.3	-6.3	-8.0

Sources: ESCAP Secretariat calculations, based on United Nations, *Monthly Bulletin of Statistics,* vol. LI, September 1997; Asian Development Bank, *Key Indicators of Developing Asian and Pacific Countries 1997* (Oxford University Press, 1997); International Monetary Fund, tape no. 92165F and *International Financial Statistics*, vol. L, No. 12 (Washington, D.C., December 1997); and United Nations, *The World Economy at the Beginning of 1998* (December 1997).

a Figures refer to the first half of 1997, annualized growth rate.

industries to higher levels. There was also a tendency for the real exchange rates to appreciate (see figure 1), as the nominal exchange rates with the United States dollar were held stable while domestic inflation rates tended to exceed those of major trading partners, including the United States. The realignments of currencies of the other countries also had an effect on the appreciation of real effective exchange rates. At the same time, new competitors emerged both within and outside the region to encroach upon the markets for the labour-intensive products of some of the countries.

The changing composition of capital inflows

The rising current-account deficit naturally had to be financed by capital inflows. To an extent, the easy access to capital inflows also provided an incentive to run into current-account deficit. As regards the composition of such inflows, private flows are the dominant component in most countries of East and South-East Asia. In these countries, foreign direct investment (FDI) has been and remains an important component of total capital inflows. However, portfolio investment and credit, including banking flows, clearly showed rising trends. In the Republic of Korea, net portfolio flows rose from an average of 2

Figure 1: Selected South-East and East Asian countries, index of real effective exchange rates,[a] 1991-1996
(1990 = 100)

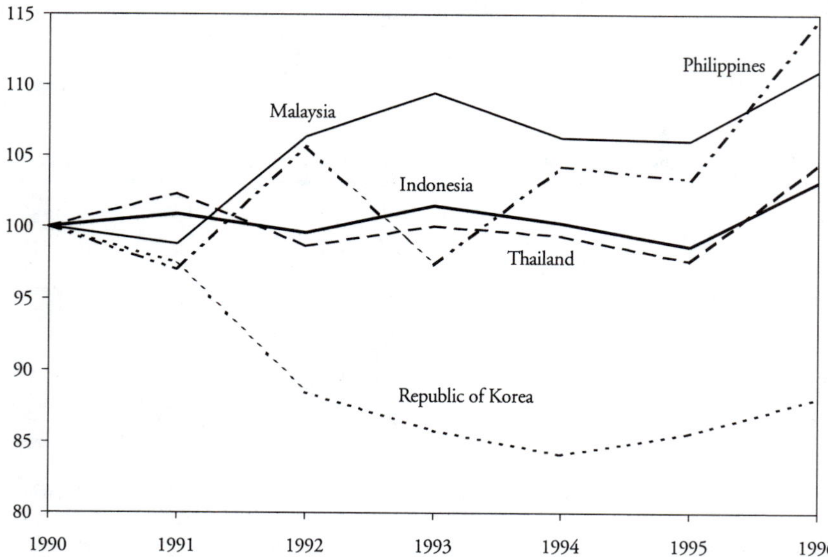

Sources: United Nations, *The World Economy at the Beginning of 1998* (December 1997).

a. Defined in terms of foreign currencies per unit of domestic currency, a rise in the index implies a fall in competitiveness.

per cent of GDP in 1990-1992 to 2.8 per cent in 1995-1996. During the same periods, they rose from –0.1 per cent to 2.3 per cent in Indonesia, from 0.1 to 2.6 per cent (1995) in Malaysia, and from 0.2 to 2.2 per cent in Thailand. Similarly, in the Republic of Korea, banking and other inflows rose from 1.4 per cent of GDP in 1990-1992 to 2.6 per cent in 1995-1996. In Indonesia, this component of capital flows recorded a significant increase between 1993 and 1995, reaching 1.2 per cent of GDP in 1995. In Malaysia, the Philippines and Thailand, non-FDI private inflows as a proportion of GDP kept rising, reaching the average level of 9 per cent of GDP in Thailand in 1995-1996. In Malaysia and the Philippines, they remained at around an average of 5 per cent of GDP during the period 1993-1995.

The substantial capital inflows took place not merely to finance the deficits in the current accounts of the balance of payments, but often also as a result of investors seeking profit opportunities in capital markets, which were seen to be expanding very fast and entry to which had recently been made easier (see section on financial liberalization). At the same time, a very significant structural change was taking place in the international financial markets. The rapid institutionalization of savings in the developed countries led to huge accumulation of resources in pension and mutual funds. The growing institutionalization of savings and the participation of institutional investors in international markets as a means to diversify their portfolios boosted the purchase of emerging market securities.

Many countries in the region pursued a policy of relatively high interest rates in order to maintain a stable exchange rate. The rather large and continuing differential between the domestic interest rates and international interest rates, in combination with the liberalization of policies noted earlier, was a further lure for capital inflows, while stable exchange rates minimized currency risks. These factors gave rise to a rapid build-up of the stock of foreign debt (see table 2), a large part of which was not hedged against currency risks. Between 1992 and 1996, the increase was about threefold in the case of Malaysia, the Republic of Korea and Thailand, and about twofold in the case of Indonesia and the Philippines. It should also be noted that a high proportion of the stock of private debt was of a short-term nature. In 1996, this ranged from 50 per cent in Malaysia to 67.5 per cent in the Republic of Korea. A high proportion of short-term debt contains the risk of a sudden reversal and crisis owing to adverse expectations with respect to either the exchange rate or the health of the financial sector, or both.

Mention should also be made of the relevance of the utilization of capital inflows which financed the deficit. The sustainability of the deficit becomes

Table 2. Stock of debt owed to foreign private creditors, 1992-1997

	Indonesia	*Malaysia*	*Philippines*	*Republic of Korea*	*Thailand*
***Total** (billions of US dollars)*					
1992	28.4	8.5	6.9	38.7	23.0
1993	30.5	13.0	5.8	41.2	29.6
1994	34.2	13.5	6.5	56.5	43.4
1995	44.5	16.8	8.3	77.5	62.8
1996	55.5	22.2	13.3	100.0	70.1
Mid-1997	58.7	28.8	14.1	103.4	69.4
***Short-term** (percentage of total)*[a]					
1992	60.5	48.1	45.7	71.4	69.0
1993	61.7	56.8	40.8	70.8	72.1
1994	61.8	48.8	47.4	71.1	71.0
1995	61.9	47.2	48.8	70.0	69.4
1996	61.7	50.3	58.2	67.5	65.2
Mid-1997	59.0	56.4	58.8	67.9	65.7

Source: Bank for International Settlements, *The Maturity, Sectoral and Nationality Distribution of International Bank Lending,* various issues.

a Up to and including one year maturity.

questionable when short-term foreign resources are used for the purpose of investments which yield returns in the medium or long term. This causes a maturity mismatch. In addition, a currency mismatch may occur when investments are made in non-tradeables such as land, buildings and infrastructure which generate returns in local currency, but repayment has to be made in foreign currency. To some extent, both of these mismatches arose over the last few years in the countries which came under attack.

Financial sector weaknesses

There is no doubt that a part of the explanation for the crisis lay in the weaknesses inherent in the overstretched operations of the financial institutions, the enabling conditions for which were created by easy access to external inflows. For example, during the period 1990-1995, the foreign liabilities of the Thai commercial banks went up from 6 per cent of their total liabilities to 23 per cent and those of the non-bank financial institutions, from about 5 to 7 per cent. Over the same period, the total assets of the principal domestic financial institutions, excluding the Bank of Thailand, expanded from $96 billion to $290 billion, and those of the commercial banks from $71 billion to $200 billion. In Indonesia, domestic credit as a proportion of GDP rose from less than 50 per cent in 1990 to 54 per cent in 1996. The corresponding figures for

Malaysia were 78 and 93 per cent; for the Republic of Korea 57 and 65 per cent; and for Thailand, 70 and 99 per cent.

There is some evidence that the rapid credit expansion was associated with some degree of inefficient intermediation. In Thailand, for example, total advances to manufacturing expanded 10-fold between 1985 and 1996, but credit to the real estate sector increased 22-fold during the same period. The stock and the property markets in Thailand, as well as in the other countries, had shot up rapidly since 1989-1990. Growing foreign portfolio investments were partly the reason for the explosive growth in the stock market.

An increasing and persistent oversupply in the property market and the downward pressure on its prices negatively affected the financial sector with its substantial exposure to the property market. A downturn in the stock markets started in 1993-1994. Thus assets pledged against loans depreciated rapidly with the decline in both these markets. Failure of businesses to repay their borrowings from the financial institutions exposed the vulnerability of those institutions as a large proportion of their credit advances became bad debts. By the first half of 1997, non-performing loans as a proportion of total loans increased rapidly, ranging from about 13 per cent in the Philippines to nearly 20 per cent in Thailand; in 1996, these proportions stood at less than 5 per cent in all cases, with the exception of Indonesia, where it was close to 9 per cent. The financial institutions could not even have effective legal recourse to foreclosures to recover defaulted loans because of weaknesses in the legal systems, particularly, inadequacies in bankruptcy laws or cumbersome procedures for their enforcement.

These institutions, in turn, found difficulty in repaying their sizeable foreign obligations. Export slowdown, falling property and stock values, and increasing revelation of accumulated bad debts of financial institutions ultimately shook investors' confidence and triggered large-scale capital flight. The domestic currencies came under pressure. Initially the central banks tried to defend their value by using available reserves. Their efforts, however, did not succeed and they had to give up as they started to suffer serious losses of reserves.

The role of foreign market players

The point can be made that foreign creditors were substantially responsible for sowing the seeds of the crisis. The outstanding credit from the foreign private sector was almost entirely contracted by the private sector in the borrowing countries. These transactions were, therefore, the result of the evaluation of risks and returns by foreign private creditors. The underlying economic causes discussed earlier should have acted as warning signals for discriminating creditors; yet overall bank lending to Asian developing countries, including the ones which suffered the crisis, proceeded unabated in the first half of 1997 (*The Asian Wall Street Journal*, 1998). And then there was a rapid withdrawal. By the end of 1997, there was a net outflow of commercial bank credit from the five affected countries amounting to $27 billion as against a net inflow of $56 billion in 1996.

This pattern of behaviour can be viewed as an instance of market failure, but not the first one in recent history. It has been argued by many that the Latin American debt crisis of the early 1980s owed its origin partly to the failure of proper risk assessment and the poor ability of transnational banks to evaluate creditworthiness (Dillon and others, 1985; and *The Economist*, 1982).

In a world of integrated financial markets, portfolio investors such as mutual funds or hedge funds tend to look upon a region or a subregion as a single market. The problems confronted in one country may prompt them to pull out of the whole region or subregion in a herd reaction. This is evidenced by the fact that many short-term investors pulled out of the markets of South-East Asian countries and the Republic of Korea more or less at the same time, following the problems in Thailand. Net portfolio equity inflows to the five affected countries amounted to $12 billion in 1996 and turned into net outflows of $4 billion in 1997. This exposes the fragility of the argument that portfolio investment should not be a matter of concern. The rationale underlying the argument is that portfolio investors share the burden of adjustment as they suffer losses in the course of withdrawal. Secondly, initial losses may be a disincentive for further withdrawal and so a self-correcting mechanism may come into play. The Asian experience clearly shows the ineffectiveness of such a mechanism. One reason is that if some fund managers start withdrawing, others feel compelled to follow suit to avoid blame in the event equity markets go down further. Moreover, any sizeable withdrawal by some investors may give rise to an expectation of devaluation and thus provide an incentive to all to withdraw early, before devaluation actually takes place.

The investors overreacted in a panic-stricken manner, even though all these countries had some strong economic fundamentals immediately prior to the crisis. In 1996, all the countries had high rates of savings exceeding 30 per cent with the exception of the Philippines; budgets were in surplus; foreign exchange reserves were rising; and inflation was moderate at less than 7 per cent except in the Philippines where it was 8.4 per cent. Besides, despite common weaknesses among the affected countries in terms of some economic indicators discussed earlier, there were considerable differences. To illustrate, the current-account deficit as a proportion of GDP in Indonesia in 1996 was less than half of that of Thailand, its exchange rate was more flexible, and it had a smaller volume of foreign private debt. Similar observations apply to the Philippines. As for Malaysia, the current-account deficit as a proportion of GDP was a little higher than that of Indonesia and the Philippines, but considerably lower than that of Thailand, and its stock of foreign private debt was higher than that of the Philippines, but less than half of that of Indonesia and a third of that of Thailand.

The various elements of the process described above are schematically presented in figure 2.

(b) The prime causes

There will probably be no overwhelming disagreement about the broad contours of the process leading to the crisis as discussed above. But there are considerable differences of views as to whether one can single out one or two essential causes, and if so, what these are.

Some analysts argue that the primary cause of the crisis was short-term debt. There is no doubt that short-term debt did play a role in causing the crisis. The growth in the volume of short-term debt and the resultant maturity and currency mismatch have been already noted. However, it can be seen from table 2 that in the affected countries there were no drastic increases in short-term debt as a proportion of total debt during the period 1993 to 1996 with the exception of Malaysia. Similarly, with the exceptions of Indonesia and Thailand, there were no major increases in short-term debt as a proportion of exports up until 1995. It was only in 1996 that there was a very large increase in this latter ratio in all the countries, primarily as a result of deceleration in export growth. As exports slowed down sharply in 1996 and early 1997, concerns arose about debt servicing capacity and short-term loans were not rolled over, leading to capital outflows and the subsequent trauma. One can therefore argue that the fall in export growth, rather than the volume of short-term debt per se, is a better explanation for the crisis.

According to others, the primary causes of the crisis lay in the weak financial sectors. Here again, it is evident that financial sector weaknesses cannot be absolved of some degree of culpability but their primacy as an explanatory factor is open to question. To some extent, the weaknesses of the financial sector were a consequence of easy access to external capital flows and, to that extent, liberalization of capital account transactions was the main cause. Besides, even if the financial sector were healthy, it is difficult to hypothesize that outflows would not have taken place in the face of a sharp slowdown in export growth which gave rise to perfectly rational expectations of devaluation. The fact is that the weaknesses in the financial sector in the affected countries have been known to exist for many years. But, the almost total liberalization of capital

Figure 2: The process leading to the crisis

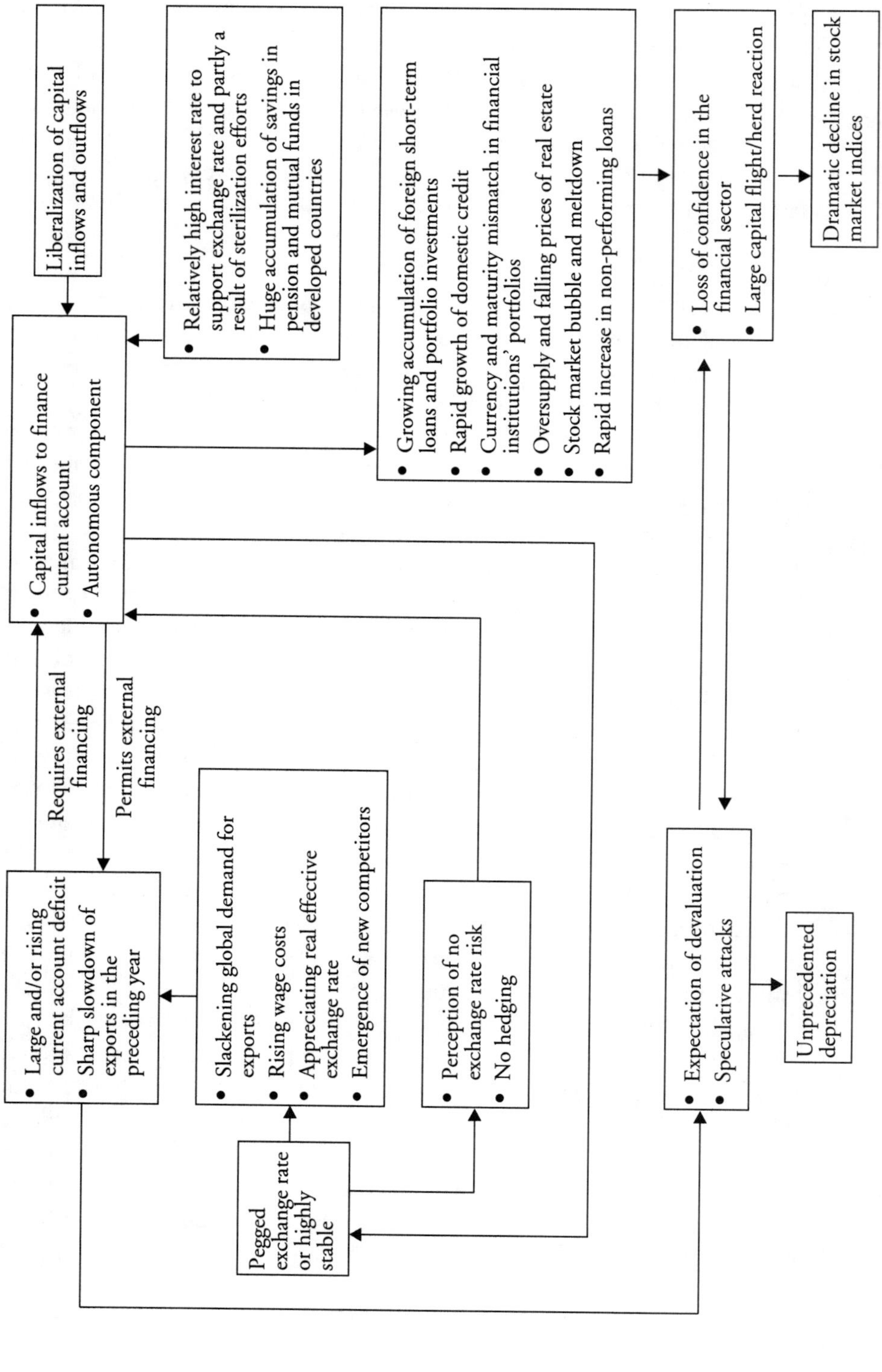

accounts aggravated the financial sector problems through increased exposure to easily reversible inflows.[1]

In this context, much blame has been laid on "crony" capitalism. The argument is that individuals or corporations favoured by powerful bureaucrats or politicians had easy access to financial institutions and could borrow large sums without due consideration for risks, returns and repayment obligations. The financial sector institutions, in turn, acquiesced in such transactions either under pressure or on the assumption that they would inevitably be bailed out. This sort of argument typically focuses on who borrowed rather than on the use of borrowed funds. For such an argument to be convincing, it is necessary to demonstrate that (a) there did exist an alternative class of borrowers and investors; (b) they would have put the borrowed funds to better use; (c) their access to funds was pre-empted by "cronies"; and (d) the financial sector institutions possessed the requisite information and expertise to apply more rational criteria in their lending decisions. It is quite possible that in some instances, access to credit was based more on connections than on soundness of investment proposals, but putting the blame on "crony" capitalism as a major determinant of a massive crisis is an oversimplification.

Some argue that the most important cause of the crisis was the pegged or highly stable exchange rate. This argument has some validity provided it is recognized that what was important was the combination of pegged exchange rate with increasingly liberal capital account regimes. In the absence of the latter, even if an inflexible exchange rate were to hurt exports, countries would be forced to reduce the current-account deficit early on, rather than continuing on the path of reliance on short-term flows to finance the growing deficit. Moreover, it is not clear how much moderating impact flexible exchange rate policies would have had on short-term inflows during the period of rapid growth of the overall economy and of exports, and the resultant perception of high returns. It should also be noted that of 116 currency crises (defined as a 25 per cent or more depreciation in a year) between 1975 and 1996, close to half were under flexible regimes (IMF, 1997a).

In light of the above, the conclusion is that there were two prime causes of the crisis. These were the sharp slowdown in export growth giving rise to a rapid deterioration in the current account and liberalization of the capital account. These were the villains of the piece, the other elements were essentially accomplices.

1 There is an argument that some degree of liberalization may provide the necessary stimulus for reforming and strengthening the financial sector. However, that does not negate the fact that liberalization was carried too far and too quickly in the affected countries.

3. The persistence of the crisis

There are a number of factors which explain the slow progress in moving to a stage of recovery from the crisis. To a great extent, these have to do with the policy packages introduced as a part of IMF assistance. These policy packages included generation of additional tax revenue and/or curtailment of government expenditure; containment of growth of domestic credit; and a variety of structural and institutional reforms which encompassed privatization of public enterprises, deregulation of business and industry, further liberalization of policies with respect to trade, foreign investment and financial flows, closure of some financial institutions, and improved transparency of the financial system.[2]

One problem with this policy approach is that it did not take into account the distinctive nature of the Asian crisis. In most of the Asian countries, there was no major private consumption boom, nor did the governments pursue profligate fiscal policies. In anticipation of continued high growth in exports as well as GDP, there was overinvestment in both tradable and non-tradable sectors. Policy measures aimed at curtailing domestic demand in the absence of compensatory export expansion have deterred capacity utilization and created enormous problems for the corporate sector.

The financial sector reforms which have included closure of institutions, more stringent capital adequacy requirements and larger provisions for loan losses contributed to the emergence of a vicious circle. The lack of credit from financial institutions, high interest rates associated with whatever credit is available, and an inability to generate internal funds have led to a serious liquidity crunch for the real sector. The increasing business failures have seriously affected the borrowers' debt servicing capacity. The rising proportions of non-performing loans in the portfolios of financial institutions, in turn, are contributing to their reluctance to extend new credit.

Based on the notion that the crisis was primarily financial, too much attention has been paid to financial sector reforms. The importance of the real sector for spearheading the process of recovery has not received adequate attention. This has not merely delayed recovery, but has also adversely affected the soundness of the financial sector.

A related consideration is that policy approaches appear to be largely motivated by the desire to restore foreign investors' confidence. It seems there is an

2 For a brief description of the conditionalities for IMF's assistance to the various countries and a critique thereof, see UN/ESCAP, 1998.

an inadequate appreciation of the fact that the return of foreign funds, whether in the form of FDI, bank credit or portfolio investment, is most unlikely when the domestic economy is sinking.

Another factor which is delaying recovery in Asia is the existence of close intraregional linkages. For example, in 1995 more than one-fifth of merchandise trade of countries belonging to the Association of South-East Asian Nations (ASEAN)[3] was intra-ASEAN. Nearly two-thirds of their trade was with the Asian and Pacific region (including all developing economies, Australia, Japan and New Zealand). Similarly, there are fairly strong linkages among countries in East and South-East Asia in respect of trade in services, particularly tourism, and foreign direct investment (FDI). The close intraregional linkage implies that recovery in any one country is contingent on the recovery of others in the region.

To a significant extent, the process of economic development in the Asian countries has followed "the flying geese" pattern in which Japan played a leading role. Japan emerged not merely as a leading source of FDI, but also as an increasingly important market for export and a major supplier of bank credit. The continued weaknesses in the economy of Japan thus remain an important hurdle for recovery in the crisis-affected Asian countries.

4. Selected domestic policy issues

(a) The constraints on macroeconomic management

Fiscal policy

One policy response to deal with capital inflows could be to pursue a flexible fiscal policy which would be contractionary during episodes of large inflows and expansionary during outflows. However, there are inherent limits to the use of fiscal policy as an instrument for dealing with capital flows. Government tax and expenditure policies are determined primarily by medium- or long-term development considerations, rather than short-term fluctuations in capital flows. It would be nearly impossible to adjust fiscal policy speedily enough to be able to respond effectively to rapid changes in short-term capital flows, in part due to legal procedures. The countries experiencing large capital inflows from private sources typically have a more liberal policy regime governing the operations of financial sector institutions which are allowed to set their own credit policies, as was the case in East and South-East Asian countries. It has often been the experience that consumer

3 Comprising Brunei Darussalam, Indonesia, Malaysia, the Philippines, Singapore and Thailand.

credit is readily made available by financial institutions during the periods of heavy capital inflows. This factor may also constrain the effectiveness of fiscal policy in curtailing aggregate demand. Similarly, during periods of rapid outflows which give rise to a mood of pessimism, governments may find it difficult and costly to raise resources from the domestic or foreign market in order to be able to finance an expansionary fiscal policy.

Monetary policy: sterilization and interest rate instruments

Sterilization policy, implemented by monetary authorities, aims at insulating the domestic economy from the effects of capital inflows. This is sought to be achieved by targeting two macroeconomic variables simultaneously: the prevention of nominal exchange rate appreciation and reduction of the domestic money supply. In order to avoid the exchange rate appreciation induced by capital inflows, monetary authorities resort to intervention in the foreign exchange market by selling local currency for foreign exchange. The instruments used to sterilize the possible adverse consequences on money supply growth consequent upon increases in foreign reserves can involve open market operations, increases in reserve requirements and shifts of government deposits and funds from the banking system to the central bank.

The experience in East and South-East Asian countries suggests that in most of the countries, sterilization has not been an effective tool of monetary control. Domestic credit expansion has remained high. Moreover, the experience of most of the economies indicates that short-term interest rates rose as sterilization efforts progressed, whereas in the absence of sterilization, domestic interest rates would be expected to decline with the inflow of foreign capital. Thus, there was the paradoxical experience of rapid growth in credit expansion and high domestic interest rates. Even with the easing or cessation of sterilization, interest rate spreads tended to remain high, attracting further inflows of short-term capital. Under a less liberal capital-account regime, even if open market operations were to result in a high interest rate regime, domestic borrowers would be constrained from accessing funds overseas.

The increase in short-term interest rates as a result of sterilization can discourage long-term investment demand as the cost of capital rises, while returns on less risky assets such as government paper become more attractive. Sterilization, therefore, may have the unintended effect of changing the composition of capital flows away from long-term to short-term.

The unintended effects of sterilization may take other forms and be magnified when the financial sector is weak. With rising interest rates, financial institutions tend to become less stringent in evaluating credit risks and expand short-term operations without careful assessment of trade-offs between risks and returns. Their institutional capacity may thus become overstretched and they may quickly run into serious problems with non-performing loans. With inadequate loan-loss provisions or capital reserves, public confidence in financial institutions may weaken, leading to large withdrawals and a precipitous crisis.

The above discussion has already indicated the ineffectiveness of high interest rate policy to contain domestic credit growth during periods of upswing with large capital inflows. On the other hand, during periods of downswing characterized by capital outflows, aggravated financial sector problems and depressed domestic demand, the high interest rate policy seems to have only limited effectiveness in securing the return of foreign flows. At the same time, a high interest rate policy intensifies deflationary forces and causes severe loss of output and employment.

The exchange rate policy

Another policy response to capital inflows would be allowing greater flexibility in exchange rates. This would imply appreciation in nominal exchange rates during periods of large inflows and depreciation during periods of outflows. The underlying rationale is that the flexibility in exchange rates would introduce some uncertainties that might discourage purely speculative and highly reversible inflows. It also allows the monetary authorities a greater degree of independence in exercising control over monetary aggregates as they become relatively free from preoccupation with stability of the exchange rate.[4]

There are, however, a number of arguments in favour of a stable exchange rate. First, the prevention of appreciation in the nominal exchange rate following large capital inflows is often a policy priority with a view to maintaining the competitiveness of exports. Second, there is apprehension that once the currency is allowed to float, it may become highly volatile, inhibiting not merely capital inflows but also trade transactions. Such a situation arises particularly because of the lack of development of deep markets for managing currency risks. Third, a stable exchange rate may be an effective anchor against inflation in the domestic economy. Fourth, a government's ability to maintain a stable exchange rate may be viewed as an indicator of its policy credibility, which can help maintain confidence in the economy.

However, a fixed or highly stable exchange rate regime is inherently vulnerable to speculative attacks, particularly when there are expectations that

4 A flexible exchange rate policy, if it does not produce wide fluctuations, may also be helpful to the real sector of the economy. For example, it can help maintain export competitiveness.

devaluation is likely (Bensaid and Jeanne, 1997). Several factors can cause an expectation of devaluation in the market. These may be related to some problems with the fundamentals of an economy, such as loss of export competitiveness or deteriorating current account or fiscal balance; political events; or actions of some strategic market participants, for example, major hedge fund operators. Once expectation of devaluation sets in, speculators are aware that a government's willingness or ability to defend the exchange rate is subject to severe limitations. The intervention in the foreign exchange market is bounded on the upper side by the stock of accumulated international reserves. Efforts to prevent devaluation by raising domestic interest rates impose heavy costs on the economy, including an increase in public debt obligations, a collapse of the property market and a dampening impact on the level of economic activities in general. Speculators recognize that these costs cannot be sustained indefinitely and therefore may persist with their attacks. In the end, the governments and monetary authorities can win if they are ready to pay a high cost, as happened in Hong Kong (China) in 1997, where the authorities permitted a drastic increase in interest rates in order to defend the exchange rate. They were also, of course, backed up by a very high level of foreign exchange reserves. But in the crisis countries, it was the authorities who were forced to succumb.

These arguments point towards the desirability of a greater flexibility in exchange rate policy. However, the potential benefit of this policy stance in terms of moderating capital flows needs to be balanced against the benefits of a stable exchange rate regime. It is not easy to precisely calculate the trade-offs *ex ante*, giving rise to errors of judgement.

The upshot of the above discussion is that macroeconomic management becomes highly complex in economies with open capital accounts. The policy instruments become severely constrained in ensuring both internal and external stability. Governments inevitably face a serious conflict of objectives such as aiming simultaneously at a stable exchange rate, financial sector openness and independence in executing monetary policy - the so-called "impossible trinity" (Frankel, 1996). In addition, the traditional indicators used to guide macroeconomic management become inadequate, if not inappropriate. For example, the consumer price index is a poor guide to inflation in the presence of a large bubble in the prices of financial assets. And the desirable level of reserves usually calculated on the basis of average import bill for a certain number of months becomes in a situation where there are possibilities of large and unpredictable capital outflows.

(b) Financial sector management

Strengthening the financial sector

The crisis has revealed particularly serious weaknesses in the financial sectors of the affected economies. The weaknesses relate not only to the operations of the individual financial institutions but also to the regulatory and supervisory regimes governing them. The intermediating entities appear to have been unaware of, or unable to gauge correctly, the underlying risk of many of the investment and lending decisions they took; in addition, they have not had the capital strength to absorb the losses that subsequently occurred. Supervisory and regulatory bodies also appear not to have been in a position to carry out their functions effectively for reasons of inadequate human resources, lack of institutional development and of regulatory tools, or laxity. The problem of ineffective regulation and supervision extended to the bank and non-bank financial institutions as well as capital markets and it allowed a climate of lack of transparency and accountability to flourish.

It is clear that governments need to establish a proper regulatory framework and be more effective in the implementation of that framework. Equally important, proper accounting, auditing and disclosure requirements need to be in place. In particular, rules regarding non-performing loans and adequate provision of capital with appropriate risk weights should follow or exceed international standards.[5] Legal lending limits to insider borrowing should be established and rigorously enforced. The rules regarding consolidation of financial reports of financial and other companies with extensive cross-holding and interlocking ownership need to be formulated and implemented. Foreign exposures of financial institutions as well as other corporate entities have to be monitored. In the absence of such regulations, any business or company evaluation rests on poor financial data, becomes either biased or meaningless and, in effect, financing decisions rely heavily on investors' confidence which can be very fragile and volatile. The rigorous efforts to restore the soundness of financial institutions should be complemented by appropriate support to debtor enterprises in the real economy that are fundamentally sound but are currently facing liquidity problems. Sound rules of corporate governance should be put in place. Also important are competition policies to restrict improper business practices in both the financial and the real sectors. At the same time, in increasing competition by allowing liberal entry in the financial

5 It has been suggested that these rules should be more stringent in emerging financial markets where the volume of business is rather thin.

arena, governments should take into account how much competition can be allowed. Too much competition can erode profit margins, encourage the financing of highly risky projects, complicate the task of supervision and eventually lead to the failure of some institutions and a crisis.

Governments have a critical role in putting in place well structured and staffed supervisory and regulatory bodies with clear mandates. Also they need to consider the viability of an integrated supervisory framework for the financial sector as a whole. There is a growing worldwide trend to adopt such an integrated framework, the recent cases being in Japan, Malaysia, the Republic of Korea, the United Kingdom of Great Britain and Northern Ireland and (to some extent) India. The main rationale for this is that many banks, non-bank financial institutions and securities and insurance firms engage in a widening variety of financial transactions in different financial markets, both directly and indirectly. In the existing supervisory framework, each separate body supervises only one type or a limited number of types of financial institutions. The supervisory body or bodies thus tend(s) to be ill-equipped to monitor the total financial activities of institutions and the cumulated risks involved, and hence to enforce prudential standards. A related issue is the role of the central bank in financial supervision in terms of both stretching its capacity too far and creating an inherent conflict of interest situation. Governments should consider assigning the supervisory functions to a separate specialized autonomous body and leaving the central bank solely with the conduct of monetary and exchange rate policy. Such a separation of functions exists in a few countries and is being implemented in some others.

Coping with risk in financial transactions

Both the increasing array of financial instruments available and the globalization of financial markets make it imperative that public and private operators have access to, and actively use, hedging instruments for managing their risks. Such risks include unanticipated changes in prices, interest rates and exchange rates etc. These can be managed or counterbalanced to a large degree through hedging techniques on forward or futures markets. However, most countries in the region do not yet possess active financial forward or futures markets, and those that do exist are very thin, with few active participants. The recent exaggerated swings in currency markets bear testimony to this. The development of viable financial risk management markets requires not only having an adequate supervisory mechanism in place but also providing training for, and encouraging its use by a wide spectrum of participants, including business enterprises, investors, financial institutions etc. The wider (in terms of different types of participants) and deeper (in terms of number of transactions per day) a market, the more robust is its price formation and the less the volatility of prices. More specifically, it can be claimed that a well-functioning forward or futures market for a currency is a necessary adjunct to a currency float, particularly for commercial transactions of various sorts, and its existence should lead to smoother variations in the exchange rate over the longer term.

Strengthening the financial sector and developing mechanisms for coping with risks are certainly desirable, with or without a crisis. Many governments in the region are taking measures in these areas.

There are several policy lessons that should be borne in mind in pursuing these reforms. First, it may be inopportune to introduce drastic reforms during a crisis as a vicious circle explained earlier may come into being. Second, it takes considerable time to establish a viable financial sector and even countries with sophisticated institutions, high levels of transparency and good corporate governance like the United States and Sweden have had to face serious problems in their financial sector (Stiglitz, 1998a). Third, it should be recognized that in an economy characterized by a liberal financial sector regime, a financial sector crisis and a currency crisis become closely intertwined. A recent empirical study has shown that in many cases the simultaneous occurrence of the two crises had their common origin in the deregulation of the financial system (Kaminsky and Reinhart, 1996). An expected devaluation, for reasons unrelated to the financial sector, changes the return profile of investment for the foreign investors and increases the perceived benefits of early withdrawal, thereby causing a significant drain on the financial intermediaries and a fall in capital markets. On the other hand, the withdrawal of funds from financial intermediaries and repatriation outside the country, for reasons unrelated to the domestic financial or real sector (for example, the emergence of a better opportunity elsewhere) weakens the financial sector, causes depletion of reserves and forces a devaluation of the currency. A strengthened financial sector may thus inhibit, but is unlikely to prevent a crisis.

(c) Policies towards short-term flows

The above arguments suggest the need for exercising some restraint on capital flows and/or a carefully sequenced and gradual process of liberalization. This is being increasingly accepted by economists who are otherwise strong proponents of openness (see, for example, Bhagwati, 1998;

Fischer, 1997; Williamson, 1997 and Stiglitz, 1998b). From the perspective of pre-empting the emergence of a future crisis attributable to external capital inflows, measures may be aimed at reducing inflows and/or influencing the composition of such flows in favour of long-term ones. One such measure is a non-remunerated reserve requirement deposited with the central bank on liabilities in foreign currency arising from borrowing by firms. The reserve requirement can be varied with the maturity of the loan, the percentage of the requirements declining with the increasing length of maturity. There can also be an explicit tax on inflows with variations across assets as well as across maturities. Such a tax can be imposed either on domestic debtors (for example, on a local firm issuing bonds abroad), or on foreigners (for example, those investing in the stock market). It is also possible to impose quantitative capital control measures such as prudential limits on or prohibitions of non-trade-related swap activities, offshore borrowing, ceilings on banks' foreign currency liability or sale of short-term money market instruments to foreign residents (see Reinhart and Dunaway, 1996).

The case of Chile is worth citing here (see Agosin and Ffrench-Davis, this volume). The experience of Chile suggests, however, that policies to influence maturity may reduce overall inflows. But, it is desirable to err on the side of caution, rather than desperation after being hit by a crisis. In addition to any regulatory measures with respect to short-term flows, countries should also examine the scope for expanding the range of financial instruments that can attract medium- to long-term flows.

5. Some thoughts on international and regional cooperation

(a) The establishment of a World Financial Organization

The globalization process that has been characterized by imbalances and disruptions in financial markets brings the issue of market stabilization to the fore. While speculative activities can be useful in correcting imbalances between national (or regional) markets, thus promoting global efficiency in the longer run, there is a valid concern that these activities may impose unacceptably high short-run costs. Hence, there is a good case for considering a mechanism for global governance of international financial flows comparable with that in the area of trade.

In this context, the proposal for the creation of a World Financial Organization (WFO) by the Committee for Development Planning (CDP) of the United Nations merits serious consideration.[6] The Committee proposed that WFO should monitor the implementation of sound international principles and practices for accounting, payments and settlements, banking supervision, security market supervision, insurance supervision and supervision of financial conglomerates. In addition, it should formulate acceptable forms of international regulation for short-term capital movements to complement national measures, as well as formulate and apply international guidelines for short-term lending and borrowing by private creditors and borrowers. According to CDP, the competence of WFO could also be extended to include the development of rules for ensuring transparency and full disclosure of information relating to both financial and non-financial corporate sectors, as well as rules for the smooth functioning of international bankruptcy regimes.

(b) Should there be an international debt strategy?

In the context of the current Asian crisis, as of mid-1998 only the Republic of Korea had succeeded in striking a reasonably comprehensive debt-rescheduling deal with creditor banks. The implementation of the deal is voluntary; creditors are not bound to join it. However, a more general issue is that a case-by-case approach is a time-consuming process and imposes high economic costs on the debtor countries in the interim. In fact, in the case of the debt crisis of the Latin American countries in the 1980s, it took seven years before the creditor community accepted the need for debt reduction. There are also inequities in the present system with foreign creditors typically enjoying an explicit or implicit seniority in their claims (IMF, 1997b). In the event of a crisis, governments are often in a hurry to reassure these creditors that all their claims will be met and the burden of adjustment falls almost entirely on domestic debtors. Besides, as long as free movement of international capital is allowed, no one can guarantee that the debt crisis will not recur in the future. These considerations point to the need for the revival of the discussion on an international debt strategy, an idea which seems to have dissipated with the resolution of the Latin American debt crisis. WFO could play an important institutional role in the formulation of an international debt strategy. It could also bring private lenders, investors and borrowers together when financial crises

---

6 The Committee for Development Planning is an independent body of experts constituted by the Secretary-General of the United Nations. Its members are chosen from a large cross-section of both developed and developing countries. [In 1998, the Committee was reconfigured by the Economic and Social Council and renamed the Committee for Development Policy — *Editor's note.*]

do erupt and thus expedite negotiations in sharing the responsibility for debt relief, for rescheduling or for delaying claims on repayments.

(c) Regional cooperation

Setting norms and sharing information

There is a strong case for greater regional cooperation in the Asian and Pacific region to address the issues of financial sector regulation, the establishment of common prudential standards for the industry, and development of early warning systems. Financial market instability has been partly aggravated by perceptions of weaknesses in financial institutions as well as other corporate entities and the lack of reliable relevant information regarding their operations. This has arisen partly from differing standards of regulation, the lack of detailed information regarding assets and liabilities, the variability as well as inadequacy of standards of corporate accounting, auditing, disclosures and problems with corporate governance generally. It would appear, therefore, that arrangements capable of generating and transmitting more accurate, transparent and timely information regarding the build-up of significant financial risks within a particular jurisdiction would be very useful for the authorities in another jurisdiction.

Much of the current crisis can be traced to doubts regarding the ability of countries to service their foreign liabilities, especially short-term debts. Doubts arose as market operators appeared to be unaware of the true extent of the affected countries' indebtedness, principally because short-term debts had not hitherto been fully included in the official debt data. Besides, detailed information about debt incurred by non-bank private sector companies is not available. All economies need to make substantial improvements in this area by providing comprehensive and timely debt information to counter the deleterious effects of rumour and speculation. Governments could cooperate in setting out common definitions, information requirements and reporting procedures and in establishing a system for sharing information. In this context, the accord recently signed by several countries of the Asian region with the Asian Development Bank for conduct of surveillance is a welcome step. Perhaps the accord can be extended to include other countries willing to join it.

The generation and dissemination of information may be certainly desirable for encouraging the adoption of corrective measures before a country falls victim to a crisis, but a *caveat* is in order. There will always be some question as to how the information will be interpreted by the relevant actors and when. For example, much, though not all, of the information relating to the weaknesses which characterized the East and South-East Asian countries immediately before the crisis was in the public domain. But neither policy makers nor the market actors took any serious notice, presumably because their interpretation was that the situation did not warrant much concern, and then suddenly there was an overreaction by the market players.

Asian Fund

The proposal for the establishment of an Asian Fund appears to have been put on the back burner. There are, however, good reasons why the establishment of such a fund could reduce the probability of a crisis, or mitigate its adverse impact. The Asian Fund would provide liquidity additional to what is at the disposal of IMF. The very existence of this liquidity would help improve market sentiment. It could be designed to be quick-disbursing in nature. Thus, it could help member countries in replenishing reserves as soon as signs of distress become visible and thereby reduce the incentive for rapid withdrawal by foreign market operators. As of now, countries have to negotiate conditionalities with IMF. The news that such assistance is being sought aggravates loss of confidence. By the time the assistance package is in final shape, too much damage has already taken place and restoration of confidence takes a very long time.

The argument that the establishment of an Asian Fund could create a "moral hazard" problem is not very persuasive. Countries are unlikely to pursue irresponsible policies simply based on the knowledge that they have access to some limited amount of funds in the event of an emergency. The moral hazard argument is hardly applicable to life insurance because people are rarely expected to commit suicide in order to realize insurance benefits. Similarly, countries are not expected to pursue suicidal policies. Besides, a system of incentives could be created to reduce the probability of moral hazard by, for example, varying interest rates with the volume and the frequency of drawing from the Asian Fund.

Another argument against the Asian Fund is that it could undermine IMF conditionalities. Once conditionalities are agreed upon, any release of subsequent assistance by the Asian Fund could be made contingent upon compliance with the conditionalities. But the Asian Fund should have a role in negotiating the conditionalities themselves. At present, negotiations take place between IMF and a country in distress and are often perceived as a one-way process. The competence of IMF in prescribing curative medicine for an ailing economy is not in question. But, some degree of plurality of views in the determination of conditionalities would most likely add to their credence and promote wider acceptance, including in the recipient country.

6. Concluding observations

This paper has argued that one of the primary causes of the economic crisis in East and South-East Asia was the large and/or rising current-account deficits resulting from slowdowns in export growth. It is therefore essential that countries pay strict attention to the size of their current-account deficit, although one cannot lay down a precise percentage of GDP that should be considered too large. Much depends on how the deficit is financed. In general, the greater the importance of short-term private flows in financing, the lower is the desirable level of deficit. Countries thus need to persist with efforts to enhance their export competitiveness through technological upgrading, improvements in the quality of human resources, and increases in the domestic value-added component of exports, including by reducing the import intensity. The underlying rationale is to ensure that import requirements are primarily financed by export earnings, rather than by short-term private credit.

The deficit in the current account reflects a savings-investment gap. The recent crisis has brought into sharp focus the unsustainability of a substantial and prolonged savings-investment gap, particularly when it is financed by short-term private inflows. Hence, the need for giving greater attention to matching the level of domestic savings to the levels of investment desired if these are to be sustained. One of the options that countries with already high savings have to consider in the future is to settle for lower levels of investment and lower rates of economic growth. Meanwhile, efforts should be continued to increase domestic saving, to the extent possible, through such measures as wider coverage of insurance services, pension systems and provident funds. More strict supervision of the credit practices of commercial banks and financial institutions may have a desirable effect of curtailing consumption credit and raising domestic savings. In this context, it should be noted that the efficacy of the interest rate policy as an instrument to encourage savings is rather constrained in a country with an open financial sector, as any sizeable differential between the domestic and foreign interest rates tends to bring about an upsurge in short-term inflows and sows the seeds of instability.

The second primary cause of the crisis was the liberalization of capital flows which not merely permitted financing of growing current-account deficits through short-term inflows but also encouraged sizeable autonomous inflows. In this situation, macroeconomic policy instruments face severe constraints in exercising control over the size of the current-account deficit. Measures aimed at strengthening the domestic financial sector and enhancing capacities to cope with risks in financial transactions may not be adequate in preventing rapid changes in the direction of capital flows. Specific policies towards short-term flows are, therefore, required. These policies may be aimed at both limiting the magnitude of short-term flows and increasing the maturity of inflows. However, one consequence of such policies is likely to be a reduction in overall inflows.

Policy measures implemented at the national level need to be complemented by actions at the international and regional levels. In the latter respect, the paper supports the establishment of a World Financial Organization and the formulation of an international debt strategy. In addition, the paper suggests regional cooperation in setting norms for the operation of financial institutions, devising systems for sharing information on their functioning and the establishment of an Asian Fund.

References

Agosin, Manuel and Ricardo Ffrench-Davis (this volume). "Managing capital flows in Chile".

The Asian Wall Street Journal (1998). "Banks continued lending to Asia in first half of 1997", p. 6 (5 January).

Bensaid, B. and O. Jeanne (1997). "The instability of fixed exchange rate systems when raising the nominal interest rate is costly", *European Economic Review*, vol. 41, No. 8, pp. 1461-1478.

Bhagwati, Jagdish (1998). "The capital myth, the difference between trade in widgets and dollars", *Foreign Affairs*, vol. 77, No. 3, pp. 7-12.

Dillon, K. Burke and others (1985). *Recent Developments in External Debt Restructuring*, IMF Occasional Paper No. 40, Washington, D. C.

The Economist (1982). "Bottomless debt", p. 12. (11 December).

Fischer, Stanley (1997). *Capital Account Liberalization and the Role of the IMF*. Washington, D.C.: International Monetary Fund.

Frankel, J.A. (1996). "Recent exchange-rate experience and proposals for reform". *The American Economic Review, Papers and Proceedings of the Hundred and Eighth Annual Meeting of the American Economic Association*, vol. 86, No. 2, pp. 153-158.

International Monetary Fund (1997a). *World Economic Outlook*. Washington, D.C., p. 91. (October).

______ (1997b). *International Capital Markets: Developments, Prospects and Key Policy Issues*, p. 40, Washington, D. C.

Kaminsky, G.L. and C.M. Reinhart (1996). *The twin crises: the causes of banking and balance of payments problems*, International Finance Discussion Paper. Washington, D. C.: Board of Governors of the Federal Reserve System.

Reinhart, Carmen M. and Steven Dunaway (1996). *Dealing with Capital Inflows: Are there Any Lessons?* Helsinki: United Nations University, World Institute for Development Economics Research.

Stiglitz, J.E. (1998a). "More instruments and broader goals: moving toward the post-Washington consensus". *WIDER Annual Lectures 2*, mimeo.

______ (1998b). "South Asia beyond 2000: lessons from East Asia and elsewhere". Keynote address to South Asia Beyond 2000, Colombo, Sri Lanka (19 March), mimeo.

UN/ESCAP (1998). *Economic and Social Survey of Asia and the Pacific 1998*. New York: United Nations publication, Sales No. E.98.II.F.59.

Williamson, John (1997). "Public policy towards international capital flows". In Istvan P. Székely and Richard Sabot, eds., *Development Strategy and Management of the Market Economy*, Volume II, pp. 325-347. Oxford: Clarendon Press.

6

Do We Know the Real Causes of the Asian Crisis?

IWAN AZIS*
University of Indonesia and
Cornell University

Introduction

It is now more than a year since several economies in Asia began to melt. Hundreds or thousands of papers, analyses and comments have been made, attempting to unravel the causes of the Asian crisis. This is not unexpected. Even now, some experts are still trying to explain the great depression of the 1930s.

At the risk of falling into "another one of those", this manuscript is intended to explore alternative explanations of the Asian crisis. It is argued that the region's "fundamentals" did not indicate fragility. The weak banking system, which indeed existed in most of the countries, also by itself could not be blamed for triggering the crisis. It is the contagion, channelled especially through huge shifts in financial flows, that may be able to explain the episode.

Yet, the severity of the crisis remains unexplained. By using the case of Indonesia, which happens to be the most serious casualty so far, it is argued that distinct political factors in each country may help clarify why the crisis ended

---

* Professor of Economics, University of Indonesia. Currently, Visiting Professor, Cornell University and Participant for the Indonesian economy in Project LINK. [The original version of this paper has been shortened and edited, in part to avoid repetition of the review of pre-crisis trends in the preceding chapter — *Editors' note.*]

up more severe in one country than in another. In the last section, issues of banking reform and debt resolution are discussed.

The fundamentals

Before the crisis kicked off, the affected countries—Indonesia, Malaysia, Republic of Korea, Philippines and Thailand—appeared quite robust in terms of several indicators. Most of the countries produced remarkably high economic growth. The only exception was the Philippines, which during 1991-1995 posted a mere 2.2 per cent annual growth rate. But even that number was higher than the annual rate of 1.8 per cent during the preceding decade.

Inflation trends were also quite positive. All affected countries managed to keep inflation at one-digit rates, although there was a slight increase in 1996. Indonesia, traditionally having the highest inflation rate, even managed to reduce the rate to 6.5 per cent in that year.

One of the factors behind the low inflation has been the management of the government budget. Practically all the countries had a budget surplus, a very different situation than that in the Latin American countries which experienced crises in the 1980s.

Export performance of the Asian crisis countries had also been relatively strong and the current-account deficits manageable, although the situation deteriorated and 1996 was a year of concern in terms of both indicators, above all for Thailand (see Islam, this volume, table 1).

One factor offered as an explanation of the current-account situation was the appreciation of the real exchange rate in the years leading up to the crisis (see ibid., figure 1). Each country had a fixed or semi-fixed exchange rate that was pegged, in essence, to the United States dollar and the dollar had strengthened during 1996 relative to other major currencies.

However, an appreciation of the exchange rate is not the same as having an overvalued exchange rate and thus the precise status of the exchange rate prior to the crisis needs to be looked at more closely. In this regard, Chinn (1998) found that even when overvaluation of the exchange rate was detected using a model that estimated the purchasing-power-parity exchange rate, the size of the overvaluation in crisis-stricken countries was smaller than that in crisis-free countries. For example, the Singapore dollar was found to be overvalued by 45 per cent, whereas the size of the overvaluation was much smaller in Indonesia, Malaysia and Thailand (see table 1).

Moreover, each of the South-East Asian crisis countries had relatively large holdings of foreign-exchange reserves. As shown in table 2, the recorded foreign reserves were 5, 4 and 3.5 months of imports in Indonesia, Malaysia and

Table 1. Deviations of exchange rates in East Asia from purchasing power parity (PPP)
(Percentage[a])

	January 1997	*February 1995-January 1997*
Indonesia	0.9	4.7
Malaysia	2.0	0.5
Philippines	-24.6	-26.4
Republic of Korea	-12.3	-0.5
Singapore	35.4	45.4
Taiwan Province of China	7.6	12.8
Thailand	2.0	3.7

Source: Chinn (1998).

a. Global currency overvaluation (+) or undervaluation (-) relative to PPP.

the Philippines, respectively. In Thailand, the number was highest among the four at 6.3 months.

On the basis of other indicators, however, the official reserve situation was less favourable. For example, one may contrast the stock of liquid monetary assets, which residents could some day try to convert into foreign exchange, with the capacity of the central bank to intervene to meet that demand were private suppliers of foreign exchange to withdraw, as during a speculative attack. One indicator that has been suggested in this regard is the ratio of broad money (M_2) to foreign reserves. The higher the ratio, the more vulnerable will be the country to speculative attack.[1] On the basis of such a ratio, table 2 reveals that in 1996 Indonesia was the most vulnerable, followed by the Philippines. Thailand had the smallest ratio. Even when a narrower measure of money is used (M_1), the ranking alters only slightly. Thailand continues to have the smallest ratio.

A complementary picture is given by a different external liquidity indicator, the ratio of short-term foreign debt to reserves. Obviously, the greater the ratio, the more vulnerable to speculative attacks a country will be. The last column of table 2 shows that the countries with the worst economic situation—Indonesia and Thailand—were precisely those that had ratios above one.[2]

A related indicator was the rapid growth of foreign debt itself, and the high and increasing share of short-term debt in the total (see Islam, this volume, table 2). However, the ratio of short-term debt to reserves did not rise

1 Calvo (1995) and Sachs et al. (1996) used a similar indicator in tests of the vulnerability of a country to speculative attack in the wake of the 1994-1995 Mexican peso crisis.

2 The Republic of Korea's short-term debt was more than twice its foreign reserves.

Table 2. Indicators of pre-crisis foreign exchange reserves in South-East Asia

	Foreign-exchange reserves (billions of US dollars)	*Import coverage of reserves (number of months)*	*Liquidity indicators (ratio to reserves)*		
			M_2	M_1	*Short-term foreign debt*[a]
Indonesia					
1992	10.2	4.5	5.7	1.3	1.7
1993	11.0	4.7	6.2	1.5	1.7
1994	11.8	4.4	6.6	1.6	1.8
1995	13.3	3.9	7.1	1.5	2.1
1996	17.8	5.0	6.5	1.2	1.9
Malaysia					
1992	16.8	5.2	2.6	0.8	0.2
1993	26.8	7.4	2.0	0.7	0.3
1994	24.9	4.9	2.6	0.9	0.3
1995	22.9	3.6	3.4	1.1	0.3
1996	26.2	4.0	3.8	1.2	0.4
Philippines					
1992	4.3	3.3	4.5	1.1	0.7
1993	4.5	3.0	4.9	1.1	0.5
1994	5.9	2.9	5.4	1.1	0.5
1995	6.2	2.7	5.9	1.2	0.7
1996	9.9	3.5	4.5	0.9	0.8
Thailand					
1992	20.0	5.9	4.1	0.5	0.8
1993	24.1	6.3	4.1	0.5	0.9
1994	28.9	6.4	3.9	0.5	1.1
1995	35.5	5.9	3.7	0.4	1.2
1996	37.2	6.3	3.9	0.4	1.2

Source: Data of IMF and the Bank for International Settlements.

a. Debt to private creditors maturing in one year or less.

significantly through 1996, which reflected the strong growth in reserves themselves. In fact, there were heavy pressures on the central banks to purchase foreign currency, especially in 1996, owing to massive inflows of capital into the region and the commitment to maintain fixed exchange rates or exchange-rate bands. By the same token, each of the countries saw rapid increases in domestic credit, fed in part by the foreign fund inflows and this should have been taken as an early warning of danger ahead.

Impact of capital inflows

By the late 1980s, most South-East Asian countries had liberalized their financial sectors, albeit to different degrees. Theoretically, the aim of financial liberalization is a more efficient financial system, from which borrowers and savers would reap the benefits. In this region, it was associated with remarkably high capital inflows (and not all of this capital was invested in the most productive sectors).

One problem for policy makers was the upward pressure on the exchange rate created by the inflows. The potential damage of appreciation on export competitiveness led the monetary authorities to purchase large amounts of foreign funds (boosting reserves), but that also added significantly to the domestic money supply. That could be inflationary, which left the authorities with an impossible dilemma.

Like anything else, the "Asian way" was to opt for a middle ground. While the Thai baht was perhaps the most stable currency in the region until 1996, in Indonesia, Malaysia and the Philippines, the selected middle ground was to manipulate the exchange-rate band by widening it when there were pressures to do so. At least until early 1997, the effort appears to have worked fairly effectively.

But high capital inflows have a far more serious impact than pressuring the exchange rate, namely their effect on the growth of bank credit and on domestic interest rates. That is, when a central bank buys foreign exchange (when it adds to foreign-exchange reserves), it pays with domestic money that thereby enters into the economy and into the domestic reserves of commercial banks; and on this basis, the banks extend more credit. However, if the monetary authorities simultaneously withdraw reserves from the banks, they may be able to sterilize the credit-expansion effect of the inflows. The problem is that to the degree that the excessive capital inflows were initially attracted by high domestic interest rates, those interest rate might well be unchanged at the end of the exercise and so the capital inflow would continue.

At a certain point, the monetary authority would have to give up sterilizing the inflows (alternatively, the strength of the inflow could overwhelm the sterilization capacity of the central bank). The story then becomes one of greater-than-desired increases in bank deposits and bank reserves, and excessive increases in domestic bank credit to the economy. Studies by Glick and Moreno (1994) and Chinn and Dooley (1995) showed that relationships of this sort existed in Indonesia and Malaysia. Indeed, table 3 shows that the four crisis countries of South-East Asia had very high credit growth. It continued

Table 3. Growth of credit to the non-government sector in South-East Asia[a]
(Annual percentage change)

	Indonesia	*Malaysia*	*Philippines*	*Thailand*
1992	18.3	14.2	21.8	31.6
1993	23.9	11.5	34.7	23.8
1994	22.8	19.6	25.2	29.8
1995	22.6	30.3	41.6	24.2
1996	21.7	28.0	50.1	14.3

Source: International Monetary Fund, *International Finance Statistics.*

a. Credit in local currency extended by commercial banks and the central bank to private and financial sectors (excluding commercial banks).

through 1996, except in Thailand, where policy tightening was necessitated by already-visible signs of difficulty.

This notwithstanding, it is one thing to detect rapid credit growth and massive capital inflows. It is a different thing to conclude that those factors *per se* explain why the crisis reached such high proportions in East Asia. It is absolutely an oversimplification, in other words, to assert that the culprits of the crisis were credit expansion and capital inflows, especially when most of the "fundamental" variables did not show any sign of trouble. Two questions suggest themselves: how was the credit used and why did the financial inflows change direction more or less simultaneously.

A weak banking system

Having found no robust explanation of the source of the crisis in the standard macroeconomic fundamentals, some analysts turned their attention to microeconomic issues, the most prominent of which is the region's weak banking system. Following deregulation of the banking sector throughout the region, the number of banks and other financial corporations grew rapidly. Many big conglomerates set up new banks, primarily to serve their own often-risky projects. Despite regulatory measures formally imposed by the monetary authority (for example, legal lending limits, capital adequacy ratios), weak enforcement impeded the development of a healthy banking sector.

Too often, Governments in the region played favourites. A few highly leveraged and well-connected groups were given special, often non-transparent access to credit. These private businesses could obtain loans from state banks without difficulty at interest rates that were much lower than the market rate and under more lenient conditions. This spelled trouble for the lending banks, as the probability of default on such loans was relatively high.

"Corruption, cronyism and nepotism", popularized as CCN, was already taking place in the 1980s, precisely the period during which the region performed its "miracle". Commenting on the Indonesian case, Hill (1998) remarked, "As long as growth was delivering benefits to practically everyone, CCN could be tolerated as annoying but not fatal." Also, as long as the volume of such practices was confined to a limited number of business deals, there was no serious threat to the economy. But as more and more public activities and state-owned enterprises were privatized, the cosy crony deals became widespread. Such practices peaked during the first half of the 1990s and coincided with the period of massive inflows of foreign capital.

The combination of CCN and cheap credit resulted in misallocated credit, as funds went to projects with the best connections, rather than those with the best economic prospects. Loans were advanced on the basis of inadequate project appraisals, many of them to the real estate sector. Indeed, average returns on capital fell sharply in the region during the 1990s, most dramatically in the Republic of Korea, Malaysia and Thailand.

Even when funded projects proved profitable, debt repayment could be slow and arduous, aggravating the problems faced by the banking sector. Indeed, dodging regular repayment to the state banks was not uncommon and the burden of missed payments was consequently transferred back to the public sector. Thus, privatization increased instead of decreased the public sector burden!

Central banks in the region were increasingly willing to become involved in efforts to bail out not only state banks but also selected commercial banks, typically those with well connected owners. The goal was to avoid the disruption that could be caused by banking defaults. But avoiding default in the short run, in effect, increased the probability of larger default in the future, as the source of weakness was not removed.

Policy errors were also made in efforts to address the problem. In particular, the policy reform advanced by the International Monetary Fund (IMF) in October 1997 in response to the weakness of Indonesia's banking system contained a miscalculation. After a frustrating two weeks of discussions with the Fund, the Indonesian Government agreed to a set of policy measures, which were to be supported with a US$43 billion international credit package. One step in the agreement was to liquidate 16 Indonesian banks, some of which were owned by well connected businessmen and members of the Suharto family. As there was virtually no deposit insurance system, the outcome could have been expected: even with 15 to 20 per cent higher interest rates in the remaining local banks, most depositors went in a panic to the foreign banks operating in Jakarta. Only in May 1998 did the IMF recognize that its demand to close the insolvent banks backfired and caused a panic.[3]

Meanwhile, confidence in the domestic financial sector continued to erode in South-East Asia. More banks lost deposits, bad loans mounted, banks called loans, companies went bankrupt, good loans went bad. Lenient disclosure rules and poor banking regulations aggravated bad credit analysis and distorted investment decisions. This in itself was enough to make the entire financial sector falter.

But that is not the whole story. A more serious blow came from another front. The huge build up of short-term foreign debt of the private sector that was noted above had to be repaid. As the debt-service burden mounted, expectations of currency depreciation grew, raising the degree of nervousness among local corporate sectors. These companies then scrambled to buy dollars to meet repayment obligations, which worsened downward pressure on the exchange rates. Currency devaluation, inevitably came, which only worsened the problem.

In other words, a weak banking system was indeed a serious trouble spot in the region. However, to say that it was the source of the crisis is incorrect. The system was already weak even long before the crisis began. Furthermore, it is not too difficult to find other countries with much weaker banking systems that are not in crisis. This is not to say that the weak banking system did not contribute to the crisis. It did. But other factors must have been playing a more critical role. Something else provided the spark and fanned the flames.

Contagion

From the time that the Thai crisis first spread to neighbouring countries in July 1997, attention has been directed towards understanding the process of contagion. Unfortunately, this is an area where economists are not known to have a solid theory.

One hypothesis is that the more a country is financially integrated with a country where a crisis occurs, the more likely it is that the crisis will be transmitted to the first country. Hence, as regional integration intensified in the 1990s, including among the member countries of the Association of South-East Asian Nations (ASEAN), the vulnerability to contagion was reinforced.

Because a sharp U-turn of foreign capital marked the start of the crisis in South-East Asia, it would be reasonable to look at the behaviour of financial

3 While closing insolvent institutions is legitimate, i.e., "free exit" must accompany "free entry", the closure of an entire bank—forcing blameless workers to be laid off—can be questioned if instead it is possible to punish only the owners and the bank's management. In either case, a policy to minimize the ripple effects of bank closures should be in place to avoid panic in the entire financial market.

variables. The stock market return is one such variable. We can measure the extent to which stock market returns in the country where a crisis originated correlate with the returns in neighbouring countries. Hence, a correlation of, say, weekly stock market returns in Thailand with returns in Indonesia, Malaysia and the Philippines would indicate whether private investor behaviour in Thailand contaminated investor attitudes in the other three countries.[4]

Another potential line of contagion is external trade. The most forceful argument pertains to what is known as "competitive devaluation". After China devalued its currency in 1994, currency pressures were detected throughout the region, especially in those countries that have similar trade patterns as China. This strand of argument suggests that the collapse of the Thai baht might have been a form of contagion from the yuan devaluation, and the subsequent collapse of the rupiah, peso and ringgit could be the result of contagion from the baht's devaluation.

The key factor in the trade-and-exchange-rate argument is the similarity of economic-*cum*-trade structures. Singapore was not infected by the contagion because it has a markedly different economic structure than the other ASEAN countries. Moreover, even if two countries export similar commodities, they may ship to different destinations. If most of Indonesia's resource-intensive products were exported to Japan, the contagion pressures from Thailand would be less to the degree that most Thai resource-intensive exports were instead bound for the US market.

Attempting to measure those two types of contagion processes, Fratzscher (1998) found that the financial markets of most economies in the region are indeed highly integrated with Thailand, causing the financial channel of contagion to be strong. Fratzscher also found most regional economies to be close trade competitors in terms of the similarity of export structures and export destinations (including intra-regional trade). However, the size and significance of the coefficients in his econometric equations suggest that the financial link was the most important channel of contagion in the Asian crisis.

The study also found little support for the hypothesis that countries with weak fundamentals and low reserves, per se, were more vulnerable to contagion. However, such countries were found to be more vulnerable to contagion

4 Obviously, other factors (for example, fundamentals and incentive policies) have to be taken into account first in order to correct for their influence on investors' decisions.

if, in addition, domestic credit had expanded rapidly prior to the crisis.[5] It is thus the credit boom and the composition of capital inflows—facilitating the sharp switch from high inflows to high outflows—that mattered most in making the East Asian countries vulnerable to crisis contagion.

In sum, unlike economic fundamentals and a weak banking system, we probably can be more certain about the role of contagion in triggering the regional crisis following the baht collapse. However, even if we know a sufficient amount about the "what" (integrated financial market), we do not yet know enough about the "why". Moreover, detecting the importance of the swing in capital movement in generating a crisis, from massive inflows to huge outflows, does not itself explain what factors fund managers look at before a "stay or exit" decision is taken or how the decision is really made. Rational or irrational, such behaviour is important for policy makers to comprehend in order to be vigilant and better able to anticipate future shocks.

Finally, while the above study sheds some light on the causes of the crisis, there are limitations to such econometric exercises. One is the exclusion of possibly relevant variables. In Thailand and Indonesia, for example, the severity of the crisis has been raised significantly by political factors, operating during the early and later stages of the crisis, respectively.

Political factors—a case study of Indonesia

When economic factors leave unanswered questions, one tends to shift to non-economic factors, more particularly to political ones. On this subject, however, each country has a uniquely different set of events and a case study approach is unavoidable. Let me now shift to the particular situation of Indonesia, where the relationship between the financial crisis and the political crisis cannot be more obvious.

When President Suharto cancelled his scheduled visit to the ASEAN summit in Kuala Lumpur, and subsequently to his wife's grave in Solo (only 35 minutes flying time from Jakarta) in early December 1997, many perceived it as a serious sign of illness. In late December, there was another rumour that Suharto had had a stroke and that there would be a military coup. In no time, the stock market tumbled and the exchange rate fell to over 5,200 rupiah per US dollar.

Entering 1998, the situation worsened. The way the 1998/1999 budget was announced on 6 January did not satisfy the market. The number of laid-off

5 This was the only result in which the null hypothesis could be rejected at the 10 per cent level and it held both for Latin American and Asian crisis countries studied. Other tests, in particular for the relevance of exchange-rate overvaluation, did not find a significant relationship (Fratzscher, 1998).

workers continued to increase, adding to the already high open unemployment. The stock market plunged again and the rupiah hit an "insane" level of over 11,000 per US dollar. Pandemonium set in when on 8 and 9 January, people went on a buying spree to hoard foodstuffs.[6]

Meanwhile, perceptions spread that Suharto had lost his touch. A popular revolt gained strength and public attacks on the Government and Suharto's leadership rose. Fearing that tensions in Jakarta could degenerate into anarchy, the armed forces were put on special alert. Investors became jittery; the stock market tumbled.

Only then did the world begin to react with serious concern. The potent mixture of continuing market panic and political uncertainty led an array of heads of state—from Washington, Tokyo and Canberra—to phone Suharto. High ranking US and IMF officials rushed to Jakarta to consult with him and to press for urgent reforms.

The revised budget, announced after the President met with the Managing Director of IMF, assumed a 20 per cent inflation rate and zero GDP growth. A controversial item in the budget was the petroleum subsidy, amounting to Rp10 trillion (US$2.5 billion). The cutbacks of monopolies, special treatments, subsidies and tariffs that were contained in the "Letter of Intent" to IMF signed by Suharto received a subdued reaction and both the rupiah and the stock market continued to slip. The market seemed to be waiting to see the extent to which the proposed policies would actually be implemented.[7] Far more importantly, the political factor had now come more forcefully into play.

After mounting pressures from Government critics who demanded economic, legal and political reforms, which also meant the removal of Suharto, Indonesian politics reached a turning point. It started on 12 May when a bloody incident took place in one of the private universities in Jakarta (Trisakti). Four students died when real bullets hit them during demonstrations. On the next day, larger demonstrations spread across the nation. All this occurred while Suharto was in Cairo attending the summit of the Group of 15.

---

6 For several weeks there was also confusion because Suharto had indicated that a currency board system (CBS) would be implemented. The argument was as follows. A considerable amount of private debt matured early that year. In such a situation, a proposal that would guarantee a peg of the rupiah to the US dollar would be appropriate. Hence, the proposal for setting up a CBS seemed to make sense to some policy makers and to the heavily indebted private sector. Yet, the requirements for a CBS to work effectively with minimum adverse repercussions were not yet present in Indonesia (e.g., unfinished banking reform, which was part of the conditionality for IMF assistance).

7 The coincidental timing of Standard & Poor's announcement to downgrade 15 Indonesian banks was also not helpful.

On 14 May, there was mob violence and more than 500 people were killed, many of them looters burned to death. From that one-day tragedy alone, the material loss was estimated at about US$250 million.[8] In this chaotic situation, the stock market plunged and the rupiah weakened to 11,500 to the dollar.

Upon his return from Egypt, Suharto tried to respond by proposing two things: revise the planned increase of fuel and electricity prices and reshuffle the cabinet. The students and the public did not receive the decision with enthusiasm.

On 18 May, the wave of students protests escalated. Thousands of students managed to enter the parliament compound, demanding an immediate special session of the People's Consultative Assembly (MPR) and Suharto's resignation.[9] Once again, investors and the market faced a lot of uncertainties. However, there was one certainty: Suharto's era was over. It was only the exact time and the mode of transition that remained uncertain.[10]Opinions seemed to polarize in response within the pro-reform groups: one group strongly rejected the proposed scenario, while another saw it as a sufficient starting point and a

8 This is the official figure, which I think is underestimated. Around 5,000 buildings were damaged or burned, close to 2,000 vehicles were torched, no less than 220 bank branches were destroyed, and about the same number of automatic teller machines were damaged. Many stores were closed for several days, as were businesses and banking operations. It is estimated that the money transactions affected by bank closures in Jakarta alone reached some US$3 billion each day. The impact across the country was devastating, as the economies of many regions outside Jakarta are significantly dependent upon money flows from the capital city.

9 By 3:30 pm, under massive pressure, the Speaker of the House, Harmoko, flanked by two deputy speakers, announced that the top leaders of the parliament were calling on Suharto to step down for the sake of national unity. The students cheered the announcement, but the hope quickly faded when in the evening of the same day at 8:00 pm the armed forces commander, General Wiranto, said that Harmoko had spoken as an individual and his call for the President's resignation had no legal power.

10 After a meeting with Islamic and community leaders, Suharto announced that he would not step down immediately. Instead, he promised to revise political laws through a reform committee, the members of which would include representatives of the student movement. The cabinet would be reshuffled immediately in order to handle the deep economic and political crisis better. Then, new elections would be held as soon as possible. However, the most important point of Suharto's announcement was that he explicitly pledged that he would not run in the new elections. Many analysts suspect that such a compromise scenario was the result of a negotiation process, in which General Wiranto was a key player.

Opinions seemed to polarize in response within the pro-reform groups: one group strongly rejected the proposed scenario, while another saw it as a sufficient starting point and a dramatic one too, given that Suharto had never before explicitly said he would not run in the elections. Followers of the first group expressed scepticism and fear that such a deal was a last shrewd political game being played out by Suharto behind the opaque screen of a Javanese shadow puppet play. They even called for mass demonstrations on 20 May, Indonesia's National Day of Awakening, to mark the anniversary of the formation of the country's nationalist movement to fight against the Dutch colonial administration in 1908.

dramatic one too, given that Suharto had never before explicitly said he would not run in the elections. Followers of the first group expressed scepticism and fear that such a deal was a last shrewd political game being played out by Suharto behind the opaque screen of a Javanese shadow puppet play. They even called for mass demonstrations on 20 May, Indonesia's National Day of Awakening, to mark the anniversary of the formation of the country's nationalist movement to fight against the Dutch colonial administration in 1908.

Then came the historic day, 21 May, when Suharto announced his resignation and Vice President B. J. Habibie replaced him. A surprise? Not quite so. The intensity of the pro-reform movements and the dynamics of high-intensity political struggles during the preceding few months should have been enough to predict the outcome. The nomination of Habibie was not a surprise either, since constitutionally the vice president was next in line.

The social repercussions of the crisis quickly became very serious. The combined forces of declining real wages and unemployment raised poverty dramatically (see Azis, 1998d). This could become a fertile ground for social and political instability.[11]

Another serious blow to the economy was the exit of money and capital, especially owned by Indonesian Chinese—it is widely quoted, albeit with no supporting hard data, that ethnic Chinese control about 70 to 80 per cent of the assets of Indonesia's top 300 companies. The exodus of expatriates and foreigners bruised the country's image and made the prospect for economic recovery gloomier. Meanwhile, the exchange rate and the stock market continued to "go south". On 18 May, the former touched 17,000 per US dollar and the latter came closer to a low of 400 (on the third week of April, the recorded rate and the stock index were still 8,024 and over 490, respectively).

The new Government has thus had no deficit of challenges. The economy had already started to slide in mid-1997, although the worst really began early in 1998. Even without the financial crisis, the country has been stricken by a long drought (related to the El phenomenon), the haze problem caused by forest fires, a fall in oil prices, and a series of diseases that occurred in some parts of the country. The financial and political crisis only exacerbated the situation. The remaining strengths of the

11 The middle income population groups were hardest hit, in particular those in the urban area. The effect of inflation on transportation services was especially devastating. Higher fuel prices and the price hike of vehicle components of up to 300 percent forced many public transport operations to close down. By the end of March, more than 30 per cent of public transport ceased to operate, affecting the mobility of millions of medium and low-income workers throughout the country. In addition, the interregional and inter-island distribution of basic commodities was upset by the limited availability of transport operations. This put further pressures on the already sharply increased prices of many food products.

country—the enormous amount of natural resources, fairly adequate physical and non-physical infrastructure, and a cohesiveness as well as harmony among heterogeneous Indonesian society—remained under threat.

To sum up, in the early stage of the crisis a combination of rampant CCN and lack of confidence over Suharto's Government did nothing to counter the damaging effects of contagion. Then the policy package prescribed by the IMF pulled the economy further down. Prolonged discussions of the possibility of adopting a fixed exchange rate under a currency board system only raised more confusion. In the next stage, repeated violence, looting, destruction and street battles elevated the economic costs further. As Suharto's term neared its end, the political temperature peaked. Financial markets continued to shun Indonesia and the currency plunged, along with the stock market.

A lot of uncertainty remains in the political and economic spheres. This uncertainty is something that investors simply cannot cope with. When investors and the market know what is going on, they vote with their money. But when they do not know, they vote with their feet. Those who were already in the region faced the "exit or stay" choice, and those who originally thought about entering or who were ready to buy cheap, might have become more reluctant to come in while political uncertainty was high.

Bank and debt restructuring

By the second half of 1998, bank restructuring was under way in all the Asian crisis countries. The objectives were clear: return to normal lending and a safer banking system. Learning from recent experience, the key goal of bank restructuring is to protect depositors and the core banking system, but not necessarily the existing owners, managers and shareholders. The main principle is, let the troubled banks not contaminate the healthy ones, and try to revive the country's troubled banks or at least those that could be salvaged.

This meant some combination of merging or selling troubled banks to new owners who would infuse capital as well as new management, and reducing the burden on banks of their stocks of non-performing ("bad") loans. It also meant more of a direct, if temporary, role of government in the banking sector.

In Indonesia, for example, the Government set up the Indonesian Bank Restructuring Agency (IBRA) and by May 1998 it had 54 banks under its control. The agency also took over the management of eight banks, including Indonesia's largest private bank, the Bank Central Asia (BCA). In taking over these banks, IBRA took charge as well of the renegotiation of the nonperforming loans of its debtors. IBRA also guaranteed the deposits held in its commercial banks. Finally, IBRA infused its banks with sometimes large amounts of liquidity obtained from the central bank. Despite these efforts, it had to suspend the operations of some of the banks.[12]

The strategy to sell troubled banks, however, has not worked as well as hoped. Despite the asset price drop (especially as measured in dollars), the response from international investors was lukewarm, primarily because of the severity of the banks' distress. Bad loans were roughly 40 per cent of outstanding bad debts in Thailand and Indonesia.[13] In Thailand, foreign banks had agreed to take majority control of only two local banks more than one year after the crisis began.[14] A similar slow response was also seen in Indonesia and Malaysia.

In a further attempt to lure capital for Thailand's 15 commercial banks—the estimated requirement was 600 billion baht—the Thai central bank made a dramatic announcement in early August 1998. It would basically guarantee through the Financial Institutions Development Fund that foreign investors who bought major stakes in troubled banks and finance companies would receive their money back after five years. This "money back guarantee" system seems attractive, but unless it is combined with other measures, its effectiveness would be questionable.[15]

In part, plans to lure foreign capital have fallen victim to domestic policies and popular sentiment (nationalist outcry). This happened throughout the region and in various sectors. In Indonesia, for example, the plan to sell a stake in a blue-chip telecommunications company had to be scrapped, and the final plan to sell 35 percent of PT Semen Gresik, a cement company, to Mexico's Cemex SA also faltered, forcing the foreign stake to be lowered to 14 per cent.[16]

However, when confronted with such disappointments, the Government voiced a more liberal tone. In particular, on 24 August, Indonesia's Minister of Finance announced that the Government would now allow foreign investors to take more than the 50 percent maximum percentage of shares previously allowed foreigners in Indonesian banks. The net result of such developments, however, is that the Government's target of raising US$1.5 billion in the fiscal year ending 31 March 1999 had to be cut to US$1 billion.

---

12 As of August 1998, seven banks had also received more than US$11 billion in liquidity support (more than 500 per cent of the capital of the banks).

13 The precise figure is actually hard to know; one extreme estimate by Moodys is as high as 75 percent for Indonesia.

14 The Development Bank of Singapore bought a 50.3 per cent stake of Thai Danu Bank and the Dutch ABN Amro Bank acquired a 75 per cent stake in Bank of Asia.

15 One of the suggested measures is to set up a "bad bank" that would manage and sell bad assets. So far, the Government only set up an Asset Management Corporation to take over the bad loans of the 56 finance companies that were shut down in 1997.

16 It is unclear, however, whether objections to the sale stemmed from a grass-roots explosion of nationalism or merely from the management who feared losing control of their enterprise.

A related concern, affecting the capacity of enterprises to service their bank debt, is the treatment of the foreign debt of the corporate (and banking sector). This has been a special difficulty in Indonesia and was the subject of long months of debate and informal negotiations with foreign creditors. Then, on 4 June 1998, an agreement covering US$80 billion in private debt was reached in Frankfurt. As part of the agreement, an Indonesian Debt Restructuring Agency (INDRA) began to function on 1 August, promoting and facilitating the voluntary restructuring of the private sector's foreign currency debt.

The basic principle in the Frankfort agreement is to save the Government from having to assume the debt-servicing obligations of the private sector, whose repayment capacity had been eaten up by the collapsing rupiah exchange rate. The plan is self-financing, albeit with some subsidies. The mechanism by which the agreement works is that debtors participating in INDRA make scheduled principal payments on their debt in rupiah, at an interest rate equal to the inflation rate plus 5.5 per cent. As their debt was in foreign currency (mainly dollars), the amount of rupiah to be paid is based on a notional exchange rate, calculated on the basis of agreed rules. This is the subsidy element, as the exchange rate can be higher than that prevailing in the spot market (but never lower). Instalments are made on a monthly basis over the life of the debt, or over a period ending 31 December 2003. Dollars are then bought to pay the foreign creditors according to the rescheduling agreement reached in Frankfort.[17]

The INDRA scheme was not the only way for the private sector to handle its foreign debt and participation is voluntary. The attractiveness to the debtors depends on the exchange rate under the scheme and the market exchange rate. In the final analysis, I suspect that a mixture of actions will have to be taken, for example, allowing the Government to take over some of the debts by using a portion of IMF financing, and permitting other alternatives such as debt buybacks, securitization of debt and debt-equity swaps.

Why is debt resolution so critical, especially in Indonesia? Aside from the direct role in improving the solvency of the private sector, it would help stabilize the exchange rate. One of the reasons is that every time there is a sign that the rupiah is strengthening, private debtors rush to buy US dollars, seeking to reduce the mismatch in their foreign currency exposure. As long as debt overhang is not resolved, the rupiah is unlikely to get stronger for a relatively long period of time.

17 The restructured debt has an 8 year maturity with a 3 year grace period and carries an interest rate of LIBOR plus a margin not to exceed 3 per cent a year. Short-term inter-bank debt was refinanced over a period of up to 4 years.

Concluding Remarks

The crisis in Asia is dramatic. It is explainable but certainly was not predictable. The verdict that weak fundamentals caused the Asian crisis is clearly misplaced. Even the weak banking system alone cannot explain the depth and severity of the crisis. It was the role of contagion that seems vital. The region's integrated financial sector made the contagion process from Thailand to other countries work very rapidly. Yet, we know little about why the change in perception of fund managers and investors happened so fast and spread so quickly to other countries.

Although the economies in the region are well integrated, each also has a distinct character that affected how the crisis unfolded. For example, political instability clearly had a substantial consequence in the Indonesian case, more so than in other countries in the region.

There have been signs of progress, albeit slow, on the debt front. It is difficult to expect a stable and strong currency when the debt overhang remains unresolved. Bank restructuring is also under way in all crisis countries. Does this mean that there is a light at the end of the tunnel? Yes and no!

The answer is yes if other supporting factors are in place and the external environment is conducive. The answer is no if the social and political repercussions of economic hardship outweigh the impact of gradual improvement on the economic front. Economic stability cannot be achieved in an unstable socio-political environment.

This is precisely the reason why in the second half of 1998 policy makers across the region changed direction. Monetary conditions eased in Malaysia, Thailand and the Republic of Korea, and Indonesia's fiscal deficit was allowed to expand to about 8 per cent of GDP, as output collapsed.

At the same time, however, the policy shift raises serious concerns. To ensure success in a stabilization programme, some basic principles should not be relinquished. An excessive budget deficit is likely to raise inflation (hyperinflation in Indonesia), and too many populist approaches could hinder the process of real recovery by distorting consumption and production.

Also, the state of the global economic environment is less than certain. In 1998 alone, we have seen the Dow tumble, the Hong Kong market slump, markets in Brazil and India feel the tremor, and the Russian Federation plunge. Signs of pressure have also emerged in China, and the prospect of Japan remained worrisome. Japan is to many Asian countries what the United States is to Mexico; and the latter recovered relatively quickly from its crisis in 1994-1995 by getting a strong boost from exports to the United States. Obviously, such a boost is absent in Asia at this moment. In short, there are many fragilities in the world economy and even the risk of a widespread recession is no remote concern. Thus, if the light at the end of the tunnel is dimly perceptible, it could also possibly be snuffed out.

References

Islam, Azizul (this volume). "The dynamics of Asian economic crisis and selected policy implications."

Azis, Iwan J., (1998). "Southeast Asian crisis: the bubble finally bursts." *The Economic Outlook for 1998*, University of Michigan, Research Seminar on Quantitative Economics.

______ (1998a). "When politics fuses with currency panic." *Capital Trends*, Nikko Research Center (America) Inc., vol. 3, No. 2.

______ (1998b). "Indonesia." *Pacific Economic Outlook, 1998-1999*. U.S. National Committee for PEC, in cooperation with The Asia Foundation and Arthur Andersen, pp. 34-36.

______ (1998c). "Indonesia's journey from boom to bust." *Braudel Papers*, Fernand Braudel Institute of World Economics, No. 19.

______ (1998d). "Transition from financial crisis to social crisis." *Social Implications of the Asian Financial Crisis,* United Nations Development Programme and Korea Development Institute, EDAP Joint Policy Studies No.9, p.139-166.

______ (1998e). "How much do we know about the causes of Asian crisis?" Paper presented at international conference on "Market Economy and the Government: International Perspective", Center for International Research on the Japanese Economy, University of Tokyo, 7-8 September.

Calvo, Guillermo, A. (1995). "Varieties of capital-market crises." Unpublished paper, University of Maryland (April).

Chinn, Menzie, D. (1998). "Before the fall: were East Asian currencies overvalued?" National Bureau of Economic Research, Working Paper Series, No. 6491 (April).

Chinn, W. and Michael Dooley P. (1995). "Asia Pacific capital markets: integration and implications for economic activity." National Bureau of Economic Research, Working Paper Series, No. 5280 (September).

Dooley, Michael P. (1997). "A model of crises in emerging markets," National Bureau of Economic Research, Working Paper Series, No 6300 (December).

Fratzscher, Marcel (1998). "Why are currency crises contagious? A comparison of the Latin American crisis of 1994-95 and the Asian crisis of 1997-98." Paper presented at the ASP Seminar Week, Jakarta (December).

Glick, R. and Ramon Moreno (1994). "Capital flows and monetary policy in East Asia." Federal Reserve Bank of San Francisco, Pacific Basin Working Paper Series, No. PB94-08 (November).

Hill, Hal (1998). "Southeast Asia's economic crisis: origins, lessons, and the way forward." Paper for ISEAS 30th Anniversary Conference, "Southeast Asia in the Twenty First Century: Challenges of Globalization", Singapore, 30 July - 1 August.

Sachs, Jeffrey D., A. Tornell, and A. Velasco (1996). "Financial crises in emerging markets: the lessons from 1995," *Brookings Papers on Economic Activity*, No. 1.

Sheng, Andrew (1998). "Asia and the crisis of money." *Braudel Papers*, Fernand Braudel Institute of World Economics, No. 19.

7

The Financial Restructuring and Reform Programme in the Republic of Korea: Progress and Constraints

SOO-WON LEE
Ministry of Finance and Economy, Republic of Korea

and

ANN ORR*
United Nations Department of Economic and Social Affairs

The restructuring and reform programme in the Republic of Korea has had financial stabilization as its near-term objective and full liberalization of the economy as its longer-term goal. The programme was formulated in conjunction with the International Monetary Fund (IMF) and supported by $58.35 billion of international funds mobilized under the leadership of IMF in December 1997.[1] It represents an acceleration of the gradual reform and liberalization of the economy that began in the latter part of the 1980s. Indeed, the President of the Republic sees full economic liberalization as a necessary step towards long-term economic development of the country.

* Consultant (on loan from the Ministry of Finance and Economy, Republic of Korea) and Chief, Developing Economies Section, respectively. The views expressed herein are those of the authors and not necessarily the views of their employers.

1 See "Letter of Intent of the Government of the Republic of Korea" at http://www.imf.org/external/np/loi/120397.htm.

To reach the short-term objective, austere monetary and fiscal policies were implemented for domestic adjustment and to regain international investor confidence, stabilize the exchange rate, and improve the foreign exchange liquidity of the economy. At the same time, the very large amounts of external private short-term debt were restructured.

For the long-term goal, policies would aim to address one of the main causes of the financial crisis: the lag in institutional reform and development relative to the pace of liberalization. The programme seeks financial and corporate restructuring and reform, complemented by measures to increase the efficiency of labour markets. This is supported by the development of regulatory and supervisory structures for the financial sector, broadening and strengthening of the social safety net, and reform of the public sector.

The Government has worked to mobilize domestic political support for new reform legislation and build consensus among the government, business and labour sectors with regard to financial and corporate restructuring. The Government also took a proactive role in the negotiated restructuring of external debt-servicing obligations of financial institutions and provided a guarantee of the amount of debt rescheduled. Furthermore, it is mobilizing large amounts of financial resources to support financial restructuring and to bolster the unemployment insurance system in response to soaring unemployment. To expedite corporate restructuring, the Government has urged commercial banks to assess the financial viability of their corporate clients and identify those that should not be extended further credit. It has also pushed for mergers of subsidiaries of the five largest conglomerates (*chaebol*) as part of their debt restructuring and overall consolidation.

With regard to results, the external financial situation has been stabilized and the level of foreign exchange reserves increased, owing in particular to sharp import reductions associated with economic recession and the lower exchange rate, as well as the negotiated improvement in the repayment structure of external debt. As to the longer-term goals, there has been some corporate and financial restructuring, but the magnitude of the task has been made even more daunting by the effects on companies and banks of the tight macroeconomic policies and the deep economic recession in 1998. In addition, the sharp rise in unemployment has led to growing resistance to further restructuring, as it is expected to lead to large-scale lay offs. While opposition from powerful labour unions increased uncertainty at mid-year about the timely and full implementation of the programme, the unions and the Government have since been able to reach a compromise on the matter.

Major factors contributing to the financial crisis

The crisis in the Republic of Korea was triggered by the 1997 financial crisis in South-East Asia, which undermined international investor confidence in "emerging markets", particularly those with strong financial and trade links to the troubled economies.[2] The massive pull-out of foreign capital from the country in late 1997 reflected an abrupt reversal of the still-positive sentiment in the first half of the year, when international banks continued to extend loans to Korean financial institutions. There had been no history of defaults by these banks and the Government was expected to bail them out should difficulties arise. International credit rating agencies had also maintained high ratings on Korean banks and corporations, which continued to facilitate their access to international funds.

The change in sentiment came with the growing realization that the riskiness of the Korean banking sector and their major clients had grown appreciably. By late 1997, a large mismatch had arisen between the maturities of the deposits and other liabilities of domestic banks and their assets (loans). Moreover, a large part of these loans were made to corporations that had weakened significantly. Indeed, 5 of the 30 largest Korean conglomerates went bankrupt during the year and the overall level of indebtedness of Korean corporations had grown quite high.

The high level of external and domestic debt arose from a number of structural and policy weaknesses in the Korean economy, the root cause of which was the lag in structural change and institutional development following the decentralization and liberalization of the economy that began in the mid-1980s.[3] By the mid-1990s, the Government bureaucracy charged with economic and financial policy-making was streamlined, effectively ending the planning function of the Government. The two top ministries in this area were merged into the Ministry of Finance and Economy, which was given complete charge of economic policy-making and economic information. The reduced direct official intervention in the economy was not, however, replaced by indirect safeguards.

In the financial sector, the regulatory and supervisory infrastructure was not developed. The structure and operation of financial institutions and

---

2 For a discussion of how the investment boom in East and South-East Asia, fuelled by large capital flows into the region, made them highly vulnerable to speculative currency attacks and financial contagion, see Park (1996).

3 For discussions of the role of the Government in the economic development of the Republic of Korea, see Amsden (1989), Wade (1990) and Kim and Leipziger (1993).

corporations, which had evolved under a system of strong industrial policy guidance and centrally controlled financial allocation, remained little changed. Banks were slow to develop their own credit and risk-assessment capabilities and continued to be influenced by the Government in extending loans. The banks provided financing for the rapid global expansion of large conglomerates, which became poor risks. The opening of the financial sector to international financial flows greatly increased demands on these structures, amplifying existing weaknesses (see Amsden and Euh, 1998 and Chang, forthcoming).

The pace of the opening of the economy accelerated in 1993 and further in 1995, partly in an effort to meet requirements to join the Organization of Economic Cooperation and Development (OECD). As part of the financial liberalization, the number of "merchant banks" and the volume of their foreign currency business grew rapidly, but without the proper regulation.[4] The mismatch of their large, mostly short-term, foreign debts with their predominantly long-term lending was one of the major culprits in the external debt crisis.

As in other Asian countries, exchange rate policy also played an important part in the lead-up to the crisis. For purposes of controlling inflation and minimizing exchange rate volatility, a virtually fixed nominal exchange rate against the United States dollar was maintained for over a decade. Under this policy, disregard of exchange-rate risk in borrowing from international creditors was common. In addition, in the early 1990s, the Japanese yen appreciated substantially against the United States dollar, which lowered the real effective exchange rate of the Korean won. This imparted a trade stimulus (and thus an investment stimulus), but only a temporary one. Starting in 1995, the yen depreciated sharply against the dollar and the real effective exchange rate appreciated (see Islam, this volume, figure 1). This, combined with a slowdown in global demand and the collapse of prices of semiconductors, a major export, led to a significant deceleration of export growth, a deterioration of the external balance and a slowdown in overall economic growth (see table 1).

The deceleration in export and economic growth, which began in late 1995, put heavy financial pressure on many large conglomerates which needed rapid economic growth to generate the revenues to service their high debt levels.[5] In short, a heavy reliance on debt financing along with, in retrospect,

4 Merchant banks in the Republic of Korea are financial institutions that specialize in selling short-term commercial paper to investors and primarily extend loans to corporations, but are not subject to the same regulations as were commercial banks prior to recent reforms. With external financial liberalization, these banks entered the business of selling short-term bonds to overseas investors.

5 The average debt-equity ratio was more than 500 per cent for the 30 largest conglomerates at the end of 1997.

Table 1. Selected macroeconomic indicators for the Republic of Korea, 1994-1998

Per cent	*1994*	*1995*	*1996*	*1997*	*1998*[a]
GDP growth rate	8.6	8.9	7.1	5.5	-6.2
Current-account balance (per cent of GDP)	-1.0	-1.8	-4.9	-1.7	9.0
Inflation	6.2	4.5	4.9	4.4	7.5
Unemployment	2.4	2.0	2.0	2.6	7.0

Source: United Nations estimates and forecasts and statistics of the Republic of Korea.

a. Estimate as of December 1998.

over-ambitious capacity expansion left many corporations vulnerable to external trade and financial shocks, as occurred during 1997.

Managing the external debt crisis

The Republic of Korea was on the verge of a national moratorium on external debt in December 1997. Short-term foreign debt of the private sector was $80.2 billion or 52 per cent of total external debt at year end, but short-term debt had been $100 billion one year before (see table 2). Korean banks and corporations had faced increasing resistance to rolling over their short-term debt with international banks, especially after October 1997, and so outstanding debt levels were falling as loans were repaid and not renewed. Meanwhile, however, usable foreign exchange reserves dropped to a low of $3.9 billion, as the Government sought to bolster the exchange rate in the face of the large net outflows of capital, in particular, late in the year.

There was also some confusion about the size of the outstanding foreign debt. Corporate external debt totalled $43.2 billion at the end of 1997, as conventionally measured. However, this excluded the external obligations that offshore subsidiaries of Korean enterprises had contracted for their overseas operations, which amounted to $32.4 billion, raising total corporate debt to $74.6 billion. The debt of offshore subsidiaries had not been included in the accounting because it did not appear in the headquarters balance sheets of Korean firms, which were following domestic accounting practices. These were, none the less, foreign obligations of Korean enterprises.

The foreign debt of Korean enterprises was not, however, considered to be impaired in general and was not included in the debt-restructuring negotiations undertaken by the Government in 1998. The corporate debt consisted mainly of trade financing that was expected to be routinely serviced. Of corporate non-trade financing, only an estimated $9.5 billion fell due in 1998.

Table 2. External debt of the Republic of Korea, 1996-1997
(Billions of US dollars at year-end)

Per cent	*1996*	*1997*
Total	160.7	153.0
Long-term	60.7	72.8
Public sector	2.4	11.0
Private	58.3	61.8
Financial institutions	44.7	44.2
Corporations	13.6	17.6
Short-term	100.0	80.2
Private	100.0	80.2
Financial institutions	78.0	54.6
Corporations	22.0	25.6

Source: Ministry of Finance and Economy, Republic of Korea, "External Liabilities of Korea", 30 December 1997.

The impending emergency in December concerned, rather, the debt of Korean banks and a severe shortage of foreign exchange for the country as a whole. It was addressed with two policy actions. First was to restore central bank liquidity through the accelerated disbursement of $10 billion from the international assistance package. Second, short-term bank debt due at the end of 1997 was rolled over to the end of January 1998. The emergency package was secured by 25 December, after the newly-elected President pledged to fulfil the terms of the IMF assistance programme, including specific deadlines for adopting measures to abolish almost all restrictions on foreign investment, including access to capital markets and the banking sector (see table 3).[6]

With persuasion by IMF and several industrialized country Governments, the major international bank creditors agreed in January to roll over and restructure the short-term debt. Although the debt was owed by domestic private entities to foreign private entities, the Government took a central role in the negotiations, including providing financial guarantees for the rescheduled loans. The decision to make the guarantee reflected the priority placed on preserving access of domestic banks to international credit, even at the risk of fostering "moral hazard"—in effect, giving a false sense of security—to international and domestic banks.

In March 1998, the Government obtained agreement from the major international banks to reschedule $21.8 billion of short-term debt into one to

6 See the letter of intent of the Government of the Republic of Korea at http://www.imf.org/external/np/loi/122497.htm.

Table 3. Major developments in restructuring and reform in the Republic of Korea

Date	*Policy measure of event*
1997	
2 December	The operations of nine ailing merchant banks were suspended.
3 December	The Government and International Monetary Fund (IMF) signed an agreement for a $58.35 billion assistance package.
11 December	The ceiling on foreign equity ownership in Korean companies was raised to 50 per cent.
	Operations of another five merchant banks were suspended.
18 December	Election of new President who pledged to fulfill the terms of the IMF agreement.
24 December	IMF agreed to an early disbursement of $10 billion from the rescue package.
28 December	The Government and IMF agreed on the definition of external liabilities of the country.
	Major international creditors agreed to roll over foreign short-term debt that was due at the end of 1997 to the end of January 1998.
29 December	The National Assembly adopted the Financial Reform Bill.
1998	
28 January	The Government and a group of 13 leading international banks reached agreement on a plan to roll over approximately $24 billion of short-term credit to Korean banks. The Government would guarantee repayment of the debt.
14 February	The Parliament passed a revision of the labour law allowing lay-offs by companies.
16 February	Ten of the suspended merchant banks were ordered closed.
25 February	Compulsory appointment of outside directors for conglomerates and listed companies.
13 March	International creditor banks agreed to exchange $21.4 billion of short-term debt for new loans with maturities of between one and three years.
1 April	Foreign hostile takeovers of corporations allowed.
	Liberalized rules for the establishment of Korean branches of foreign banks and securities companies.
8 April	The Government sold $4 billion of global bonds.
25 April	End of cross-debt guarantees between subsidiaries of conglomerates and listed companies.
13 May	Eliminated the ceiling on foreign ownership of stock in Korean companies.

/.....

(Table 2, cont'd.)

Date	*Policy measure of event*
20 May	The Government unveiled a comprehensive economic restructuring programme, including the financing plan for financial sector restructuring.
25 May	Strengthened voting rights of minority shareholders of conglomerates and listed companies.
18 June	The Government announced a list of 55 troubled companies that would be forced to close.
29 June	The Government announced that five out of a total of 27 commercial banks will be closed and their assets and liabilities transferred to stronger banks.
30 June	Allowed foreign ownership of real estate and land .
1 July	Liberalized corporate foreign borrowing through loans and bonds with maturities over one year.
Beginning in fiscal year 1999	Adoption of consolidated financial statements by conglomerates and listed companies.

three-year loans. As a result, the share of short-term debt dropped to 30 per cent of the total external debt. In addition, by March the current-account deficit changed into a growing surplus and an additional $11 billion disbursement was made from the IMF programme. By the end of March, the level of usable foreign reserves increased to $24 billion.

A successful issue of $4 billion of global bonds by the Government in April further raised foreign exchange reserves (which reached $34.3 billion by the end of May 1998). This bond issue marked the return of the Republic of Korea to the international capital market from which it had been excluded since the crisis erupted. On the other hand, the "real" economy was in the midst of a major contraction.

Restructuring and reform of the financial sector

The December 1997 crisis had made clear that major financial-sector reform was needed. However, the quality of bank loan portfolios further deteriorated after the onset of the financial crisis, as the increase in interest rates led to much higher debt-servicing burdens, while the deflation of asset prices and economic contraction weakened the debt-servicing capacity of corporations. Also, the domestic-currency burden of servicing external debt increased sharply following the large depreciation of the exchange rate. As of March

1998, 7.7 per cent of loans were non-performing in commercial banks.[7] Capital adequacy ratios averaged about 7 per cent for commercial banks and 6.7 per cent for merchant banks, compared to the international standard of 8 per cent. In this situation, there was a credit squeeze on the corporate sector, making financial sector restructuring one of the most urgent tasks in restoring financial stability and increasing liquidity in the economy.

Stronger official oversight

At the end of December 1997, 13 financial reform bills were legislated to provide the basis for a strengthened regulatory and supervisory structure. The new Acts substantially reinforced the independence of the central bank, the Bank of Korea (BOK). Thus, the Monetary Board, the supreme policy making body of the BOK is now chaired by the Governor of the Bank instead of the Minister of Finance and Economy. The responsibility of the BOK was also narrowed to maintenance of price stability, whereas earlier it had also been responsible for maintenance of exchange rate stability and regulation of the financial system.

A new Financial Supervisory Commission (FSC) was established in April 1998 outside the BOK. The FSC is to function as a neutral and independent supervisory and policy making body and play a central role in financial restructuring. In addition, the existing supervisory bodies were to be merged into a new Financial Supervisory Board (FSB) by the end of 1998, which is to be directly accountable to the FSC. The aim in creating the FSB is to allow for more effective supervision of the financial system on a consolidated basis.

Bank restructuring and reform

In order to strengthen the banking sector, some banks had to be closed, while others could be reorganized or assisted through purchase of their "bad" debt. For example, the Government wrote down the equity in two large commercial banks that were insolvent and recapitalized them. The plan was to subsequently offer them for sale to domestic and foreign investors. The FSC also required the submission of rehabilitation plans by 12 commercial banks that did not meet the 8 per cent capital-adequacy ratio as of December 1997. After review by the FSB, the plans of five small banks (constituting about 7 per cent of total deposits) were found to be unviable. In June 1998 they were ordered closed and their assets and liabilities transferred to five stronger banks. This

---

7 This compares with 19.7 per cent in Thailand, 8.2 per cent in the Philippines and 7.6 per cent in Malaysia (see Rhee, 1998, p. 10).

was, however, only the beginning of the process and many more closures or mergers were expected.

In addition, the Government intended to help recapitalize the banks by purchasing non-performing loans (NPLs) through the Korean Asset Management Corporation (KAMC). The KAMC was to purchase about $35.8 billion worth of NPLs, at a market value of $17.9 billion. In addition, the Korea Deposit Insurance Corporation (KDIC) was slated to inject about $11.4 billion toward recapitalizing financial institutions. An estimated $6.4 billion was made available if needed to meet deposit withdrawals that might arise in the course of restructuring non-bank financial institutions.

Several insolvent non-bank financial institutions were suspended or closed. Fourteen of 30 merchant banks were closed in February 1998 and one merchant bank was suspended. Merchant banks were expected to self-finance their recapitalization and have become subject to regulation and supervision by the FSB. In addition, one investment trust company and two securities brokerage houses had their licenses revoked.

Complementing the financial restructuring, banking practices were to be reformed. By the end of 1998, new laws and regulations were scheduled to be adopted to ensure that commercial banks meet international standards in accounting and auditing. In the past, banks have been more like public-sector corporations than private enterprises, in particular, in extending preferential loans to officially targeted industries or firms. Now, improved risk assessment and management practices and enhanced transparency are needed and are objectives of the reforms. This notwithstanding, no explicit measures were planned to insulate the banks from Government intervention and strengthen their autonomy.

Financing restructuring

The Government estimated that public funds of about 50 trillion won ($28 billion) would be necessary for financial restructuring. Measures were taken to attract more foreign investment in financial institutions, as through joint ventures or mergers and acquisitions. For example, as part of the liberalization measures, limits on foreign ownership in banks have been lifted. However, because of the financial and operational weakness of Korean banks, the response from foreign banks in 1998 was muted.[8]

---

8 Another source of funds could be strong domestic conglomerates which were interested in acquiring a stake in a bank, but this would require an end to the ban on bank ownership by conglomerates. It also would aggravate concerns about the influence of corporations over the lending decisions of banks.

The Government estimated that the overall cost of its plan of financial support for restructuring would be about 75 trillion won ($42 billion), equivalent to about 18 per cent of GDP. Most of the amount would be financed by issuing Government-guaranteed bonds in 1998 and 1999. At the same time, financial institutions were expected to raise about 25 trillion won($14 billion). Nevertheless, the already large demand on fiscal resources could rise substantially were there to be more large-scale corporate bankruptcies or if private capital became less available than anticipated.

Corporate sector restructuring and reform

As in the financial sector, the restructuring and reform of the non-financial corporate sector entails both financial flows and new rules of the game. Attention has focused on the 30 largest conglomerates, which account for about one-third of total value added and fixed assets in the manufacturing sector. Their contribution to exports and employment is also very important. In addition, because their business activities are diverse, and because they are sector leaders, their economic influence is even greater than their sheer size. However, their over-expansion and over-diversification has been a major source of their low profitability and they have been strongly urged by the Government to focus on their core business as well as to exit unviable businesses.

One concern was that the Government could consider the conglomerates as "too big to fail" and not follow through on the reform agenda. Indeed, in May 1998, the FSC asked banks to extend a low interest loan to a large construction conglomerate that was on the verge of bankruptcy, with the justification that its demise would have wiped out hundreds of small subcontractors. Although the director was removed and the creditor bank took over management control through a form of debt-for-equity swap, this raised doubts about the Government's commitment to corporate restructuring. However, the Government subsequently indicated that this would not be a precedent for future corporate restructuring.

Finance for corporate restructuring

To strengthen the balance sheets of the large conglomerates, some mechanisms for debt reduction and or increased equity capital were necessary. Indeed, the Government was aiming at a reduction of conglomerate debt-equity ratios from an average of over 500 per cent to under 200 per cent by the end of 1999.

Under the restructuring plan, in early 1998 conglomerates submitted their debt-reduction plans to the Government and to their main creditor banks. To expedite the process, the Government initiated a procedure in April 1998 to facilitate the smooth exit of unviable companies without resorting to legal procedures. Companies judged to be financially unviable, based on the assessment of their debt reduction plans by creditor banks, would not be extended any further credit and would be forced to close. Their operations would be purchased by foreign or domestic investors. The Government announced that there were 55 such companies in June 1998, including 20 subsidiaries of conglomerates, and it expected to announce more casualties in the ensuing months.

One source of funds for corporate recapitalization was expected to be the international capital market. To help raise funds, restrictions on foreign capital inflows were lifted in February 1998. Regulation of mergers and acquisitions has also been liberalized, including permitting foreign takeovers of domestic corporations.

The sale of real estate is another potentially important avenue for mobilizing resources for repaying debt, as most conglomerates have had sizeable real estate holdings. But because of depressed market conditions, the Government itself expected to purchase such real estate through the publicly funded KAMC. At the same time, to attract foreign investment in such real estate, acquisition of land by foreigners was fully liberalized in July 1998.

Corporate governance and transparency

One major problem in the management of conglomerates has been the lack of transparency and accountability, aggravated by lax financial accounting standards and disclosure requirements. These practices had been tolerable in a policy environment in which the Government formulated detailed industrial policy and allocated financing based on industrialization targets and strict performance criteria. With the greatly diminished role of such policy in the 1990s in a more liberalized economy, such management practices became problematic.[9]

Thus, the Financial Supervisory Commission has planned to set new accounting and auditing rules in line with internationally accepted standards. All listed companies will be required to establish committees of external auditors, and conglomerates have to produce consolidated financial statements by 1999, providing comprehensive corporate information to investors.

The rights of minority shareholders have also been strengthened by reducing the share of ownership required to be able to demand a financial review, remove corporate officers, or take legal action against managerial abuse. The role of institutional investors as monitors of corporate management will also be

9 For a discussion of governance of conglomerates, see, for example, Hattori (1997).

strengthened, as the ban on their right to vote in general shareholder meetings was eliminated.

To improve financial management, moreover, companies belonging to the same conglomerate have been prohibited from issuing new loan guarantees for each other and financing institutions have been prohibited from demanding such "cross-debt" guarantees. This practice had allowed subsidiaries of the same parent company to provide loan guarantees for each other, or parent companies would provide guarantees for subsidiaries, often without collateral. In addition, the guarantees did not appear on the balance sheet of the guarantor, as conglomerates had not been required to disclose consolidated financial statements. Thus, creditors did not necessarily know the full extent of guarantees already outstanding, which helped conglomerates to accumulate excessive levels of debt.

Labour market reform

Traditionally, workers in the corporate sector in the Republic of Korea, as in the public sector, expect virtual lifetime employment, in particular through the negative as well as the positive phases of the business cycle. Lay-offs were regarded as the last resort, even in corporate rationalization. The Labour Standard Act had established restrictive legal provisions relating to job placement and employment which applied to all businesses with five or more employees.

Now, shifting to the liberal-economy model, the Government and corporations have sought to ease restrictions on lay-offs, in particular in cases of troubled corporations that were undergoing restructuring, as discussed above. However, labour unions have put up strong resistance.

Thus, after tripartite consultative talks between labour, business and Government, the Labour Standard Act was amended in March 1998. It established circumstances and procedures for lay-offs for purposes of restructuring, incorporating a number of concessions made by labour in this regard. For its part, the Government pledged to strengthen the capacity of the unemployment insurance system and to expand coverage in response to sharply rising unemployment resulting from the soaring number of bankruptcies. As unemployment continued to rise (reaching an average of 7 per cent in 1998 compared to 2.6 per cent in 1997) resistance from the labour unions intensified resulting in their withdrawal from tripartite talks in July 1998 and an organized strike to protest Government efforts to push through restructuring. A more accommodative stance has since been taken by all sides and lay-offs in major corporations have taken place, although not on a large scale.

Capital-account liberalization

Foreign financial participation in the economy is seen as critically important in the Republic of Korea, especially with respect to the restructuring exercises described above, as well as for promoting long-term, sustainable growth. This represents, in fact, a sharp acceleration in the pace of financial liberalization.

That is, a five-year comprehensive financial reform programme had been adopted in 1993 and further reforms were scheduled for 1997-2000, before the financial crisis erupted (see Johnston and others, 1997 and Oh, 1998). By 1998, restrictions on foreign investment in the equity of domestic companies, foreign takeover of management, and foreign land ownership have been mostly eliminated, as noted above. In addition, more domestic industries have been opened to foreign direct investment, with only 31 (out of 1,148 industries) remaining fully or partially restricted. Also, to facilitate investment and prevent selective treatment, the numerous remaining regulations and restrictions related to foreign investment were to be streamlined and unified into a single legal framework under the Foreign Investment Promotion Act.

Restrictions on foreign borrowing have also been reduced substantially, with the lifting of all limits on foreign investment into domestic government, corporate, and special bond markets as of the end of 1997. Restrictions on overseas borrowing by Korean banks and corporations have also been lifted on debts with maturities of over one year. A plan has also been announced for the replacement of the existing Foreign Exchange Control Act with a new law that will simplify the current cumbersome regulations on foreign exchange transactions.

Indeed, the goal of the reform programme is to eliminate all controls and complete the restructuring by the year 2000. This pace of liberalization appears very ambitious, however, and might be questioned in the light of heightened concerns in many quarters about the potentially destabilizing effect of short-term capital inflows on developing countries.

Constraints on restructuring and reform

As of late 1998, the two major constraints to the further implementation of financial and corporate restructuring were the magnitude of financial resources needed and the growing social resistance to the programme. Both have been made more difficult by the recession and the deflation of asset prices following the onset of the crisis. Meanwhile, resistance to the Government's restructuring efforts, led by powerful labour unions, was being galvanized by rapidly rising unemployment. As large-scale restructuring will aggravate already high unemployment, the programme is becoming politically more difficult to implement.

Restoring economic growth would mitigate unemployment and help bolster financial resources for restructuring (both fiscal revenues and private incomes). However, prospects for economic growth in the near term are highly uncertain. Any exogenous stimulus to growth from exports, in particular, will be constrained by the continuing recession in many Asian markets and moderating demand from the United States.

The priority of the Government has thus been shifting toward stimulating growth, but here, too, the near term constraints are daunting. In 1998, a larger fiscal deficit would be accommodated than previously targeted, and it will probably be increased further in 1999. This has largely been in recognition of the need for additional social expenditures in light of rising unemployment and lower fiscal revenues owing to the deeper than anticipated contraction. In addition, interest rates fell to pre-crisis levels by the end of 1998, as the exchange rate strengthened. But even with the limited dose of fiscal easing and interest rate reduction, liquidity in the economy has continued to be in short supply, as the financial restructuring process requires more time. Economic recovery was thus not yet on the short-term horizon.

References

Amsden, A. (1989). *Asia's Next Giant: South Korea and Late Industrialization.* New York: Oxford University Press.

______ and Y. Euh (1998). "Rapid deregulation led to the Korean crisis". In *Perspective on International Financial Liberalization*, United Nations Development Programme, Office of Development Studies, Discussion Paper, No. 15, pp. 38-40.

Chang, H. (forthcoming). "Korea: the misunderstood crisis". In *World Development.*

Hattori, T. (1997). "Chaebol-style enterprise development in Korea". In *The Developing Economies*, vol. 35, No. 4 (December), pp. 458-477.

Islam, A (this volume). "The dynamics of Asian economic crisis and selected policy implications.

Johnston, R. B. and others (1997). "Sequencing capital account liberalization: lessons from the experiences in Chile, Indonesia, Korea and Thailand". IMF Working Paper, WP/97/157, November.

Kim, K. and D. Leipziger (1993). *The Lessons of East Asia: Korea, A Case of Government-led Development.* Washington, D.C: The World Bank.

Oh, J. (1998). "Financial reforms, their effects and management issues: a Korean experience". Paper prepared for the Conference on Improved Management of the financial sector for its enhanced stability and support to trade and investment flows, United Nations Economic and Social Commission for Asia and the Pacific (ESCAP), Bangkok, March.

Park, Y. C. (1996). "East Asian liberalization, bubbles, and the challenge from China". In *Brookings Papers on Economic Activity*, No. 2, pp. 357-371.

Rhee, S. Ghon (1998). "Financial sector reforms". Asian Development Bank, ESCAP, IMF and World Bank High-Level Seminar on Managing Financial Flows: National and International Dimensions, Bangkok, 15-16 June.

Wade, R. (1990). *Governing the Market: Economic Theory and the Role of Government in East Asian Industrialization.* Princeton: Princeton University Press.

8

Discussion – Asia

MICHAEL W. CASEY
ROBERTO S. MARIANO
ROBERT WADE

MICHAEL W. CASEY*

In the past few years the International Monetary Fund (IMF) has taken on three tasks of direct importance for emerging debt markets. Two of these tasks: confidential consultation with member States on macroeconomic and especially balance-of-payments matters; and acting as a source of funds for temporary relief of balance-of-payments problems, are specifically mandated in the Fund's charter. In addition, over the past few years, the Fund has taken on a new task by becoming an increasingly important source of information on the state of members' economy and government finance for private investors. Not only has the Fund used both carrot and stick to urge Governments around the world towards greater transparency in their official accounts, it has helped publicize the data and has spoken off the record with many private investor groups

* Vice President and Portfolio Manager, Federated Investors. The opinions expressed in this comment are strictly his own and do not necessarily reflect the views of Federated Investors.

as to the state of the markets it monitors closely. I am not suggesting that the Fund or its agents have engaged in any improper disclosure of confidential information, but rather that private financial markets have come to rely, perhaps rather too closely, on information from the Fund when making private investment decisions.

The push towards greater transparency of international financial data championed by IMF has not only improved the quality of information used in international investment, but has probably also led to improved financial disclosure within some countries, furthering the open democratic assessment of government operations. Certainly, in several cases where the international data were found to be faulty or misleading, the internal transparency of government operations was also found to be seriously impaired. Despite the advantages of additional transparency to sound international investment and democratization, I wish to suggest that the Fund's effort to undertake all three tasks (consultation, lending and information dissemination) simultaneously necessarily leads to practical dilemmas known by the economist's term, "moral hazard".

The essential element of moral hazard as it pertains to financial decision-making is that one party to a transaction has more information on the underlying risks of a transaction than the other parties to the transaction. Having superior knowledge allows a party to secure better terms than would otherwise have been available and may also lead to increasingly risky behaviour by that party, especially if such behaviour is associated with very high potential rewards. As the theory applies to the practice of emerging market lending in the past few years, the "hazards" are twofold: first, since private investors realize that IMF has inside knowledge of its client countries' public finances and international reserve positions, the investors may simply mimic IMF, lending to those countries and only those countries currently part of an IMF plan. This may encourage increasingly reckless behaviour by Governments believing themselves eligible for IMF programmes. In addition, public officials with inside knowledge of their country's finances may try to bluff both IMF and the private investors, hoping to be saved from their risky actions by IMF packages, designed to maintain orderly global trading conditions.

There are possible and plausible reforms to IMF's structure that will eliminate the first sort of moral hazard mentioned above. I know of no reform that will totally eliminate the second sort since local government officials will always have an information advantage over outsiders, including IMF, before a surveillance programme is put in place. IMF reform can at best be structured so as to make this sort of behaviour as painful as possible *ex post*. Because IMF's attempt to undertake the three tasks mentioned above necessarily leads to increased moral hazard, attempts at IMF reform should begin by considering which of the three to drop. The size of this comment does not allow a full treatment of this question, but I wish to suggest that the alternative that is likely to get the least consideration is perhaps the most promising; if IMF were to drop all confidential consultations with its member Governments, many of the problems inherent in the current system could be avoided.

This suggestion appears to fly in the face of the Fund's chartered mandate to coordinate and consult with member States on questions pertaining to their foreign exchange markets and balances of international payments. I wish to suggest, however, that the Fund would be better off trying to fulfill this mandate in a very different way than it has in recent years. Rather than acting as an arbiter of acceptable economic practice on any number of macroeconomic, microeconomic and international topics, I suggest the Fund should draw up a list of acceptable practices regarding balance of payments and currency questions. Individual member States would be free to choose from a variety of acceptable practices, all of which would be consistent with the Fund's major objectives, which include preserving liberalized current accounts so as to enhance the volume of world trade and avoiding exchange rate regimes which are designed to confer unfair trade advantages. These practices and objectives should be understood as the basic rules of the game. The Fund should *not* undertake to advise member Governments on the adequacy, desirability or elegance of their financial, macro- and microeconomic institutions. There are other, superior, forums for such discussions. Should the current forums be found inadequate, the United Nations might want to consider establishing such an institution itself or assigning this task to a World Financial Organization (WFO). The Fund, in contrast, would limit itself to providing public information and making short-term loans to Governments in compliance with the rules of the game that nonetheless find themselves in temporary balance-of-payments difficulties. A look at the Fund's charter suggests that this was the spirit of the Fund's original mandate, although I concede that consultations with national Governments were specifically provided for in the charter.

The Fund would thus limit itself to waiting for requests for help by member Governments, evaluating those requests, including whether the Government was in fact in compliance with international financial standards, and disbursing currency as needed. The Fund would be compelled to release *immediately* all documentation pertaining to the member Government's request. This is a much more severe standard of information release than is currently practiced by any national lender of last resort. It is, however, justified by the fact that there can be no binding regulation of national Governments or central banks in the same way that commercial banks are regulated by national authorities where they are domiciled. The increased potential for moral hazard at the sovereign level needs especially severe penalties as an offset.

The immediate and full disclosure of all information by the Fund in the course of its lending operations would help insure the safety of the Fund's capital since all Fund members as well as other international capital market participants could evaluate the scope of the liquidity problem as well as the Fund's response. It would also provide a strong disincentive for a national Government to seek liquidity from the Fund. A short-term liquidity line from commercial banks for that Government would not be subject to the same scrutiny, leaving a request to the Fund as either a last resort by a Government in trouble or the act of a Government with nothing to hide. A WFO might eventually also set general guidelines for commercial bank lending to sovereign states—especially to IMF or WFO members. The penalty for providing false information to the Fund, and thus to its member States, would be expulsion from the Fund with the loss of the capital invested when the country entered its IMF membership.

In such a system, the Fund would retain its role of providing liquidity to Governments in temporary need of it, but would do so in a much more transparent way. In addition, it would not be seen as meddling with the economic institutions of member States. At the moment, the Fund's involvement with these institutions may sometimes be seen as generating a conflict of interest as the Fund seeks to reward Governments following its strictures, rather than simply supplying temporary liquidity to Governments acting in accordance with IMF's basic objectives. This strictly limited method of operation for the Fund would allow more diversity of member State financial institutions without interference by Fund managers as long as the Fund's basic objectives were met.

Briefly, how might this more modest approach for the Fund have worked in the East Asian crisis of 1996-1998? It goes without saying that it would not have solved or even helped solve many of the problems which the Governments and financial markets in the region faced. But, I believe it would have helped in some key respects. One key element of moral hazard, which I believe could have been avoided, was the sense in the financial markets that IMF's consultations with the Thai Government placed a sort of IMF imprimatur on the liberalized banking arrangements that the Thai Government had introduced to promote foreign bank lending into the kingdom. A similar problem existed with IMF's acquiescence to the Thai Government's fixed basket exchange rate policy, of which we now know IMF (gently) disapproved. Some in the markets believed that because the Fund was consulting with the Government and had not publicly objected to the system, it would provide more or less unlimited cover to the Thai Government if the fixed basket system came under attack.

This was, of course, a totally erroneous reading of the Fund's position. But, the informational misunderstanding could have been avoided entirely if the Fund had not been in the business of providing advice on exactly these types of questions to member Governments. If the Fund had simply certified that the system was in accord with the rules of the game—as the system was—but *not* implicitly certified the system's robustness or suitability, lenders would have been forced to make those determinations for themselves. They would have had no excuse for the mistakes of overlending to a fragile system that clearly were made.

The Thai Government would have been able to go off its basket system without any complaint from the financial markets that the Fund had been remiss in its advice to the Thai Government or in its explanations to the financial markets. What if the Thai Government had asked the Fund for assistance in maintaining its peg? The Fund would have been obliged to publish the Thai Government's international balance sheets at the central bank and the Ministry of Finance before making any loan. The extent of the purchases of baht on the central bank's forward book would have been revealed. An important and difficult question appears at this point: should the Fund be required to lend in support of situations it may find cannot be maintained, as long as the member Governments are playing by the rules? Without wanting to give this question a full treatment here, it seems fair to suggest that the Fund should be required to release the national Government's own capital held at the Fund, but that additional loans should be decided on the basis of whether the Fund has a reasonable chance of recouping its investment. This is a question that has much to do with whether the institutions under attack are robust enough to withstand that attack. Thus, at some point, the Fund might indeed be drawn into questions of evaluation as it performs its function of international lender. In the proposed regime, however, the Fund's member States and the international capital markets would have a full and clear understanding of the Fund's reasoning in making what are often very difficult decisions. The ability of the member States and the markets to evaluate the Fund's performance in these difficult cases should contribute to a clearer understanding by all concerned of which decisions have worked well and why.

The case of Indonesia presents another set of dilemmas. The Indonesian Government, which had been in constant contact with IMF for several years and enjoyed reasonably good relations with the Fund, received a fairly generous support package early in the crisis. Only when it became apparent that the Government was not willing to honour the terms set out in the conditionality agreement did the markets lose faith and attack the rupiah more forcefully than other East Asian currencies. This raises several questions. First, should IMF have been in the position of demanding conditionality in return for making a normal liquidity loan? Second, what terms should IMF be reasonably expected to extract in order to ensure the repayment of its loans? In the case of Indonesia, IMF officers in the country demanded, and obtained, the closure of several poorly-run Indonesian commercial banks as a condition of releasing one tranche of its support. At least one of these banks was controlled by a son of the President at that time. The Fund appeared to believe that the money lent to the central bank was simply destined to flow back out of the country, as capital flight in private accounts, as long as these banks were left open.

My suggestion for a revision of the Fund's method of operations would have also had a few advantages in this case. The Fund would not have been in contact with the Government prior to the crisis. The impression would therefore not have been left in anyone's mind that the Fund was in the least sympathetic to the way the commercial banking system was structured in Indonesia; in fact, that structure would have been none of the Fund's business. If the Fund decided that leaving certain banks open would have seriously jeopardized the prompt return of its capital after the crisis, it would certainly have been free to stipulate conditions for ensuring the safety of its investment over and above the return of Indonesia's capital in the Fund. But, it would not have been in a position to demand a restructuring of the Indonesian commercial banking system simply to force a desirable outcome on the Indonesian authorities. Only conditions clearly devoted to ensuring the returning of IMF's funds would be acceptable in my more modest system. The Fund would not have the power to use conditionality to attempt to force micro-, macro- or financial changes on member Governments, even if those changes would be very desirable in terms of efficiency or equity. The Fund would further have been required to show why it was requesting the closure of a commercial bank in order to ensure the return of its loan.

Questions surrounding the relationship between public and private financial institutions have been at the heart of many of the most difficult decisions the Fund has been confronted with in Asia. In general, confining the Fund to making loans solely to foreign Governments on their own credit forces these questions into the hands of the national authorities where they belong. If these authorities are manifestly unable to achieve desirable outcomes in structuring their commercial banking systems, the Fund would not be required to lend them funds beyond the return of their capital. Perhaps one positive lesson from the Asian financial crisis is that intimate relationships between public and private financial institutions are rarely a source of strength in the long run. A more widespread appreciation of the need for prudent and careful regulation of private financial institutions would be a positive development in both emerging and developed financial markets.

This comment has not attempted to treat many aspects of the financial debacle that began in South-East Asia more than a year ago. Questions of the pace of financial liberalization, pegged currencies, deliberately opaque financial reporting and flawed relations between public and private financial institutions have hardly been touched on. These questions can be extremely difficult, but are best left in the hands of national Governments to sort out as best they can in the light of recent experience. Some Governments will no doubt be better than others at drawing conclusions to promote the well-being of their citizens.

I have attempted to outline some of the aspects of the crisis where the role of IMF was central. The need for reform of this institution is now being debated in financial circles throughout the world. I hope to have shown that while the need for such an institution has not diminished in recent years, and may well have increased owing to increased financial deregulation, its current method of operation leads ineluctably to dilemmas of moral hazard. A reform aimed at changing the Fund's methods of operation so as to reduce moral hazard while continuing to promote the Fund's basic goals therefore seems both timely and well-advised. In addition, the establishment of a World Financial Organization to set common "rules of the game" for international financial transactions seems worthy of consideration, even if the exact nature of such an organization would need to be the subject of extended consideration.

ROBERTO S. MARIANO*

I would like to comment on five main topics that were covered or discussed in the papers:

- Japan's importance in the recovery process
- Crony capitalism
- Macroeconomic projections in the region
- Assessment of financial and sovereign risks
- Recovery strategy

---

* Professor of Economics and Statistics, University of Pennsylvania.

Japan's importance in the recovery process

There is double trouble in Japan—an economy in recession with dormant domestic demand and a distressed banking sector exposed to bad loans worth close to US $1 trillion and backed by real estate collateral.

Japan is an important export market of the region. It is also a critical source of investment funds that go into the region. Withdrawal of Japanese investments can hurt badly some domestic economies in the region. For example, real estate and tourism in Hong Kong (China), have been depressed partly because of this Japanese pull-out.

A faltering economy and a weakening yen can precipitate another round of currency devaluation in the region, this time for export competitiveness—such as in China, Hong Kong (China), Taiwan Province of China, the Republic of Korea and South-East Asia.

Crony capitalism

I feel strongly that behest loans and concessions to special individuals and groups is a major factor in the onset of the crisis and a serious deterrent to a speedy recovery. In fact, a survey of Asian executives in *Far Eastern Economic Review* rates this factor as the most critical obstacle to recovery.

And this is a problem not only in Indonesia, but also in Thailand, the Republic of Korea, Malaysia and the Philippines. Special concession loans, grants and project financing with unusual government guarantees led to useless investments in the Philippines in the early 1980s and eventually fuelled the deep recession in 1984-1985. Just before this crisis hit the Philippines, the incremental capital output ratio (ICOR) was roughly 10 times its normal level.

Macroeconomic projections in the region

Fast-developing events can quickly overtake the projections reported in the papers—especially at a time of crisis. Consequently, such projections require frequent updates.

Information available in June and July 1998, however, already indicated deeper-rooted problems that could prolong the economic difficulties in the region, compared to forecasts made slightly earlier.

For the Philippines, official government projections of real GDP growth in 1998 were lowered during the year. El Niño seriously hampered agricultural harvests, especially in Mindanao. Onerous interest rates following the financial crisis in 1997 have made it extremely difficult for small businesses to access capital. Interest rates eventually came down to more manageable levels (to the mid-teens for 91-day treasury bills by mid-1998).

The recovery period for countries such as Indonesia and Thailand, badly affected by the crisis, may be prolonged. In its debt crisis in 1983-1985, the Philippines contracted by about 5 per cent per annum for two consecutive years before posting positive growth, and it took the country four years to reach decent growth rates of 4 per cent to 5 per cent.

Assessment of financial and sovereign risks

International credit rating agencies indeed have failed in anticipating the Asian financial crisis. A tabulation of macroeconomic events and rating adjustments immediately before and during the crisis would show this dramatically.

Credit rating agencies, in assessing sovereign risks, have not paid much attention to sectoral and micro-information and instead have focused on macroeconomic indicators.

Lawrence Lau had a study in 1995 which used 10 macroeconomic indicators of sovereign risk and, two years before the crisis, flagged down the Philippines and Thailand as two countries in imminent risk, while Malaysia and Indonesia were assessed to be in reasonably good shape. His list of indicators includes:

- Falling exchange rate
- Lowered rate of GDP growth
- High relative rate of inflation
- High interest rate differential
- Rising interest rate differential
- High real rate of interest
- Low domestic saving rate
- Large negative trade balance
- Large negative current-account balance
- High ratio of foreign portfolio investment to foreign direct investment

In the present environment of globalized finance, we need to develop a better understanding of international financial flows and financial risks need to be taken into account in the assessment of sovereign ratings.

There are early warning systems that have been constructed by researchers in academe, various organizations and commercial outfits. It would be interesting to go beyond the qualitative matching of movements of indicators and measures of crisis or the fitting of a logit or probit model to data sets with artificially constructed series on incidence of a crisis. At the very least, sectoral indicators should complement the usual macroeconomic variables, such as those listed above, in these predictive models of a crisis. Such additional indicators can include measures of the health of sectors at risk -- such as the banking sector and the real estate sector. The variables most commonly mentioned along these lines are exposure of banks to non-performing loans and office vacancy rate in central business districts.

Creation of an international public rating agency to "supplement or replace the private Western rating agencies,"—mentioned by some authors—may not be feasible. Instead, regional associations of domestic credit rating agencies (such as AFCRA—the ASEAN Forum of Credit Rating Agencies) can be encouraged for regional cooperative efforts in information and technology sharing, economies of scale in training, and harmonization of rating procedures, accounting standards and information requirements.

Recovery strategy

The IMF programme of monetary and fiscal austerity must be supplemented with social safety nets and funding support for development projects (for example, infrastructure).

Prudential regulations on lending, requirements of more transparent disclosure of financial information etc., may already be in place in countries like the Philippines; in such cases, the real question is implementation.

Creation of derivatives to hedge Asian investments—to help limit foreign exchange exposure and perhaps the pace of capital reversals—has to be considered with care and deliberation (as Thailand did). If established too soon, without adequate infrastructure support and regulatory supervision and proper understanding on the part of intermediators and participants, formal derivatives markets can backfire, as in recent experiences in Malaysia (KLOFFE), China and the Philippines. KLOFFE suffered from a thin market and an unenthusiastic pool of investors. China and the Philippines both closed down futures exchanges.

Let me end my comments with some questions on the Republic of Korea. Are the adjustments and new liberalization moves, undoubtedly precipitated by IMF , happening too fast? Does the Republic of Korea have enough resources (financial, political will etc.) to assure social stability as it goes through restructuring?

ROBERT WADE*

The world is awash with proposals for new crisis-fighting mechanisms. The United States, Canada, France and Germany have all recently expressed serious interest in the idea of an expanded International Monetary Fund (IMF), or a financial supervisory organization parallel to IMF, or even a second Bretton Woods conference to rethink world financial architecture from scratch. Part of the hidden agenda is to prevent the Asians from going off on their own.

In August 1997, the Japanese Government proposed an Asian Monetary Fund to deal with the crisis in South-East Asia. It secured pledges of $100 billion mostly from itself, China, Hong Kong (China), Taiwan Province of China and Singapore. The United States Treasury pulled out all the stops to kill the proposal, and it died. The Treasury explained that IMF should be the sole coordinator of the rescue effort.

Now the idea is again being seriously discussed in the region. This time the West must encourage it. The Asian fund could make an important contribution to recovery in Asia and the rest of the world. Too much is at stake to worry about Asia going its own way.

How would the fund help? It would be better able to appreciate and build on the strengths of Asian financial systems than IMF has proven to be. It would allow Asian Governments and corporates to refinance their high-cost Western loans and provide selective new loans for recovery programmes. And the creation of the fund would send a signal that Asians were taking charge of their own destiny and no longer dependent on bail-outs. This may prompt Western bankers and portfolio managers to rush to take positions in the early stages of recovery—which should help to solve Asia's current short-term funding problems with the West. We now elaborate these arguments.

The Asian Model

Talk of "the Asian financial system" is no doubt too simple. But countries of East and South-East Asia share enough features to make a simple picture tolerably accurate. Above all, they share high levels of savings compared to Western norms, and the savings are done mostly by households. The high levels of savings promote high levels of domestic debt, held mostly by firms. High levels

---

* Professor of Political Science and International Political Economy, Brown University. This note was co-authored with Frank Veneroso.

of domestic debt must be buffered by long-term financial relations between firms and banks, with the government standing ready to support both firms and banks in the event of shocks (such as sharp rises in interest rates, or sharp falls in demand, that impact large swathes of the economy at once). In the absence of long-term relations, such shocks cause creditors to call their loans and liquidate firms. Where debt levels are high, the failure of some firms propagates the failure of others to a greater degree than where debt levels are low. This is the financial rationale for what used to be called Asian "alliance capitalism", and has now come to be maligned as "crony capitalism". It is also the rationale of the "convoy" system of Japan, where strong companies support weak ones under various kinds of government encouragement.

Until the mid-1990s Asian alliance capitalism generated the highest sustained economic growth rate for any region in world history. It worked not only as a "catch up" strategy for countries far from the world technological frontier, but also for Japan as it reached the frontier in the 1980s.

Asian alliance capitalism did this almost entirely with domestic savings. (Foreign direct investment mattered as a source of technology, management and marketing, but amounted to a small proportion of total investment.) Domestic savings rates are approximately twice that of the United States. In the United States most household savings go to finance households' own investment in housing, and most corporate investment in real productive fixed capital is financed by depreciation funds and retained profits. Asia has savings rates 15 or more percentage points of GDP higher than the United States, and corporate investment rates 10 or more percentage points of GDP higher. This corporate investment gets financed to an important degree through savings transfers from households. Households typically put most of their savings into (low-risk) banks rather than into (higher-risk) equities. High levels of bank indebtedness tend to go with high levels of household savings and corporate investment.

In some Asian countries, more household savings have been transferred to the enterprise sector through equity markets. Singapore and Malaysia have specialized institutions, such as pension and provident funds financed partly by payroll taxes, which purchase large quantities of equities. In Taiwan Province of China, both government- and party-directed funds buy equities. However, these are all forms of government-sponsored forced investment regimes. They share with the debt transfer systems long-term relationships between government, financial sector and enterprise sector.

In a pure Anglo-American free market regime, competition and short-term profit maximizing cause high debt structures to become unstable in the face of shocks that interfere with debt service payments. Creditors seeking to safeguard their assets call in loans and liquidate firms. Bank depositors "run" on banks that might be too exposed to defaults. This collective behaviour causes contractions of the whole financial system, spilling over into price deflations and depressions. To avoid these outcomes Anglo-American nations long ago agreed that the state had to create a lender of last resort and a body of regulation that placed limits on the indebtedness of private firms, banks and households. These limits of prudent indebtedness were set far below the levels permitted in Asian alliance capitalism.

The build-up to crisis

For a variety of reasons most Asian governments opened their economies to financial capital movements in the 1990s. Global banks and portfolio investors seeking to participate in the Asian economic miracle flooded in. After 1995 the rise of the United States dollar and the depreciation of the Japanese yen and the Chinese renminbi led to a loss of export competitiveness in those Asian economies whose currencies were pegged to the United States dollar. The capital inflows exacerbated the real appreciation of the exchange rates and the loss of export competitiveness, resulting in large, and out-of-character, current-account deficits in Thailand and Malaysia. The inflows also contributed to domestic asset bubbles, credit excesses, and a growing fringe of inefficient investments.

However, Western banks and portfolio investors, keen to participate in "miracle Asia", were providing funds to Asian firms with debt ratios and long-term alliance relationships that would have been unacceptable in the West. When the crisis hit, the violence of the outflow owed much to the realization that much of the funds should not have been committed in the first place, by Western prudential standards.

Enter IMF

When the Fund negotiated its programmes with Thailand, Indonesia and the Republic of Korea, it imposed a prescription of high real interest rates and fiscal restriction. This was based largely on the Fund's experience in Latin America. There, fiscal deficits tended to be large and inflation chronic. Currency devaluations set off hair-trigger inflationary expectations. The cure, quite plausibly, was IMF-style austerity. High real interest rates could be tolerated because corporate debt/equity ratios were quite low as inflation eroded the real debt burden. In Asia, the Fund failed to see the inappropriateness of fiscal restriction where budgets had long been roughly in balance. And more seriously, the Fund failed to see the inappropriateness of high real interest rates in economies with high levels of private indebtedness and low inflationary expectations. Here, high real interest rates have disastrously deflationary consequences.

Further, the Fund attempted to strengthen weakened Asian financial structures by imposing Western measures of financial restructuring. Basle rules of capital adequacy ratios were to be applied. Highly-indebted firms and banks were to be closed. Labour laws were to be changed to make it easier to fire workers, facilitating the closures. Regulations on foreign ownership were to be lifted in order to allow foreign banks and firms to buy domestic banks and firms, injecting needed capital and skills.

Somewhat similar measures were applied in a much narrower setting to solve the American savings and loan crisis in the late 1980s, and they worked. But it is one thing to undertake such reforms where real interest rates are very low and indebtedness not high (as in the United States), and another thing to undertake them where both real interest rates and indebtedness are high. In these conditions such restructuring leads to closures and lay-offs, with deflationary knock-on effects throughout the economy.

Asian resistance

This is why IMF's strategy for Asia has not worked. The currencies did stop falling in early 1998. But by May the deepening economic contraction, the rising unemployment and the fear of social unrest combined to produce a second wave of capital outflows and renewed falls in currencies and stock markets.

The second quarter resumption of the collapse is what finally forced Asian Governments to begin to turn away from the IMF strategy. They began to bring down interest rates and turn fiscal restriction into fiscal expansion. Malaysia slapped on exchange controls in September, the better to engineer an expansion at home without risking further currency falls. The Republic of Korea has used government funds to buy out bad loans and finance bank mergers. Japan is seriously discussing nationalizing the banks so as to break out of its current trap, in which the attempt to maintain Basle standards of capital adequacy while bank equity falls prevents the needed expansion of credit. Japan is also discussing the reintroduction of exchange controls to allow rapid monetary expansion without depreciating the yen (which might destabilize other currencies in the region and make trade frictions worse). China has suspended the restructuring of state enterprises and banks, because of the deflationary consequences of restructuring in crisis conditions.

The Asian Monetary Fund

There is a gathering insistence in the region that Asian arrangements have strengths that have been denied in the West since the crisis broke and that must be built upon as part of the solution. The two labour federations of the

Republic of Korea gave a statement in early July to the United States Secretary of Treasury, Robert Ruben, that made this plain: "The Asian development model, while containing some of the key elements which gave rise to the current crisis, also contains the very dynamic elements which made the 'miraculous' growth over such a short period.... The IMF policy regime, however, has overlooked... the positive and dynamic elements in its virtual blanket disavowal of the Asian economy.... It may be necessary, therefore, for Asian nations to build a body... which can serve as an Asian monetary fund".[1]

Asia is the world's great savings surplus region. Its foreign exchange reserves of almost $800 billion dwarf those of all other regions. Virtually all of these reserves are claims on the United States (Treasury bills and deposit holdings) and to a lesser degree Europe. The private sectors of Japan, Taiwan Province of China and Singapore are also large net lenders to the West. It is ironic that a region with such massive savings surplus and net foreign assets should be plunged into crisis by the flight of capital belonging to institutions that reside for the most part in the United States, a massive net debtor with a savings deficit.

An Asian Monetary Fund, or AMF, builds on Asia's savings surplus, foreign exchange reserves and net creditor status (including reserves, treasury bills and the like). The most severely affected countries—the Republic of Korea, Thailand, Malaysia and Indonesia—have gross external debt of perhaps $400 billion, of which over $100 billion has long-term maturities and favourable terms and does not need refinancing. The amount of debt needed to be refinanced in order to completely stabilize the situation is small compared to the aggregate net creditor position of Asia—less than $300 billion. The high level of economic interdependence within Asia that has built up over the past decade means that crisis in one country hurts other Asian countries above all. The all too evident neighbourhood contagion effects give each creditor country a strong interest in pooling resources with others in order to avoid further disruption.

The Asian Monetary Fund would have core financing from subscriptions by member governments. The fact that pledges of $100 billion were quickly secured in August 1997 suggests that sizeable sums would be forthcoming. Additional financial resources could be tapped by issuing World Bank-type bonds on regional financial markets, guaranteed jointly by the members.

The Fund would make quick disbursing loans available to members in difficulty, with conditionalities limited to stabilization rather than to IMF-type structural reforms. It would operate to reinforce the demonstrated strengths of Asian-type financial systems, and not to disavow them.

---

1 "The KCTU proposal", document presented at KCTU-FKTU meeting with the United States Treasury Secretary Rubin, 1 July 1998.

The Fund would save Asia money. At present, Asia lends much of its savings to the West at United States treasury bill and deposit rates of 5 per cent, while it borrows from Western creditors at 10 per cent or more. With the AMF, Asian lenders would lend to it at slightly better than 5 per cent, and Asian borrowers would borrow at only slightly more, say 6 per cent. The borrowing governments could repay the more expensive Western loans. Asia would then earn the risk premium in the interest rate on emerging Asia's external debt that is now paid over to Western creditors.

Would Asia not suffer by having Western financial markets less involved in resource allocation, as Treasury Secretary Rubin and Federal Reserve Chairman Alan Greenspan have been saying? No. Western financial institutions have failed to discriminate correctly among both sovereign and private borrowers. They piled in to fuel a speculative bubble, and after the crisis they departed even in the face of high-risk premiums, cheap assets, and current-account surpluses. The economic performance of the emerging Asian economies prior to the crisis suggests that Asian Governments and their financial institutions can allocate resources more efficiently than that.

Would the United States suffer as Asia sells United States treasuries and dollar bank deposits to fund its Monetary Fund? Probably not. Every dollar of Western credit that is refinanced is a dollar that must be redeployed. If the Government of Taiwan Province of China sells its US treasuries and puts the funds with the Asian Monetary Fund, the Fund can refinance Citibank's loan to the Republic of Korea and pay off Citibank. Citibank now has cash. In the fungible world of funds the redeployment of Citibank's cash will result, perhaps several transactions later, in the purchase of US Treasuries.

Finally, isn't an AMF by now redundant; aren't the current efforts—some bilateral, some involving the existing multilateral machinery—quite adequate? No. The existing machinery propagates a "bail-out of basket cases" image. The Asian Monetary Fund propagates an image of an Asia which is unique in having ample financial resources to handle the external financial difficulties of its weakest regional members. It propagates an image of Asians taking charge of their own destiny, and even partly closing the door to the West. The threat of the door will encourage capital flows back to the region, as Western bankers try to hold on to their Asian markets and as portfolio managers, now underweight in Asia, seek to build up their positions in order to ride up the recovery curve.

Of course the AMF would compete with IMF. But IMF wants competition for others, and should not be averse to it for itself. The only serious losers are the Western speculators who extract a risk premium they do not deserve.

Part Three

LATIN AMERICA

Edited by

Alberto Padova

9

Introduction – Latin America

ALBERTO PADOVA*
United Nations Department of Economic and Social Affairs

The rapid spread of the current global instability, initially from one country to the next in East Asia and later to financial markets on every continent, has led to renewed interest in—and economic research on—the phenomena of spillover effects and contagion (Corsetti and others, 1998). When investors' information is insufficient to distinguish among economic conditions in different emerging markets (for instance, either not up to date or hastily analyzed), a crisis in one country can trigger a sudden loss of confidence and speculation against other emerging markets (or "flight to safety"), even if underlying conditions do not warrant it. A deficit perceived as sustainable until yesterday may become unsustainable today. Sudden changes in perceptions and the herd instinct of short-term lenders and investors are a common element in recent financial crises. These kinds of situations have been a focus of concern in Latin America and in the papers that follow.

In contrast to the crises of the 1980s and 1994-1995, when Latin America was at the center of the problem, in the current financial turmoil the region found itself almost as an "innocent bystander", hit by consecutive shock waves in financial and commodity markets. As José Antonio Ocampo, Executive Sec-

* Economic Affairs Officer, Developing Economies Section. The views expressed herein are those of the author and not necessarily the views of the United Nations.

retary of the Economic Commission for Latin America and the Caribbean (ECLAC) noted , "The instability in international markets has generated speculative pressures that do not reflect the soundness of the underlying macroeconomic variables of the region's economies, or the speed and efficacy with which their authorities respond. The measures they have been obliged to adopt in reaction to external speculative movements are far more stringent than the economic fundamentals would warrant and entail high costs to the Latin American economies." (Ocampo, 1998)

At the onset of the Asian crisis, economic fundamentals differed substantially in countries across Latin America. In general, however, the health of the region's financial systems has improved since the Mexican fiasco of 1994, as a result of bank restructurings and the strengthening of financial supervision, notably in Argentina and Brazil. Moreover, the old policy lesson about the importance of a stable macroeconomic environment which had been learned at high cost during the 1980s and early 1990s, has led to declining inflation rates and budget deficits, gradually improving debt ratios, and longer maturities on external liabilities.

Still, Brazil showed widening fiscal and current-account deficits (rising from 4 per cent of GDP in 1996 to over 6 per cent in 1997 and from 3 per cent to over 4 per cent, respectively), and the latter was interpreted by the market as a sign of an overvalued currency. In addition, Brazil continued to implement a dangerous mix of tight monetary and loose fiscal policies. Not surprisingly, therefore, it rapidly became a focal point of the ripples from the Asian and later the Russian turmoil, especially through financial channels.

At the other end of the spectrum, Chile, the "model economy" of the region for the last decade, displayed a fairly stable fiscal surplus, in the order of 2 per cent of GDP up to 1997. It also had sustained economic growth and domestic saving, and a solid financial system. As pointed out by Cristián Ossa in the discussion below, with respect to the management of capital inflows, it had made "all the right moves". Yet, Chile's Achilles' heel was the continued concentration of its export revenues on copper, still accounting for around 40 per cent of the total, despite rapidly growing non-copper exports. Its otherwise successful geographical diversification towards Asia (around 30 per cent of total exports, about half of which to Japan) exacerbated the negative impact of the copper prices drop in the wake of the Asian crisis. Chile's current-account deficit increased rapidly, and growth had to be slowed to bring it under control. Together with Peru and Venezuela, Chile was therefore also hit by the crisis, particularly through trade channels.

In any event, irrespective of domestic conditions, in both Brazil and Chile and across the region, bond spreads soared, access to international financial capitals became more limited and equity markets collapsed.

Policy responses had an important role in determining the size and shape of the impact of the crisis. Defending the exchange rate through sharp increases in interest rates and/or cuts in public expenditure can be costly in terms of losses of foreign exchange reserves, output and jobs, as seen most recently in Brazil. On the other hand, absorbing the external shock partially through a depreciation of the exchange rate, as Mexico did in 1998, caused a rise in inflation and a fall in real wages, which in Mexico wiped out the slight recovery in real wages achieved in 1997. It also increases the cost in domestic currency of servicing external debt.

The above issues, namely the vulnerability of Latin America to the spillover effects and the response mechanisms adopted by the Governments of the region, are the focus of the paper by ECLAC. The paper examines the two channels of trade and finance through which the spillover effects are transmitted, and their effects on the external and fiscal accounts, output and income. In addition, it provides a number of policy lessons that can be drawn from the events of the last 18 months, both at the domestic and international levels.

Many of its conclusions, which apply beyond regional boundaries, are now widely accepted, if not always applied in practice. This is the case for the importance of the consistency among macroeconomic, institutional and competitiveness policies, as well as the need for counter-cyclical fiscal and monetary policies, in particular an improved management of periods of boom, when governments have more room for manoeuvre to smooth private and public spending over time, as through temporary taxes or stabilization funds. ECLAC also recommends increased attention to the sequencing of financial reforms. The call for better governance of the international financial system and an increase of the resources available to multilateral institutions to confront international crises were also shared by the discussants, although the proposal to introduce a "Tobin tax" at the global level, as "sand in the financial wheel", is more controversial.

Only tentative lessons can be drawn on exchange rate policy. Daniel Lederman, in the discussion, calls for more flexibility in exchange rate management, aimed at preventing excessive foreign exchange exposure by the private sector and facilitating the response to market pressures. Indeed the trend towards greater participation by developing countries in global financial markets has been accompanied by an increased reliance on exchange rate flexibility (Collins, 1996). Admittedly, the optimal mix of interest rate and exchange rate policies remains elusive. The use of an exchange rate anchor to fight inflation, a strategy adopted by several Latin American economies plagued by very high inflation, appears most effective when strong institutional commitments to this policy are established, as with a currency board, to enhance its credibility. The political will to follow policies consistent with the chosen currency arrangement is also essential. The trouble is that if the exchange rate becomes unsustainable, attempts at even modest adjustments often lead markets into panic. Exchange-rate regimes such as wide bands, with sometimes a crawling peg element, appear to have provided some flexibility with some guidance to the market and anchor for monetary policy (Griffith-Jones and Kimmis, 1998).

Capital inflows returned to Latin America in the 1990s, reversing the negative transfer of the previous decade, and reached an all time high in 1997, exceeding 4 per cent of the regional GDP. Over two thirds of these flows consist today of foreign direct investment (FDI), the most stable component of foreign capital. Complementing domestic savings, the latter can lead to higher investment and growth, and is especially crucial in low-saving Latin American economies. However, concerns about the management of large inflows of potentially reversible short-term capital have been heightened by the current financial turmoil.

In this context, much attention has focused on the Chilean experience in dealing with foreign capital inflows, and especially on the use of capital controls. Chilean-type measures to discourage short-term inflows, though not without costs and some inevitable evasion, are market-based and not excessively complex to administer.

The paper by Agosin and Ffrench-Davis examines the policies adopted by Chile vis-à-vis these inflows and their effects on growth and investment. The policies adopted have included the imposition of a non-remunerated reserve requirement on all financial inflows (excluding FDI), active sterilized intervention on foreign exchange markets to prevent undue appreciation of the peso, and the use of a crawling exchange rate band. In addition, fiscal policy has remained very conservative and prudential banking regulation was introduced after the 1982 banking crisis, and subsequently strengthened.

These policies appear to have prevented an even larger surge of foreign capital to Chile, kept real exchange-rate appreciation within bounds, fostered a higher share of FDI in total inflows, and partly contributed to the country's positive growth performance. However, between late 1995 and mid-1997, they tended to become insufficient as capital inflows accelerated. By late 1997, demand for foreign exchange had surged, as a consequence of spillover effects from the Asian crisis, and a part of the exchange rate appreciation of the past two years has been reversed. As a result, the reserve requirement was first reduced in 1998 from 30 per cent to 10 per cent and then to zero, but could be restored in case of future need.

The Chilean experience points to the need to face sharp temporary surges in capital inflows with a flexible and pragmatic mix of policy tools (including temporary controls on capital inflows) rather than with a single and rigidly used instrument. Monitoring the final use of the inflows, to prevent excessive asset price booms, is also essential. As pointed out by Ossa, to the degree that inflows could increase investment, rather than consumption, then "the trade-off would be between less volatility and a slightly higher investment rate". Finally, the relative success with controls in Chile has not always been repeated in other countries, as mentioned by Lederman with reference to Brazil, where their effectiveness appears to have been temporary.

In summary, Latin America's management of current external shocks has been followed closely not only within the region, but also by other countries in search of models of effective response to contagion. However, the region's external vulnerability, both on the trade and financial fronts, has exposed many of its economies to considerable adjustment costs, whose full magnitude has yet to be entirely realized. In some countries, such as Brazil and Ecuador, external turbulence has compounded internal weaknesses, presenting authorities with politically difficult options.

References

Collins, S. M. (1996). "On becoming more flexible: exchange rate regimes in Latin America and the Caribbean". *Journal of Development Economics,* Vol. 51, Issue: No. 1 (October), pp. 117-138.

Corsetti, G. and others (1998). "Trade and contagious devaluations: a welfare-based approach". New York: New York University (October); and other papers available in N.Roubini's Asian Crisis Homepage (http://www.stern.nyu.edu/~nroubini/asia/AsiaHomepage.html).

Griffith-Jones, S. and J. Kimmis (1998). "Capital flows: how to curb their volatility". Sussex University, Brighton. Mimeo. Paper prepared for United Nations Development Programme (UNDP) as background for the *1999 Human Development Report.*

Ocampo, J. A. (1998). "Towards a global solution". *ECLAC Notes,* Issue No. 1 (November), p. 2. Economic Commission for Latin America and the Caribbean.

Perry, G. E. and D. Lederman (1998). "Financial vulnerability, spillover effects, and contagion: lessons from the Asian crises for Latin America". *World Bank Latin American and Caribbean Studies Viewpoints* (July). Washington, D. C.: The World Bank.

10

Impact of the International Crisis on Latin America

UNITED NATIONS ECONOMIC COMMISSION FOR LATIN AMERICA AND THE CARIBBEAN*

1. A Brief Overview of the Crisis

The nature of Latin America's participation in the international crisis has been a changing one. Until October 1997, there was little impact in the region; indeed, the year 1997 was extremely successful for most countries. In the last quarter, however, the first of several waves of the crisis hit Latin American shores. The impact took two interrelated forms. The more dramatic of the two centered on volatile financial flows. Through December 1998, four phases of the financial crisis can be identified in the region. (1) October-November 1997: The Brazilian currency was attacked, but the government response was quick and effective. Regional stock markets suffered their first drop, and the bond market contracted, but recovery was fairly rapid. (2) January-February 1998: The stock markets declined again in January, and some additional countries (especially Chile and Colombia) suffered pressure on their currencies;

* This chapter was drafted by Barbara Stallings, who assumes full responsibility for its content. It draws on a document prepared earlier by ECLAC, *The Impact of the Asian Crisis on Latin America* (LC/G.2026), May 1998. The earlier document was prepared jointly by the Economic Development Division and the Division of Statistics and Projections. In addition to Stallings, others who participated actively included Pedro Sáinz, Alfredo Calcagno, José Miguel Benevente, Sandra Manuelito, and Guillermo Mundt. José Antonio Ocampo and Ricardo Ffrench-Davis offered many helpful comments.

interest rates were raised. (3) May-June 1998: A third stock market drop occurred, due to falling oil prices and gloomier perceptions about Japan. (4) August-September 1998: After the spread of the crisis to the Russian Federation, all emerging markets entered in crisis. Credit again dried up, and most countries faced severe currency problems.

The second way in which the crisis affected Latin America was via trade links. This channel was dominated by a decline in commodity prices, partially but not totally related to events in Asia. The price effect was exacerbated by a quantity effect through weak demand in Asia, both in Japan and the developing Asian economies, although this was only important for a few countries. Two additional trade channels—Asian export competition with Latin America in its own and in third markets—have not emerged as of late 1998. In contrast to the financial volatility, the trade aspect of Latin America's problems has been relatively constant, in the sense that most prices have been falling on a fairly continuous basis since mid-1997.

Fortunately for the region, Latin America had some important advantages going into the crisis period. Budget deficits had been sharply curtailed, inflation was declining and at the single-digit level in more than half the countries, and the domestic banking sector had been strengthened. International reserves were high, and the debt profile had been lengthened so that short-term obligations no longer posed an imminent danger. In addition, nearly two-thirds of foreign capital inflows consisted of foreign direct investment, whose owners take a longer-term perspective and are less likely to flee in response to short-term fluctuations.

Moreover, since they had been through many crises in the past, Latin American Governments were better prepared than their Asian counterparts to deal with the new shocks. When problems appeared in a given country, finance ministers and central bank governors were fairly quick to take action. With the exception of Mexico, the initial responses tended to center on defending exchange rates through raising interest rates and sometimes cutting fiscal expenditure. Over time, however, more countries have opted to include devaluation as part of their policy packages when faced with the alternative of falling output and loss of reserves.

Despite this relatively positive backdrop, Latin America has clearly been hurt by the international crisis. The average of the price indexes for the major Latin American stock exchanges had already fallen by 30 per cent in the three quarters ending 30 June 1998. With the new round of selling between July and September, the losses reached 42 per cent, with a small upturn in the fourth quarter. The plunge in stock market prices was closely associated with capital outflow from the region, since both foreign and domestic investors wanted to exchange their Latin American holdings for dollars. At the same time, capital inflows of other types also fell off, especially through the bond market. Investors' lack of interest in Latin American paper was such that many governments and corporations from the region postponed planned issues. In the few cases where bonds were placed, the terms deteriorated sharply.

As a result of the outflows associated with the stock market, the lack of new capital to replace them and the growing trade deficit, international reserves fell from their high levels in mid-1997. Between October 1997 and the beginning of 1998 reserves fell by US$10 billion, but they later more than regained their initial level. In the six months from July through December 1998, there was a new fall of US$33 billion (mostly centered in Brazil).

As a consequence of the multiple waves of the crisis, projections for economic growth in Latin America and the Caribbean in 1998 were continually adjusted downward. ECLAC's own estimates, made in September and March of each year for the LINK Project, showed in September 1997 that output in the region would expand by around 4.5 per cent. In March 1998, after the initial effects of the crisis had begun to manifest themselves, the figure was lowered to 3.2 per cent. In actuality, growth for the year was only 2.3 per cent. As a result, unemployment increased, and it is a virtual certainty that poverty will rise as well.

Discussion in the region at the beginning of 1999 centers on two interrelated sets of issues. On the one hand, there is obviously concern about ways to halt the negative impact of the current crisis in the region. In this aspect, Latin American leaders have been joined by the entire international financial community since halting the crisis in Latin America, and especially in Brazil, is seen as key to getting it under control on a worldwide basis. For this reason, a large support package for Brazil was set up. On the other hand, there is also concern in the region to study the lessons of the crisis so as to be in a better position to prevent—or at least moderate—the impact of future crises. Some of these lessons concern international institutions; others deal with policies that the Latin American countries themselves might adopt in the coming years.

The rest of this paper will discuss these themes further. The second section will elaborate on the impact of the crisis on Latin American economies: the trade and financial channels through which the crisis has affected the region, the policies followed by different governments, and the impact on growth and the balance of payments in 1998. The third section will provide a summary of the main lessons, both international and domestic, that can be drawn from the events of the last year and a half.

2. Effects of the Asian crisis on Latin America

(a) Channels of transmission

One of the most disturbing aspects of the current international crisis is the way it has spread from one country or region to others. This "contagion" process is not well understood and requires further study. In the Latin American case, there appear to have been three main transmission mechanisms: financial, commercial, and government policies.

Financial channels

It was through financial channels that Latin America first became dramatically aware of the crisis. In October 1997, speculators attacked the Brazilian real in a process that would be repeated elsewhere in the region later. The aim is to profit from an expected devaluation by selling a currency "short," that is, by borrowing the currency and selling it with the hope of repurchasing it more cheaply before repaying the lender. While this mechanism is usually not sufficient to force a devaluation, it can put pressure on a currency. The outcome depends on a government's response. It can defend its currency by selling reserves and/or raising interest rates, or it can allow the devaluation to occur.

A related financial mechanism for transmitting crises involves stock markets. Much short-term capital came into emerging markets during the mid-1990s, leading to a boom in the price of stocks. When investors lost confidence, those same funds were quickly withdrawn, driving prices down. This first occurred in Latin America about the same time as the attack on the real, in October 1997, as the South-East Asian market crash spread to other markets in that region (for example, Japan, Singapore, Taiwan Province of China, and Hong Kong (China), and even to the United States and Europe. It should be noted that the catalyst for a sell-off need not be in the same country or region where it is taking place. For example, some international investors felt the need for profit-taking in Latin America in order to make up for their losses on other stock markets and to maintain their liquidity.

A third financial channel relates to other types of foreign capital. During the first half of 1997, emerging markets enjoyed improved access to international financing and narrower spreads on Eurobonds and Brady bonds. The result in Latin America was a gross influx of capital amounting to some US$90 billion between January and September 1997, two thirds of that long-term capital. Foreign direct investment maintained an upward trend with flows of US$55 billion. After the crisis broke in July, spreads increased for some of the Asian countries affected, but held steady or declined in Latin America and other regions. This situation changed in October, with the abrupt stock market declines. The risk premiums for many emerging economies, including Latin American countries, shot up suddenly. A similar development occurred in August and September 1998, after the spread of the crisis to the Russian Federation undermined investor confidence in all emerging markets.

By changing the climate in the international financial markets, especially for emerging economies, the crisis has had a direct impact on the sectors most sensitive to external capital movements. With much variation from country to country, the stock market declines, combined with tougher terms of access to external capital, have affected not only foreign exchange markets and banking systems, but all those looking to the international capital markets for financing (including governments).

Trade channels

Currency devaluation and economic recession in the Asian countries caused them to import less, and this is having an impact on the whole of world trade. The eight main developing countries of East and South-East Asia, most of which were affected by the crisis,[1] represented 15 per cent of world trade in 1996; they accounted for 31 per cent of the increase in world imports between 1990 and 1995 and 28 per cent of the increase in exports. Including Japan, also in a deep slump, the percentage of world trade the region accounted for in 1996 rises to 22 per cent. Lower demand by these countries affects not only volume traded, but also the prices of products for which they constitute a major market.

The contraction of imports by East and South-East Asia has a direct impact on demand for Latin American exports. In volume terms, however, the effect has been relatively minor, because the market is not an important one for Latin American countries, with the exception of Chile and Peru, which in 1996 sold 14 per cent and 9 per cent of their exports, respectively, to the eight Asian countries in question. Sales to Japan added another 16 per cent for Chile and 7 per cent for Peru.

Much more importantly, via the contraction of imports, the Asian crisis also has had an impact on the prices of Latin America's export products, especially commodities for which the East and South-East Asian countries constitute an important part of world demand. In 1995, for example, these countries accounted for around 15 per cent of world imports of agricultural raw materials, minerals and metals and petroleum. Moreover, their share of world imports of minerals and metals was rapidly increasing.

1 They include Hong Kong (China), Indonesia, Malaysia, the Philippines, the Republic of Korea, Singapore, Taiwan Province of China and Thailand.

At the same time that the crisis led to a contraction of Asian imports, it is also likely to increase their exports. Sharp currency devaluation, lower domestic demand and underutilized installed capacity should all favour the exports of the Asian countries. Up until now, the difficult financial conditions brought on by the crisis (tighter credit, higher interest rates, the increased burden of debt denominated in foreign currencies) have tended to hinder rapid expansion of export supply; for that reason, most of the trade adjustment so far has been in the form of import reduction. It can be anticipated, however, that the Asian countries will eventually increase the quantity of their exports of manufactured goods, and that this will result in an increase in value exported despite the expected decline in unit value. This process could put competitive pressure on the Latin American countries in both their domestic and external markets.

Determination of the possible magnitude of the effect is complicated by the fact that Asian exports do not compete directly with Latin American and Caribbean exports in the markets of the member countries of the Organisation for Economic Cooperation and Development (OECD). The Asian countries export consumer manufactures and capital goods (such as electronic and electrical products, computers and other machinery); the Latin American and Caribbean countries export a larger proportion of raw materials and semi-manufactures to OECD countries, particularly to the European and Japanese markets. The situation is different in the North American and Latin American markets, the destination for most of the region's exports of manufactures, where competition from Asian products could intensify in categories such as chemical products, steel, textiles and footwear. Here there could be a bigger impact when Asian exports increase.

Policy measures

The principal economic measures taken in response to the crisis have been in the areas of monetary, fiscal and trade policy. Monetary measures have been taken by countries whose financial and foreign exchange markets have experienced volatility, either as a direct consequence of short-term capital flows or as a reaction to a fall in prices of exports. Fiscal measures—chiefly budget cuts—have been applied in response to declining fiscal revenues in countries that derive an important part of their revenue from the sale of commodities by government-owned companies, that is, oil in Ecuador, Mexico, Venezuela and, to a lesser extent, in Colombia and copper in Chile. Budget cuts have also been made to shrink aggregate demand so as to reduce current-account deficits. In the particular case of Brazil, its fiscal packages, which have included tax rises, were also necessary in order to finance the increase in interest payments on the domestic public debt, which resulted from the monetary measures, and to send a signal to financial investors of a capacity for timely response. Lastly, some countries have adopted anti-dumping and safeguard measures to protect domestic producers threatened with competition from Asian products and to improve the current account balance.

It is evident that Governments are reacting to the consequences of the crisis with measures that tend to slow economic activity, in that they tighten monetary policy, raise taxes and cut public spending. Table 1 shows the primary kinds of measures adopted by selected countries.

(b) Magnitude of the effects of the Asian crisis and of policy measures

The impact on the financial sector

The channels by which the crisis has spilled over into the Latin American region vary from country to country. As noted above, the financial factors basically came into play in October 1997 and in August-September 1998 , when stock market and foreign exchange crises spread further and internationally-based investors began to flee the emerging economies, especially the countries that appeared to suffer from external imbalances similar to those of the Asian countries in crisis, and to move their money to developed economies considered safer. In Latin America, the country hardest hit was Brazil, which has been experiencing a growing deficit on its fiscal accounts and a large current account deficit. In international crisis situations, the markets usually interpret the latter as a sign of an overvalued currency.

Table 1. Economic policy measures adopted in response to the international crisis in 1997 and 1998

Country	*Fiscal adjustment*	*Monetary tightening*	*Trade measures*
Argentina	X		X
Brazil	X	X	X
Chile	X	X	
Colombia	X	X	X
Ecuador	X		X
Mexico	X	X	
Paraguay		X	
Peru		X	
Venezuela	X	X	

Until the events of October 1997, the region's stock exchanges were maintaining the gains made earlier in the year, spreads on Latin American Eurobonds were continuing to narrow, and capital inflows showed no signs of slackening. In fact, in the third quarter of 1997, international bank credit balances rose by US$10 billion, a figure roughly equal to the increase for the entire first half. Then, at the end of October, the perceived "country risk" for the region's economies abruptly shot up in international financial markets and caused stock prices to drop sharply, by 20 per cent on average. An even larger reduction occurred during a similar situation in the third quarter of 1998, when stock prices fell by 30 per cent (see figure 1).

The influx of portfolio capital dropped off noticeably during the last quarter of 1997: international bond issues declined to under US$4 billion, compared with US$20 billion the previous quarter (see figure 2). To a great extent, the decline was due to the severe deterioration in the terms offered by the market, which, by demanding wider spreads and shorter maturities, pushed potential issuers into a holding pattern. Beginning in November 1997, a number of governments and firms postponed issues they had planned, although some

Figure 1: Stock market quotations
(Index June 1997 = 100)

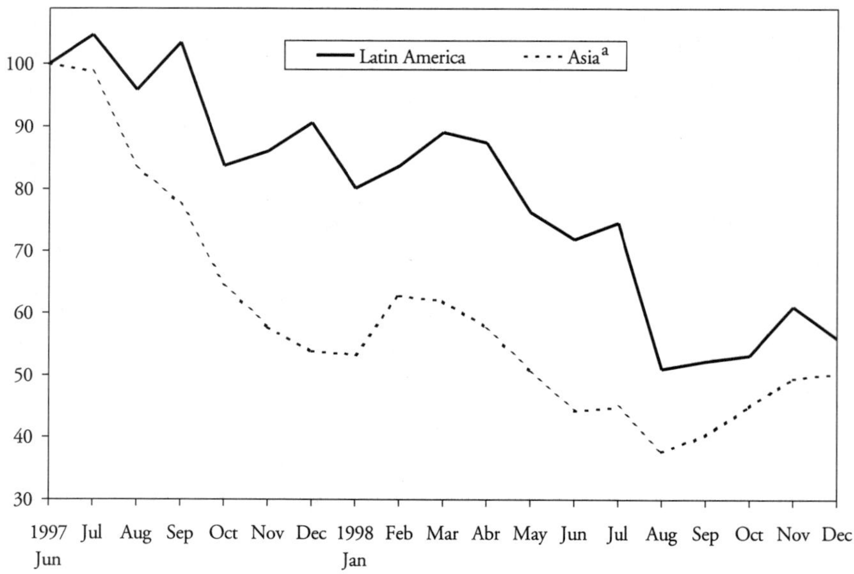

Sources: ECLAC, on the basis of figures from the International Finance Corporation.

a. Includes China, India, Indonesia, Malaysia, Pakistan, the Philippines, Republic of Korea, Sri Lanka, Taiwan Province of China and Thailand.

Figure 2: International bond issued by Latin American borrowers

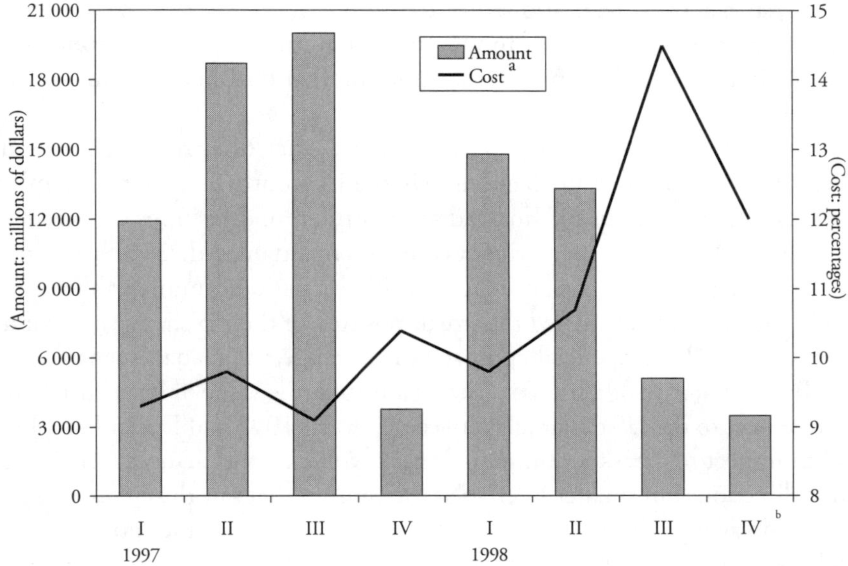

Sources: ECLAC, on the basis of figures from national sources, the World Bank and the International Monetary Fund.

a. Sum of the average spread for bond issues plus the yield of long-term United States Treasury bonds.
b. Preliminary estimates.

returned to the market shortly thereafter: the Governments of Argentina and Colombia placed debt paper beginning in January, Brazil in February and Mexico in March 1998. For the region as a whole, bond issues rebounded during the first half of 1998; at that time, the Government of Argentina was particularly active, using the funds raised primarily to pay off maturing debt .This favorable situation did not last long, however. Another major credit squeeze began in the second half of 1998, following the Russian crisis. Only a handful of bonds were issued in the fourth quarter because of the enormous interest premium being demanded.

Along with a decline in bond placements, some countries experienced flight of short-term capital; such outflows from Brazil reached US$8 billion in October 1997 and US$17 billion in September 1998, in effect an attack on the currency. In Venezuela, the estimated outflow for October 1997-September 1998 was US$5 billion. Chile experienced currency pressures in December 1997 and January 1998 and in June-July 1998; during those months it suffered a cumulative drop in international reserves of US$2.6 billion. On the other hand, there is no evidence that foreign direct investment in Latin

America has been affected significantly by the international crisis. Long-term factors, such as the privatizations due to come in some countries, the liberalization of service markets and the funds attracted by integration programmes (especially in Mercosur), support the assumption that foreign direct investment will persist.

Despite the losses of international reserves that occurred principally in Brazil, Chile, Colombia and Venezuela in the 15 months ending in December 1998 (see figure 3) , this did not lead to important modifications in real effective exchange rates. The majority of countries maintained their exchange rate systems. In particular, Brazil kept on with its periodic mini-devaluations. Chile and Colombia adjusted the size or position of their exchange rate bands but maintained their general approach to exchange rate management.

In the majority of Latin American countries, the value of local currencies with respect to the US dollar fell between October 1997 and December 1998. (With respect to a basket of international currencies, the changes were in the same directions but smaller.) Peru was the country that saw the largest real depreciation against the dollar (around 13 per cent); Brazil, Chile and Colombia each devalued about 8 per cent, while the Argentine currency was steady.

Figure 3: Changes in international reserves
(Millions of dollars)

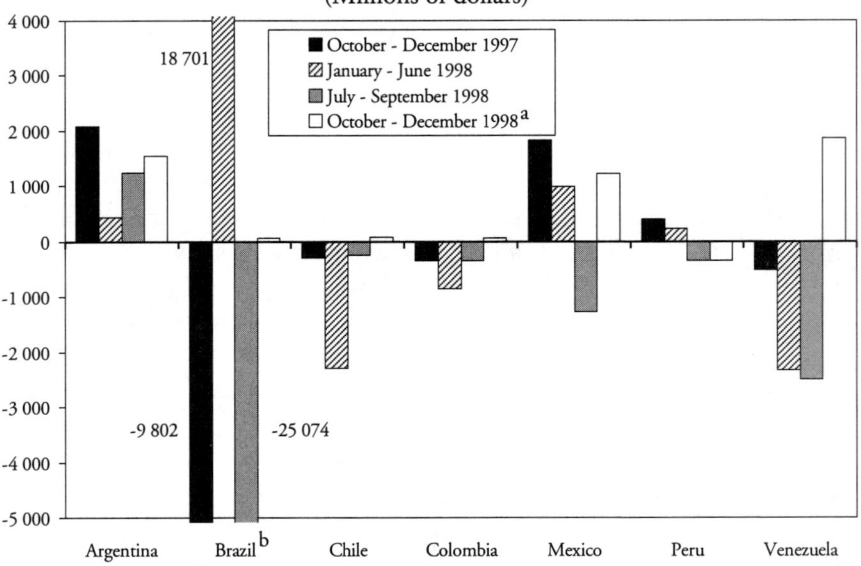

Sources: ECLAC, on the basis of official figures.

a. Brazil: Preliminary estimates.

b. In December 1998, figure includes US$9 billion from the International Monetary Fund and Bank for International Settlements.

Although through the middle of 1998 Mexico had only a moderate depreciation, the process speeded up substantially in the third quarter. In Venezuela, in contrast, the currency continued to appreciate with the exception of the third quarter of 1998 (see figure 4).

In order to staunch (or prevent) the loss of reserves and the flight of deposits from the banking system, various countries resorted to raising domestic interest rates significantly (see figure 5) . Thanks to these measures and the perception that banking systems were sounder (in comparison with their condition when the "tequila effect" hit), the tension in the foreign exchange markets was not accompanied by an appreciable loss of bank deposits. Had it been otherwise, the pressures on exchange rates might have been much greater, and a loss of deposits might have forced banks to cut lending, further slowing the pace of economic activity, as happened in Mexico and Argentina in 1995.

The country hardest hit by the financial repercussions of the international crisis was, as already mentioned, Brazil. At the end of October, the drop in the prices of its external debt paper reduced the interest rate differential by which it attracted external capital (domestic interest rates became insufficient, owing to

Figure 4: Changes in real values of local currencies[a]
(In percentages)

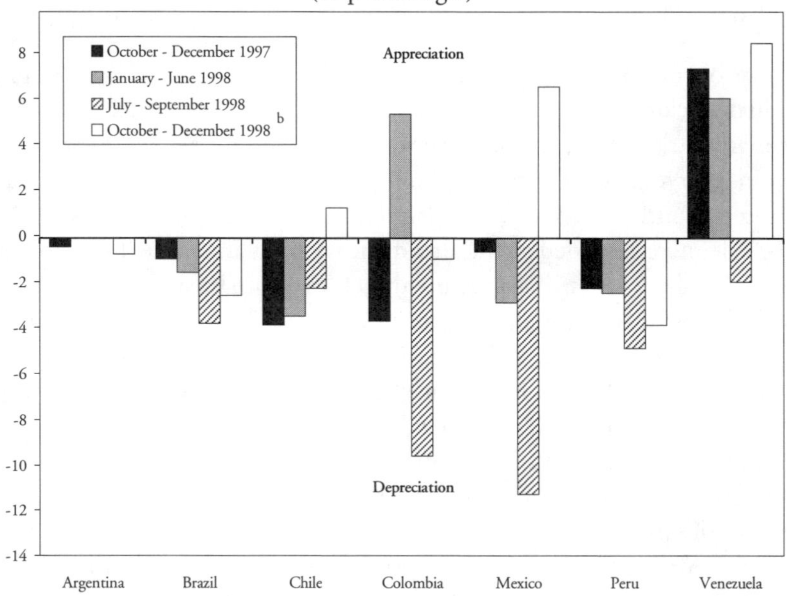

Sources: ECLAC, on the basis of official figures.

a. With respect to the US dollar.

b. Preliminary estimates.

Figure 5: Changes in nominal interest rates
(Percentage points of variation in different periods)

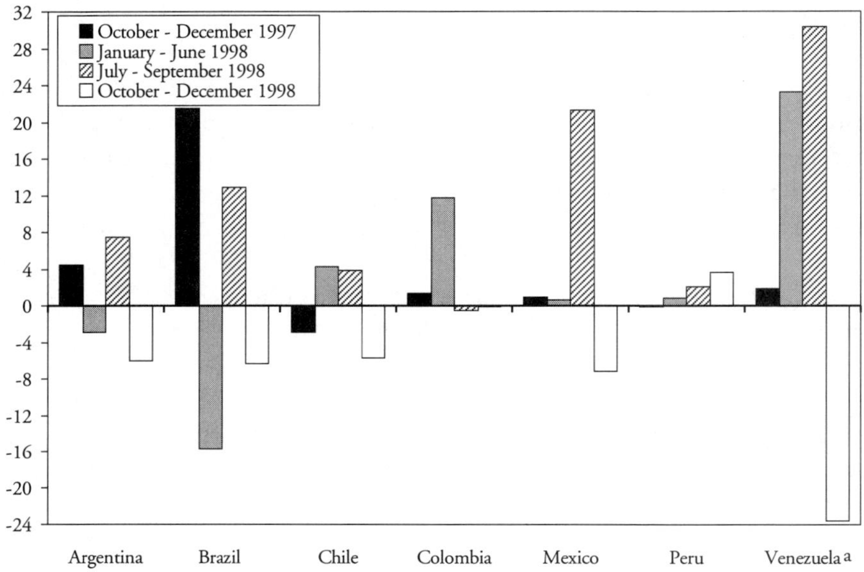

Sources: ECLAC, on the basis of official figures.

a. November.

the level of country risk), while at the same time the decline of the main international stock markets induced foreign investors to realize their gains on the Brazilian market. Both factors gave rise to a strong net demand for dollars, a drop in reserves and a contraction in liquidity; in response, the Central Bank increased its interest rate ("CBR") from 21.6 per cent to 43.4 per cent per annum. The increase added to the already heavy pressure of the domestic public debt on fiscal accounts. The measure therefore had to be supplemented in November by fiscal adjustments equivalent to nearly 2 per cent of GDP. From a longer-term perspective, in February 1998 Congress gave preliminary approval to two bills that should bring about a reduction in public expenditure; one bill sets a limit to salaries of civil servants and makes it easier to dismiss them; the other is aimed at reducing pension payments.

Following a period of recuperation of reserves and lowering of interest rates, Brazil's problems flared up again in the third quarter of 1998. Economic difficulties were exacerbated by the upcoming presidential elections. The attention of the international financial community centered on the situation in Brazil because it was believed that if Brazil "fell", then the international crisis would expand substantially. Thus a large financial rescue package was put together in return for Government measures to cut the fiscal deficit.

Chile and Colombia are two other countries that have faced especially severe financial problems during 1998. In Chile, the prospects of a major deterioration of the current-account balance because of the fall in the price of copper led to greater demand for dollars on the part of individuals and financial institutions. When the demand began to take on a speculative slant, the Central Bank, after a modest devaluation of the peso, decided to intervene. The Central Bank raised the real reference interest rate from 6.5 per cent to 7 per cent in January 1998 and then again in February to 8.5 per cent.

When the current-account deficit continued to expand, a more comprehensive package was introduced in June. It adjusted the exchange rate band and provided for new dollar-linked securities. But its most controversial measure was to lower the reserve requirement that Chile had used to help prevent the inflow of short-term capital; the rate was dropped from 30 per cent to 10 per cent. It was interesting that, just when other countries and the multilateral organizations were beginning to praise the Chilean controls, the Central Bank lowered them. A few months later, they were reduced to zero, since Chile's problem was no longer an excess of capital inflows but a scarcity. (On Chile's capital controls policy, see Agosin and Ffrench-Davis in Chapter 11 of this book.)

The problem of capital flight also confronted the Government of Colombia. The Bank of the Republic increased the supply of foreign exchange by drawing on its reserves to the tune of over US$500 million in the first two months of 1998; it also lowered the reserve requirement on external credits (from 30 per cent to 25 per cent), shortened the length of time such deposits are held from 18 to 12 months and announced the country's receipt of foreign exchange obtained through privatization and bond issues (US$800 million pending receipt at the end of 1997). In addition, in order to influence general liquidity in the system, it raised the interest rate on its 30-day bonds (*títulos de participación*) to 23 per cent (21.5 per cent in August 1997) and in mid-February increased from 27 per cent to 30 per cent the interest rate on its one-day repurchase agreements. These measures caused the interbank rate to rise from 24 per cent to 40 per cent, later dropping back to 33 per cent. These policy decisions and others that followed threatened to undermine seriously the country's growth rate. Consequently, when faced with similar choices in the second half of 1998, the Government allowed a devaluation.

For the region as a whole, for the first time since the tequila crisis, it was necessary to draw on international reserves to finance the current account deficit. While the deficit increased from US$64 to US$84 billion between 1997 and 1998, capital inflows fell from US$80 to US$62 billion. The large volume of reserves on hand meant that the shortfall could be covered relatively easily, assuming that it only lasted for a single year. In addition, the gap was partially filled by Brazil's drawing on the large rescue package put together by the international community. Beyond the external sector problems, the main impact of the financial components of the crisis should come from the restrictive monetary policies and high domestic interest rates that governments have been obliged to apply in order to avoid a loss of international reserves and bank deposits.

The impact on trade

Though the effects of the Asian crisis in Brazil and Colombia, and, temporarily, Argentina were mainly felt through financial channels, in several other countries trade was the area most affected. In Chile, the financial effects were felt later than, and to a large extent were due to, the effects on trade. The available data show that in the majority of the countries the main impact of the crisis on trade was a drop in prices for some commodities, rather than a contraction in export volumes. The main reason is that Asia, where the recessions are centered, is not a major market for most Latin American countries; the two main exceptions are Chile and Peru (see figure 6).

Figure 6: Latin American exports to Asia
(As a percentage of each country's total exports)

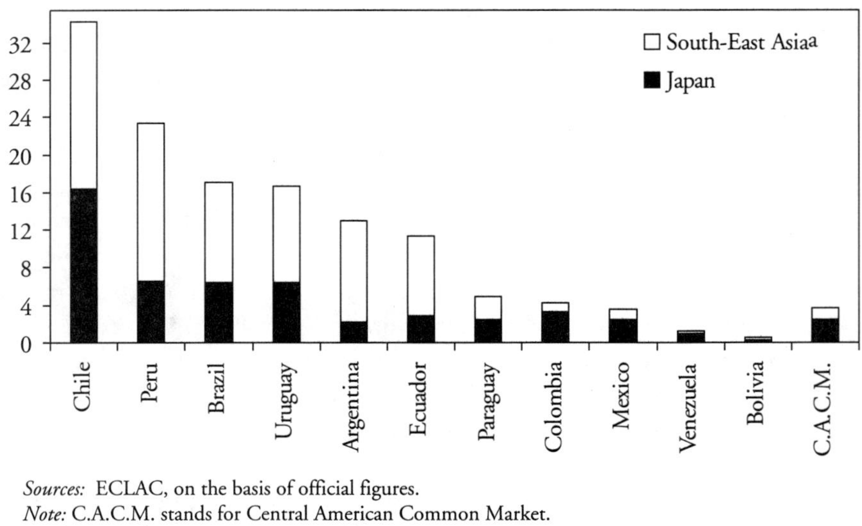

Sources: ECLAC, on the basis of official figures.
Note: C.A.C.M. stands for Central American Common Market.

a. Includes Australia, China, Hong Kong (China), Indonesia, Malaysia, New Zealand, the Philippines, Republic of Korea, Singapore, Taiwan Province of China and Thailand.

The information available on Latin America's exports for 1998 showed a generalized slowdown throughout the region, with at least half of the countries suffering a decline in the absolute value of export revenues in comparison with 1997. The sharpest falls, more than 10 per cent, have occurred in Chile, Ecuador, Nicaragua, Peru and Venezuela.

Taking account of the price trends of the main Latin American export products, it can be inferred that the worsening of export sales was due to the sharp fall in prices rather than to variation in volume. The primary product price index of *The Economist,* for example, continued to fall throughout the year, such that at the end of the fourth quarter it was more than 16 per cent below the level of the previous year. The metals category has experienced the biggest fall, almost 25 per cent, but almost all the prices of primary products fell. (See figure 7 for a representative group of commodities.)

Petroleum exporters suffered especially serious problems because of the falling price of oil. Venezuela, for example, saw the prices of the blend of petroleum it exports fall to less than US$10 per barrel in June 1998, compared to US$16.3 dollars in 1997. This obliged the Government to make several budget cuts to reduce the projected deficit. Venezuela's access to the international bond market was closed after August, eliminating an alternative to budget cuts. The fall in the price of petroleum, in turn, increased speculation against the bolívar. Since the Government did not want to devalue, it had to raise interest rates and use part of its ample supply of reserves to support the currency. Ecuador also suffered from the fall in oil prices, together with that for bananas. The fall in export revenues (15 per cent during 1998) was responsible for the country's trade balance shifting into the red, worsening the deficit on the current account. Given its large budget deficit, Ecuador was eventually forced to allow its currency to depreciate.

The other oil producers have a smaller share of their export revenues coming from petroleum. In Mexico, for example, oil export revenues fell by 34 per cent during the first part of the year, but non-oil exports (especially the *maquila*) rose by 13 per cent; the combination left Mexico with an overall increase of 6 per cent. While this was quite positive in comparative regional terms, imports continued to outpace exports, leading to a widening of the current account deficit. The 7 per cent devaluation in 1998 makes Mexico's exports even more competitive in its main market, the United States, although the fall in the value of the currency also presages higher inflation. Also, while Mexico's export portfolio does not depend heavily on petroleum, its fiscal accounts do. This led to several budget cuts and slower than predicted growth.

Other commodity producers with especially serious problems were the

Figure 7: Commodity prices
(Index 1990 = 100)

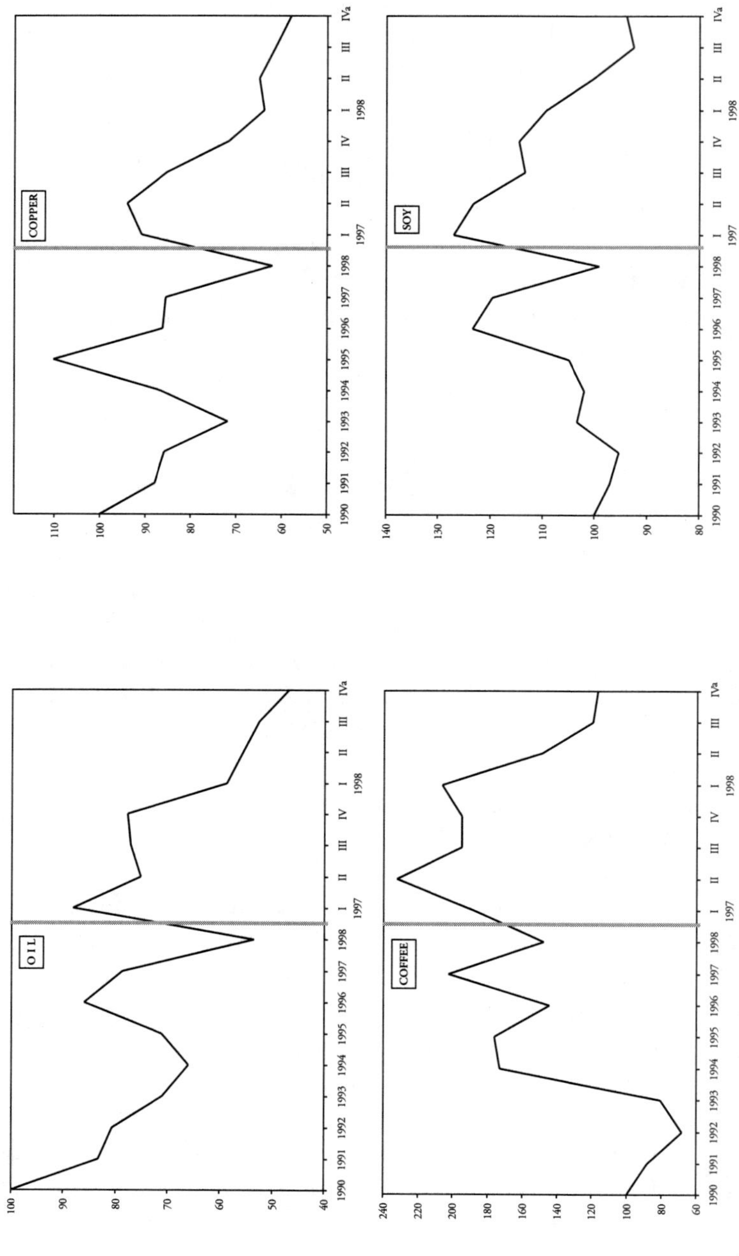

Sources: ECLAC, on the basis of official figures.

a. Preliminary estimates.

copper exporters: Chile and, to a lesser extent, Peru. Copper prices for 1998 were down more than 25 per cent with respect to 1997. Since around 40 per cent of Chile's export revenues derive from copper, this was the major source of the 11 per cent fall in overall export revenues during the year. Although the Government owns the country's largest copper company, fiscal revenues were somewhat protected by the Copper Stabilization Fund, which was used last year. Peru's exports, although more diversified than Chile's, are down by a larger amount (17 per cent); part of this fall was due to the El Niño phenomenon, in addition to low prices for various metals. At the same time, Peru's main mines are privately owned, so again the fiscal impact was cushioned. It will also be remembered that Chile and Peru are the two countries in Latin America with a significant share of their trade with Asia. Thus, unlike their counterparts in other countries, they suffered from volume as well as price effects because of Asia's problems.

Argentina's trade situation held up surprisingly well (virtually no change in 1998), given the earlier fears about the negative impact of slower growth in Brazil. Argentina is also a commodity exporter, especially oil and grains, whose prices were both down. But a bumper grain crop partially compensated for the reduction in prices. At the same time, modest export growth presents the Government with a dilemma, since the output elasticity of imports remains high, so that the maintenance of a rapid rate of growth could generate ever larger external imbalances. The exports of Paraguay and Uruguay were also affected by lower growth in the Brazilian economy.

Except in specific cases and categories, there was no drop-off in export volumes: falling demand for Latin American commodities in the Asian countries was balanced, at least in part, by the relative strength of other markets. For example, the available data for 1998 show that, in the case of Brazil, declining demand from Asia was more than offset by sales to the countries of the Latin American Integration Association (LAIA) and the European Union. Chile also managed to shift some of its output to other customers.

Preliminary figures for Latin American trade for 1998 indicate that there was no massive influx of goods from East and South-East Asia. This would appear to be further proof of the difficulties countries of that region faced in expanding their exports rapidly, despite having devalued their currencies. In fact, China, which did not devalue its currency, is one of the Asian countries that continued to increase its market share in Latin America and the Caribbean. However, the difficulties of East and South-East Asian countries will eventually be overcome, and for that reason a number of Latin American countries have adopted or announced anti-dumping or safeguard measures in view of the risk of an influx of certain goods at very low prices. In Colombia, for instance, in late January the Supreme Council on Foreign Trade considered introducing safeguard measures which could block for up to four years the entry of foreign goods that threaten local production; Argentina streamlined procedures for anti-dumping investigations in the case of Asian imports (including watches, toys, footwear, textiles, electronic goods, food products and tools); and in Peru and Uruguay, manufacturers are demanding the introduction of safeguard clauses to protect the apparel and footwear industries.

The possibility that Latin American goods may lose ground in third country markets as a result of renewed competition from Asia is a latent threat that may materialize in the future when Asian exports have overcome their present difficulties. It is important, however, to remember the advantages that trading areas confer on a number of countries in the region. Thus, Mexico's *maquila* industry (one of the categories potentially threatened) is covered by agreements that protect its share in the United States market. Preliminary data for Mexico for 1998 point not to a slowdown, but rather to sustained growth of exports.

To sum up, in 1998, declines in some prices and in the volumes exported to East and South-East Asia were offset by increases in the volumes produced and exported to other markets (including the intraregional market). Most countries experienced worsening terms of trade and export revenues performed far less well than they might have, had the international crisis not occurred.

Overall results for 1998

Latin America did not experience the negative growth that struck many Asian countries or that occurred in parts of Latin America itself in 1995 (Argentina, Mexico, and Uruguay). There is a feeling of modest satisfaction in the region regarding the Governments' handling of the crisis, but the policies adopted to deal with the international turbulence entail high costs in terms of growth opportunities, employment and, in some cases, inflation.

Any attempt to quantify the impact of the crisis on the region involves the difficulty of isolating that impact from the effects of other contemporary events which also influence the economic performance of the Latin American countries. To the extent that these events are manifested through trade and financial channels, their effects are superimposed upon those of the international crisis; it is therefore difficult to make reliable estimates of the causal relations.

An example of this overlapping of factors is seen in the pricing of certain commodities, especially oil. Lower demand in the countries of East and South-East Asia is not the only factor weakening oil prices, nor does it appear to be the most important one. On the demand side, lower energy consumption in the developed countries due to the exceptionally mild winter of 1997-1998 in the northern hemisphere also played a part; on the supply side, there has been a substantial increase in production, both within and outside the Organization of Petroleum Exporting Countries (OPEC). A combination of factors also seems to have influenced the fall in prices for other commodities. In addition to falling demand in Asia, good grain and oilseed harvests occurred in 1998. While copper prices are perhaps the most deeply affected by events in Asia, the market had already been anticipating a fall from relatively high levels in the first half of 1997, owing to increases in production levels and stocks.

Many countries of the region were also affected by the climatic phenomenon known as "El Niño". By altering ocean temperatures and rainfall patterns it not only caused human and material losses, but also affected fisheries and agriculture by producing drought in some areas and excess rainfall and floods in others. This led to problems with hydroelectric power generation (particularly in Central America), forest fires, and widespread destruction of dwellings and infrastructure. As a result, independently of the international crisis, the El Niño phenomenon reduced growth and export forecasts for a number of countries; it also affected fiscal accounts.

Finally, in addition to all other factors, growth forecasts for 1998 had to take into account the difficulty certain countries would experience in maintaining growth rates at their high 1997 levels, given the rapid increase in external imbalances and/or the fall in unused production capacity. Argentina, Mexico, and Peru are examples of particularly high growth rates in 1997 that probably could not have been maintained in 1998, even in the absence of special international problems.

Some of these factors had already been taken into account in forecasts prepared by ECLAC in September 1997, before the crisis struck the region. Therefore, comparisons between those estimates and later ones (March, September and December 1998), shown in table 2 , provide an approximate picture of the impact of the crisis on GDP growth. Thus, although GDP is now projected to have grown by 2.3 per cent in 1998 (a fall of more than three percentage points with respect to 1997), it had already been expected to fall by one percentage point regardless of the international crisis. The latter cut GDP growth in the region by two more points. If the worsening terms of trade are taken into account, income growth in the region fell by even more. This reduced growth rate has begun to affect employment levels, making it more difficult to solve the problems of social marginalization that characterize the region.

The balance-of-payments deficit also widened as a result of the crisis. This came about mainly because the value of exports fell for the first time in the decade, mostly owing to the decline in commodity prices. Slower growth in imports also occurred, although they continued to grow faster than exports. Again, other factors, especially El Niño, were also relevant to the explanation for deterioration in the trade balance and the current account. For lack of a September 1997 (pre-crisis) forecast, table 3 compares the actual result for 1997 with the latest forecast for 1998. This comparison shows a widening of the deficit from 3.3 per cent to 4.1 per cent of GDP (0.8 percentage points).

A comparison of tables 2 and 3 suggests that Brazil, Chile and Venezuela were especially hard hit by the crisis. Brazil's growth rate fell because its vulnerability, arising from its fiscal deficit and overvalued exchange rate, led speculators to conclude that they could make money by betting against its currency. Policies to protect the real had the side effect of slowing growth. In the case of Chile and Venezuela, the effects of the crisis came mainly by a fall in commodity prices (oil and copper, respectively). In Venezuela, the drop in oil prices manifested itself in a large budget deficit, whose main remedy was large cuts in expenditure, leading to a fall in growth. In Chile, the fall in copper prices led to

Table 2. Projections for 1998 GDP made in different periods
(Variation with respect to 1997 at constant 1990 prices)

	September 1997	*March 1998*	*September 1998*	*December 1998*	*Difference*
	(1)	*(2)*	*(3)*	*(4)*	*(4) - (1)*
Argentina	5.5	4.5	4.5	4.0	-1.5
Bolivia	5.0	4.5	4.5	4.5	-0.5
Brazil	3.5	1.1	1.1	0.5	-3.0
Chile	6.5	5.5	4.3	4.0	-2.5
Colombia	3.5	4.0	2.5	2.0	-1.5
Costa Rica	3.5	3.5	4.0	5.5	+2.0
Dominican Republic	6.0	6.0	5.0	7.0	+1.0
Ecuador	3.5	2.5	1.7	1.0	-2.5
El Salvador	5.0	4.5	4.5	3.5	-1.5
Guatemala	3.5	5.0	4.0	4.5	+1.0
Honduras	4.5	4.5	4.5	3.0	-1.5
Mexico	5.0	5.0	4.1	4.5	-0.5
Nicaragua	4.0	4.5	4.5	3.5	-0.5
Panama	3.5	4.5	4.5	3.5	0.0
Paraguay	3.0	2.5	2.0	0.0	-3.0
Peru	4.5	4.5	3.1	1.0	-3.5
Uruguay	4.5	3.0	3.0	2.5	-2.0
Venezuela	5.0	3.0	-1.0	-1.0	-6.0
Regional average	4.4	3.2	2.6	2.3	-2.1

Source: ECLAC, Statistics and Economic Projections Division.

a current account deficit that was considered dangerous, so domestic growth had to be reduced to keep it under control. In the case of Brazil, by contrast, an improvement occurred in the balance of payments, as slow growth reduced imports. But the fall in Brazil's current account deficit was small and did little to neutralize the reversal of Venezuela's traditionally large surplus in the regional average figures.

(c) Pending problems that influence regional prospects

A return to the macroeconomic conditions that prevailed before the crisis, with the costs being limited to those shown in the tables above, depends upon a set of circumstances that are mostly beyond the control of Governments in the region. One positive factor is the strength of the United States and European economies. Despite the marked volatility in their stock markets, the fundamentals of those economies remain sound. Their real income has benefited from an improvement in their terms of trade, and lower prices for raw materials have reduced previous estimates of inflation. Now that interest rates are being

Table 3. Projections for 1998 current-account deficit made in different periods
(As a percentage of GDP)

	Actual 1997 (1)	*March 1998 (2)*	*September 1998 (3)*	*December 1998 (4)*	*Difference (4) - (1)*
Argentina	-2.9	-3.8	-3.5	-3.6	-0.7
Bolivia	-9.1	-8.6	-10.2	-9.7	-0.6
Brazil	-4.3	-3.7	-3.8	-4.2	+0.1
Chile	-5.3	-6.2	-6.5	-6.7	-1.4
Colombia	-6.0	-4.7	-5.8	-6.5	-0.5
Costa Rica	-3.5	-6.1	-4.5	-3.6	-0.1
Dominican Republic	-1.5	-0.5	-0.8	-3.2	+1.7
Ecuador	-3.8	-5.0	-6.3	-8.5	-4.7
El Salvador	+0.8	-2.3	-1.3	-1.8	-2.6
Guatemala	-3.1	-3.7	-2.9	-3.7	-0.6
Honduras	-4.0	+0.9	-2.0	-5.4	-1.4
Mexico	-1.8	-2.9	-3.6	-3.6	-1.8
Nicaragua	-40.3	-21.0	-22.6	-36.9	+3.4
Panama	-3.6	-4.3	-2.9	-6.7	-3.1
Paraguay	-6.5	-8.6	-9.4	-2.6	+3.9
Peru	-5.2	-5.6	-6.0	-6.4	-1.2
Uruguay	-1.6	-1.2	-1.4	-2.1	-0.5
Venezuela	+5.4	+2.8	-0.5	-1.5	-6.9
Regional average	-3.3	-3.5	-4.0	-4.1	-0.8

Source: ECLAC, Statistics and Economic Projections Division.

lowered, there is the hope that normality will return to the credit markets and that these countries will provide an engine of growth for emerging market economies including Latin America.

The Asian situation, by contrast, stills presents great potential risks. Developments in Asia in the first half of 1998 were positive. Agreements on debt renegotiation helped redress the lack of liquidity, stock markets were gradually recovering, and the market value of several Asian currencies appreciated. Financial systems made progress towards stabilization. However, many of these gains have been reversed following the Russian crisis and increased international turbulence in the second half of the year, indicating that the economies remain extremely fragile.

While China has thus far played a positive role in the Asian region, especially by maintaining the value of its currency, Japan continues to pose problems for its neighbors and for the world economy as a whole. With a second year of recession now looming, Japan has been unable to absorb Asian exports in the way that the United States took additional Mexican exports in 1995. On the contrary, Japan's economy has been an additional drag on growth. Its banks, already in difficulties for years, saw their condition deteriorate further as a result of the Asian crisis. The latest measures in 1998 to revive the economy and refinance the banks may prove insufficient yet again.

In view of the fact that Asia's balance-of-payments adjustment is basically being achieved through a sharp cut in imports, and that the prospects for Japanese growth have deteriorated and may lead to a reduction in forecast imports, it is to be feared that a downswing in intra-Asian trade will provoke greater recessionary pressures than had been expected. In particular, there is a potential risk for Latin America and the Caribbean that the affected countries will pursue an aggressive policy of exporting manufactured goods at reduced prices. In such a case, some sectors, especially labour-intensive goods, could be adversely affected by greater competition both in internal sales and in exporting to third markets. Such pressure could intensify if the Asian crisis were to lead to new competitive devaluations in that region.

Lastly, it is being debated how long the affected countries will take to pull out of the crisis and what their economic momentum will be in the medium and long term. The speed and extent of the Asian economies' recovery will play an important role on certain markets that are significant for Latin America, and will be important elements in international forecasts for the medium and long term.

One market with an uncertain future that has a strong influence (albeit varying in nature and intensity) on countries in the region is the oil market.

Asian recovery could strengthen demand, but a more crucial factor appears to be the trend in supply from the oil-exporting countries (whether members of OPEC or not). The behaviour of the principal Latin American exporters in this respect will have a direct effect on their economic growth, depending on the share of the oil industry in overall output.

3. Lessons of the International Crisis for Latin America

An examination of the origins and magnitude of the international crisis, and of the mechanisms through which its effects are being transmitted to Latin America, reveals the nature and inherent danger of current international movements of capital. Several lessons can be drawn concerning the need to strengthen countries' capacity to respond. In addition, since the Asian part of the crisis arose partially as a result of domestic economic problems, these may also provide useful lessons for Latin America. Some proposals about both finance and economics are set out below. Although interrelated, for the purposes of analysis they are separated into national and international categories.

(a) National aspects

The diverse origins of the Asian crisis reflect the growing number of factors that increase countries' external vulnerability in the current international context. The three sets of factors involved are macroeconomic, institutional and those relating to production structure and competitiveness. Assigning responsibility to any one of them in isolation is generally not a sufficient explanation of vulnerability, and does not take into account the interrelationship among the various factors. By way of example, it was not in itself the weakness of the banking system that led to the crisis; this weakness coincided with strong growth and stable prices and reserves until the balance-of-payments capital account was liberalized and short-term foreign capital flooded in. All the same, financial openness would cause fewer problems if there were a well-regulated banking system and if macroeconomic policies were governed by medium- and long-term criteria. The combination of large balance-of-payments deficits, loss of confidence in export potential and competitiveness, and high-risk local bank portfolios created a climate of distrust, the effect of which was far greater than that of any one of these factors taken separately. In short, an important lesson to be learned from the Asian experience is that macroeconomic, institutional and competitiveness policies should be coordinated and should be consistent.

In the macroeconomic area, there is a need to examine the policies that preceded the crises. In both the Asian and the Latin American cases, policy management in periods of expansion had a considerable influence on subsequent difficulties. Beginning in the 1970s, countries in Latin America had to confront abrupt changes in external capital flows, in addition to the usual fluctuations in commodity export earnings. This accentuated outside influences on the sharp changes in output levels characteristic of most developing countries. There were thus successive periods of expansion and contraction, the contraction of the 1980s attaining the level of a prolonged crisis.

In the periods of expansion, external flows were channelled into a rapid expansion of public and private spending, with the encouragement of creditors. The external flows led many agents into overindebtedness, which prompted foreign banks to withdraw their loans abruptly in subsequent periods. When the flow of external capital was re-established at the beginning of the 1990s, several countries adopted policies to differentiate between different types of capital and to guard against inflows leading to situations of overindebtedness during periods of expansion. Nevertheless, the crisis that affected Mexico at the end of 1994 showed that not every country implemented policies capable of preventing such situations.

It would therefore seem desirable to adopt fiscal and monetary policies designed to even out spending over time. During periods of expansion, it is possible to exercise greater selectivity with regard to kinds and amounts of capital flows and to levy temporary taxes to discourage private spending. Such measures can act as a brake on the private spending boom in periods when there is a surge in external inflows, and vice versa. Moreover, instead of setting fiscal goals on the basis of the current deficit, policy makers might use a structural deficit indicator, as OECD countries do. This approach preferably entails sterilizing the transitory tax revenues characteristic of expansionary periods and setting up stabilization funds to manage the less stable types of fiscal revenues. Many countries may also find it beneficial to offset short-term trends in private spending (both expansionary and contractionary) in whole or in part through compensatory changes in public expenditure or revenue.

In macroeconomic management, short-term approaches must be replaced by a vision for the medium or long term. As the Asian crisis has shown, in order to assess the dynamic equilibrium of the balance of payments, trends in four areas must be examined jointly: exports, imports, foreign capital and reserves. When changes in the evolution of any of these variables give rise to a significant deficit in the current account, it is vital to be able to assess the sustainability of that deficit. A relevant example is that of imports growing faster than exports, systematically sustained by the inflow of capital; this proved to be the prelude to crisis in both Latin America and Asia. The internal counterpart of this disequilibrium relates to the evolution of public and private spending and the behaviour of the banking sector. In this and other cases, vulnerability, and especially the opinion in that regard formed by important external agents, is linked to the level and fluctuation of reserves. In addition, any assessment concerning the entry of capital must take into consideration the purposes for which such capital is intended, and in particular whether it is being invested in export sectors or is strengthening competitiveness in the production of tradable goods.

With respect to monetary policy, measures can be introduced to give it greater autonomy. One such measure is the use of mechanisms to discourage excessive inflows of short-term capital, such as the reserve requirements imposed in Chile and Colombia, and variable taxes on financial movements in Brazil. There is growing consensus that, despite their flaws, such mechanisms play a positive role in discouraging excessive inflows and decreasing the proportion of short-term flows. The latter action, in particular, makes a country less vulnerable to exchange crises. Discouraging excessive capital inflows, moreover, helps lessen pressure to strengthen the value of the national currency excessively; this in turn helps to maintain export competitiveness and dynamism and to control the size of the current account deficit. (For a discussion of capital controls, see Agosin and Ffrench-Davis in Chapter 11 of this book.)

In the institutional sphere, Latin America has made progress towards correcting an extremely weak banking situation, the legacy of the 1980s and 1994-1995 crises, and the lack of prudential control. In several countries, Brazil for example, this has involved reform of the state banks and intervention in some private banks. Other countries, such as Argentina, have preferred to consolidate and recapitalize the banking system, allowing for a higher proportion of foreign banks. And, in general, there has been increasing awareness of the need to ensure that bank portfolios do not present serious risks of insolvency.

Nevertheless, much still remains to be achieved. These reforms now require new capital investment and, in many cases, public resources. To be successful, the policies need to be backed by appropriate legislation and budgetary resources. There is wide consensus concerning the need to strengthen prudential control of banks. Among other measures, a much higher capital-to-assets ratio should be required for banks than is recommended by the Basle Committee, since currency crises in Latin American countries can be particularly detrimental to bank assets. In any case, as the Asian crisis again demonstrates, in the developing countries, financial openness should be strictly conditional upon the prior existence of strong prudential regulation.

The policies that are established in this area must coincide with a medium- and long-term macroeconomic vision. Prudential policy, and especially the rating of bank portfolios, should be based on relative prices that are not limited to current prices, since the latter can be influenced by cyclical factors, such as the inflow of short-term external credits.

With respect to changing production patterns and competitiveness, study of the crisis and prospects in Asia is of special interest. It reveals the rapid changes in international goods and non-financial services markets and permits an evaluation of Latin American external trade from that standpoint. For example, the entry of countries like China and India into the market for certain manufactured products can seriously affect prices and limit small countries' chances for market access, because of the huge production potential of continent-sized countries. On the other hand, the sharp fall in prices on semi-conductor markets is an example of how manufactured goods can be subject to price fluctuations that used to be considered more typical of raw materials.

While the Asian crisis per se is more useful for understanding markets for manufactured "commodities," the way the crisis has spread to Latin America holds lessons with respect to the more traditional types of commodities. Specifically, the latter underscores the need for the countries of Latin America and the Caribbean to continue promoting export diversification. The impact of the crisis via the fall in commodity prices, especially of oil and copper, shows the continued dangers of specialization in these products. Moreover, the expansion and diversification of exports so far achieved by a number of countries in the region cannot be considered self-sustaining. Continuous monitoring of competitiveness and of the evolution of external markets, including their possible saturation, is essential.

(b) International aspects

As far as international financial arrangements are concerned, the crisis has brought out two problems: the major flaws in the international capital market and the great vulnerability of developing economies to shocks emanating from this market. With respect to the first of these phenomena, it has to be said that, if lack of adequate prudential regulation of their internal financial markets has been evident in the majority of the Asian countries affected by the crisis, the absence of appropriate international institutions to manage such a sophisticated but unstable financial market has been an even more damaging factor. The successive waves of excessive expansion followed by financial panic show that the market tends to grow and then contract much further than the fundamentals of the economies would warrant.

A common factor in the recent crises has been the great volatility of the most rapidly growing segment of international financial markets. The causes of this volatility are partly to do with the nature of money. But they are also related to inadequacies in macroeconomic coordination among the countries that have most influence in world markets and to the limitations of the international institutions in the areas of regulation, policy coordination and information at the global level. These inadequacies are not compatible with a balanced and efficient globalization process. No international institution exists that helps prevent unsustainable financial booms developing, and the International Monetary Fund only has limited capacity to manage the subsequent crises.

For their part, the rating agencies, which play a role on this front, tend to heighten these trends rather than to moderate them, as a recent OECD Development Centre study shows. These agencies, like financial traders, play a very useful microeconomic role in development. They have also, however, perhaps without meaning to, played a role that has macroeconomic effects. Through their ratings (in the case of agencies) and with their expectations widely published in the economic press (in the case of financial traders), they have helped to strengthen financial flows towards "winner" countries, with the resulting continued rise in the price of financial and real estate assets and marked currency appreciation in the recipient markets. Regardless of the quality of prudential supervision of those markets, such macroeconomic signals help prolong a process that appears to be very efficient and sustainable (with good profits and loan collateral supported by the high prices of assets and the low prices of liabilities in dollars), but which in reality generates bubbles that, sooner or later, burst. At that point, all these signals, including the risk ratings, are reversed, accentuating the slide and deepening the crisis.

In theory, the countries that receive funds have a certain leeway to define their national policies regarding capital flows. They can passively allow external capital to be transmitted to their internal markets, or they can attempt to moderate or graduate the flows over time, to alter the composition of the flows and soften their effects on the exchange rate and aggregate demand. The predominant practice has been for recipient countries to be urged to adopt, and praised for adopting, a policy of accepting all the resources offered to them at the stage when capital inflows are increasing. With the pressures to open up the capital account, these countries are pushed into the disequilibrium which then provokes the crisis. The recriminations for having become excessively indebted come later, during the periods of massive outflow. There is an obvious contradiction between these two attitudes. There is also a contradiction in the fact that more energy is spent resolving crises than preventing them.

The existence of major imperfections in international capital markets clearly justifies considerable expansion of IMF resources, to ensure that, in collaboration with other institutions and governments, it can reduce the harmful effects of large-scale exchange rate and financial crises in individual countries and prevent the contagion from spreading to other emerging economies.

Moreover, steps should be taken to avoid the existence and activities of the IMF leading to the problem of "moral hazard"; that is, international private investors and lenders taking on excessive risks, knowing that they will be rescued if the situation becomes critical. In the event of a crisis, private lenders should do their part to overcome it by rolling over loans as they become due without demanding higher interest or government guarantees, so that the resources of international financial institutions and governments can be devoted to financing the recovery of economies in crisis, rather than to paying off prior debts. Of course, the ideal is to prevent such situations from occurring, by taking action at the international level during periods of excessive optimism, in order to moderate the cycle of capital flows to emerging economies and thus ensure that such flows are more sustainable.

For this reason, it is important to improve and above all complete international prudential supervision arrangements. There appear to be two topics that require priority attention. First, it seems essential to improve the existing prudential supervision and regulation of short-term international credit in the developed countries. Second, some degree of prudential regulation of the portfolio investments of institutional investors, such as mutual funds, would also appear to be vital. There is a parallel here with the prudential measures of the central banks of developed countries, whereby provisions weighted by risk are required to balance possible losses resulting from bank loans to developing countries. The prudential requirements for institutional investors would follow the same principle, but would be duly adapted to the institutional characteristics of the mutual funds.

The prudential supervision of international credit and capital markets could be complemented by an international tax measure. A small tax at the global level on all foreign currency transactions would act as a relatively strong disincentive to very short-term speculative flows (which would involve frequent payments), and would have a very marginal impact on long-term flows. Such a tax would increase somewhat the autonomy of national economic authorities in making monetary policy. Moreover, by cutting back the more volatile flows, it would help emerging economies' exchange rates to reflect long-term fundamental variables to a greater degree, and to a lesser degree marked changes in short-term perceptions of risks or profitability.

11

Managing Capital Inflows in Chile*

MANUEL R. AGOSIN
University of Chile

and

RICARDO FFRENCH-DAVIS**
United Nations Economic Commission for Latin America and the Caribbean

1. Introduction

Towards the end of the 1980s, private capital inflows began to return to Latin America (see Calvo *et al.*, 1993; Ffrench-Davis and Griffith-Jones, 1995; and Ocampo, 1994). Chile was one of the first countries to attract the renewed flows of foreign capital, and one that attracted the largest supply, in relation to its size. The reversal of the drought in capital inflows of the 1980s was undoubtedly welcome.

* Abridged and revised version of a paper prepared for a project of the World Institute for Development Economics Research of the United Nations University. The outcome of the project will be published in Stephany Griffith-Jones, Ed., *Short-term Capital Flows and Economic Crisis*, Oxford University Press, forthcoming. We wish to thank Stephany Griffith-Jones, Manuel Montes, Stephen Fidler, and other participants at a seminar on the project, held at Sussex University, for useful comments. We also appreciate the comments of Cristián Ossa and Daniel Lederman presented at the meeting of the United Nations Expert Group in New York, 22-24 July 1998. We thank Julio Cáceres and Heriberto Tapia for efficient research assistance.

** Professor of Economics, University of Chile and Principal Regional Adviser, ECLAC, respectively. The views expressed herein are those of the authors and not necessarily the views of the United Nations.

It relaxed the binding foreign exchange constraint under which most countries laboured during the debt crisis. However, both the large magnitude of the new capital flows and their composition—prone to volatility—have caused problems for which the recipient countries, by and large, have been ill-prepared.

In the first place, there is the problem of domestic absorption. If they are to contribute to long-term development, capital inflows should lead to a significant increase in the investment rate, something which, with the exception of Chile, has not taken place in most countries in the region. In Chile, it will be argued that one reason for the greater degree of success in channeling foreign capital to investment has been the discouragement of short-term flows and the large share of foreign direct investment (FDI) in recent capital inflows. The Chilean experience does indeed suggest that when capital inflows take the form of FDI, there is a greater likelihood that the investment rate will rise than when foreign capital is in more liquid or short-term forms.

Secondly, large inflows pose difficult dilemmas to policy makers. Without intervention on foreign exchange markets and in the absence of regulations on capital inflows, the real exchange rate will appreciate, which may be undesirable from the point of view of other important policy objectives (for example, encouraging export growth and diversification, attaining higher domestic investment rates or meeting targets for the current-account deficit consistent with sustainable capital inflows). On the other hand, intervention in the foreign exchange market tends to swell the domestic money supply and increases the difficulties in controlling inflation.

Thirdly, a significant proportion of the recent inflow to emerging markets has taken the form of short-term or liquid capital. There have been two components of capital inflows that are clearly of a short-term nature: short-term credits and deposits, on the one hand, and portfolio flows, on the other. In the case of Chile, short-term inflows (mostly, but not only, in the form of bank lending) fluctuated between 2 and 3.5 per cent of GDP between 1990 and 1993. Thereafter, they have fallen sharply as a consequence of measures to discourage them.

On the other hand, portfolio inflows are new to the Chilean economy. Since they began in 1993, net portfolio inflows have represented between 1 and 2 per cent of GDP, except in 1995, when they disappeared altogether as a consequence of the Mexican peso crisis. Portfolio flows are not usually thought of as short-term capital, but in practice they are. Portfolio investments can be liquidated at a moment's notice and, therefore, may be just as short-term in nature as short-term indebtedness. Typically, portfolio investors operate with imperfect information, seek short-term capital appreciation and are prone to bandwagon effects, either in taking positions or in liquidating them. This has clearly been in evidence in the financial crises that have stricken first Mexico (December 1994) and more recently the Asian economies (since mid-1997, and still unfolding as of this writing). In both cases, the original crisis spread to other "emerging market" countries, as investors lost confidence not only in the economy where the crisis had started but also in those of other developing countries that had received large capital inflows. Large portfolio inflows were thus followed by large outflows, with sharp reversals of initial appreciations in exchange rates and stock market prices.[1]

Up to the mid-1970s, Chile had a tradition of capital controls. Since then policy makers have maintained a fairly open capital account. However, recent policies represent a significant move towards greater pragmatism. In a nutshell, the policy response during the current surges in the supply of foreign capital can be described as an attempt to discourage short-term capital inflows while maintaining liberal policies towards long-term inflows. In particular, policies have been geared to increasing the cost of short-term inflows via non-interest-bearing reserve requirements and the introduction of greater uncertainty as regards the exchange rate. The authorities have also resorted to sterilized intervention in order to slow down real exchange rate appreciation and thus protect a development strategy whose main elements are export growth and diversification.

Policy has been effective in achieving its targets in most parts of the 1990s. However, in 1996-1997, this policy mix and the intensity with which it was applied remained unchanged, in spite of a new vigorous surge in capital flows to most countries in the region. This surge should have been met with increased restrictions.

As a consequence of such lack of action on capital inflows during 1996-1997, despite heavy intervention in foreign exchange markets, the Central Bank was unable to prevent a sharp real exchange rate appreciation and rise of the deficit on current account. Evidently, as stated above, the new surge should have been met with an increased reserve requirement or other equivalent measures. As of this writing (July 1998), the contagion effects of the Asian currency crisis had begun to make themselves felt. The large inflows of financial capital that had taken place in 1996-1997 were giving way to outflows, and the nominal exchange rate had started to depreciate. But, in our view, up to now all the

1 Nationals of the countries concerned have been observed to behave much in the same way as foreign portfolio investors. In fact, it is believed that in Mexico, the first ones to lose confidence in the peso and to shift to dollar-denominated assets were Mexican investors. Thus the ultimate cause for exchange rate and asset price volatility appears to be the openness of the capital account and the ease of moving into and out of assets denominated in foreign currency, rather than just the behaviour of foreign investors.

depreciation has been a move toward a sustainable equilibrium, only partly correcting the disequilibrium generated in 1996-1997. Thus, there is a need to assess the policy options to further improve the management of financial flows in the future, so as to discourage excessive inflows and protect the economy from excessive exchange rate volatility. A more flexible use of a comprehensive policy mix, matching the intensity of surges, should be at hand.

This paper studies the phenomenon of massive capital inflows in Chile in the 1990s, the policy approaches utilized to deal with it and its effects on the domestic economy. The next section describes the dimensions and composition of capital inflows. Section 3 discusses the policy approaches utilized to deal with inflows and their impact on the economy and section 4 draws some policy lessons.

2. Recent capital inflows: magnitudes and composition

It is important to place recent capital inflow in historical perspective. This is done in table 1, which shows total capital inflows in the period 1960-1996 as a proportion of GDP, both in current prices and in 1986 prices.[2] The transformation of the data to a constant-dollar basis was undertaken because the real exchange rate has experienced very wide fluctuations which distort the meaning of changes in the ratio in current dollars. In table 1, we use a periodization that we maintain below in the analysis of growth, saving and investment data. We take the period before 1971 to reflect a sort of long-run steady state for the Chilean economy, before the wide policy swings that followed. The 1971-1973 period corresponds to the socialist experiment. The period from 1974 to 1981 represents the first complete business cycle of the military government, during which the authorities introduced most of the free-market reforms with which Chile is associated. It begins with the deep recession of 1974-1975 and ends with the peak of the boom of the late 1970s and early 1980s. The 1982-1989 period coincides with the debt crisis and is also of a somewhat greater pragmatism in economic policy. The first four years are marked by depressed economic conditions, followed by quick recovery in 1986-1989. This latter year also represents a cyclical peak. Finally, the period since 1990 corresponds to the return to democratic rule and is roughly coincident with the latest episode of foreign capital abundance. During this entire period of the 1990s, the economy has been expanding briskly and has been

2 The constant price series was derived by deflating the dollar inflow series by an index of foreign prices faced by the Chilean economy. As for the denominator, GDP at constant 1986 prices was transformed to 1986 dollars using the 1986 peso-dollar exchange rate.

Table 1. Net capital inflow, as a percentage of GDP

	Current prices	*1986 prices*
1960-1970	2.6	4.3
1971-1973	1.2	2.1
1974-1981	9.0	12.4
1982-1989	5.3	6.3
1990-1996[a]	5.8	6.4

Source: Central Bank of Chile.

a. Excluding debt prepayments in 1995-1996.

close to capacity output.[3]

The data show that capital inflows, as a proportion of GDP, were substantially larger in the 1990-1996 period than in the 1960s and, surprisingly, only slightly higher than during the debt crisis (1982-1989). However, it should be taken into account that Chilean GDP is much larger now (by any measure, but certainly in dollar terms) than in previous periods. Consequently, in absolute terms, capital inflows are of a much larger order of magnitude. Moreover, since 1995, total inflows have soared, reaching levels that are much higher than earlier in the decade and accounting for over 10 per cent of GDP (in 1986 prices).

Detailed and (almost) consistent disaggregated capital account data are available since 1983. Figure 1 shows the breakdown of total flows into their private and public components.[4] In the mid-1980s, and in spite of the debt crisis, as previously mentioned, capital inflows were relatively large, both in nominal terms and as a proportion of GDP.[5] The disappearance of voluntary bank lending was partly compensated by substantial support from the multilateral financial institutions. Thus, public flows became the main form of international financial resources available to the Chilean economy during the 1980s.

The story of the return of private foreign capital inflows has been told before (see Agosin, 1995; Ffrench-Davis, Agosin and Uthoff, 1995), so a brief summary will suffice. Private capital began to return to Chile in 1986, well ahead of the foreign capital surge to Latin America as a whole. The initial spurt

3 In 1990, there was a policy-induced slowdown in economic growth, as the economy was overheated (for electoral reasons) during the last year of military rule (1989). Thus one can distinguish a "mini" business cycle with a peak in 1989, a trough in 1990 and a subsequent peak in 1992, a year of exceptional economic growth.

4 Public flows in figure 1 are those that have the public sector as recipient. The creditor could be either public or private (for example, the private international banks).

5 This partly reflects the effects of the debt crisis itself, which led to the dramatic real devaluations of the period 1982-1985, with the consequent fall in the dollar value of Chilean GDP.

Figure 1: Private and public sector net inflows, 1983-1997
(Millions of US dollars)

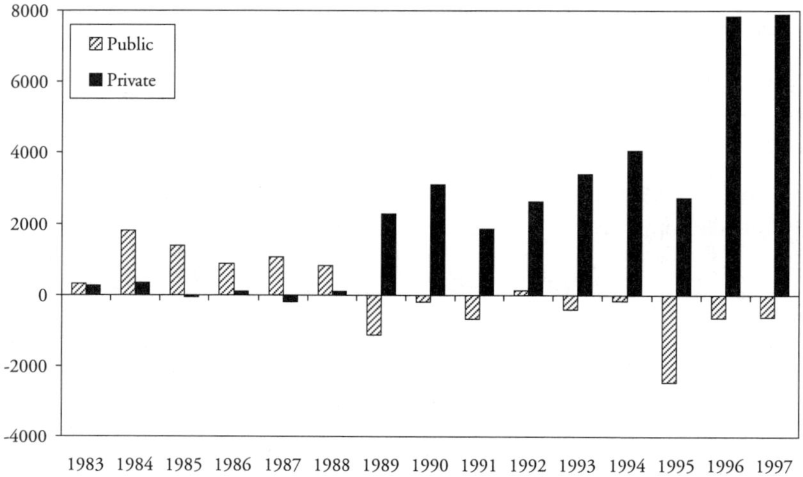

Source: Central Bank of Chile. Figures for the private sector include as "inflows" debt-equity swaps, that were large in 1987-1990.

was associated almost exclusively with the debt-equity swap programme instituted by the authorities in the second half of 1985. It was not until 1989 that other private flows became significant (see figure 2). In part owing to the large exchange rate subsidy implicit in the swap scheme, the programme was successful in attracting significant amounts of FDI in the form of swaps (Ffrench-Davis, 1990). The swap programme stopped being used by foreign investors in 1991, mainly because the rise in the international price of Chilean debt made it no longer profitable to invest via debt swaps. However, FDI not associated with swaps continued to grow apace. Thus, FDI represents a large part of the capital inflows into Chile over this decade. About 60 per cent of FDI through regular channels has gone into copper mining, the remainder concentrating in services.

As already noted, short-term private inflows have also figured prominently in the recent capital surge, though at a much lower scale than FDI. For interest-arbitraging capital inflows to take place, the domestic interest rate must exceed the international rate by a margin that is more than sufficient to compensate for the expected exchange rate depreciation and the country risk premium. These conditions have prevailed in Chile since the late 1980s. On the one hand, domestic interest rates have remained high, owing to lingering

Figure 2: Composition of private capital flows, 1983-1997
(Millions of US dollars)

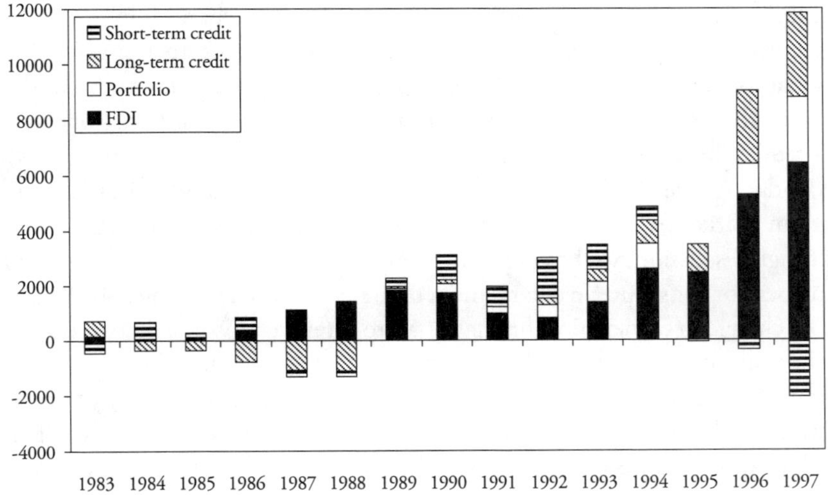

Source: Central Bank of Chile.

inflation and restrictive monetary policies. On the other hand, in 1992 and 1993, international dollar interest rates reached a 30-year low and, while they have risen since then, they have remained moderate and are still much lower than they were in the 1980s.

The other two terms in the interest arbitrage condition have also been favourable to capital inflows. As Chile began to emerge from the debt crisis, expectations regarding the real exchange rate turned from depreciation to appreciation. Improving terms of trade also contributed to the change in expectations. Moreover, expectations of exchange rate appreciation, owing to the capital inflow itself and to an improved current-account position, made short-term roundtripping appear very profitable. Also, as in other countries in the region, there was a decline in the country risk premium. The "emerging markets" mania of recent years in international stock markets can be interpreted as a dramatic reduction in perceived country risk. Chile's relatively developed domestic stock market, plus the burgeoning use of American Depositary Receipts (ADRs) for placing shares in the United States stock markets, made Chilean stocks a prime candidate for investors seeking new and more exotic financial vehicles. Short-term private flows were very important until 1993, when they began to fall off as a consequence of the measures adopted to stem them (see below).

Portfolio inflows have taken two forms: investments through mutual funds set up in the major international capital markets and the issuance of ADRs by a handful of large Chilean corporations. The ADR is a mechanism by which foreign corporations can issue new shares on the United States stock markets. The original (or "primary") issue of ADRs represents an opportunity for expanding the capital of firms at relatively low cost, since capital costs in international markets tend to be lower than in Chile. However, there is also what is known as the "secondary" issue of ADRs through the purchase of the underlying stock in the Chilean market by foreigners and its subsequent conversion into ADRs (for a thorough discussion, see Ffrench-Davis, Agosin and Uthoff, 1995). This operation does not constitute an enlargement of the capital of the issuing company but only a change in ownership from nationals to foreigners. While there is nothing intrinsically negative about these operations, at a moment when foreign exchange is overabundant and there are significant downward pressures on the exchange rate,[6] it may be necessary to discourage them. These shifts in ownership involve exposing the economy to an additional degree of uncertainty and volatility, since when foreign investors' mood changes they can easily reverse the operation and convert their ADRs into the underlying stock in national currency for sale on the domestic stock market.[7]

The Mexican and the more recent East Asian crises are illustrative of these dangers. In the case of Mexico, as emphasized by Sachs and Velasco (1995 and 1996), domestic policy failures, particularly the large increase in domestic credit that resulted from a poorly regulated domestic financial system, were important factors. Domestic credit booms were, however, in both of these crises triggered by large capital inflows. The herding behaviour displayed by foreign portfolio investors has been increasingly recognized as a critical element in the crisis (Calvo and Mendoza, 1996). Since assets of firms from a particular developing country are normally a very small proportion of international investors' portfolios, it may not pay to go to the trouble of obtaining information, which is very costly. Therefore, they tend to go on "signals". The positive

---

6 This paper follows the Latin American convention of defining the exchange rate as units of domestic currency per unit of foreign exchange. Therefore, an appreciation is a downward movement.

7 It has been argued that foreigners who become pessimistic about a country will sell their ADRs in the United States stock market, therefore having no impact on the domestic stock and foreign exchange markets. However, this argument ignores the fact that the issuance of ADRs implies that stock prices in the domestic and United States markets must tend to equality through arbitrage. This is in fact what has happened: movements in stock prices of Chilean companies that have issued ADRs in United States stock exchanges are highly correlated with those in the Santiago exchange.

signal at the end of the 1980s was that Mexico was undertaking market-oriented reforms (and entering the North American Free Trade Agreement (NAFTA)) that would, in the eyes of the international banks, raise returns on Mexican corporate assets. However, the rush to invest in Mexico created conditions which turned the positive signal into a negative one. In the case of Mexico, the "signal" for a reversal of the financial capital inflow was the notion that current-account deficits had become "unsustainable" and that the exchange rate had appreciated "excessively". Of course, the large current-account deficits and outlier macroeconomic prices, particularly an appreciating exchange rate, had been principally a consequence of the exogenous (and collective) behaviour of foreign investors in the first place.

What this boils down to is that a large component of capital inflow, particularly portfolio capital, is not only volatile but is largely exogenous from the point of view of the recipient country. Even short-term credit has an exogenous component, since the so-called country risk premium has a large subjective element. Hence, paradoxically, a successful country can see its fundamentals—such as deficit on current account, exchange-rate, domestic savings and bank portfolio—worsened by a large capital surge (see Devlin, Ffrench-Davis and Griffith-Jones, 1995).

From a theoretical point of view, what we have here is the possibility of multiple equilibria: an appreciated exchange rate with large capital inflows and a depreciated exchange rate with capital outflows. Moreover, there are dynamics involved: capital inflows appreciate the real exchange rate, and the latter, if it is gradual, encourages additional inflows. This can proceed for several years, as happened in 1976-1981 and 1990-1994 in several Latin American countries. After a while, the deficits on current account accumulate and the stock of external liabilities rises, the appreciation trend is replaced by expectations of depreciation, which, in turn, leads to a reversal of the direction of flows. This would suggest that there is a need for policies that reduce the more volatile components of capital inflows; and that the "fundamentals" are not independent of policies towards inflows. Moreover, some equilibria are more "desirable" than others, in terms of effects on economic growth and sustainability.

While private flows have increased, public debt has been reduced with public outflows. During 1989-1991, these net outflows were caused mainly by the counterpart public debt operations involved in debt-equity swaps. More recently, they represent mostly debt prepayments. These were particularly large since 1994. These prepayments have been undertaken to alleviate the large accumulation of international reserves by the Central Bank so as to relieve appreciating pressures on foreign exchange markets and to improve the balance of the Bank.

Since 1991, several large Chilean corporations have been making direct investments abroad. These flows are now significant and account for almost 2 per cent of GDP.[8] The destinations are mainly neighbouring countries. The largest investments have been in electricity generation and distribution (mostly in recently privatized companies, first in Argentina and then in other Latin American countries), but other sectors such as light manufacturing and retailing are also represented (Calderón and Griffith-Jones, 1995).

3. The policy response and its effects

In the 1990s, the Chilean monetary authorities have deployed a wide array of policies to regulate the surge in capital inflows. On the one hand, the Central Bank has attempted to discourage short-term and speculative capital inflows while maintaining open access to the economy for FDI. On the other hand, it has sought to insulate partially the domestic economy from the impacts of capital inflows by intervening in foreign exchange markets so as to prevent an excess supply from unduly appreciating the real exchange rate and by sterilizing almost completely the monetary effects of the rapid accumulation of international reserves (see Ffrench-Davis, Agosin and Uthoff, 1995).

Two other policy factors have contributed to the successes achieved in managing capital inflow. First, fiscal policy has been very conservative. Chile has been running a significant public sector surplus during the 1990s, amounting to 1 to 2 per cent of GDP. The prudent stance of fiscal policy, including the compliance with the rules of a copper stabilization fund, has eased the task of the monetary authorities in the management of capital inflows and in preventing undue exchange rate appreciation. Second, as a result of the 1982-1983 banking crisis, prudential banking regulations were introduced and have been improved over the years. This, again, prevented the capital inflow from unleashing a lending spree by the commercial banks, which, in turn, eased the task of keeping the current account and the exchange rate within bounds.

Inflow management policies

The main consideration of exchange rate and inflow management policies has been to protect the growth model adopted by the authorities, which is one based on the expansion and diversification of exports. In order for exports to continue to be an engine of growth of the Chilean economy, the level

8 Balance-of-payments data underestimate the size of these investments, because a large share of them is financed with funds raised on international capital markets and which never enter the country.

and stability of the real exchange rate are crucial. This objective could have been placed in jeopardy if capital inflows caused excessive exchange rate appreciation and greater future volatility when the direction of net flows went into reverse.

The Chilean authorities opted to regulate the foreign exchange market in order to prevent large misalignments in the real exchange rate relative to its long-term trend. The option chosen to make the long-term fundamentals prevail over short-term factors influencing the exchange rate assumes (correctly, in our view) that there exists an asymmetry of information between the market and the monetary authorities, because the latter have a better knowledge of the factors driving the balance of payments; and that they have a longer planning horizon than agents who operate intensely at the short-term end of the market. However, in the face of uncertainty, rather than a unique price, the authorities have used an exchange rate band centred on a reference price linked to a basket of three currencies, in which the dollar, the deutsche mark and the yen are represented with weights associated with their share in Chilean trade.

The excess supply of foreign exchange began in mid-1990. A summary of policy actions to tackle the excess supply can be found in table 2. Here we give an analytical account relating policy changes to the events that elicited them. The changes taking place in global markets, the increasing international approval of Chilean economic policies, high interest rates in Chile and a smooth transition to democracy stimulated a growing inflow of capital to Chile.

In June 1991, a non-interest bearing reserve requirement of 20 per cent was established on external credits (covering the whole range of foreign credits, from those associated with FDI to trade credits). The reserves had to be maintained with the Central Bank for a minimum of 90 days and a maximum of one year. At the same time, a stamp tax on domestic credit, at an annual rate of 1.2 per cent on operations of up to one year, was extended to apply to external loans. In July, an alternative to the reserve requirement was allowed for medium-term credits which consisted in making a payment to the Central Bank of an amount equivalent to the financial cost of the reserve requirement. The financial cost was calculated by applying the London interbank offered rate (LIBOR) plus 2.5 per cent (at an annual rate) to the amount of the reserve requirement. The reserve requirement, the option of paying its financial cost and the tax on foreign credits all have a zero marginal cost for lending which exceeds one year, and, as discussed below, the first two are particularly onerous for flows at very short maturities.

With continuing capital inflows, over time the system of reserve

Table 2. Regulations on capital movements in Chile, second quarter of 1998

Foreign direct investment:

The only restriction on FDI inflows is the requirement that investments remain in Chile for a one-year period. There are no restrictions on profit remittances. FDI must be financed with a maximum debt component of 30 per cent (70 per cent equity). This limit was reduced from 50 per cent in October 1997.

Portfolio investment inflows:

Minimum amount of ADR issue is U.S. $25 million, reduced from U.S. $50 million in September 1994. Minimum risk rating of BBB required for non-financial firms and BBB+ for banking companies. 30 per cent reserve requirement on secondary ADRs since July 1995.

Other financial and portfolio inflows:

Subject to the 30 per cent reserve requirement up to June 1998. These include trade credits, foreign currency deposits, loans associated with FDI and bond issues. Bond issuers face same quality-enhancing restrictions as ADR issuers.

Foreign investment by the Chilean non-financial private sector:

Investors not wishing to have access to official foreign exchange market need only inform the Central Bank of their investments abroad. Those wishing to have access to the official market need permission from the Central Bank. This is not difficult to obtain. At the present time, the formal and free market exchange rates are similar.

Foreign investments of Chilean institutional investors:

Foreign investments by pension funds, mutual funds and life insurance companies are subject to certain limits as to the amounts and types of foreign assets that they can hold. Pension funds are allowed to hold up to 12 per cent of their total assets in foreign assets, and stocks are limited to one half of total foreign holdings.

Foreign investments by banks:

Foreign financial investments by commercial banks are limited to 25 per cent of bank capital and reserves and restricted to fixed income securities issued or guaranteed by foreign governments or Central Banks. Banks are authorized to use foreign currency deposits to finance trade among countries belonging to the Latin American Integration Association (LAIA). Commercial banks may hold equity in foreign banks provided they have a capital adequacy index of at least 10 per cent.

Source: Adapted and updated from Budnevich and Le Fort (1997).

requirements was tightened and extended to most international financial transactions. Since May 1992, reserve requirements on external credits stand at 30 per cent and were extended to time deposits in foreign currency and to purchases of Chilean stocks ("secondary ") by foreigners.[9] The period during which the deposit must be maintained was extended to one year, regardless of the maturity of the loan. The spread charged over LIBOR in the option of paying the financial cost of the reserve requirement was increased to 4 per cent, up from the original 2.5 per cent. In order to close a loophole through which the reserve requirements were being evaded (since equity investment is exempt), the authorities are now screening FDI applications; permission to enter the country as FDI exempt from the reserve requirement is denied when it is determined that the inflow is disguised financial capital. In such cases, foreign investors must register at the Central Bank their funds as financial investments subject to the reserve requirement.

With the Asian crisis and the sharp scarcity of financial flows, the reserve requirement rate was reduced to 10 per cent and then to zero. The authorities announced, however, that the policy tool remained available in case of future need.

Since 1991 an attempt has been made to ease capital outflows as a way of alleviating downward pressures on the exchange rate (see Ffrench-Davis, Agosin and Uthoff, 1995). In particular, Chilean pension funds have been allowed to invest abroad up to 12 per cent of their total assets. The policy was effective in encouraging significant flows of FDI and purchases of foreign firms by Chilean companies in neighbouring countries (Calderón and Griffith-Jones, 1995). However, higher rates of return on financial assets in Chile than abroad and expectations of peso appreciation discouraged foreign financial investments by Chilean pension funds and recently authorized closed-end mutual funds for international financial investment. These investments had been rising slowly as domestic firms and pension funds obtain more and better information about foreign financial assets.[10] An immediate effect of liberalizing outflows has probably been to encourage additional

9 It is not difficult to impose reserve requirements on foreign portfolio investments. If the funds that will be used for the investment are deposited with a Chilean bank, the foreign deposit is liable to reserve requirements. For those funds that do not use a Chilean bank as intermediary, the reserve requirement can be imposed at the moment the asset is registered in the name of an agent with a foreign address. In order to be converted into ADRs, they must also go through registration with the Central Bank.

10 One obstacle to the liberalization of outflows by institutional investors is the lack of knowledge that regulators have of foreign financial assets. Thus, the fear that liberalization will lead to a worsening of the asset quality of institutional investors has been a key factor in explaining the gradual approach taken to the liberalization of outflows.

inflows (Williamson, 1993; Labán and Larraín, 1997). Furthermore, outflows by pension funds rose sharply only when expectations changed from appreciation to depreciation, since late 1997. Actually, net outflows by pension funds in January-September of 1998 climbed to the equivalent of 2 per cent of the GDP of that period.[11]

Exchange rate policy

Exchange rate policy has also experienced substantial change over time. The use of a fixed nominal exchange rate in 1979-1982, in the context of an increasing and eventually complete liberalization of capital account transactions, was abandoned after the crisis of 1982 during which GDP declined by 15 per cent. In 1983 through 1989 the authorities utilized a crawling peg, with a floating band of ± 2 per cent (widened to 3 per cent in 1988 and ± 5 per cent in mid-1989). The "official" rate was devalued daily, in line with the differential between domestic inflation and an estimate of external inflation. On a number of occasions, discrete nominal devaluations were added, helping to achieve a remarkable real depreciation following the 1982 crisis: 119 per cent between 1981 and 1988 (see Repetto, 1994).

Since early 1992, the exchange rate band has been gradually widened (with the band standing at 12.5 per cent on either side of the official rate by mid-1998), and the official rate has been revalued discretely on a number of occasions.[12] The dollar peg of the official rate has also been replaced by a peg to a basket of currencies as the new benchmark exchange rate. Given the instability of international exchange rates, these measures were intended to make interest rate arbitrage between the dollar and the peso less profitable by introducing greater exchange-rate uncertainty for speculative capital flows, that are denominated mostly in dollars. In order to lower the floor of the band,

11 The approach to liberalizing capital outflows adopted by the authorities has been gradual. The essential idea is that a hasty financial liberalization risks leaving too many doors open for outflows, which could be massive in case of market nervousness and shifts to expectations of currency depreciation, as we advised in due time (see Agosin, Ffrench-Davis and Uthoff, 1995). This could make more difficult the achievement of exchange rate and macroeconomic stability. The recent international financial crises are clear examples of this.

12 It must be noted that Chile was coming out of a profound debt crisis which was accompanied by a sharp exchange rate depreciation. Consequently, there was space for some appreciation. However, as Chile was moving from a restricted to an overabundant supply of external savings, the authorities wanted to avoid an overadjustment of the exchange rate. One specifically troublesome feature is that, as expectations of foreign agents change from pessimism to optimism, they seem to reach a new desired stock of investment in the "emerging market" over a short period. This implies excessively large inflows for a while. Obviously, these are transitory rather than permanently higher levels of periodic inflows.

the authorities have tinkered in 1997 with the weights assigned to each currency, making the peg to a currency basket rather than the dollar less credible.[13] In addition, they have factored in a 2 per cent annual appreciation into the calculation of the central rate, ostensibly to account for higher productivity growth in Chile than in its main trading partners.

Given that the market exchange rate was for several years close to the floor of the band, with little variation in the nominal dollar-peso rate, the policy of maintaining an increasingly wider band has lost effectiveness in dissuading speculative capital inflows. With expectations overwhelmingly in favour of real currency appreciation, the large interest rate differential between the peso and the dollar (together with good prospects for large Chilean companies) gave foreign portfolio and short-term investors what amounts to a very profitable one-way bet, in spite of the toll they must pay for entering domestic financial markets (in the form of the reserve requirement). This trend towards appreciation (see figure 3) could have been softened by intensifying price restrictions on inflows (that is, the height of the reserve requirement). The risky temptation to reduce fastest domestic inflation with exchange-rate appreciation weakened somewhat a highly successful policy of sustainable macroeconomic equilibria.

The authorities have been facing a respite from exchange rate appreciation by the contagion effects of the Asian crisis. Incipient financial capital outflows and greater demand for dollar-denominated assets by nationals have caused the market price for the dollar to rise, for the first time in five years, well above the floor of the band.

Effectiveness of measures

What have been the financial costs imposed on foreign borrowing by the system of reserve requirements and taxes on foreign lending? The total tax consists of the extra interest costs imposed by the reserve requirements and the tax on foreign credits. The calculations can be seen in table 3. As a result of the lengthening (in late 1992) of the reserve requirement holding period to a full year, regardless of the maturity of the financial transaction, the implicit tax rate on foreign borrowing increases dramatically as maturities shorten. This characteristic of the system, which likens it in its effects to a unilateral Tobin tax (Tobin,

13 In November 1994, the weight of the US dollar was reduced from 50 per cent to 45 per cent, reflecting the falling incidence of that currency in Chilean trade. In January 1997, it was arbitrarily raised to 80 per cent. For a comparative analysis of bands in Chile, Israel and Mexico, see Helpman, Leiderman and Bufman (1994). For an analysis of Chile, Colombia and Israel, see Williamson (1996).

Figure 3: Real exchange rate, 1960-1997
(1986=100)

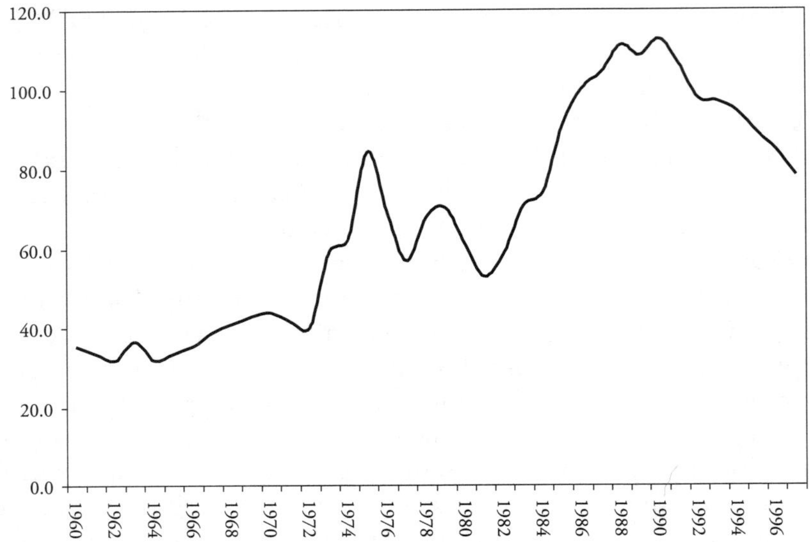

Source: Central Bank of Chile.

Table 3. Chile: Implicit taxes on foreign borrowings, 1991-1996
(annualized rates)

	1991 II	*1992 I*	*1992 II*	*1993*	*1994*	*1995*	*1996*
Reserve requirement (per cent)	20	20	30	30	30	30	30
Minimum reserve period (months)	3	3	3	12	12	12	12
LIBOR	5.5	4.5	3.6	3.4	5.0	6.1	5.6
Total tax, annual	2.9	2.6	3.3	3.2	3.9	4.3	4.1
6-month	3.0	2.7	3.3	5.0	6.2	7.2	6.7
3-month	3.0	2.7	3.4	8.0	11.0	13.2	12.2

Source: Authors' calculations, based on data of the Central Bank of Chile.

1978), is the rationale behind the requirement that reserves be held for an entire year. Before its imposition, the implicit tax rate (on an annualized basis) was identical on transactions as short as a quarter (the minimum holding period up to late 1992) or as long as a year. These very large estimates of the implicit tax rate on short-term operations suggest that if the regulations were not evaded, they must have discouraged short-term and portfolio flows.

How effective has been the reserve requirement (together with exchange rate management) in deterring short-term flows and preventing excessive exchange rate appreciation? There are two kinds of evidence to which one can resort. The first kind is qualitative. Chile faced a larger supply of external finance (relative to its GDP) than other countries in the region, because of its better economic performance and greater political stability. However, exchange rate appreciation and the current-account deficit (as a share of GDP) have both been smaller than in other countries in the region that have been large recipients of foreign capital. In addition, FDI has been a much larger proportion of inflows in Chile than in other countries. Second, there is econometric evidence that policies towards the capital account have worked rather well. A recent study indicates that the combination of disincentives to short-term inflows with the reforms in the exchange rate regime, at least up to 1994, had been able to reduce significantly the inflow of short-term, interest-arbitrage funds (Agosin, 1995 and 1998; Larraín, Labán and Chumacero, 1997). As noted below, the situation has changed markedly in more recent years, in face of both a new capital surge towards the emerging economies and restrictions that paradoxically were kept unchanged by the autonomous Central Bank.

Some observers have claimed that the efficacy of measures to discourage capital inflows is only temporary, as private sector operators find ways to evade them (for an example of this literature, see Valdés-Prieto and Soto, 1996). In principle, this can be done through several mechanisms. One is the underinvoicing of imports or the overinvoicing of exports. The second one is to delay payment for imports or accelerate export receipts. Thirdly, it is possible to bring in funds through the informal foreign exchange market. Fourth, there is also the possibility of registering short-term funds as FDI. However, this could be a costly option, since Chilean law requires that FDI remain in the country for at least one year before repatriation.[14] Nonetheless, it was becoming a significant loophole, which, as already noted, the authorities have moved to close. Fifth, it is possible for agents to arrange back-to-back operations in which, for example, an agent pays for imports with a bank deposit in Chile rather than with foreign exchange; at the same time, the exporter is paid in foreign exchange by a bank in his country. All of these (and other forms of evasion, as well) are possible, but they are not without cost, and

14 It should be noted that the loans associated with FDI are subject to the reserve requirement. Since the average maturity of these loans is about seven years, the incidence of the restriction is low.

some of them may have undesirable effects on tax liabilities. While some evasion is inevitable, there is no hard evidence that the measures to discourage short-term capital inflows have been massively evaded.

However, it is clear that maintaining the reserve requirement at an unchanged rate and/or failing to supplement it with other measures became insufficient in face of the new capital surge in 1996-1997. In addition, depressed stock market prices in late 1995 and a real exchange rate that was widely expected to appreciate further over time, exerted attraction on portfolio inflows, as witnessed by the very heavy inflows into the Chilean stock market in 1996-1997. But large financial inflows are inevitably bound to turn into outflows at some point. Contagion from the Asian crisis is now having that effect.

In addition, actual exchange rate management (in contrast to what the authorities claimed they were doing) did not contribute to discouraging speculative inflows. In spite of its formal adherence to a crawling band in 1996-1997, the Central Bank was in effect managing a quasi fixed nominal price for the dollar.

Since 1993, the secondary issue of ADRs had became a large source of short-term capital inflow with particularly volatile characteristics. Thus, the extension of reserve requirements to these inflows in 1995 can be considered to have been an attempt to deal with an incipient problem which was already causing difficulties in policy management and which could become even more important in the future. It is likely that in the absence of reserve requirements, portfolio inflows would have been much larger. However, after a temporary lull in 1995, they again bulged beginning in early 1996. It would seem that foreign investors are considering the reserve requirement as a sort of option price for investing in Chile (see Herrera and Valdés, 1997). As already noted, the entry fee may very well be perceived as cheap in the face of positive fundamentals and a strong likelihood of further real exchange rate appreciation.

Another line of attack against the use of disincentives to short-term capital inflows has been to claim that, as regards their behaviour, it is impossible to distinguish between capital inflows such as FDI or long-term lending, on the one hand, and short-term flows, on the other. Claessens, Dooley and Warner (1995) claim that balance-of-payments categories have little to do with the stability of flows themselves, long-term flows being just as likely to be unstable as short-term flows.[15]

---

15 Part of the explanation for their result that FDI is just as likely to be volatile as short-term flows may stem from the fact that, for the countries that they chose, FDI flows are a very small percentage of total foreign financing, at least as reported by IMF statistics (which, by the way, sometimes seriously underestimate FDI). Fluctuations of small numbers tend to be larger than fluctuations of large ones.

In order to check their hypothesis for Chile, a series of tests were run to determine the degree of persistence of different types of private flows. In the first place, after determining the optimal lag for each type of flow,[16] we did an autoregressive analysis of quarterly data on FDI, portfolio capital, long-term private borrowing and short-term private borrowing for the period 1983-1995. The results are shown in table 4, which reveals that, indeed, FDI and long-term borrowing have the most persistence, judging by the significance of their own lags. For FDI, the second and third quarterly lags are very significant predictors of contemporaneous levels; for long-term private borrowing, it is the first and third lags. On the other hand, for portfolio flows and for short-term private borrowing, there just is no persistence at all.

Secondly, we calculated the coefficient of variation and the R^2s of the time trends of the same four categories of flows (also shown in table 4). The coefficients of variation are indicators of the variability of flows around their mean; and $1 - R^2$ is an indicator of their variability around their time trend. On both counts, FDI is more stable than short-term borrowing and portfolio flows.

Thirdly, we ran unit root tests for FDI and other net capital inflows in real annual terms for the rather long period of 1960-1995.[17] It is interesting that FDI turns out to have a unit root, while other flows are stationary (without constant or trend). Therefore, at least in Chile, FDI behaves as a "permanent" variable and other flows as "transitory" disturbances. The behaviour of these two series is shown in figure 2.

Thus we can conclude that FDI is considerably less volatile than other kinds of capital inflows, and that it is worthwhile to target policies on the latter. This is what the Chilean authorities have attempted to do, with more success in the early years of application than more recently. Undoubtedly, short-term and portfolio inflows would have been much larger in the absence of the reserve requirement. Second, sterilized intervention in foreign exchange markets prevented undue exchange rate appreciation and a consumption boom, thus keeping the current-account deficit within reasonable bounds, except in 1996-1997.

The policy mix used also had financial costs. The accumulation of large volumes of foreign exchange reserves imposes a social cost on the economy, since the returns on these assets have been inferior to the interest payments on the Central Bank liabilities that have been issued to sterilize the monetary effects of

16 The minimum lag which produces white-noise residuals.

17 "Real" flows are calculated by deflating nominal dollar flows by the index of foreign prices estimated by the Central Bank of Chile for the period 1977-1995. For earlier years, the index of foreign prices was spliced backward to 1960 using the index of foreign prices calculated by Ffrench-Davis (1984).

Table 4. Persistence analysis for components of private flows, quarterly data, 1983-1995

Autoregressive equations

Lags (Number of quarters)	FDI	Portfolio	Private borrowing	
			Long-term	Short-term
1	0.201 (1.34)	0.156 (0.74)	0.643 (4.57)[a]	-0.158 (-1.09)
2	0.495 (3.61)[a]	0.055 (0.26)	-0.226 (-1.36)	-0.064 (-0.42)
3	0.491 (3.56)[a]	0.153 (0.72)	0.339 (2.63)[a]	0.241 (1.65)
4	-0.244 (-1.53)			
Constant	47.255 (1.344)	77.695 (1.57)	-10.200 (-0.539)	118.24 (2.11)[a]
R^2	0.908	0.460	0.500	0.192
Other indicators				
Coefficient of variation (%)	84.2	118.5	-568.4	338.4
R^2 of time trend	0.840	0.438	0.148	0.114

Source: Authors' calculations based on data of the Central Bank of Chile.

a. Significant at the 1 per cent level.
b. Significant at the 5 per cent level.

reserve accumulation, generating large losses for the Central Bank (estimated at about one half of a percentage point of GDP per annum). The disincentives on short-term capital inflows have lessened these costs and have eased the task of sterilizing the monetary consequences of reserve accumulation.

The strengthening of banking supervision

As already noted, a tough bank supervision and regulatory environment prevented excess liquidity of banks from fuelling a consumption boom and a deterioration in the quality of bank assets (as clearly took place in Mexico). This was a legacy of the banking crisis of 1982-1983, in the aftermath of the preceding foreign capital surge, which led to a virtual collapse of the entire banking system.[18]

18 For a lucid description of that crisis, see Díaz-Alejandro (1985).

Some elements of prudential supervision adopted over the years since then include the continuous monitoring of the quality of bank assets; strict limits on lending by banks to related firms; the existence of automatic mechanisms of bank equity adjustment when the market value of equity falls below the limits required by the regulators; and faculties to freeze banking operations, impede fund transfers outside of troubled banks, and restrict the payment of dividends to institutions that fail to comply with capital adequacy requirements (Aninat and Larraín, 1996). Chilean financial markets have also acquired a depth that allows for the orderly infusion of new funds and also for their withdrawal, without affecting the quality of bank portfolios (Larraín, 1995).

Capital adequacy ratios along the lines of the 1988 Basle accord have been incorporated in the new banking law approved by Congress in 1997. But banks' capital, in practice, is well above the Basle norm of 8 per cent. In addition, the Central Bank imposes limits on banks' open positions in foreign exchange, but these are still fairly crude, in that they do not differentiate between loans made in foreign currency to firms that earn foreign currency and to firms whose earnings are in domestic currency. Neither do these limits differentiate as between different foreign currencies. Currency risk is only one aspect of credit risk evaluation systems, which as a whole are quite good in Chile. Therefore, this compensates for the weaknesses in the norms on open positions in foreign exchange.

Saving, investment and growth

The period since 1989 marks a clear-cut improvement in growth performance, not only in comparison with the 1971-1989 period, but also to the more favourable 1960s (see table 5). The ratio of gross fixed investment to GDP has risen steadily since its trough in the early 1980s, from about 15 per cent of GDP in 1983-1984 to over 30 per cent in 1995-1997. Even taking longer averages, for 1982-1989 and 1990-1997, the ratio of fixed investment to GDP can be seen to have risen sharply, from 19 per cent to 28 per cent. This increase in the investment ratio has allowed Chile to sustain a growth of GDP averaging close to 8 per cent per annum in the 1990s. The increase in the national saving rate was even stronger than the increase in the investment rate, going from 13 per cent in the 1980s to 25 per cent in the 1990s. At the same time, foreign saving declined sharply, from 6 per cent of GDP to 2 per cent. This is indeed surprising, since, as discussed in section II above, foreign capital inflow averaged about 6 per cent of GDP in the 1990s. This shows that the policies of sterilizing capital inflow and fiscal austerity, by preventing undue real exchange rate appreciation, made the economy absorb less foreign capital than

Table 5. Chile: Investment, foreign saving and growth indicators, 1960-1997
(as a percentage of GDP)

	Gross fixed investment	*Gross investment*	*Machinery & equipment*	*Foreign saving* [a]	*Per capita GDP growth*
1960-1970	23.2	25.1	11.1	2.5	2.2
1971-1973	18.4	16.9	8.5	2.9	-1.1
1974-1981	18.4	22.2	11.0	5.0	1.2
1982-1989	18.7	19.8	8.9	6.2	1.1
1990-1997	27.6	31.4	15.7	3.3	6.0

Source: Authors' calculations, based on national accounts data of the Central Bank of Chile in 1986 prices.

a. The foreign saving is the deficit of the current account of the balance of payments as a share of GDP, both in Chilean pesos of each year.

what was on offer. The counterpart of the difference between capital inflow and foreign saving (that is, the current-account deficit) was, of course, the accumulation of foreign assets by the Central Bank.

The long-term behaviour of saving and investment rates shows much less spectacular increases. During the 1990s, they barely exceed the averages achieved during the 1960s, and it is only since 1993 that the investment rate has overtaken its 1963 peak. The real difference between the earlier and the later periods is in the behaviour of private and public investment.[19] In the light of the long-run data, it is not the most recent period that appears as much of an outlier, but the periods between 1971 and 1989, which exhibit strong declines in domestic saving and investment rates. There has been a clear downward trend in public investment, compensated only in the 1990s by a vigorous increase in private investment. The main culprit for the fall in public investment has been the decline in investment in infrastructure, schools, hospitals and the like. This is perhaps one of the weakest links in the so-called Chilean model: steady increases in international competitiveness (the basis of the growth strategy for over two decades) require *increases* in investment in social and economic infrastructure, not declines.

Nonetheless, the rise in domestic saving and investment rates since their troughs in the mid-1980s has been remarkable. Moreover, it has taken place at the time of strong capital inflow and even stronger increases in the availability of foreign capital to the Chilean economy. In other countries (for example,

19 To obtain private investment, central government investment (excluding that of public enterprises) was subtracted from gross fixed capital formation. Therefore, private investment is here defined as corporate gross capital formation, including the investment of public corporations, plus household investment in housing.

Mexico or Argentina), in the face of large capital inflows, investment rates have risen modestly and domestic saving rates have fallen, partly owing to the income and wealth effects of real exchange rate appreciation and sky-rocketing stock and real estate prices.

The Chilean policies to restrain capital inflow and to moderate exchange rate appreciation can be credited with at least part of the success achieved with regard to investment, saving and growth rates. On the one hand, the management of inflows has had a positive impact on macroeconomic stability and has contributed to keeping effective demand close to productive capacity, which is essential for investment expenditures to rise. On the other, there is evidence that foreign and domestic saving tend to have a high degree of substitutability, perhaps because foreign saving stimulates consumption through its exchange rate and asset price effects. Thus success in keeping the current-account deficit within reasonable bounds contributed to the increase in saving rates (see Agosin, 1998; and Agosin, Crespi and Letelier, 1998).

4. Some policy lessons of the Chilean experience

The Chilean experience with the management of capital inflows leaves us with several important lessons. For developing countries, the swings in capital flows can be of extraordinary magnitude relative to the size of their economies. Over the past 15 years, Latin American countries have gone from the Scylla of the debt crisis (and the shorter-lived Tequila crisis) to the Carybdis of foreign capital abundance during most of the 1990s. Totally passive policy stances will inevitably result in enormous volatility in key domestic macroprices (exchange rates and interest rates) and economic aggregates. By depressing investment, these fluctuations have adverse effects on long-term growth.

Chile has held on to steady policies towards capital inflows and exchange rate management. By and large, these policies appear to have discouraged the more volatile forms of inflows and have prevented excessive exchange rate appreciation. However, in 1996-1997, financial capital inflows overwhelmed the capacity of the authorities to limit them with the unchanged intensity of policy tools they were using. Inflows were very large relative to GDP (over 10 per cent), jumping to what we judge to be unsustainable levels.[20] Then, the Central Bank was unable to

---

20 It might be reasonably argued that interest rates are too high in Chile, and that this was one of the causes for excessive capital inflows. Unfortunately, there was not much room for lowering interest rates, since the economy had been operating at close to potential output for several years. Nor is it easy to tighten fiscal policy. The need to increase spending on health and education, and professionalization of the government, precludes any significant decline in public expenditure.

prevent a significant real appreciation of the peso, in spite of heavy purchases of foreign exchange. The ensuing real exchange rate appreciation contributed to a widening of the current-account deficit, that exceeded 5 per cent of GDP. There was clear evidence that a strengthening of the instruments to deal with financial surges had become necessary. Now the economy is experiencing the downside of large financial inflows: outflows of financial capital began in late 1997 and accelerated in 1998, with an over 12 per cent nominal exchange rate depreciation. However, in response to the active management of inflows in the first half of the 1990s, the accumulated deficit on current account was moderate, the stock of external liabilities was rather low and the share of volatile funds was minor. Together with large international reserves, it allows Chile to face the sharp terms of trade shock brought on by the Asian crisis.

Contrary to conventional wisdom, it is possible to discriminate between flows which are stable, of a long-term nature and that do contribute to the country's growth (such as FDI) and those which are basically speculative and lead to excessive domestic volatility. In the Chilean case, the discouragements applied to speculative flows have had no adverse effects on FDI, which has continued to exhibit unprecedented levels, in spite of the Asian crisis. The large share of FDI in capital inflows will, in effect, mitigate the effects of Asian contagion on the Chilean balance of payments.

In order to regulate capital flows, it is best to use instruments which are as non-discretionary as possible. Non-discretionary and (semi-) automatic instruments have the advantage in that they minimize corruption and evasion. Some evasion is inevitable: any system of discouragements makes it attractive for some operators to attempt to circumvent them. In the Chilean case, it has been necessary to close loopholes as it became obvious that agents were using them. However, circumvention can be kept to a minimum with a well-designed, automatic and transparent system.

The objective of sustaining economic growth in the face of volatile capital flows (or volatile export prices, for that matter) requires the use of a battery of policy instruments. In the Chilean case, the combination of tax-like instruments to deter speculative inflows, increasing short-term exchange rate uncertainty and sterilizing the monetary effects of capital inflow worked well for several years. It should be remembered that reserve requirements alone (or any other policy that increases the cost of external borrowing), while clearly useful, do not deter speculative attacks when large exchange rate changes are anticipated. Thus a flexible policy package, rather than a single rigid policy tool, is desirable when a new capital surge emerges.

There are series of possible complements to the present set of policies, in face of a new surge. One possibility is to raise substantially the withholding tax on interest rate remittances, which now stands at 4 per cent. Raising it to 30-35 per cent (the tax rate on profit remittances) would discourage foreign borrowing at all maturities.[21] With respect to portfolio inflows, in case of capital surges, the period of application of the reserve requirement could be increased over one year, in order to raise the cost of financial investments in Chile; evidently the pressures to eliminate a capital gains tax on stock dealings should be resisted, for the sake of macroeconomic stability and social equity.

As regards the exchange rate regime, the Central Bank must show a greater commitment to its crawling band policy and prevent the exchange rate from sticking to the floor of an easily punctured band. If it wishes to have credibility in its commitment to short-term exchange rate uncertainty, the Central Bank must keep the exchange rate well within the band and must practice vigorous dirty floating within the band (active intramarginal intervention). The weights assigned to each currency in the basket used to determine the central rate must reflect long-term real factors and must not be arbitrarily changed to achieve short-term exchange rate objectives.

FDI projects of the nature undertaken in Chile are large relative to the size of the economy. In addition, they are lumpy, with periods of heavy investments followed by others in which investment essentially disappears. This is typically an upward stock adjustment problem, which may involve heavy net inflows of FDI over a period of time. It may pay countries that suddenly become attractive to multinationals to try to spread out over time the adjustment to higher stocks of FDI. This can be done through the auctioning of FDI rights or some queueing mechanism for foreign investors. It also suggests that countries in this situation can be selective with FDI, giving priority to projects with large development payoffs and that allow the host nation to capture the economic rent of natural resources.

21 Since taxes on interest remittances are much lower than taxes on dividends, foreign investors have tended to bring in capital in the form of loans from parent companies (and international capital markets), rather than as equity. Thus the effective tax rate they are actually paying is extremely low, which encourages excessive inflows. This would be corrected if, as proposed above, the interest remittance tax is raised to a rate closer to that on dividends.

References

Agosin, M.R. (1998). "Capital inflow and investment performance: Chile in the 1990s", in R. Ffrench-Davis and H. Reisen, eds., *Capital Inflows and Investment Performance: Lessons from Latin America*, ECLAC/OECD Development, Paris and Santiago.

______ (1995), "El retorno de los capitales extranjeros a Chile", *El Trimestre Económico*, No. 248 (October-December).

Agosin, M. R., G. Crespi and L Letelier (1998). "Explaining the increase in saving in Chile", Network of Economic Research Centers, Inter-American Development Bank, Washington, D.C.; forthcoming in a book edited by M. Gavin and R. Hausmann.

Aninat, E. and C. Larraín (1996). "Flujos de capitales: lecciones a partir de la experiencia Chilena", *Revista de la CEPAL*, 60 (December).

Budnevich, C. and G. Le Fort (1997). "Capital account regulations and macroeconomic policy: two Latin American experiences", in UNCTAD, *International Monetary and Financial Issues for the 1990s*, vol. VIII, New York and Geneva.

Calderón, A. and S. Griffith-Jones (1995). "Los nuevos flujos de capital extranjero en la economía Chilena: acceso renovado y nuevos usos", *Serie Desarrollo Productivo*, No. 24, CEPAL, Santiago.

Calvo, G., L. Leiderman and C. Reinhart (1993). "Capital inflows and real exchange appreciation in Latin America: the role of external factors", *IMF Staff Papers*, vol. 40, No.1 (March).

Calvo, G. A. and E. G. Mendoza (1996). "Petty crime and cruel punishment: lessons from the Mexican debacle", *American Economic Review*, vol. 86, No. 2 (May).

Claessens, S., M. P. Dooley and A. Warner (1995). "Portfolio capital flows: hot or cold?", *The World Bank Economic Review*, vol. 9, No. 1 (January).

Devlin, R., R. Ffrench-Davis and S. Griffith-Jones (1995). "Surges in capital flows and development: an overview of policy issues", in Ffrench-Davis and Griffith-Jones (1995).

Díaz-Alejandro, C. F. (1985), "Goodbye Financial Repression, Hello Financial Crash", *Journal of Development Economics*, vol. 19, No. 1/2 (September-October).

Elbadawi, I. A. and R. Soto (1994). "Capital flows and long-term equilibrium real exchange rates in Chile", World Bank, Washington, D.C., manuscript.

Ffrench-Davis, R. (1984). "Indice de precios externos: un indicador para Chile de la inflación internacional", *Colección Estudios CIEPLAN*, 13 (June).

______ (1990). "Debt-equity swaps in Chile", *Cambridge Journal of Economics*, vol. 14 (March).

Ffrench-Davis, R., M. R. Agosin and A. Uthoff (1995). "Capital movements, export strategy, and macroeconomic stability in Chile", in Ffrench-Davis and Griffith-Jones (1995).

Ffrench-Davis, R. and S. Griffith-Jones, eds. (1995). *Coping with Capital Surges—The Return of Finance to Latin America*, Boulder, Colorado: Lynne Rienner Publishers.

Helpman, E., L. Leiderman and G. Bufman (1994). "A new breed of exchange rate bands: Chile, Israel and Mexico", *Economic Policy*, No. 19 (October).

Herrera, L. O. and R. Valdés (1997). "Encaje y autonomía monetaria en Chile", Central Bank of Chile, Santiago, manuscript.

International Monetary Fund (1995). "Evolution of the Mexican Peso crisis", in *International Capital Markets—Developments, Prospects, and Policy Issues*, Washington, D.C. (August).

Labán, R. and F. Larraín (1997). "Can a liberalization of capital outflows increase net capital inflows?", *Journal of International Money and Finance, vol. 16, No. 3.*

Larraín, C. (1995). "Internacionalización y supervisión de la banca en Chile", *Estudios Públicos*, 60, Santiago (Spring).

Larraín, R., R. Labán and R. Chumacero (1997). "What determines capital inflows? an empirical analysis for Chile", *Faculty Research Working Paper Series*, No. R97-18, John F. Kennedy School of Government, Harvard University (April).

Ocampo, J. A., ed. (1994). *Los Capitales Extranjeros en las Economías Latinoamericanas*, Red de Centros de Investigación Económica Aplicada, FEDESARROLLO y Banco Interamericano de Desarrollo, Bogotá.

Repetto, A. (1994). "Políticas macroeconómicas y tipo de cambio real: Chile, 1980-91", *Colección Estudios CIEPLAN*, No. 39 (June).

Riveros, L, J. Vatter and M. R. Agosin (1996). "La inversión extranjera directa en Chile, 1987-93: aprovechamiento de ventajas comparativas y conversión de deuda", in M. R. Agosin (ed.), *Inversión Extranjera Directa en América Latina: Su Contribución al Desarrollo*, Fondo de Cultura Económica, Santiago.

Sachs, J., A. Tornell and A. Velasco (1995). "The collapse of the Mexican peso: what have we learned", *Economic Policy*, No. 22.

______ (1996). "Financial crises in emerging markets: the lessons from 1995", *Brookings Papers on Economic Activity*, No. 1.

Tobin, J. (1978). "A proposal for international economic reform", *Eastern Economic Journal*, 4 (July-October).

Valdés-Prieto, S. and M. Soto (1996). "New selective capital controls in Chile: are they effective?", Pontificia Universidad Católica de Chile, Santiago, processed.

Williamson, J. (1993). "A cost-benefit analysis of capital account liberalization", in H. Reisen and B. Fischer (comps.), *Financial Opening: Policy Issues and Experiences in Developing Countries*, Paris: OECD.

Williamson, J. (1996). *The Crawling Band as an Exchange Rate Regime: Lessons from Israel, Chile, and Colombia*, Washington, D.C.: Institute for International Economics.

12

Discussion – Latin America

DANIEL LEDERMAN
CRISTIAN OSSA

DANIEL LEDERMAN*

The study by the Economic Commission for Latin America and the Caribbean (ECLAC) presents many similarities with a report recently published by the World Bank, which I co-authored (Perry and Lederman, 1998). On the dynamics of the effects of the crisis, we come to very similar conclusions. However, within the second semester of 1997, we made a slight distinction between the period of July and October 1997. On 21 October 1997, the stock exchange of Hong Kong (China), and its currency, came under attack and that is when we believe the Asian crisis started to have global financial effects. The United States stock market fell and so did markets in Japan and the United Kingdom of Great Britain and Northern Ireland. Not surprisingly, therefore, most Latin American stock markets also fell dramatically after October. However, three countries in the region were hit through their stock or asset prices almost

---

* Economist, Office of the Chief Economist for Latin America and the Caribbean, World Bank. The views expressed herein are those of the author and not necessarily the views of the World Bank.

immediately following the Thai baht devaluation of 2 July. They were Chile, Peru and Brazil, and there seems to be a logic to this. Both Chile and Peru have the highest trade exposure to the Asian countries, and they also depend heavily on copper and other commodity prices that plunged in the aftermath of the Asian crises. Brazil has been on an unsustainable fiscal path for some time and has struggled to consolidate the macro-stabilization gains from the *real* plan. It is not surprising, therefore, that the market reflected some skittishness regarding Brazil. Fortunately, the Brazilian authorities reacted swiftly in October 1997 to the second round of volatility, but as a result the Brazilian economy slowed down and unemployment rose. Despite the promise of fiscal adjustment, the fiscal situation actually worsened in 1998.

On the spillovers from Asia to Latin America, I agree with ECLAC's conclusion that in most of the large economies in the region the main effect was the terms-of-trade deterioration associated with the decline in the aggregate demand of Asian economies. On the other hand, I believe there is one exception and the ECLAC document mentions that Brazil has actually gained from the decline in commodity prices since it imports some of those commodities. It is also notable that Brazil has been perhaps the only major Latin American economy that has suffered mainly through financial effects and the associated policy response.

In fact, at times, trade transmission effects cannot be easily separated from financial effects, since borrowing requirements change with the changing trade situation. Indeed, the deterioration of aggregate demand in Asia led to a deterioration in commodity prices and in trade balances, in turn making international investors jittery about widening current-account deficits, while demands for external finance increased just at a time of greater uncertainty and falling availability of foreign capital.

On the causes of the crisis, ECLAC's paper emphasizes the role played by volatile international capital flows. We also, though more softly, advocate on the grounds of prudential regulation, the imposition of certain types of capital controls similar to the one that Chile had prior to the crisis. On the issue of prudential regulation, I agree that prudential regulation should be at the core of development strategies that aim to limit financial vulnerability. It would be unreasonable to expect that there will not be similar crises in emerging markets in the future. However, I think that ECLAC's paper missed two important elements of prudential regulation. While ECLAC emphasizes capital requirements, there are two other elements, besides supervision and monitoring of the banks, in a framework for prudential regulation. One is transforming explicit or implicit onerous deposit insurance schemes into limited deposit insurance schemes. In the paper on Chile, Agosin and Ffrench-Davis do not mention this point, but the prudential regulation scheme in Chile in a sense "outlawed" systemic banking crisis because, given the memory of the 1982-1983 intervention, for which the central bank is still paying the price, the law essentially excludes any possibility of rescue. I do not think that is advisable, since, as Kindleberger and others have shown, in the face of systemic banking crises all government financial safety nets change "ad hoc". So perhaps some sort of deposit insurance might be desirable to limit the extent or the possibility of a systemic banking crisis due to asymmetric information regarding the quality of different financial institutions within the economy. However, it should be limited and depositors, as well as creditors, should recognize that they will have to cover some of the losses associated with bad banking practices. Perhaps, we should examine a little closer what Argentina has accomplished since 1995 on this front, namely the establishment of deposit insurance partly funded by private commercial banks themselves. Still, it is very difficult to differentiate a credit boom or an asset price boom brought about by implicit deposit insurance or other sources of moral hazard or by euphoria. But we do know that the government guarantees tend to stimulate excessive risk-taking and thus should be limited.

The other element that I do not see mentioned in ECLAC's paper is the issue of bank closure and bankruptcy law. Should not bank superintendents have explicit rules telling us when a bank should be considered to be bankrupt, or when to intervene at an early stage in order to attempt to prevent the spread of bad lending practices from bad institutions to better institutions?

Regarding exchange rate policy, in the World Bank's paper, we conclude that some exchange rate flexibility may also be useful almost as another element of prudential regulation. When de facto rigid nominal exchange rates are sustained for a long period of time—as in the Asian economies—they may lead economic agents to think that the probability of severe devaluations are very low and therefore the risks involved in taking up foreign denominated liabilities are low. If, in addition, domestic lending rates are higher than foreign interest rates, then that is a recipe for disaster. Therefore, some nominal exchange rate volatility may be useful in providing the correct incentives for domestic economic agents to get a more accurate picture of what are the risks involved in foreign borrowing. This would be in addition to limitations on holding open foreign exchange positions in the balance sheets of domestic financial institutions.

Both documents mention commodity stabilization funds, such as the one used in Chile. Such funds should allow governments to implement counter-cyclical fiscal policies. During periods of commodity price booms, you accumulate reserves and so you do not promote a boom in domestic absorption, and thus prevent excessive appreciation of the real exchange rate. Then in periods of sudden declines in commodity prices, you can draw on those accumulated reserves to feed into the fiscal revenues of the government, so that the fiscal contraction will not have to be proportional to the fall in export revenues, as Mexico is currently experiencing.

What is happening in Chile? Despite the existence of a copper-price stabilization fund, the Government is implementing contractionary fiscal policies, or at least reducing the fiscal impulse. Why? It is a sort of a puzzle. Of course, the authorities are concerned about the behaviour of capital markets, an inflation target, and controlling the extent of nominal depreciation. So, if the markets are interpreting this decline in Chile's terms of trade as permanent, they will demand a once-and-for-all adjustment in absorption as well, and perhaps a depreciation of the exchange rate. Despite the amount of reserves accumulated in the stabilization fund, if there is no fiscal adjustment, international investors will demand a premium. So, when the country premium is endogenous to the trade balance or to the current-account balance, then a stabilization fund is not a very useful instrument for promoting counter-cyclical fiscal policies, because the market is going to impose a certain fiscal discipline and the Government is not going to be able to tap the financial revenue accumulated in the fund when prices drop. It may be useful for preventing real exchange rate appreciation and the Dutch disease effects during the period of booms; but one would have to evaluate the rules of operation of the commodity stabilization funds, since they are not fully satisfying one of the objectives that it was meant to achieve. In particular, it may be useful to look at the rules governing the use of the reserves in the commodity stabilization funds. Perhaps, during the periods of bust they should be converted into foreign exchange reserves and allow the central bank to use those reserves to manage the exchange rate rather than the fiscal authorities.

There is a broader issue which was not directly addressed by either paper. It is the proper fiscal-monetary mix in response to balance of payments or currency crises. Some would argue in favour of a Keynesian fiscal policy, deficit spending in the downturn, complemented by monetary expansion to hold interest rates down and help the recovery, while the International Monetary Fund (IMF) recommends exactly the opposite. What is the optimal policy mix? I would say that we do not know. We do know that in the case of Mexico in 1994-1995, the Government followed IMF prescriptions. The rate of growth of industrial production turned positive after about 12 months. It was a severe crisis nonetheless. How much pain should emerging markets sustain or what is the proper combination of interest rates and nominal exchange rate depreciation? These remain open questions.

Let me comment on ECLAC's proposal to diversify exports and increase export competitiveness. It seems clear to me that export diversification and competitiveness are not policy instruments. They are goals: it is almost like recommending that a country develop, because export diversification occurs with development. So, what are the policy instruments for export diversification? Are we suggesting that we should have an export subsidy programme, or directed credit programmes? I would take a closer look at the Asian experience with those programmes. Are those programmes linked to the falling profitability of investment? These are open questions.

Upon reading the paper by Agosin and Ffrench-Davis, one senses that they are arguing in favour of "exchange-rate protection". That is, they seem to favour a monetary policy that aims to protect the domestic tradables industry by maintaining a competitive exchange rate. On the one hand, they argue that the concept of equilibrium of real exchange rate is not very useful. On the other hand, they are concerned about deviation from trends of the real exchange rate. Are they advocating that countries should aim towards a secular depreciation of the real exchange rate? One has to wonder how fast productivity can rise on a year-to-year basis relative to the productivity growth of foreign competitors. This is an important consideration for assessing what is the appropriate path for the real exchange rate, and it is difficult to assess, indeed. But in general, it may be important to prevent drastic real exchange-rate appreciations that seem to be abnormal relative to the long-term trend, which can be defined in various ways. If we are also concerned about dramatic increases in domestic credit to the private sector, then what we are really saying is that we should be careful not to have "overheating" economies, which tend to be more susceptible to sudden reversals. However, these arguments are quite different than those that view any real exchange-rate appreciation as harmful to the economy.

Finally, let me come back to the issue of capital controls. Chile was held as a model for its capital controls, especially the 30 per cent reserve requirement. On 25 June 1998, the Central Bank announced that it was reducing the latter to 10 per cent, and they were reduced to zero more recently amidst the continuing international financial turbulence. In the case of Brazilian capital controls, it appears that rather than capital controls having an impact on capital flows, capital controls in Brazil are determined by capital inflows. The impact of the controls themselves is negligible in terms of volumes and limited in time in terms of composition, as shown in a recent paper by Eliana Cardoso and Ilan Goldfajn (1997). If the justification for capital controls is their use as a proxy for prudential regulation, that is not an argument for a variable capital control. Only if the argument in favour of capital controls is to affect the magnitude or the volume of capital flows and one is convinced that they have an impact on the magnitude of capital flows, independently of their effect on the composition of flows, then it is wise to have variable capital controls. However, if the justification is for prudential regulation, that is not a justification for endogenous capital controls. Now, if we are going to change capital controls every time there is a change of heart by international investors, any sort of signalling effect that these capital controls may have withers away.

CRISTIAN OSSA*

I liked the two presentations on Latin America, in particular, focusing on the conditions to avert crises. The attention paid by Ms. Stallings to anticipatory moves to avoid crises, especially "managing the boom" is, in my view, well placed. Improved monitoring—particularly of key components of the balance of payments—is critical, as well as are anticyclical policies and measures tending to avoid large fluctuations in short-term flows.

I find a bit surprising that the term external debt has not hitherto been used in these discussions. All the focus has been on only two components of the balance of payments: short-term credits and portfolio investments. Yet, debt levels and the dynamics of change in debt ratios are a good clue to anticipate some serious problems. Likewise, medium-term debt service profiles can often be good indicators as to whether the recovery will be L, U or V- shaped (for example, to lower a high debt-to-export ratio in a crisis environment might take a very long time). It is true that short-term debt—if there are enough reserves—can be repaid virtually instantaneously. But the inertia of long-term debt may complicate restoring balance-of-payments equilibrium in a reasonable time.

High and growing international reserve levels are not necessarily a good signal. They might presage increasing disequilibria and lead to an excessive appreciation of the national currency. That is why, as Ms. Stallings said, there is a

* Adviser, Latin American Bureau, United Nations Development Programme. The views expressed herein are those of the author and not necessarily the views of United Nations Development Programme.

need to follow closely asset prices (stocks, real estate.). She also underlined the importance of trying to isolate as much as possible the real sector—output and productive investments—from the inevitable financial fluctuations. Yet, the recommendation towards diversification seems too broad. It could make sense for large- and medium-sized economies. But should we recommend outright diversification for Central American countries, Caribbean countries and other small Latin American economies? Perhaps a concentration on a few lines of export products might be better as the only way to achieve efficiency—or competitiveness—in production and marketing.

Quite probably, better governance of the international financial system could have prevented many of the worst features of the present crisis. It is disturbing, as Ms. Stallings pointed out, that no international institution exists that helps prevent unsustainable financial booms from developing. This is an argument for either much improved supervision or tighter regulations for suppliers of capital—most of them in developed countries—or the creation of an international financial organization to design and monitor the rules of the game. The existing institutions—multilateral financial organizations and rating agencies—have not been of much help in restraining booms. On a few occasions, their reporting or analyses have led to intensifying excesses rather than preventing them.

Finally, I agree with Ms. Stallings on the need to increase the financial capability of the International Monetary Fund to confront subsequent crises. Often, time is of the essence and delays in gathering the required financing in a rescue package might become very costly for the country directly involved as well as for others. The Fund should have the required resources to facilitate prompt action and to ensure that the size of the rescue package and the conditionality be tailored to the degree of difficulty in arranging international finance.

Reading the paper on Chile of Agosin and Ffrench-Davis reminded me of a movie called "All the Right Moves". In this movie the hero, after overcoming all the difficulties and finessing the dangers faced by young men in today's world, conquers the nicest girl in town and gets a sports scholarship that allows him to go on with his studies at a good college. Despite all the past right moves, he is eager to continue to learn as, inevitably, he will have to face new realities and challenges. The Chilean policy stances on capital inflows in the 1990s as the paper explains, are quite close to what can be considered "all the right moves". Still, the learning process in Chile goes on, and the authors propose some additional measures to improve the scheme in a way that volatility of short-term inflows is reduced further, while still taking advantage of the benefits that such flows might entail.

I strongly agree with most of the analysis and recommendations of a paper that addresses all the key policy and institutional issues. Yet, there are a few statements that might deserve some qualifications. The policy to slow inflows is credited to have led Chile to a higher rate of investment, saving and growth. It is true that in the period considered there is little underutilization of resources. In other words, the economy seems to be approaching full employment. But what is not fully evident is that additional inflows could not have increased investment more than consumption. If that were the case, the trade-off is not between more short-term inflows and more investment, savings and growth, but between less volatility and a slightly higher investment rate, at least in the short term and, probably, also in the long term.

Regarding exchange rate policy, it is stated that in 1996 and 1997, rather than moving the rate according to established criteria, actual management resembled more a fixed exchanged rate system, as the dollar had fluctuated little, sticking to the lower end of the band. Gradually this fed the notion—in the country and abroad—that a fixed rate vis-à-vis the dollar is the preferred option by the Central Bank. This has two consequences: it diminishes the credibility of the stated Central Bank policy of moving the exchange rate according to established criteria; and, as the authors say, it becomes counterproductive to restrain capital inflows, as the perceived exchange rate risk is reduced. It is not clear what was behind the stickiness in the exchange rate in 1996-1997, but if the main reason was to reduce inflation further it was no doubt quite dangerous. The results of a fixed exchange policy have not been good in Chile, and at least in two episodes have proved disastrous.

The paper has an elegant test to show the comparative persistence of FDI, and long-term and short-term loans from private sources. The test is persuasive in proving the hypothesis in the Chilean case; FDI and long-term inflows are more stable than short-term inflows. Moreover, there is no evidence that discouraging short-term inflows has had any adverse impact on FDI in Chile. The paper goes on and states that there is no sign that FDI flows are declining owing to the Asian crisis. Yet, the considerable fall in copper and timber prices have been partly the result of the Asian crisis. Is it true that foreign investors are persisting with their original investment plans in Chile despite the substantial price declines in these commodities? One could expect, if not cancellations, at least suspension of some projects.

Finally, it would be interesting to have a better idea of the political background and the general business situation in Chile that allowed for such a rational behaviour of policy makers. In times of rapid growth, increasing profits and ample availability of capital, it might not be difficult to embrace the policies and measures suggested in the paper. In periods of distress, such measures could be more contested. Also, it would be useful to have more detail on the institutions involved in the decisions, who have been the main players or decision makers, the pressures they have been submitted to and the way they have interacted to achieve coherence in the results. A glimpse at the key actors involved might improve our understanding of a process which up to now can be considered very successful.

References

Cardoso, Eliana and Ilan Goldfajn (1997). "Capital flows to Brazil: The endogeneity of capital controls". IMF Working Paper, WP/97/115 (September). Washington, D.C.: International Monetary Fund.

Perry , Guillermo E. and Daniel Lederman (1998). *Financial Vulnerability, Spillover Effects, and Contagion: Lessons from the Asian Crises for Latin America,* World Bank Latin American and Caribbean Studies Viewpoints. Washington, D.C.: The World Bank.

Part Four

AFRICA

Edited by

Ana Cortez

13

Introduction – Africa

ANA CORTEZ*
United Nations Department of Economic and Social Affairs

It is often argued that among the developing regions Africa is the one that is least integrated into the world economy and would therefore be relatively protected from a financial crisis emanating from elsewhere. Indeed, the region generated only about 2 per cent of world exports in 1997 (down from 3.7 per cent in 1985) and absorbed 4 per cent of private net capital flows to developing countries in 1996, most of which reached a reduced number of countries in the region. Africa is also a region where capital markets are mostly incipient and underdeveloped. Within this context, what possible lessons could Africa learn from the Asian crisis? Several, as the papers presented at this section of the expert group meeting and the discussions they generated made clear.

But before presenting these lessons, it is worth saying that Africa is actually more integrated into the global economy than the data cited above would suggest. These figures tell only part of the story. If one takes the ratio of exports and imports of goods and services (interest payments excluded) to GDP as an indication of the openness of an economy—and therefore of its integration in global markets—African data indicate a great deal of integration. Indeed, the share for the region in 1993-1995 was actually higher than the one observed in Latin America during the same period and comparable to that of Asia, once

* Senior Economic Affairs Officer, Secretariat, Committee for Development Policy. The views expressed herein are those of the author and not necessarily the views of the United Nations.

Hong Kong (China), Myanmar and Singapore are excluded from the regional average.[1] African integration into the world economy is perhaps not of the ideal type as commodities dominate exports and manufactures dominate imports. Yet, the region has produced some success stories of a more dynamic type of integration such as Mauritius and Tunisia, where manufactures generate a significant share of export revenues.

Issues of insufficient integration become more apparent in the financial sphere than in the production sphere as financial markets are poorly developed in the region, and usually dominated by a few commercial banks. Except for a few countries, stock exchanges have just recently been established in the region and are usually small. Capital inflows going into the region are limited and highly concentrated in four countries (Egypt, Morocco, Nigeria and Republic of South Africa). This, however, has not insulated the continent from possible contagion effects arising from capital account liberalization. South Africa, for instance, has recently experienced a foreign exchange crisis, which—in contrast to some Asian countries—was not followed by a banking crisis as a result of the preventive measures adopted earlier.

Notwithstanding the above, it is through trade links that the negative effects of the Asian crisis are being mostly felt in Africa. Except for a few countries, Africa does not have strong trade links with the crisis-stricken countries of Asia, but it has been affected nevertheless owing to the fall in commodity prices in international markets. Oil and mineral prices (copper in particular) have been severely hit. African countries are also finding it more difficult to compete in tropical product markets as Asian countries, having suffered considerable currency devaluation, may be able to afford lower dollar prices for their exports. In his paper, Befekadu Degefe places export revenue losses at about $25 billion in 1998, roughly 20 per cent of the region's exports in 1997, most of which will be shouldered by the oil exporting countries (which also account for a large share of the regional GDP).

Lack of diversification in the productive structure may also negatively affect private capital inflows—both short and long-term—within a context of depressed commodity prices. Foreign direct investment mostly

---

1 During the period 1993-1995, the ratio of exports and imports to GDP ranged from 70 to 77 per cent both in Africa and in Asia, while it ranged from about 66 to 72 per cent in Latin America. The Caribbean was the region that showed the greatest degree of trade integration, with its ratio constantly over 100 per cent of the GDP during that period. Hong Kong (China) and Singapore were excluded from the Asian sample as a result of the importance of re-exports for those economies, while Myanmar was atypical to the region, showing an extremely low degree of integration (about 3 per cent of GDP). Figures are based on data from the World Bank, *World Development Indicators 1998*, CD-ROM version.

goes to commodity-based industries, particularly in the mining sector, while commodity-related corporations dominate the stock markets emerging in the region.

As most of the regional economy is dominated by the production of commodities, the continent remains vulnerable to the vagaries of the weather and the fluctuations of international commodity prices. Poverty is rampant. Economic growth has been further constrained by civil strife, political instability and the external debt overhang. Nevertheless, some progress has been achieved in Africa, as the rate of growth improved during the past few years and macroeconomic indicators are at more sustainable levels.

Yet, there is recognition that there is more to be done on macroeconomic management, on institutional and structural reforms, on economic governance—not only public but also private—and on financial sector development. GDP growth rates of 4 to 5 per cent per year are not enough to pull the continent up from the its current state. Mr. Degefe argues in his paper that the current development strategy followed by African countries should be revised, as results obtained so far have been disappointing. If anything, Africa should look at Asia to learn how to better integrate into the world economy and achieve fast and equitable growth. There is therefore a lesson to extract from the good Asian experience of the past few decades. The temporary setback being felt in Asia should not obscure its spectacular achievements in poverty reduction, human resource development and economic growth. All these successes were achieved through the positive leadership of local governments, which guided the markets in allocating scarce resources. This is, in his opinion, the major lesson that Africa can learn from Asia.

Henk-Jan Brinkman's paper, by focusing on issues particular to financial markets, stresses those policy measures adopted in Asia which should not be followed elsewhere, that is, the bad part of Asia's recent experience. For Africa, he argues, the timing of such lessons could not be more opportune as financial sector reforms are approaching the top of the reform agenda in the region. In fact, some 30 African countries have already undertaken some form of financial reform, with some positive trends being produced. There has been a movement towards more private banks and towards positive real interest rates.

Financial reforms in Africa have not led to expected outcomes. Institutions are not necessarily more solid, and despite the increased competition, borrowing and lending spreads have not declined. In countries with unstable macroeconomic conditions, interest rate volatility has not subsided. Deregulation and low barriers to entry—without adequate prudential regulation and strong supervision—have contributed to the emergence of banking crises in several countries.

Therefore, reforms have recently emphasized issues related to regulatory and supervisory capacity. However, while these measures will improve risk management, they will certainly not eliminate risk altogether. As Mr. Brinkman reminds us, financial markets are not like ordinary markets for goods. Financial markets are imperfect, prone to herd behaviour, volatility and failures, which can have pervasive effects on the rest of the economy. The Asian crisis has been witness to all these features. Hence, he suggests, African countries should proceed rather cautiously with financial sector reforms and especially with the liberalization of their capital account. Some controls may indeed be required to address the volatility of external flows within a market that can never be perfect, and adequate regulation cannot address all risks involved.

We come now to one lesson that may be extracted from an especially disheartening side of the recent Asian experience and which has not attracted sufficient attention from policy reformers: its social costs. Indeed, the possible impact of economic reforms and liberalization needs to be carefully assessed before they are implemented. Policy makers should be constantly reminded of the human implications of liberalization and deregulation policies that are poorly phased and sequenced. Wages decline and unemployment soars, but costs are not restricted to the "organized" sector of the economy. The informal sector suffers as well, given the effect of usually high interest rates that are evoked to defend the currency and the overall demand contraction. Rural areas are also negatively affected because they rarely are completely isolated from the rest of the economy. There is often some kind of income diversification taking place and it will most likely be negatively affected by the decline of activity in the formal economy. Fiscal revenues are compromised which may, in turn, reduce social expenditures. And within the African context, this usually implies cutting what is already under-supplied. There is therefore a need to think about the economic reforms in a more comprehensive way, thus integrating the social component before liberalization is launched, and not after when it is causing pain. Hence, when thinking about sequencing of reforms, perhaps the introduction of social reforms—including the establishment of safety nets and measures to promote human capital development—should be adopted concurrently with, if not prior to, the adoption of economic reforms, a point raised, in particular, in the discussion of the African papers that follow.

14

South-East Asia's Economic Crisis and Africa: A view from the African Region

BEFEKADU DEGEFE*
United Nations Economic Commission for Africa

1. Introduction

The economic crisis of the South-East Asian (SEA) countries engendered by the currency and financial instability of 1997 has had important repercussions on the world economy. According to the International Monetary Fund (IMF, 1998) global economic growth will decelerate by two percentage point from 4.1 per cent of 1997 to 2.1 per cent in 1998. This is mainly due to the negative impact emanating from countries mostly affected by the financial crisis in SEA (Indonesia, Malaysia, the Republic of Korea and Thailand), whose GDP—taken as a group—is projected to shrink by 8.7 per cent and by the economic recession in Japan.

The economic consequences of the SEA's instability have spread to the rest of the world in different ways depending on the nature and intensity of the link the various countries and regions have with these countries. Africa's major link with the SEA region is in the main mediated through the global commodity markets where the two meet either as trading partners or as competitors. Thus,

---

* Director, Beaman Centre for Economic Studies, Addis Ababa. This article was prepared while the author was consultant to the Economic and Social Policy Division at UN/ECA. The views expressed in the paper are strictly those of the author and do not necessarily reflect the views of ECA. The author would like to express his gratitude to Professor A.G. Ali for his critical comments and suggestions.

it is not surprising to note that the SEA crisis has affected Africa through its impact on world prices, especially those of primary commodities. In addition, two relatively minor impacts on Africa having their source in the SEA instability relate to foreign direct investment (FDI) and the exchange rate. Regarding FDI, some South-East Asian economies (the Republic of Korea and Malaysia) have been investing in the southern African countries particularly in Botswana, the Republic of South Africa and Zimbabwe. Following the crisis, on-going projects have been terminated and planned ones shelved. On the financial front, Africa has been spared the distress by the virtue of its capital markets being grossly underdeveloped. The only country that was affected by a currency shock was the Republic of South Africa, where the initial trauma was contained by the defensive measures taken by the authorities in that country.

From an African perspective, it is grossly inappropriate to talk about the current financial, economic and social instability in SEA as a crisis. For that matter, crisis of any nature or dimension anywhere in the world is likely to pale relative to Africa's past experience and current status. Despite their current difficulties, the SEA countries have their fundamentals correct. They had been enjoying unprecedented rates of growth during the last three decades, the highest savings rate in the world, very high rates of employment, an equitable income distribution and very low inflation. Above all they have succeeded in creating and nurturing a peaceful social and political environment conducive to a dynamic and robust economic activity. In contrast, Africa lacks all of these attributes and is mired in crises of unprecedented magnitude.

It is against this background and the challenge of extricating Africa from its crisis that we should reflect on the impact of the SEA's instability and the lessons that the region's policy makers and their development partners should learn. While an understanding of what triggered the crisis and the modalities for its containment are certainly interesting and profitable, it is equally, if not more, appropriate for Africa to benefit from the strategy that led to their success that engendered the crisis. In the rest of the paper we would make a brief interlude into the nature and impact of the SEA crisis on Africa in section 2 and take stock of what this means on the region's economy in 1998 in section 3. In section 4 we would focus on the problematic of the African countries and suggest a broad based agenda in sections 5 and 6. Section 7 would conclude the paper.

2. South-East Asia's economic crisis and Africa

The economic interface between the SEA and Africa is mediated mainly through trade flows between the two regions and competition in the global market. The impact of the SEA crisis on Africa deriving from trade with each other is insignificant. The ASEAN four (Indonesia, Malaysia, the Philippines and Thailand) and the Republic of Korea account for about 3 per cent of the region's exports, of which 50 per cent is oil, 20 per cent is agricultural raw materials and 13 per cent is non-fuel minerals. On the other hand, only 1.6 per cent of Africa's imports originate from these countries. The slowdown in SEA countries has depressed both the value and volume of African exports to that region. On the import side, the devaluation of South-Asian currencies has reduced import costs for Africa, although the extent of such benefit has been partially offset by the high rate of inflation in these countries.

However, the more significant impact of the SEA crisis has been channelled to Africa through the world market via commodity prices. The crisis in SEA itself affected world prices as the declining demand by the region contributed to a downward pressure on the prices of those commodities of which they are among the major importers. For Africa these included, among others, oil, minerals and agricultural raw materials. In addition, the prices of those commodities, which are exported to the world market by the SEA and in which African producers are also major participants (for instance, beverages), were also depressed for a variety of reasons. In consequence, the average price of agricultural raw materials compared to average level in 1997 declined by 14 per cent, metals by 12 per cent, beverages by 9 per cent and oil by 30 per cent at the end of the second quarter of 1998.[1] Assuming that Africa will maintain in 1998 the same volume of exports as in 1997, the Secretariat of the Economic Commission for Africa has estimated that Africa would lose between $20 and $25 billion of foreign-exchange earnings. Up to 80 per cent of such loss would be borne by the oil-exporting countries.

3. Africa's economy in 1998

The decline in commodity prices and the resulting loss of foreign exchange earnings were expected to affect economic activity in Africa. Initially, the Economic Commission for Africa projected a growth rate of between 4 per cent and 5 per cent for 1998, depending on the possible outcome of the two major determinants of economic activity in Africa—weather conditions and the external economic environment. Under a plausible scenario of negative out-turn in either one of these determinants, the lower figure was expected to hold, while it was expected that the higher bound might prevail if the two determinants were more auspicious.

Half way into the year we noted that the negative impact on the external

1 Calculated from IMF, International Financial Statistics, June 1998, pp. 68-71. Note the price of oil (petroleum) is the average crude price.

environment seemed to be offset by the positive effect of the weather condition, as a result of which the region's economy seemed to be on course. Lower oil prices, although detrimental to oil-exporting countries, have allowed oil-importing countries in the region to reduce the pressure on their limited foreign exchange resources, while the export market in the OECD countries remains vibrant (excluding Japan). We were therefore reasonably confident that Africa's economy would increase by no less than 4.5 per cent in 1998. Towards the end of the year, however, that forecast started to look optimistic. Estimates for some of the major economies in the region have been revised downwards due to lower than anticipated commodity prices, export volumes and higher interest rates. For instance, the Republic of South Africa, the largest economy of the region, is expected to grow by less than 1 per cent in 1998 as compared to a previous forecast of 2.5 per cent.

4. The African crisis

For the past three years, a number of African countries have begun to experience stronger rates of economic growth, but at its peak the average annual increase in output for Africa as a whole has not exceeded 4 per cent. This is not satisfactory. It is not sufficient to make up for the loss in per capita income during the last decade, except over an inordinately long period of time. As shown by very high rates of growth of some countries, particularly those of the SEA, the potential exists for faster growth in Africa. This notwithstanding, the current growth rate is an improvement over the region's weak economic performance in the past. If Africa succeeded in maintaining a GDP growth rate of about 4 per cent per annum, not only would it end its slide into poverty, but it would also be able to regain the per capita income of 1980 in about a decade and half.

Unfortunately, at the turn of the century, Africa is the continent which is the most vulnerable to exogenous and persistent shocks, the most poverty-stricken, the most debt-distressed and the most technically backward. Civil unrest and political instability, born of deepening poverty and years of misrule, have destroyed the most basic of the social and physical infrastructure on which a dynamic economy can thrive.

Since the 1980s, all the misery indices have been continuously on the rise in Africa. Real GDP growth averaged 2 per cent, while population increased at an annual average of 3 per cent. In consequence, per capita income declined by an average of 1 per cent per annum. As a result of this dismal performance, the number of Africans living in absolute poverty increased from 105 million in 1985 to 216 million by 1990. This number was projected to increase to 304 million which roughly corresponds to half of the population of the region at the turn of the century (World Bank, 1990).[2] Measures to contain the crisis by the governments were to no avail, triggering unsustainable deficits in both the budget and the current account.

Furthermore, and this is purely a personal view, the recent policy paradigm has not been helpful in reviving the economy either. The policy package that was exported to Africa to contain the crisis and resuscitate the economy has not been sufficiently powerful to reverse the continent's trajectory of decline.[3] Budget deficits were reduced, but at the expense of a shrinking state. The current-account deficit was increasingly financed by the international financial institutions and the donor community. These measures had important repercussions on the economy and the society. The debt burden increased, inflation soared and the states were reduced to a shadow of their past, unable to provide the most basic of services, including maintenance of law and order. Despite bright spots here and there, the region-wide growth and development momentum of the 1960s and 1970s were derailed. The number of African least developed countries increased from 17 in 1980 to 28 in 1990 and currently reaches 33. The deteriorating social and economic conditions have given rise to civil unrest, ethnic strife and wars, which in turn reduced new investment, both domestic and foreign, encouraged capital flight, thus further aggravating instability.

It is compared to these social and economic conditions that we find the South-East Asian crisis a non-crisis, although the slowdown in these countries and the resulting decline in world commodity prices do affect African economies. But as pointed out earlier this is not an unexpected or unusual development. For most of this century, and more so since 1980, primary commodity prices and African terms of trade have been experiencing secular decline.[4] What is new in this round, therefore, is the source rather the substance of what happened.

5. Understanding the African tragedy

As the only region steadily defying conventional theory and policy packages derived therefrom, Africa has posed and continues to pose the greatest

2 For a recent review of the status of poverty in Africa, see Plenary paper African Economic Research Consortium (AERC), Workshop on Poverty, Income Distribution and Labour Market Conditions in Africa, May 1998.

3 Critiques of Structural Adjustment Programs inspired and financed by the Bretton Woods institutions are legion, including the Economic Commission for Africa's , African alternative framework to structural adjustment programmes (1989). For a recent view see, for example, Joseph E. Stiglitz (1998).

4 For a review of global price behaviour see for example Enzo R. Grilli and Maw Cheng Yang (1998).

challenge to both researchers and policy makers. If the 1980s was the lost decade (Singer, 1989), Africa's history of the 1960-1990 period has been an era of "growth tragedy" (Easterly and Levine, 1997).

The challenge to better understand Africa by Western intellectuals and researchers was triggered, among others, by Barro. In a seminal paper (Barro, 1991), Barro's cross-country regressions failed to account for a significant proportion of the causes of the poor performance of the region's economy. That is, a "dummy" variable (one for an African country, zero for non-African country) was a statistically significant "explanatory" variable. Ever since, attempts to unlock and understand the "African dummy" have been a growth industry. The range of hypotheses marshalled to explain the region's poor performance extends from purely economic reasons to other factors such as geography, politics, psychology and culture. The geographical factor[5] (Sachs and Warner, 1997; Ram, 1997), neighbourhood effects and ethnicity (Easterly and Levine, 1997), institutional weaknesses and associated risks (Mauro, 1995; Knack and Keefer, 1995), policy reversals of social capital and lack of integrity of leaders (Collier and Gunning, 1997) illustrate the range of non-economic factors economists have picked up in the course of their research in recent years.

6. The way ahead

While the studies mentioned above and the large volume of analysis of more purely economic nature have helped to understand the problems and challenges facing African policy makers, a viable policy framework has yet to be developed to anchor and guide Africa's social and economic development. The more or less permanent nature of the crisis, the frequently disrupted attempts at recovery and the plethora of economic and non-economic factors that are called upon to explain the poor performance of the African economies only stress that existing programmes are not powerful enough to overcome the problem and that the path of development taken as a whole has not been making progress.

This raises the important issue of understanding how the East Asians succeeded in transforming their economies and societies in the short span of three decades so that Africa could learn from their strategies. The most important lesson from the experience of these countries is the absolute necessity of a strong state and visionary leadership.[6] The need for a strong state is a theme that has been picked up lately by institutions such as the

5 The idea of the tropics affecting economic activity is not new. In a book published in 1976, Andrew Karmarck argued the case strongly and his argument was resurrected in the 1990s. See Karmarck (1976).

6 For an entertaining and perceptive reading of the East Asian case, see Robert Wade (1990).

World Bank (World Bank, 1997) as well as by individual researchers (Sachs and Sievers, 1998).

The point of departure for the new and bold strategy should be the reinventing of the state as well as the broadening of the growth and development objective beyond the narrow confines of efficiency as measured by international prices. Moreover, the mechanism for price stability should shift from the current demand deflating policies to a supply increasing framework.

There are essential points that should define the development strategy in Africa. First, Africa suffers from extensive unemployment of both human and natural resources. Current production locus in virtually all the countries of the region is well within their production possibility frontier. Second, inflation in Africa is driven not by excess demand as much as by the shortages of basic goods in the face of a growing population. Under such circumstances, demand deflation to institute a regime of stable prices would only exacerbate the situation.

With the limited resources that are available in Africa, the free market is incapable of channelling adequate amounts to priority areas. The market needs to be assisted and guided. This is the one inexorable lesson that the SEAs success teaches the African policy makers and their development partners.

7. Conclusion

The South-East Asian crisis has had important repercussions on the global economy. In the African context its negative impact has been mediated through depressed commodity prices.

However, the external shock for Africa that accompanied the crisis in the SEAs is nothing new to Africa. If anything, what is new is the source of the shock, since Africa has experienced a regime of deteriorating terms of trade in the past, the origin of which can be traced to developments taking place in the developed economies.

Much more than the crisis emanating from SEA, the cause of the African tragedy lies elsewhere. Vulnerability to external shocks, poverty, undeveloped technical capacity and a heavy external debt burden can be easily evoked when characterizing the region. It is precisely these characteristics of Africa that need to be faced and addressed in the course of developing a sufficiently robust economic policy. To this end, the current policies need to be revised and a more appropriate and robust strategy put in place. Africa has a lot to learn both from the successes and errors of the SEA countries. Two basic lessons to be learned from these countries are that there is need for strong and visionary state and that the market must be assisted in the allocation of the limited resources in the region.

References

Barro, Robert J. (1991). "Economic growth in a cross section of countries". *Quarterly Journal of Economics*, Vol. 56, pp. 407-443.

Collier, P. and J. Gunning (1997). "Explaining African economic performance". Center for the Study of African Economics, Working Paper Series, WPS/97-2.1.

Easterly, William and Ross Levine (1997). "Africa's growth tragedy: policies and ethnic divisions". *Quarterly Journal of Economics*, Vol. 62, pp.1203-1250.

______ (1995). "Africa's growth tragedy: a retrospective, 1960-89". *Policy Research Working Paper 1503*. Washington, D.C.: The World Bank (August).

Economic Commission for Africa (1998). *Economic Report on Africa 1998*, Economic and Social Policy Division (mimeo).

Grilli, Enzo R. and Maw Cheng Yang (1998). "Primary commodity prices, manufactured goods prices and the terms of trade of developing countries: what the long run shows". *The World Bank Economic Review*, Vol. 2, pp. 1-48 (January).

IMF (1998). International Financial Statistics (June).

______ (1988). *World Economic Outlook* (October).

Karmarck, Andrew (1976). *The Tropics and Economic Development*. Baltimore, Maryland: Johns Hopkins University Press.

Knack, S. and P. Keefer (1995). "Institutions and economic performance: cross country tests using alternative institutional measures". *Economics and Politics*, Vol. 7, No. 3, pp. 207-227.

Mauro, P. "Corruption and growth" (1995). *Quarterly Journal of Economics*, Vol. 110, pp. 681-712.

Ram, Bati (1997). "Tropics and economic development: an empirical investigation". *World Development*, Vol. 25, pp. 1443-1452.

Sachs, Jeffery and Sara E. Sievers (1998). *The Africa Competitiveness Report 1998*.

Sachs, J.D. and Andrew M. Warner (1997). "Sources of slow growth in African economies". *Journal of African Economies*, Vol. 6, pp. 335-76.

Singer, Hans W. (1989). "Lessons of postwar development experience". *African Development Review*, Vol. I, No. 2.

Stiglitz, Joseph E. (1998). "More instruments and broader goals: moving towards the post-Washington consensus". *1998 WIDER Annual Lecture*. Helsinki: World Institute for Development Economics Research, United Nations University (January).

Wade, Robert (1990). *Governing Market: Economic Theory and the Role of Government in East Asian Industrialization*. Princeton, New Jersey: Princeton University Press.

World Bank (1990). *World Development Report 1990*. New York and London: Oxford University Press for the World Bank.

______ (1997). *World Development Report 1997. The State in a Changing World*. New York and London: Oxford University Press for the World Bank.

15

Financial Reforms in Africa and the Lessons from Asia

HENK-JAN BRINKMAN*
United Nations Department of Economic and Social Affairs

1. Introduction

There are a number of lessons Africa can learn from the financial crisis in East Asia despite the fact that the financial sector in Africa is relatively underdeveloped, Africa gets only a fraction of the international capital flowing to emerging markets and Africa has hardly been affected by the contagion of the financial crisis in East Asia. Financial sector reform is approaching the top of the reform agenda in Africa and policy makers can learn from what went wrong in East Asia. Moreover, total external private finance might be small compared to other regions, but it is increasingly important and certainly large enough to trigger a financial crisis in some countries.

---

* Economic Affairs Officer, Developing Economies Section. The views expressed herein are those of the author and not necessarily the views of the United Nations. The author has benefited from the papers presented and discussions at the "Asia-Africa High-level Workshop on Advancing Financial Intermediation in Africa", held in Mauritius on 20-22 April 1998 and organized by the Office of the Special Coordinator for Africa and the Least Developed Countries of DESA in collaboration with the Government of Mauritius and the Special Unit for Technical Cooperation among Developing Countries of the United Nations Development Programme. The author wishes to thank Jorge Braga de Macedo, Ana Cortez, Barry Herman, Richard Morgan and Temitope W. Oshikoya for their comments and Ivy Lee for assistance with the figure.

The present paper is organized as follows. First, some theoretical issues regarding the role and nature of financial markets will be discussed in section 2. In the next section, features of the financial sector in Africa will be described. Section 3 will also address the state of domestic financial liberalization in Africa. The following section will move to the external side. Section 4 will first present some data on private capital flows to Africa and discuss the vulnerabilities associated with these flows that are peculiar to Africa. South Africa is used as an example. Some aspects of the financial crisis in East Asia are recounted in section 5. The final section presents some lessons that can be drawn from the previous sections.

2. On the nature and functioning of financial markets

Well-developed financial markets perform important functions in advanced capitalist economies. They mobilize savings and intermediate between savers and investors, select and allocate investments, monitor managers, enforce contracts, operate the payment system and transfer, share and pool risk (Hellmann and Murdock, 1997; Stiglitz, 1993, p. 23; Levine, 1997).

Market failures

All markets can fail but failures in financial markets and institutions are more pervasive and because of their crucial functions in an economy the effects of a crisis are more widespread. Thus, they are typically regulated. Indeed, financial markets are critically different from markets for goods. Banks are not butcher shops (Diaz-Alejandro, 1985). In financial markets, money is exchanged for a promise to repay. Banks want loans to be repaid, hence they do not lend to just anyone and they do not lend all that all customers want at the prevailing interest rate. The problem, called "asymmetric information", is that the bank does not know as much as the borrower about the capacity to repay. Thus, trust and the borrower-lender relation play a crucial role. Another key aspect of banking is that an investor who borrows part of the cost of his investment shares the risk of bankruptcy with the bank, but shares none of the profit after interest is paid. The greater the leverage available, the more attractive it is to undertake a high-risk venture, creating a "moral hazard" (excessive riskiness) potential. Also, if interest rates are high, it will crowd out the low-risk projects and banks will have higher risk portfolios whose overall expected returns will be sub-optimal (called "adverse selection"). Higher interest rates make moral hazard and adverse selection problems worse and banks thus do not raise interest rates as high as possible. Credit is therefore rationed and the market invariably imperfect (Stiglitz and Weiss, 1981; Stiglitz, 1993, pp. 29-30). Moreover, if a butcher fails, it will not have much of an effect on the rest of the economy; but when a bank fails, it can have economy-wide implications. This is because banks are repositories of information about their borrowers. When one bank lends to a particular borrower or sector, that sends a signal about its credit-worthiness to other lenders. A bank failure means that the information that the bank has about its borrowers would probably mostly disappear (Stiglitz, 1993, p. 26). Moreover, other banks might fail as well because of interbank lending and externalities of monitoring and selection. Monitoring and selection are thus public goods (Stiglitz, 1993). As a result, the credit supply and payment system of the economy could be severely disrupted, which is why regulators try to prevent bank failures.

Self-fulfilling prophecies and volatility

There is another way in which financial markets fundamentally differ from other markets: financial markets are subject to herd behaviour and are much more volatile than other markets. Financial market participants do not act upon true virtues of particular projects or upon the true value of assets (as they are unknown), but upon average opinion; i.e., a financial market participant needs to determine what everybody else believes. If everybody believes that a particular asset you own is overvalued, you will be wise to sell irrespective of whether you agree or not. Keynes (1936) compared this phenomenon to a beauty contest, popular in the 1930s, where the judges did not choose the person closest to his or her preference but ranked the contestants according to what they believed average opinion to be. This can lead to self-fulfilling prophecies and multiple equilibria. Average opinion, or confidence, can quickly change, inducing herd behaviour. Multiple equilibria create a sense of indeterminacy and rumours and sudden shifts in sentiments can quickly shift an economy from one equilibrium to another. The consequence is volatility. The equilibrium is not determined by real fundamentals to which the financial markets react but financial markets in part determine the equilibrium itself. The "true model" is not independent from financial markets. For example, if market participants believe that higher budget deficits will lead to higher interest rates, then that will be the case (Eatwell, 1997).

This implies that a crisis can be self-fulfilling as well. What is sustainable policy is itself a function of the self-fulfilling behaviour of financial markets. A rumour (as in South Africa; see below) can trigger a speculative attack that is unwarranted by economic fundamentals but that can create an unsustainable path that can lead to a crisis and is fuelled by self-fulfilling expectations. In a self-fulfilling speculative attack, previously sustainable policies become unsustainable only after the attack. The markets did not anticipate a crisis but provoked it. Economic events or fundamentals can play a role in triggering an attack but the "magnitude of the crisis is often incommensurate with any plausible change in fundamentals" (Rodrik, 1998, p. 58). The self-fulfilling character of attacks and multiple equilibria have played a central role in the second generation of speculative attack models, whereas the first generation had only emphasized policy inconsistencies as a trigger for an attack.[1]

Volatility and rapid shifts in sentiment are more frequent in emerging markets because of highly imperfect information as reporting and accounting systems are often inadequate (for example, on the external debt of Indonesia). Better information and more transparency will help but this cannot eliminate volatility. Stiglitz (1998b) compared better information to better navigation charts: they are useful but not everything. Indeed, all the crisis countries in Asia (Indonesia, the Republic of Korea, Malaysia, the Philippines and Thailand) as well as Hong Kong (China), subscribed to the Special Data Dissemination Standard of IMF during 1997. (However, existing information was not used by markets; the Bank for International Settlements, for example, warned about short-term debt in summer 1996 but banks lent anyway.) Africa in particular is vulnerable because of weak accounting and information and undeveloped telecommunications systems.

Financial liberalization increases risks because it increases the volatility of interest rates, asset prices and capital flows (Cornford and Brandon, 1998, p. 24). Banks face increased interest rate risk (when assets and liabilities are mismatched), liquidity risk and credit risk. Liquidity risk is likely to increase after liberalization because a bank might not be able to sell assets to raise cash as asset price volatility increases. Competition can mean that banks lend to more risky projects, especially if foreign banks can "cherry pick" the best credits. Credit risk is higher because the higher volatility in financial markets affects the creditworthiness of borrowers. Indeed, Demirgüc-Kunt and Detragiache (1998) provide evidence that a banking crisis is more likely in a liberalized financial environment.

Risks are also higher for countries because sudden capital inflows reversals can cause a balance-of-payments crisis and because disruptive effects of a banking crisis are larger in developing countries. Banking crises are often associated with external crises in developing countries but not as frequently in developed countries (compare, for example, the savings and loan crisis in the United States

1 See, for example, Tavlas (1996) and Sachs and others (1996) and other articles in the same issues of the *Open Economies Review* and the *Journal of International Economics*. Several articles in both issues are devoted to the Mexican currency crisis of 1994-95.

or the crises in the European Exchange Rate Mechanism in 1992 and 1994). Large capital inflows (as in East Asia) or large outflows can make the banking sector weaker and create a self-fulfilling crisis through its effect on the banking sector. Countries are particularly vulnerable to the negative effects of capital inflows if their banking system is unsound because they expose banks to exchange rate risk on top of other difficulties and they could lead to more risky lending or to the augmentation of moral hazard and adverse selection problems if interest rates increase as a result of the sterilization of capital inflows (Kasekende and others, p. 74). Moreover, if inflows reverse, the risk of a financial crisis is large with an unsound banking system (Schadler and others, 1993, p. 19).

The private sector and Governments need to develop capacity (for example, through hedging) to manage and monitor these higher risks, which are associated with a more liberal financial environment. (Increase in short-term, unhedged, foreign debt in East Asia was an important cause of the crisis. See below.) Moreover, in a more liberal environment with higher levels of risk, the capacity to regulate and supervise financial institutions becomes more important. Although risk can be managed, risk and uncertainty can never be eliminated. Moreover, the development of the institutions and capacity to manage these risks takes time and some humility with regard to the possibilities for risk management in Africa could be derived from the fact that even in North America only four out of the 64 largest banks practice state-of-the-art portfolio risk management (Rodrik, 1998, p. 59).

Financial liberalization

Given the market imperfections, the volatility, the higher risks and the possibilities of severe financial crises, one has to raise the questions of how and with what speed properly functioning financial markets can be established. There are two additional empirical regularities that should be considered in this regard. Firstly, several studies have shown that there is very little correlation between savings and interest rates (Clarke, 1996; Gibson and Tsakalotos, 1994; Giovanni, 1985; Muradoglu and Taskin, 1996; Mwega, 1997). This goes to the core of the traditional argument against interest rate controls that states that low or negative real interest rates discourage savings and therefore growth. The reasons for this low elasticity might be that the interest rate sensitive portion of deposits may be very small because the transaction demand for money dominates, bank branches are remote (and have a spatial monopoly) and because of large denominations of treasury bills (Roe and Sowa, 1997, p. 236). Indeed, for smallholder farmers, the intermediation function of the formal financial sector is largely irrelevant as a large portion of their savings *are* investments when, for example, saving occurs on the hoof. Higher interest rates have in some cases led to a shift of funds from informal to formal savings institutions, increasing measured savings, but leaving aggregate savings unchanged. Moreover, a switch to formal financial institutions reduces the amount of finance available to small producers and traders as they often lack access to formal credit. In addition, the formal sector is subject to reserve requirements, possibly diminishing the amount of total credit if the reserve multiplier is small. Moreover, the evidence on the relation between interest rates and investment is mixed. There is research that shows that once real rates are positive there is no effect on investment (Hellmann and Murdock, 1997, p. 299).

Secondly, there is substantial evidence that most investment is financed by retained earnings and very little investment is financed through equity and bond issues, although institutional and historical factors have to be taken into account to explain some of the variation across countries (Athey and Laumas, 1994; Collier, 1994; Jenkins, 1998; Shafik, 1992; Singh, 1995; Stiglitz, 1993). In Africa in particular, investment is largely financed by retained earnings because most firms lack reputation and trust with financial institutions. Moreover, bank lending is on the basis of the break-up value of the firm (not resale value) because banks in Africa generally don't have the skills to manage the firms and the private sector is too small to buy the firm in case of failure (Collier, 1994, pp. 228-229).

Given these arguments and evidence, one can have some doubts about the benefits of financial liberalization. The arguments in favour of financial liberalization are largely based on the analogy between goods and financial markets. This analogy, however, is deceptive because goods markets are not subject to asymmetric information, herd behaviour and external effects to the same extent (if at all) as financial markets. The benefits of liberalization can thus, not as quickly be assumed or concluded in the case of financial markets as in the case of goods markets (Bhagwati, 1998; Rodrik, 1998; Stiglitz, 1993). One researcher argued that "financial market liberalisation is at the disappointing end of the spectrum of market liberalisations... That is, the eventual gains are not as large as commonly supposed, the period of transition is likely to be very long, and the short-term effects may well be negative, especially when financial liberalisation is combined with liberalisations in other markets." (Collier, 1994, p. 226).

It is, therefore, not surprising that the evidence on the relation between financial development and economic growth is mixed. Some studies show that certain indicators of financial development are correlated with economic growth but most studies rely on cross-section analysis, which is criticized because it does not account for institutional differences. Moreover, most researchers agree that the evidence so far does not resolve the direction of causality, nor does it prescribe the beneficial effects of particular patterns of financial development or financial structure (Arestis and Demetriades, 1997; Demetriades and Hussein, 1996; Levine, 1997, pp. 703-710, 715-720; Montiel, 1996). Indeed, "we do not have a sufficiently rigorous understanding of the emergence, development, and economic implications of different financial structures." (Levine, 1997, p. 702).

Yet, the financial sector plays a critical role in a market-based economy. And the development of the financial sector should be an important part of a development strategy. The question is how to reach that stage of development where the financial sector is sound, well-developed and regulated so that it can perform its functions with the minimum number of crises. The seminal studies of McKinnon (1973) and Shaw (1973) on financial development emphasized the distortions created by Governments, particularly through interest rate controls. Such a regime became known as financial repression. Subsequently, the policies have almost entirely focused on liberalization, particularly of interest rates, with scant references to institutional developments. However, the focus on the interest rate is misguided, as the discussion above indicates. Indeed, it can be argued that it is not the intermediation function and the role the interest rate plays in performing that function that is most important, but rather, the other functions. Financial sector reforms if accompanied by proper regulation and supervision might have a more important effect on the efficiency of investment rather than its volume.

3. The financial sector in Africa

Weak financial sector

The financial sector in nearly all African countries is rather underdeveloped, weak and dualistic with a concentrated banking sector and a large informal sector (Soyibo, 1997). The major exception is South Africa, which has a very advanced and diversified financial sector. Indeed, the capital of the 12 largest South African banks accounts for 72 per cent of the 100 largest banks in sub-Saharan Africa (*The Banker*, December 1997).[2] The financial sectors in Côte d'Ivoire, Ghana, Kenya, Mauritius, Nigeria, Zimbabwe and northern Africa are also more advanced than in other African countries, but certain weaknesses, such as an oligopolistic banking sector and an immature capital market, remain. In Egypt, for example, the four largest banks, which are publicly

2 Capital of the 28 largest banks in northern Africa is about equal to that of the dozen largest banks in South Africa, $7.8 and $7.5 billion, respectively. See *The Banker*, November 1997.

owned, account for 70 per cent of commercial bank assets, 68 per cent of loans and 60 per cent of deposits.

In almost all African countries, the formal financial sector is dominated by a small number of commercial banks which are still often state-owned or controlled by the Government and mostly located in urban areas. The banking sector is thus highly monopolistic or oligopolistic. Indeed, there is evidence of collusion among banks in, for example, Tunisia and Zimbabwe (Moore, 1991, p. 78; Ncube and Senbet, 1997, p. 80). Within the banking sector, development banks, often state-owned as well, have a prominent position. Development banks have been used to direct credit to specific sectors and have been largely financed by Governments or by foreign donors.

The non-bank financial sector is dominated by insurance companies but is mostly small or non-existent outside of northern Africa and such countries as Mauritius and South Africa. There are currently only 18 stock exchanges in Africa, all very small except in South Africa which has the fourth largest stock exchange (as measured by capitalization) in the developing world (see table 1). Several new stock exchanges have been established since 1989 and a number are in the process of being established (for example, in Algeria and Cape Verde) and other countries consider the establishment of a stock exchange. The stock exchange of Côte d'Ivoire was transformed in 1998 into a regional stock exchange (Bourse Régionale des Valeurs Mobilières) for seven members of the Union Économique et Monétaire Ouest-Africaine (Benin, Burkina Faso, Côte d'Ivoire, Mali, Niger, Senegal and Togo). The participation of Guinea-Bissau, which only joined the Union in 1997, has been postponed because of political turmoil. The Union is particularly suited for a regional stock exchange because members share a currency, the CFA franc. A number of nearly dormant stock exchanges have in recent years gained new momentum as a result of privatization programmes, for example, in Egypt, but they remain shallow and illiquid with concentrated ownership (which also is the case in South Africa) and high transaction costs. For example, only three countries had in 1997 more than 100 companies listed and turnover ratios are mostly below 10, compared to 8851 and 90, respectively, in the United States[3] (see table 1).

Another aspect of the financial sector is the importance of the informal financial institutions. Informal financial institutions are rather vital, particularly in rural areas because of limited access to formal institutions, institutional barriers to formal credit, such as lack of collateral, and the higher flexibility. The informal financial sector is very heterogeneous with several different kind of

3 Combined data for NASDAQ, New York (NYSE) and American Stock Exchange.

Table 1. Stock exchanges in Africa
(ranked by capitalization)

	Year established[a]	*Capitalization ($ billions) end-1997*	*Number of stocks end-1997*	*Turnover ratio*[b] *1997*
South Africa	1887	232.1	642	18.3
Sudan[c]	1995	43.5	34	8.0
Egypt	1883	20.8	650	33.5
Morocco	1929	12.2	49	10.2
Tunisia	1969	2.3	34	8.3
Zimbabwe	1947	1.9	64	17.1
Nigeria	1960	3.6	182	3.9
Kenya	1954	1.8	58	5.7
Mauritius	1989	1.7	40	8.2
Swaziland	1990	0.1	4	122.7
Ghana	1990	1.1	21	3.7
Côte d'Ivoire	1974/76	1.3	35	2.3
Namibia	1992	0.7	13	4.0
Botswana	1989	0.6	12	12.3
Zambia	1994	0.7	6	1.8
Malawi[d]	1995/96	0.02	1	
Uganda	1997		0	
Tanzania	1998			

Sources: IFC (1998) and *African Stock Exchanges Handbook 1997.*

a The first year refers to year of establishment and the second to the year trading started.
b Traded value as a percentage of market capitalization.
c Data refer to 1995.
d Data refer to 1996.

participants but a common element is that they are deposit taking and/or lending resources and are not legally licensed or registered and are outside direct control of monetary authorities. Generally, informal financial institutions such as Rotating Savings and Credit Associations (ROSCAs) and other group-based associations are flexible, based on personal relations and have low fixed and variable costs and a narrow geographical base. On the other hand, there are also semi-formal institutions that do not mobilize savings but give small loans (microfinance) and are funded by Governments and donors. They are better defined and generally are registered, directly controlled by monetary authorities, moderately flexible, based on relatively impersonal relations, more complex and have moderate fixed and variable costs and a broader geographical base.

Perhaps most importantly, the institutional framework of the African financial sector is very weak and this has contributed to its poor performance.

The accounting and legal framework is in several countries inadequate and there is a dearth of professionals such as accountants, regulators, supervisors and managers. Accounting standards, rules for loan classification and loan-loss provisions and reporting and disclosure requirements in some countries do not even exist. Another handicap is the fact that the financial press is also underdeveloped in most African countries.

> Government inspection and supervision of banks is grossly inadequate. Indeed, supervision is essentially non-existent in countries where the banking system has been nationalized. Even in countries with nominally private banks, there may be a conflict of interest because members of the supervisory agencies often sit on the boards of the banking institutions. In most instances, prudential ratios have been ineffective in preventing the degradation of loan portfolios. The ratios sometimes were poorly designed, and banks sometimes lacked rules for classifying credit according to risk and for defining and handling loans. Not surprisingly, adjustment under such conditions has been slow and difficult. (World Bank, 1994, pp. 113-114).

To exemplify the dearth of information, when *The Banker* published surveys of 100 banks in sub-Saharan Africa and 28 banks in northern Africa in November and December 1997, a BIS capital adequacy ratio was available only for 17 banks in sub-Saharan Africa and 2 in northern Africa if Egypt, Mauritius, Nigeria and South Africa are excluded.[4]

Weak supervision and regulation and lack of professionals also had its counterpart at the level of the financial institutions. Banks often suffered from inadequate expertise to screen and monitor borrowers and from poor loan documentation and internal controls (Brownbridge, 1998). Moreover, in some countries insider lending was a major contributor to bank failures (Brownbridge, 1998). Politicians who were shareholders or directors often received loans in return for deposits from parastatals or other favours. Political connections were also used to obtain banks licences or prevent action by regulators, reducing constraints to imprudent lending and worsening moral hazard problems.

The performance of the financial sector in Africa has been hindered by a number of additional factors. Firstly, the poor economic performance in most of Africa since the late 1970s has affected the financial sector as well. The commodity boom of the 1970s led to an investment boom in several countries but the slow growth that followed in the 1980s and early 1990s limited the returns to

4 The BIS ratio was published for 28 banks in Mauritius, Nigeria and South Africa (4, 18, and 6, respectively) and 7 banks in Egypt.

investment and increased the number of non-performing loans. If banks borrowed abroad—often to sustain the investment boom after commodity prices declined—they were also affected by the higher interest rates of the early 1980s. Moreover, since some of the liabilities were in foreign currencies, these banks suffered when exchange rates depreciated (United Nations, 1995). Secondly, macroeconomic instability has had negative effects on the financial sector. High and volatile inflation rates have discouraged savings and generated large windfall gains and losses, transfers that are unrelated to improving efficiency (Collier, 1994; Seck and El Nil, 1994). High budget deficits, which have partly been financed by borrowing from the central bank, have often fueled inflation. Budget deficits have also been funded by borrowing from banks with negative effects on their soundness. Yet, high growth and low inflation rates are no guarantee for a sound banking system, as the crisis in East Asia has shown. Thirdly, although directed credit programmes and other government intervention have worked under certain circumstances in, for example, East Asia,[5] they have in several cases in Africa contributed to poor performance among banks. Government-directed lending to state-owned enterprises, which have been running losses, have, for example, led to a large number of non-performing loans.

Africa thus suffered several banking crises. Since the early 1980s, 40 countries faced a significant or serious banking problem of which 11 were classified as a crisis and 32 spilled over into or started in the 1990s. The bulk of the problematic banks were confronted with very high shares—some over 90 per cent—of non-performing loans. Recent banking crises occurred in Kenya, Nigeria, Zambia and Zimbabwe in 1998, 1994-98, 1995-96 and 1998, respectively.

Financial sector reforms

Banking crises and poor performance of the financial sector put financial reforms on the adjustment agenda. Financial sector reforms started in most countries not before the late 1980s and progressed slowly and with limited results. Reforms in the financial sector in most countries were first aimed at establishing positive real interest rates. The liberalization of interest rates in many cases did not result in positive real interest rates and led to larger spreads between lending and deposit rates—because of the existence of monopolistic banks, for example, in Kenya, Madagascar and Malawi—and high volatility in

5 In general, success of directed credit depends on whether targets are well-defined (for example, in terms of exports or productivity growth), rigorous monitoring, non-discretionary rules (i.e., no political interference) and whether the capital market is closed (otherwise capital might flee the country) (Hellmann and Murdock, 1997, pp. 310-12; Stiglitz, 1993; United Nations, 1996, pp. 103-108).

nominal and real interest rates in some countries (Collier, 1994; Montiel, 1996; Pill and Pradhan, 1997). The high and volatile interest rates have been partly a result of macroeconomic instability. In Ghana, Kenya, Nigeria, Zambia and Zimbabwe, for example, inflation and budget deficits were not under control when interest rates were liberalized. High interest rates followed their liberalization in these countries, making budget deficits even worse as they have been partly domestically financed. Real interest rates in Ghana, Kenya, Nigeria, Zambia and Zimbabwe reached double digits at one point and stifled investment and purchases of output and intermediate inputs, drove up debt-servicing costs for the Government and caused bankruptcies in some cases. In sum, liberalization of interest rates has often failed to reach its primary aim: the generation of more savings and investment.

After interest rate liberalizations, other reforms have come to the fore. In such countries as Benin, Burkina Faso, Cameroon, Egypt, Ghana, Kenya, Mauritania, Morocco and Senegal, the supervisory role of the central bank has been strengthened, regulation improved, many banks have been recapitalized, restructured and/or privatized, many insolvent banks have been liquidated and institutions to take over non-performing loans have been created (see, for example, World Bank, 1994, pp. 110-120; African Development Bank, 1997, p. 129; *West Africa*, 22 December 1997-11 January 1998). Algeria, Botswana, the Gambia, Kenya, Madagascar, Mozambique, Niger, Nigeria, Tanzania and Uganda also have recently undertaken bank reforms. Recapitalization of banks has, however, often failed as banks continue to suffer losses and has been very expensive, amounting in Mauritania to nearly 15 per cent of GDP. The performance of privatized banks has also not been satisfactory (World Bank, 1994, pp. 116-117). Continuing poor performance of banks can be partly attributed to weak economic performance, lack of skilled professionals and inadequate regulation and supervision.

During the 1980s, financial reforms usually neglected regulatory issues (World Bank, 1994, p. 118). In several countries checks on expertise were loose and minimum capital requirements were low, partly because they were not raised in line with inflation. Low entry barriers and profit opportunities in newly created or liberalized foreign-exchange or treasury-bill markets led to an increase in the number of banks.[6] However, low entry barriers without adequate prudential regulation and supervision has contributed to banking crises in Kenya, Nigeria, Uganda, Zambia and Zimbabwe (Brownbridge, 1998). In Nigeria, deregulation allowed the number of banks to increase

6 The number of commercial banks in 28 sub-Saharan countries rose from 213 to 245 between 1982 and 1992 with the percentage of banks without government participation rising from 28 to 47 per cent (World Bank, 1994, p. 119).

from 26 in 1980 to 120 in 1991. Many of these banks were established with little capital and a small deposit base and they were mainly active in the profitable foreign exchange market. The rise was halted by the ban on new merchant and commercial banks, issued by the central bank in mid-1991. By the end of 1994, the Nigerian Deposit Insurance Corporation estimated that 40 per cent of loans were non-performing. In early 1995, the central bank issued licences to only 68 banks but many banks have continued to suffer from insolvency problems (Lewis and Stein, 1997). In early 1998, 26 banks were liquidated after they were not able to recapitalize; but 23 are still categorized as "distressed" and need to recapitalize by the end of 1998. A similar process occurred in Kenya. A rapid increase in financial institutions, often established with very little capital, did not contribute to a healthy financial sector. In Kenya—as in Nigeria—lack of supervision by the central bank allowed many banks to lend to the owners or their friends, leading to the term "political banks" in Kenya. Whereas in Nigeria the foreign exchange market provided windfall profits, in Kenya it has been the market for treasury bills with very high real interest rates which boosted profits—at the expense of lending for investment. Provisions for loan losses have, however, been poor and some 33 banks have failed since 1984, among them a number of "political banks". In 1994, central bank supervision was tightened in Kenya, after a corruption scandal in which the central bank was defrauded of $230 million, and in 1998 new rules to curb insider lending were issued. Nonetheless, the 1996 Annual Supervision Report of the Central Bank of Kenya classified only nine out of 50 banks as "strong" and the 1997 Report only seven out of 53. In the middle of 1998 the Central Bank warned that 14 non-bank financial institutions and 26 of the 53 commercial banks face the risk of closure in 1999 when new minimum capital requirements come into effect. And more banks are likely to fail when interest rates on treasury bills come down (Collier, 1994; Ngugi and Kabubo, 1998; Steel and others, 1997, p. 826; *Financial Times*, African Banking and Development Survey, 2 June 1998).

The number of banks has continued to increase in Africa in the 1990s, partly owing to foreign investment (see, for example, *West Africa*, 18-31 May 1998). The most extreme case is South Africa where 10 foreign banks established subsidiaries, 9 operated new branches and 59 opened representative offices between the end of apartheid in 1994 and December 1997 (*Financial Times*, African Banking and Development Survey, 2 June 1998). On top of that, South African banks have been investing heavily in other African countries since 1994.

The increase in the number of banks is usually regarded as positive. More banks might increase the availability of credit and foreign banks are an important source of skills, capital and technology. However, more banks can also mean that the higher level of competition pushes banks into risky lending or reduces lending rates and profit margins, making banks weaker (see section 2).[7] It appears that this has happened in a number of African countries. Liberalization and deregulation led to a rapid increase in the number of financial institutions in countries such as Kenya, Nigeria and Zimbabwe, causing these countries to be "overbanked". This has led to competition that has weakened the financial sector.

There are particular arguments in favour of restrictions on foreign banks. Stiglitz (1993) listed three. Firstly, the public can have more confidence in foreign banks that is not necessarily warranted but that leads to a shift of deposits from domestic to foreign banks or high deposit rates in local banks.[8] Smaller deposits and high deposit rates in local banks have caused high-cost interbank borrowing and risky lending in a number of African countries (Brownbridge, 1998). Secondly, foreign banks lend mostly to multinational corporations because of an informational disadvantage they face with regard to domestic firms. Thirdly, authorities have less leverage over foreign banks because a Government can only close branches but not the whole bank.

In the 1990s, more attention has been paid to strengthening the skills to manage, supervise and regulate banks. But this is a slow process and much remains to be done. The building of capacity (public and private) to manage risk and payment systems and the creation of regulatory and accounting systems takes time. For example, a senior member of the Basel Committee on Banking Supervision has said that it takes as much as a decade to train banking supervisors (Cornford and Brandon, 1998). Nonetheless, progress is being made. The strengthening of supervision and regulation in recent years in several African countries—although uneven—is a positive sign. For example, supervision, regulation and legal frameworks have been strengthened in Algeria, Egypt, Ghana, Kenya, Madagascar, Morocco, Mauritania, Tunisia and the franc zone (World Bank, 1994, p. 119). In the franc zone, two regional supranational supervisory banking commissions, which are separate but subordinate to the two

7 Claessens and others (1998) present evidence that entry of foreign banks reduces bank profits in developing countries.

8 In Indonesia, for example, the deposit rate of foreign banks was 12 per cent while the rate at domestic banks was 32 per cent at one point during the crisis but domestic banks, nonetheless, received little deposits. See also *Financial Times* (African Banking and Development Survey, 2 June 1998) on a similar phenomenon in Zimbabwe.

central banks and have jurisdiction in each country, were created and began operations in 1990 in the western part of the franc zone and in 1992 in the central part (Clément and others, 1996, p. 78). Yet, concerns remain even in countries where supervision has recently been strengthened, such as Côte d'Ivoire and Tunisia.

In sum, the financial reforms in Africa have yielded disappointing results, partly because insufficient attention has been paid to the structural constraints (Aryeetey, 1997b; Collier, 1994; Montiel, 1996; Pill and Pradhan, 1995, 1997; World Bank, 1994). The characteristics of financial markets, such as high administrative and transaction costs compared to loan size, lack of collateral and the difficulties banks have in assessing credit risk, have precluded an increase in bank lending for investment as a result of financial liberalization in Africa (Collier, 1994; Steel and others, 1997). Moreover, financial liberalization did not lead to enhanced financial deepening and improved credit allocation in cases where non-performing loans have taken up a large share of the loan portfolio and where insider lending and government interference have persisted.

The financial sector in Africa remains underdeveloped and several structural and institutional weaknesses remain. Particular attention needs to be paid to the speed and sequencing of the financial sector reforms (Hellmann and Murdock, 1993; Stiglitz, 1993). An early and quick interest rate liberalization can have negative effects, especially when macroeconomic stability has not yet been achieved. Privatization and deregulation of the banking sector without adequate supervision and prudential regulation can be a disaster and supervision and regulation remain inadequate in several countries. Another concern is the early push to establish stock exchanges. Their role is often overstated. Stock exchanges are volatile, are focused on the short-term, provide generally little financing of investment and have limited monitoring capacity if ownership is diversified (Harris, 1997; Jefferis, 1995; Singh, 1997; Singh and Weisse, 1998). (See Kenny and Moss (1998) for a more positive view.) Finally, restructuring and regulating the banking sector so as to increase competition among banks without increasing risks need careful study.

The case of Tunisia

The intricacies of financial sector reforms can be illustrated by the case of Tunisia.[9] Until the early 1980s, the volume and direction of credit and interest rates were very much under the control of the Government. For example, banks were required to lend 43 per cent of their total deposits (excluding foreign

9 This section is partly based on United Nations (1996, pp. 159-164).

currency deposits of non-residents and convertible dinar deposits) in the form of medium- and long-term loans—25 per cent in public sector bonds and 18 per cent for the private sector and certain public enterprises. In addition to government policy, credit allocation was also influenced by personal relations and other non-market phenomena. Moreover, credit was controlled through ceilings on rediscounting. However, credit for certain activities, such as export financing, was not limited. Interest rates were subsidized through either the Government's budget or the preferential rediscount window of the Central Bank.

Tunisia has had a rather well-developed banking system[10] and aside from retained earnings, finance for investment came mainly from commercial banks during the 1960s and 1970s. Up to the mid-1980s, banks were able to remain profitable partly because the rediscount rate of the Central Bank was lower than the lending rate. But profitability decreased between the mid-1970s and the early 1980s (Nabli and Nugent, 1989). Banks had suffered from negative real interest rates, controls on asset composition and credit and, according to one estimate, non-performing loans amounted to 20 per cent of their collective portfolio at the end of 1988 (Moore, 1991, p. 77).

Liberalization of the financial sector started in the early 1980s but reforms only became comprehensive with the structural adjustment programme of 1986. Indeed, the programme focused on the financial sector. Already in January 1987, interest rates were partially liberalized—although banks, brought together under the *Association Professionelle de Banques*, immediately colluded to fix interest rates. About a year later, the prior approval requirements for loans and for rediscounting and all the refinancing facilities, except for priority sectors, were abolished. Preferential interest rates were increased and the number of activities eligible for preferential credit was reduced in 1990 and 1992. By the end of 1992, only 10 per cent of total credit was granted at the preferential rate. By 1997, financial reforms had significantly progressed with the introduction of several new financial instruments since 1988; the issuance of new prudential regulation and the strengthening of Central Bank supervision in 1991; the requirement that all banks meet the BIS capital adequacy ratios by 1999; the opening of the banking sector to foreign banks since 1986; the adoption of a new banking law in 1994 which established the legal basis for investment banks, credit institutions and deposit insurance and increased the competition between

10 In 1956, Tunisia counted 79 bank branches which increased to 100 in 1970 and 496 in 1988 (Moore, 1991, p. 87). In 1998, the banking system consisted of 12 commercial banks of which five are, at least partly, publicly owned and these five control about 70 per cent of total bank assets. In addition, there were eight development banks, all public, eight offshore banks, a savings bank, a merchant bank and offices representing foreign banks.

development and commercial banks; the end of the obligation for banks to hold treasury bills in 1994; the removal of the cap on the spread of lending rates over the money market rate in 1994; and the elimination of obligatory sectoral lending ratios and the associated preferential interest rates for priority sectors in late 1996. Bank restructuring and recapitalization is still going on and in early 1998 two banks, a commercial and a development bank, both controlled by the Government, merged. The Government took over non-performing loans to public enterprises and has signed performance contracts with the public banks, which still dominate the banking sector (Jbili and others, 1997).

It is perhaps too early to assess the full impact of the financial sector reforms. Nonetheless, some observations are warranted. Firstly, lending rates do not seem to have had a major impact on investment as both have increased since 1987. Secondly, the extension of domestic credit to the private sector increased rapidly between 1986 and 1997 but it decreased from 55 per cent of GDP in 1986 to 50 per cent in 1997. Moreover, the share of total loans going to public enterprises basically remained the same. This share was 17 per cent in 1989 and 16 per cent in 1993.[11] Thirdly, the profitability and operating costs of banks for the period 1987-1993 are broadly in line with banks in the developed countries. Fourthly, competition in banking remains limited in part because of explicit understandings between banks to limit competition on interest rates. Fifthly, the stock exchange and the market for government paper are still rather illiquid, hindering open market operations. Finally, there is a danger that the liberalization of the financial sector will negatively affect the amount of credit lent to small- and medium-sized enterprises. Hence, publicly supported funds and other institutions will continue to play an important role in providing financing for such enterprises as they lack access to formal credit.[12] Indeed, the Government plans to establish a new bank, Banque Tunisienne de Solidarité, to this purpose.

4. Private capital flows to Africa

As domestic financial liberalization is a recent phenomenon in Africa, external financial liberalization is even more recent and remains very limited. Different kinds of capital controls for external finance are in force in

11 The definition of public enterprises was changed in 1989. Hence no comparison is possible with data before 1989. The IMF doesn't publish data on credit to public enterprises after 1993.

12 According to a recent survey, the *Fonds National pour la Promotion de l'Artisanat et des Petits Métiers* provided the bulk of the formal finance of micro-enterprises, amounting to 8.6 per cent of total finance. Self-financing and loans from family or friends accounted for 91 per cent of total finance. See Morrison and others (1994).

most countries. According to IMF (1997b), nearly all African countries have controls on at least eight out of the 10 different categories of capital transactions it distinguished.[13] Yet, the capital account is becoming more and more liberalized. For example, foreign ownership of stocks has been liberalized in a number of countries. At the end of 1997, listed stocks are freely available to foreigners in Botswana, Côte d'Ivoire, Egypt, Ghana, Mauritius, Namibia, Nigeria, South Africa and Zambia and relatively free in Kenya and Zimbabwe. In all these countries repatriation of income and capital was free at the end of 1997 (IFC, 1997, 1998). Moreover, foreigners could generally own 100 per cent of a company in Côte d'Ivoire, Egypt, Mauritius (except for sugar companies), Morocco, Nigeria and South Africa. Foreigners could own 74 per cent of the stocks in Ghana and between 40 and 49 per cent in Botswana, Kenya, Tunisia and Zimbabwe (IFC, 1998). Furthermore, in order to attract foreign direct investment (FDI), many African countries have recently revised their investment codes and signed bilateral treaties which include tax and tariff incentives, allow for the repatriation of profits and provide for fair and equitable treatment and ownership guarantees (UNCTAD, 1995). As of 1 January 1997, about 300 bilateral investment treaties had been signed by African countries (UNCTAD, 1997).

This more liberal environment has not remained unnoticed. At least 19 investment funds oriented on Africa have been established since 1992 when there were none. Indeed, foreign portfolio investment (FPI) is the fastest growing component of private capital flows to Africa. Portfolio equity flows increased from zero in 1992 (excluding South Africa) to $5 billion in 1995. They declined to $3.5 billion in 1996 but increased probably to about $6 billion in 1997 as the region was not much affected by the contagion from the financial crisis in East Asia (see figure 1 and annex table 1). The bulk of the foreign equity investments, however, has gone to South Africa with the rest concentrated in Egypt (since 1996), Ghana (in 1994), Mauritius and Morocco. Foreign investments in African bonds turned positive in 1994 and amounted to about $1 billion per year in the period 1994 to 1996, but probably reached about $4 billion in 1997. Egypt, Mauritius, Morocco, South Africa and Tunisia have been particularly active on the international bond market. The contagion of the crisis in East Asia did not affect the bond market much either in 1997, except for a relatively minor outflow from South Africa in October 1997. This,

13 The exceptions are Democratic Republic of the Congo (which has 6), Djibouti (none), Egypt (4), the Gambia (one), Ghana (7), Kenya (5), Liberia (none), Mauritius (1), Uganda (7) and Zambia (none). However, for some countries information is incomplete. If there is no information, it is assumed that a control is in place.

however, changed in May 1998 when foreign investors suddenly became net sellers of South African bonds (see below).

Foreign direct investment in Africa has also increased in the 1990s and reached about $4.5 billion in 1997 (see figure 1 and annex table 1). Yet, Africa's share in total developing country FDI has declined. FDI has partly responded to opportunities created by steadily expanding privatization programmes and favourable investment regimes, particularly for the mining sector. The concentration of FDI, geographically and by sector, has declined in the 1990s but continues to be rather high. Seven countries (Angola, Egypt, Ghana, Morocco, Nigeria, South Africa and Tunisia) accounted for about 70 per cent of the FDI inflows in 1996 and 1997. FDI in energy and mining continues to be important but FDI in manufacturing (for example, in electronics and automobiles) and tourism has increased in recent years in a number of African countries, such as Botswana, Namibia and Mozambique. Because the mining and especially the energy sector is rather isolated geographically in such countries as Algeria and Angola, they continued to receive FDI even when politically unstable. South Africa has also enjoyed higher levels of foreign direct investment inflows since the end of apartheid in 1994, amounting to about $4 billion, but only 18 per cent has been "greenfield" foreign investment.

Figure 1. Private net resource flows to Africa
(Billions of US dollars)

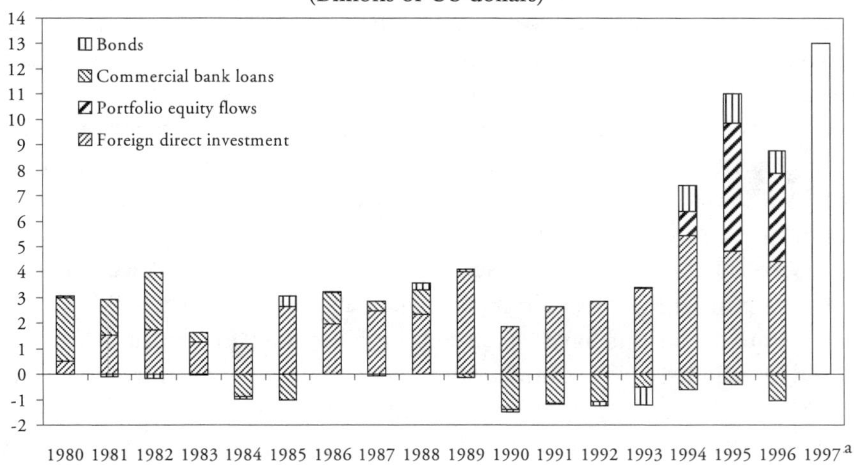

Source: Annex table 1.

Note: Totals for Africa exclude South Africa for 1980 to 1993 (except for FDI).

a Preliminary estimate, decomposition unavailable.

One interesting recent trend is the emergence of Asian foreign direct investment in Africa, which has increased rapidly in the 1990s. FDI from five Asian countries amounted to at least $541 million between 1990 and 1996 (UNCTAD, 1997, p. 63). Some major direct investments from Asia were announced in 1997 but the financial crises in East Asia might put some of these plans in jeopardy.[14]

Access to international bank loans is also highly concentrated, with Algeria, Angola, Côte d'Ivoire, Morocco, South Africa, Tunisia and Zimbabwe accounting for the bulk of the disbursement. However, the net resource flow (disbursement minus principal repayments) has been negative since 1989 (see figure 1 and annex table 1).

Vulnerability

Africa is particularly vulnerable to the negative effects of capital inflows for a number of reasons. Firstly, for a proper policy response it is essential to identify the size, character, sustainability and causes of the capital inflows (Ul Haque and others, 1997). This is, however, particularly difficult in Africa because recording mechanisms are frequently inadequate (Kasekende and others, 1997, pp. 60-61, 75). Moreover, financial markets are generally not well developed in Africa—as discussed above—which would, if they were more developed, usually give some indications about the causes underlying the capital inflows. It is, for example, in several African countries difficult to separate private transfers from capital flows or to separate foreign direct investment from portfolio investment when companies are privatized through a stock exchange (Kregel, 1996). Indeed, without knowledge about the size, character, sustainability and causes of the capital inflows, the appropriate policy response is not clear and there is a risk of taking inappropriate measures that would exacerbate the negative effects associated with capital inflows (Kasekende and others, 1997, p. 78). It is thus essential that institutions are developed before the capital account is liberalized.

Secondly, the number of instruments available to most African Governments is more limited than in many other developing countries. Many African countries do not have a well-developed market for treasury bills that could be used to sterilize capital inflows. A number of African countries have established markets for treasury bills in recent years but they remain thin and volatile and subject to manipulation. Moreover, using supplementary

14 For example, a bank from Malaysia that bought part of a privatized Ugandan bank was granted a payment extension after the financial crisis hit Malaysia.

measures to sterilize, such as foreign exchange swaps[15] or the forward exchange market,[16] are even less frequently within the realm of possibilities.[17] The size of the fiscal deficit in a number of African countries makes sterilization also problematic because sterilization can push up domestic interest rates, causing significant budgetary implications. Finally, the poor enforcement of taxes and controls on capital flows makes these instruments less effective (Kasekende and others, 1997, pp. 75-79).

Thirdly, Africa suffers from a bias towards short-term capital inflows because in many African countries the conditions to attract long-term capital, foreign direct investment in particular, are deficient. Determinants of FDI, such as infrastructure, skilled labour and the size of the domestic market, are often inadequate and take much longer to improve than macroeconomic stability and liberalizing markets which are determinants of both FDI and portfolio investment. Thus, when macroeconomic stability is established and markets are liberalized, portfolio investment might flow in but direct investment not because other conditions are not yet met. Indeed, capital flows to Africa have been particularly volatile because they have been associated with commodity prices, high real treasury bill interest rates in countries where macroeconomic stability had not been achieved (such as Kenya, Zambia and Zimbabwe) and because portfolio investments have accounted for an increasing share of capital inflows in recent years, as described above, which has made countries more vulnerable (Kasekende and others, 1997, pp. 68, 70).[18]

The case of South Africa

To illustrate the vulnerability that African countries face, South Africa can be used as an example. South Africa has faced a currency crisis two times in the past two years, one during 1996 and another between May and August 1998. In

---

15 Capital inflows could be sterilized by a foreign exchange swap when the central bank sells foreign exchange to domestic banks against domestic currency and buys it back at an agreed date using the forward exchange market (Lee, 1997, p. 8).

16 The central bank can make capital outflows more attractive by intervening in the forward exchange market, allowing hedging at a favourable rate for domestic investors (Lee, 1997, p. 10).

17 As an illustration, there are 21 banks in Uganda which could participate in the interbank foreign exchange market but only one bank has a professional foreign exchange dealer and even in that bank staffing levels are too low to allow a proper participation in the market (Collier, 1997, p. 659).

18 Volatility is even higher if private transfers are considered part of the capital flows. Large amounts of capital inflows are actually misrecorded as private transfers (Kasekende and others, 1997, pp. 61, 70).

February 1996, the exchange rate fell suddenly. The fall was initially triggered by rumours about the health of the President, by a study stating that the exchange rate was 7 to 10 per cent overvalued[19] and by the expectation that the end of foreign exchange controls was imminent. A fall in capital inflows from abroad and intervention in the foreign exchange market led to a decline in the foreign exchange reserves of $1.9 billion between the end of 1995 and May 1996. However, downward pressure on the exchange rate continued during the rest of the year, even after the initial triggers were either falsified or corrected, as a result of perceived policy uncertainties, fear for renewed political instability and speculation. The raising of the discount interest rate twice during 1996 did not stem the tide.

The events in South Africa show that a speculative attack triggered by non- or relatively minor economic events and unwarranted by economic fundamentals can create an unsustainable path, fuelled by self-fulfilling expectations as described in section 2. Indeed, economic fundamentals, such as those relating to growth, inflation and the fiscal and current-account deficits, were not unsustainable before the attack occurred in early 1996. The current-account deficit was in 1995 only 2.1 per cent of GDP and smaller in the second half of 1995 than in the first half. The consumer price inflation and the yield on long-term government bonds had declined quite sharply in the second half of 1995 as well. Moreover, credit growth and the public sector borrowing requirement decreased during 1995. The market for government bonds did not perceive economic fundamentals and policies as unsustainable. In fact, the spread between the South African bond yield and the United States yield declined by 2.5 percentage points between June 1995 and January 1996. Moreover, the net sales of bonds by foreigners followed the exchange rate depreciation rather than caused it.[20] Thus, markets did not think that economic fundamentals and policies were unsustainable.

During the course of 1996, there was some deterioration in economic indicators, partly as a result of the turmoil in the foreign exchange market. Yields on South African bonds increased, particularly during February, March and April. Inflation rose as well, partly as a result of the higher import prices caused by the depreciating exchange rate. With lower foreign exchange reserves and lower capital inflows, a smaller current account deficit became imperative.

The level of foreign exchange reserves was very low after intervention by the Reserve Bank, providing for less than 5 weeks of import cover. The Reserve Bank

19 During 1995, the exchange rate was generally considered to be overvalued, in part because of large capital inflows during 1995.

20 LSE Centre for Research into Economics and Finance in South Africa, *Quarterly Review*, July 1996.

was unable to defend the currency against a speculative attack and market participants were able to make a quick profit by selling foreign exchange short. The net inflow of capital, however, remained positive in 1996. R19.2 billion flowed into South Africa in 1995 and R3.9 billion in 1996, of which R3.3 billion in the last quarter of 1996. Fortunately, South Africa still had a number of exchange controls in place for residents, preventing them from substituting foreign for domestic assets. That is, insurers, pension funds and unit trusts, held nearly R600 billion ($138 billion) in securities and shares at the end of June 1996,[21] compared with $1 billion of foreign exchange reserves. If these institutional investors had only shifted one per cent of their assets, foreign exchange reserves would have been completely depleted. Indeed, domestic investors led the pack in the case of Mexico (Frankel and Schmukler, 1996).

It was only in January 1997 that the exchange rate started to appreciate significantly, anticipating government policy announcements and reacting to improved economic indicators. The most encouraging economic statistic was the declining current-account deficit in the second half of 1996—after peaking in the second quarter of 1996 at 2.7 per cent of GDP. This was particularly owing to a good export performance which had benefited from the depreciated exchange rate. Despite the fact that the annualized monthly inflation rate had increased since mid-1996, the inflation rate for 1996 was only 7.4 per cent, its lowest rate since 1972, as the impact of the depreciation was smaller than expected. The foreign exchange and bond markets also reacted positively to the presentation of the budget in March 1997, which relaxed some foreign exchange controls and forecast a declining deficit.

Between May and August 1998, another speculative attack on the exchange rate occurred, as speculators took advantage of the vulnerability of South Africa. When the financial crisis hit East Asia in 1997, South Africa was relatively free from the contagion effect and received record capital inflows (see annex table 1). But international financial-market participants had in general become more cautious in placing money in emerging markets and South Africa became a victim in 1998. Rumours again played a role, this time about the dismissal of the Reserve Bank governor, Reserve Bank intentions and an impending 20 per cent devaluation—all were incorrect. Economic fundamentals were again generally considered relatively sound and in the words of the

21 Most was domestically held because of the foreign exchange controls. At the end of 1995, the non-monetary private sector held less than R10 billion in foreign securities and shares. Since July 1995, South African institutions have been allowed to swap assets with foreign institutions in a partial liberalization of foreign exchange controls. As of early 1998, R77 billion had been approved by the Reserve Bank and R38 billion had been transacted.

Governor of the South African Reserve Bank, "Nothing of substance had ... changed in the fundamental domestic economic situation from April to May 1998" (*Financial Mail*, 31 August 1998). The banking system is sound, with only about 3 per cent of loans non-performing. Inflation was about 5 per cent and the current account deficit was 1.4 per cent of GDP in the first quarter of 1998. Yet, the current account deficit was mostly financed by portfolio investment and foreign exchange reserves were rather low. Moreover, the South African authorities were hesitant to raise interest rates as GDP growth was low and unemployment high. This left South Africa vulnerable, a situation easily exploited by international currency traders. Indeed, one, unnamed, hedge fund based in the United States has been blamed in the 1998 turmoil. Authorities had few options but to raise interest rates.

One conclusion from this case is that capital controls are in many cases essential to counter negative effects of international capital flows and might be one of the few instruments available in the case of a speculative attack on the exchange rate.

5. Financial crisis in East Asia

Much has been written about the sudden reversal of fortune in East Asia and economists will for a long time be analyzing the events that abruptly turned the cards. One of the intriguing questions is how these countries—for which prospects looked bright, according to nearly all analysts, and which had enjoyed high economic growth, low inflation and budget surpluses for such a long time—could so suddenly collapse. The answer to that question should partly be sought in developments in the financial sector.

As other papers in this book address in detail the causes and consequences of the financial crisis in Asia, it is sufficient here to summarize only some stylized facts. As a result, many differences between the crisis countries (Indonesia, the Republic of Korea, Malaysia, the Philippines and Thailand) and much country detail will be ignored.

The crisis in East Asia appears to have been caused by a number of coinciding factors.[22] Firstly, there were developments in the current account that played a role. The real exchange rate appreciated in several countries, resulting partly from capital inflows or from the appreciation of the dollar to which some currencies were pegged. This contributed to lower export growth and widening current account deficits. The decline in the growth of export earnings also resulted from

22 See, for example, Akyuz (1998); IMF (1997a, 1998); United Nations/ESCAP (1998); United Nations (1998); and Wade (1998).

slow GDP growth in Japan and a depreciating yen, making imports more expensive, and a decline in the terms of trade. The unification of the exchange rate and effective devaluation by China in 1994 might also have been a factor in reducing the relative competitiveness of the economies in East Asia, although its role is often overstated (United Nations, 1998, box III.1).

Secondly, several countries liberalized the financial sector and capital account rather quickly. This led to capital inflows and large increases in assets and liabilities in a few years, which stretched the capacity to manage these flows and the associated risks in the private and public sector. The capital inflows led to a growth in the number of banks and non-financial institutions and risky lending. Crucially, this growth occurred at a time that the capacity to supervise was inadequate and regulation outdated or not enforced. For instance, supervision of and regulations on the currency and maturity compositions of assets and liabilities were weak or abolished in some countries. The Republic of Korea, for example, had eliminated or eased in a few years many regulations, among them controls on external borrowing, partly as a requirement to join the Organisation for Economic Cooperation and Development (OECD) (Akyuz, 1998; Rodrik, 1998; Wade, 1998). And Thailand abolished limits on lending to the real estate sector (Stiglitz, 1998a). However, supervision and regulation have been stronger in Malaysia and the Philippines and they have fared better in the crisis (Farooq, 1998).

Typically, after deregulation, short-term borrowing abroad increased rapidly. This lending was considered relatively safe by foreign creditors as exchange rates were pegged. Moreover, there might also have been a moral hazard problem associated with government guarantees (implicit or explicit; too big to fail). For example, the legal framework for bankruptcy and foreclosure was inadequate in Thailand, which could be interpreted by creditors that the Government would bail the borrower out in case of insolvency. Borrowed funds were lent domestically in local currencies to long-term, risky projects, particularly in the real estate sector where an asset price bubble had been in the making. As short-term borrowing was unhedged, a burst of the bubble immediately caused a currency crisis.

Many factors that contributed to the crisis in East Asia have been mentioned but probably none alone is sufficient to explain the crisis. Even a combination of factors might not be sufficient. For example, the banking sector was weak in the 1980s and East Asia suffered from declining export revenues in the mid-1980s as well (Dowling, 1998). Yet, even if there were several factors that can be identified *ex ante*, why did nobody see disaster coming? If economic fundamentals cannot explain the crisis, the existence of self-fulfilling prophecies might have played a role in causing a financial crisis as explained in section 2.

A number of lessons can be drawn from the financial crisis in East Asia. Capital inflows can add to the resources available for investment and relieve a balance-of-payments constraint. However, East Asian economies did not seem to have a lack of resources for investment with savings rates generally above 30 per cent of GDP. Financial liberalization allowed an increase of capital flows to East Asia, helping to finance current account deficits. But the capital inflows and their uses were poorly monitored, supervised and regulated. Overborrowing and risky lending went unnoticed and unregulated. Inadequate supervision and regulation—not overregulation as some assert—was an important factor that contributed to the crisis. The experience of East Asia also exemplifies—once again—the volatility of capital flows and how quickly a change in market sentiment can move capital flows. This volatility can even make economies vulnerable that were considered robust.

A strong supervisory and regulatory institutional framework needs to be in place before the financial sector is liberalized. This can perhaps prevent and contain some financial crises. Yet, it cannot eliminate crises altogether. For example, in East Asia a sizeable part of the external short-term borrowing was done by private companies which would not have been covered by the normal supervisory and regulatory framework of the financial sector even if it had existed.

Finally, it has long been recognized that macroeconomic stability needs to be achieved before the financial liberalization commences. However, the experience of East Asia demonstrates that macroeconomic stability is not a sufficient guarantee against a financial crisis.

6. Conclusions: Policy implications for Africa

Financial markets are fundamentally different from the markets for goods because of asymmetric information, herd behaviour, volatility and the external effects of a financial crisis. Moreover, financial crises will always happen, they cannot be exterminated—not with better supervision and regulation, not with better information and not with stronger institutions, although all might reduce the likelihood of a crisis. The benefits of financial liberalization are generally overstated and are mostly realized in the long run. This should give some caution in the extent and speed of financial liberalization. The question is how to reach that state where the benefits of the financial sector can be fully grasped and outweigh the increased risk that comes with a liberalized environment. This process is likely to be long and requires careful planning, sequencing and pacing of the reforms.

The creation of legal and accounting systems and the capacity to supervise, regulate and monitor financial institutions is essential before domestic liberalization commences (Montiel, 1996, pp. 78-79; Stiglitz, 1998a). "The key issue should not be liberalization or deregulation, but the construction of the regulatory framework that ensures an effective financial system" (Stiglitz, 1998a, p. 16). For example, if interest rates are liberalized and rise, moral hazard and adverse selection problems increase and if the banking system is unsound or prudential supervision inadequate, a financial crisis becomes more likely. Thus, banking crises are more likely when the financial system is liberalized but this effect is weaker—yet still existent—when the institutions are strong (Demirgüc-Kunt and Detragiache, 1998). Structural reforms and strengthening institutions take time to design, to implement and to yield results. They cannot be accomplished by the stroke of a pen, as liberalization measures often can. In East Asia, financial sector reforms were generally initiated relatively late, i.e., in the 1980s or 1990s, but the speed, however, was in some cases rather high, which has partly contributed to the crisis because essential institutions were not in place. Capacity (public and private) has to be built up over time. This also implies that financial liberalization should be gradual.

Domestic financial sector reforms have often focused on interest rate liberalization but other (institutional) reforms actually should precede. For example, with an oligopolistic and weak banking sector—as prevalent in several African countries—it cannot be expected that an auction-like market system will determine the interest rate after it is liberalized. Indeed, deep markets with a large number of participants and many traded securities are needed for indirect monetary policy to work. For example, indirect monetary policy requires the quantification, monitoring and forecasting of more than a hundred variables—many on a daily basis—which is beyond the capacity of many central banks in Africa (Roe and Sowa, 1997, p. 244).

Some capital account controls are needed because international capital flows are volatile, information can never be perfect and symmetric and is particularly meagre in Africa and because regulation and supervision are important but cannot address, for example, corporate external borrowing (Bhagwati, 1998; Rodrik, 1998; Stiglitz, 1998b). Capital controls have been rather successful in Latin America. Chile imposed reserve requirements on foreign loans and foreign-owned deposits of short maturity which lengthened the maturity of capital inflows. Other countries (Brazil, Colombia) have taxed short-term inflows or imposed minimum stay periods for portfolio flows.

There are no easy solutions to the problems in the financial sector. The manner in which reforms are designed depends largely on the initial conditions and specific circumstances of the country involved. Nonetheless, generally it has been recommended that macroeconomic stability should be established before financial liberalization is initiated and that domestic liberalization should precede liberalization of the capital account (Funke, 1993; Gibson and Tsakalotos, 1994; Greeneway and Morrissey, 1993; Hehran and Laurens, 1997; Pill and Pradhan, 1997; Stiglitz, 1998a). Given the previous analysis, this sequence is adjusting in the following way.[23]

1. Creation of macroeconomic stability (sustainable fiscal and current-account deficits, manageable inflation);

   Development of capacity for prudential supervision and regulation; development of accounting and legal systems and for risk management; development of regulation that encourages sound and prudential behaviour and competition among financial institutions;

   Structural reforms to improve soundness of the domestic financial sector (recapitalization, restructuring, liquidation);

2. Gradual liberalization of domestic financial sector (for example, interest rates); caution is necessary because in thin markets volatility is usually high; sequencing of liberalization of interest rates: (a) wholesale (interbank) interest rate; (b) lending interest rate; (c) deposit interest rate; and

3. Gradual, selective and limited external financial liberalization; certain controls to reduce volatility of short-term capital flows might be kept in place.

---

23 Postponing liberalization and deregulation until after structural and institutions reforms have not always been clearly recommended nor followed in practice. See, for example, World Bank (1994, pp. 112-113) which stated that "The first objective is to reduce financial repression—by aligning interest rates toward market equilibrium levels and reducing directed credit programs. The second is to restore solvency and improve the incentives under which banks operate. (...) The third objective is to improve the financial infrastructure, strengthening supervision, auditing, and accounting practices (...) [and] improving the legal framework".

References

Akyuz, Yilmaz (1998). "The East Asian financial crisis: back to the future?", mimeo. UNCTAD, (January).

Arestis, Philip and Panicos Demetriades (1997). "Financial development and economic growth: assessing the evidence". *Economic Journal*, vol. 107, No. 442, pp. 783-799. (May).

Aryeetey, Ernest and others (1997a). "Financial market fragmentation and reforms in Ghana, Malawi, Nigeria, and Tanzania". *The World Bank Economic Review*, vol. 11, No. 2, pp. 195-218 (May).

Aryeetey, Ernest, Lemma W. Senbet and Christopher Udry (1997b). "Financial liberalization and financial markets in sub-Saharan Africa: a synthesis". *Journal of African Economies* (AERC Supplement) vol. 6, No. 1, pp. 1-28.

Athey, Michael J. and Prem S. Laumas (1994). "Internal funds and corporate investment". *Journal of Development Economics*, vol. 45, No. 2, pp. 287-303 (December).

Bhagwati, Jagdish (1998). "The capital myth: the difference between trade in widgets and dollars". *Foreign Affairs*, vol. 77, No. 3, pp. 7-12 (May/June).

Brownbridge, Martin (1998). "The causes of financial distress in local banks in Africa and implications for prudential policy". *UNCTAD Discussion Papers*, No. 132 (March).

Claessens, Stijn, Asli Demirgüc-Kunt and Harry Huizinga (1998). "How does foreign entry affect the domestic banking market?". *World Bank Policy Research Working Paper*, No. 1918, Washington, D.C.: World Bank (May).

Clarke, Roland (1996). "Equilibrium interest rates and financial liberalization in developing countries". *The Journal of Development Studies*, vol. 32, No. 3, pp. 391-413 (February).

Clément, Jean A.P. and others (1996). "Aftermath of the CFA Franc Devaluation". *Occasional Paper*, No. 138, Washington, D.C.: IMF (May).

Collier, Paul (1994). "Financial liberalization". In *Adjustment and Development: The Experience of the ACP*, Patrick and Sylviane Guillaumont, eds. Paris: Economica, pp. 225-242.

______ (1997). "The trade policy review of Uganda". *The World Economy*, vol. 20, No. 5, pp. 649-664 (August).

Cornford, Andrew and Jim Brandon (1998). "The WTO negotiations on financial services: problems of financial globalization in practice", mimeo, UNCTAD (January).

Demetriades, Panicos and Khaled Hussein (1996). "Does financial development cause economic growth? Time-series evidence from 16 countries". *Journal of Development Economics*, vol. 51, No. 2, pp. 387-411 (December).

Demirgüc-Kunt, Asli and Enrica Detragiache (1998). "Financial liberalization and financial fragility". *World Bank Policy Research Working Paper*, No. 1917, Washington, D.C.: World Bank (May).

Diaz-Alejandro, Carlos (1985). "Good-bye financial repression, hello financial crash". *Journal of Development Economics*, vol. 19, No. 1/2, pp. 1-24 (September-October).

Dooley, Michael P. (1996). "A survey of literature on controls over international capital transactions". *IMF Staff Papers*, vol. 43, No. 4, pp. 639-687 (December).

Dowling, Malcolm (1998). "The Asian currency and economic crisis: macroeconomic performance and policy", paper presented at the Project LINK meeting, New York (March).

Eatwell, John (1997). "International financial liberalization: the impact on world development". *Discussion Paper Series*, No. 12, New York. UNDP: Office of Development Studies.

Eisenbeis, Robert A. (1997). "Bank deposits and credit risk as sources of systemic risk". *Federal Reserve Bank of Atlanta Economic Review*, vol. 82, No. 3, pp. 4-19 (third quarter 1997).

Farooq, Janet (1998). "Managing the external sector", paper presented at the Project LINK meeting, New York (March).

Frankel, Jeffrey A. and Sergio L. Schmukler (1996). "Country fund discounts and the Mexican crisis of December 1994: did local residents turn pessimistic before international investors?". *Open Economies Review*, vol. 7 (Supplement), pp. 511-534.

Funke, Norbert (1993). "Timing and sequencing of reforms: competing views and the role of credibility". *Kyklos*, vol. 46, No. 3, pp. 337-362.

Ghate, P.B. (1992). "Interaction between the formal and informal financial sectors: the Asian experience". *World Development*, vol. 20, No. 6, pp. 859-872 (June).

Gibson, Heather D. and Euclid Tsakalotos (1994). "The scope and limits of financial liberalization in developing countries: a critical survey". *Journal of Development Studies*, vol. 30, No. 3, pp. 578-628 (April).

Giovanni, Alberto (1985). "Saving and the real interest rate in LDCs". *Journal of Development Economics*, vol. 18, No. 2/3, pp. 197-217.

González-Hermosillo, Brenda, Ceyla Pazarbasioglu and Robert Billings (1996). "Determinants of banking system fragility: a case study of Mexico". *IMF Staff Papers*, vol. 43, No. 4, pp. 639-687 (December).

Greeneway, David and Oliver Morrissey (1993). "Structural adjustment and liberalization in developing countries: what lessons have we learned?" *Kyklos*, vol. 46, No. 2, pp. 241-261.

Hardy, Daniel C. and Ceyla Pazarbasioglu (1998). "Leading indicators of banking crises: was Asia different?", *IMF Working Paper*, No. 98/91, (June).

Harris, Richard D.F. (1997). "Stock markets and development: a re-assessment". *European Economic Review*, vol. 41, No. 1, pp. 139-146 (January).

Hehran, Hassanali and Bernard Laurens (1997). "Interest rates: an approach to liberalization". *Finance and Development*, vol. 34, No. 2, pp. 33-35 (June).

Hellmann, Thomas and Kevin Murdock (1997). "Financial sector development policy: the importance of reputational capital and governance". In *Development Strategy and Management of the Market Economy*, vol. II, István P. Székely and Richard Sabot, eds. Oxford: Clarendon Press, pp. 269-323.

International Finance Corporation (1997). *Emerging Stock Markets Factbook, 1997.* Washington, D.C.: IFC.

______ (1998). *Emerging Stock Markets Factbook, 1998.* Washington, D.C.: IFC.

International Monetary Fund (1997a). *World Economic Outlook, Interim Assessment.* Washington, D.C.: IMF.

______ (1997b). *Exchange Arrangements and Exchange Restrictions*, Washington, D.C.: IMF.

______ (1998). *World Economic Outlook.* Washington, D.C.: IMF (May).

Jbili, Abdelali, Klaus Enders and Volker Treichel (1997). "Financial sector reforms in Algeria, Morocco and Tunisia: a preliminary assessment". *IMF Working Paper*, No. 97/81 (July).

Jefferis, F.R. (1995). "The development of stock markets in sub-Saharan Africa". *The South African Journal of Economics*, vol. 63, No. 3, pp. 346-363 (September).

Jenkins, Carolyn (1998). "Determinants of private investment in Zimbabwe". *Journal of African Economies*, vol. 7, No. 1, pp. 34-61 (March).

Kasekende, Louis, Damoni Kitabire and Matthew Martin (1997). "Capital inflows and macroeconomic policy in sub-Saharan Africa". *International Monetary and Financial Issues in the 1990s: Research papers for the Group of Twenty-Four*, vol. VIII, Geneva: UNCTAD, pp. 59-85.

Kenny, Charles J. and Todd J. Moss (1998). "Stock markets in Africa: emerging lions or white elephants?". *World Development*, vol. 26, No. 5, pp. 829-843 (May).

Keynes, John Maynard (1936). *The General Theory of Employment, Interest, and Money*. New York: Harcourt, Brace and Company.

Kregel, Jan (1996). "Some risks and implications of financial globalization for national policy autonomy". *UNCTAD Review*, pp. 55-62.

Lee, Jang-Yung (1997). "Sterilizing capital flows", *Economic Issues*, No. 7, Washington, D.C.: IMF.

Lewis, Peter and Howard Stein (1997). "Shifting fortunes: the political economy of financial liberalization in Nigeria". *World Development*, vol. 25, No. 1, pp. 5-22 (January).

Levine, Ross (1997). "Financial development and economic growth: views and agenda". *Journal of Economic Literature*, vol. 35, No. 2, pp. 688-726 (June).

McKinnon, Ronald I. (1973). *Money and Capital in Economic Development*, Washington, D.C.: Brookings Institutions.

Montiel, Peter J. (1996). "Financial policies and economic growth: theory, evidence and country-specific experience from sub-Saharan Africa". *Journal of African Economies* (AERC Supplement) vol. 5, No. 3, pp. 65-98 (October).

Moore, Clement Henry (1991). "Tunisian banking". In *Tunisia: The Political Economy of Reform*, I. William Zartman, ed. Boulder and London: Lynne Rienner Publishers.

Morrison, Christian, Henri-Bernard Solignac Lecomte and Xavier Oudin (1994). *Micro-Enterprises and the Institutional Framework in Developing Countries*. Paris: OECD Development Centre.

Muradoglu, Gulnur and Fatma Taskin (1996). "Differences in household savings behavior: evidence from industrial and developing countries". *The Developing Economies*, vol. 34, No. 2, pp. 138-153 (June).

Mwega, F.M. (1997). "Saving in sub-Saharan Africa: A comparative analysis". *Journal of African Economies*, AERC Supplement, vol. 6, No. 3, pp. 199-228 (October).

Nabli, Mustapha K. and Jeffrey Nugent, eds. (1989). *The New Institutional Economics and Development: Theory and Applications to Tunisia*, Amsterdam: North-Holland.

Ncube, Mthuli and Lemma W. Senbet (1997). "Perspectives on financial regulation and liberalization in Africa under incentive problems and asymmetric information". *Journal of African Economies* (AERC Supplement) vol. 6, No. 1, pp. 89-99.

Ngugi, R.W. and J.W. Kabubo (1998). "Financial sector reforms and interest rate liberalization: the Kenyan experience". *AERC Research Paper*, No. 72, Nairobi: African Economic Research Consortium (March).

Pill, Huw and Mahmood Pradhan (1995). "Financial indicators and financial change in Africa and Asia". *IMF Working Paper*, No. 95/123 (November).

______ (1997). "Financial liberalization in Africa and Asia". *Finance and Development*, vol. 34, No. 2, pp. 7-10 (June).

Reinke, Jens (1998). "How to lend like mad and make a profit: a micro-credit paradigm versus the start-up fund in South Africa". *The Journal of Development Studies*, vol. 34, No. 3, pp. 44-61 (February).

Rodrik, Dani (1998). "Who needs capital-account convertibility?". In *Should the IMF Pursue Capital-Account Convertibility?, Essays in International Finance*. No. 207. Princeton, New Jersey: Princeton University, Department of Economics (May).

Roe, Alan R. and Nii K. Sowa (1997). "From direct to indirect monetary control in sub-Saharan Africa". *Journal of African Economies*, AERC Supplement, vol. 6, No. 1, pp. 212-264.

Sachs, Jeffrey, Aaron Tornell and Andrés Velasco (1996). "The Mexican peso crisis: sudden death or death foretold". *Journal of International Economics*, vol. 41, No. 3/4, pp. 265-293 (November).

Schadler, Susan and others (1993). "Recent experiences with surges in capital inflows". *Occasional Paper*, No. 108 (December). Washington, D.C.: IMF.

Shafik, Nemat (1992). "Modeling private investment in Egypt". *Journal of Development Economics*, vol. 39, No. 2, pp. 263-277 (October).

Shaw, Edward S. (1973). *Financial Deepening in Economic Development*. New York: Oxford University Press.

Singh, Ajit (1995). "Corporate Financing Patterns in Industrializing Economies". *Technical Paper*, No. 2, Washington, D.C.: International Finance Corporation.

______ (1997). "Financial liberalization, stock markets and economic development". *Economic Journal*, vol. 107, No. 442, pp. 771-782 (May).

Singh, Ajit and Bruce A. Weisse (1998). "Emerging stock markets, portfolio capital flows and long-term economic growth: micro and macroeconomic perspectives". *World Development*, vol. 26, No. 4, pp. 607-622 (April).

Soyibo, Adedoyin (1997). "Financial liberalization and bank restructuring in sub-Saharan Africa: some lessons for sequencing and policy design". *Journal of African Economies*, AERC Supplement, vol. 6, No. 1, pp. 100-150.

Steel, William F. and others (1997). "Informal financial markets under liberalization in four African countries". *World Development*, vol. 25, No. 5, pp. 817-830 (May).

Stiglitz, Joseph (1993). "The role of the state in financial markets". *Proceedings of the World Bank Annual Conference on Development Economics*, pp. 19-52.

______ (1998a). "More instruments and broader goals: moving toward the post-Washington consensus". *Wider Annual Lectures*, No. 2 (January).

______ (1998b). "Boats, planes and capital flows". *Financial Times* (25 March).

Stiglitz, Joseph and Andrew Weiss (1981). "Credit rationing in markets with imperfect information". *The American Economic Review*, vol. 71, No. 3, pp. 393-410 (June).

Tavlas, George S. (1996). "Currency crisis: introduction". *Open Economies Review*, vol. 7 (Supplement), pp. 431-436.

Ul Haque, Nadeem, Donald Mathieson and Sunil Sharma (1997). "Causes of capital inflows and policy responses to them". *Finance and Development*, vol. 34, No. 1, pp. 3-6 (March).

UNCTAD (1995). *Foreign Direct Investment in Africa* (United Nations publication, Sales No. E.95.II.A.6).

______ (1997). *World Investment Report, 1997* (United Nations publication, Sales No. E.97.II.D.10).

United Nations (1995). "Towards advancing financial intermediation in Africa". Report of the Secretary-General, A/50/490 (October).

______ (1996). *World Economic and Social Survey 1996* (United Nations publication, Sales No. E.96.II.C.1).

______ (1998). *World Economic and Social Survey 1998* (United Nations publication, Sales No. E.98.II.C.1).

UN/ESCAP (1998). *Economic and Social Survey of Asia and the Pacific 1998* (United Nations publication, Sales No. E.98.II.E.59).

Wade, Robert (1998). "The Asian debt-and-development crisis of 1997-?: causes and consequences", mimeo, New York: Russell Sage Foundation (March).

World Bank (1994). *Adjustment in Africa: Reforms, Results, and the Road Ahead.* Oxford: Oxford University Press.

Annex table 1. Private net resource flows to Africa, 1990-1997
(Millions of US dollars)

	1990	*1991*	*1992*	*1993*	*1994*	*1995*	*1996*	*1997*[a]
				Total private net resource flows				
Africa	389	1484	1614	2192	6819	10598	7692	13000
sum of large four	1145	1147	-31	2170	5735	8084	4508	11000
				Foreign direct investment (net)				
Africa	1869	2663	2867	3382	5449	4830	4405	4500
sum of large four	1487	1282	1778	2329	4100	3420	1614	..
Egypt	734	253	459	493	1256	598	636	800
Morocco	165	317	422	491	551	290	311	..
Nigeria	588	712	897	1345	1959	2201	1391	700
South Africa	0	226	-25	-27	334	993	758	1725
				Portfolio equity flows				
Africa	0	0	0	17	938	5021	3472	..
sum of four	0	0	0	0	308	4729	3219	..
Egypt	0	0	0	0	10	2	1233	..
Morocco	0	0	0	0	63	150	222	..
Nigeria	0	0	0	0	17	6	5	..
South Africa	..	..	..	..	219	4571	1759	5686
				Commercial bank loans *(net resource flows = disbursement - principal repayments*				
Africa	-1373	-1148	-1071	-515	-596	-414	-1065	..
sum of four	-341	-135	-1809	-159	-176	-796	-1845	..
Egypt	55	15	-382	-242	-167	-105	-255	..
Morocco	7	-49	-85	94	247	110	-102	..
Nigeria	-403	-101	-1342	-10	-10	-10	-10	..
South Africa	..	..	..	..	-246	-791	-1478	..
				Bonds *(net resource flows = disbursement - principal repayments)*				
Africa	-107	-32	-181	-693	1029	1161	880	..
sum of four	-1	0	0	0	1503	731	660	..
Egypt	-1	0	0	0	0	0	0	..
Morocco	0	0	0	0	0	0	293	..
Nigeria	0	0	0	0	0	0	0	..
South Africa	..	..	..	..	1503	731	367	3646

Sources: World Bank, *Global Development Finance, 1998* and IMF, *International Financial Statistics.*

Note: Totals for Africa exclude South Africa for 1990 to 1993 (except for FDI).

a Preliminary estimates.

16

Discussion – Africa

RICHARD MORGAN
TEMITOPE W. OSHIKOYA

RICHARD MORGAN*

Consideration of the effects of and lessons from the financial crisis in emerging-market economies needs to include, centrally, the impact on people, especially those most vulnerable. Effects on low-income families through the labour market, including the informal sector, form one area. Linked to this is the question of the probable need for household consumption stabilization through income-related safety net measures, such as public works and, where possible, well-targeted subsidies. The second major area of concern in terms of the impact on people is through possible reductions in public sector capacity for the financing and delivery of essential services, including primary health care, water supplies, sanitation and basic education. Unless public spending in such areas is protected and cushioned from financial crisis, the short-run effects in terms of deteriorating social and environmental conditions are likely to be serious. Equally, if social development spending is not safeguarded, the

---

* Deputy Director, Programme Division, UNICEF, New York. The views expressed herein are those of the author and should not be attributed to UNICEF.

e *positive* lessons of the East Asian experience over the past three decades—including the need for sustained and high levels of investment in people through quality basic education and health care if high rates of economic growth and human development progress are to be achieved—risk being jettisoned.

Mr. Degefe clearly raised the question of "who is really in crisis?". He focused on the still-valid positive lessons of Asian experience for Africa over a relatively long period, and on the fact that, even in the context of recent setbacks in parts of Asia, social indicators in Africa are still much worse; further, prospects for their rapid improvement are heavily constrained by complex and structural factors such as debt distress, downward pressure on commodity prices, the vulnerability of households to climatic fluctuations, weaknesses of governance and the AIDS pandemic. While some Asian economies are struggling to regain stability, African societies and people—not least children—are struggling for survival.

Nonetheless, Africa has its own success stories which provide, to some extent, pointers for the continent itself. Mauritius and Botswana have, to a considerable degree, mirrored the Asian tigers in terms of the highly active role played by the public sector to ensure sustained investments in their people ("human capital") through public health, mass-access quality basic education, and—in times of climatic and other crisis—safety nets for the most vulnerable (Mehrotra and Jolly, 1997). These public policy measures have been an essential part of both sustained human development and rapid economic progress in these countries, in addition to their good records of macroeconomic management and relative economic "openness". (Botswana's diamonds do not rule it out, as some may suggest, as an irrelevant special case—several other African countries have or have had large investible surpluses arising from extractive industries—while its inability in recent years to stem the spread of HIV indicates that it does not, on the other hand, entirely out-perform other African countries).

These examples, and others in Africa, albeit less clearly sustained, also provide partial confirmation of Mr. Degefe's implication that we cannot leave it entirely to the free market to deliver or safeguard the basic development goals to which families, societies and their leaders aspire. Active public policy must, on moral as well as efficiency grounds, also play its part, in bad as well as better times—and perhaps particularly during the former.

Looked at in another way: financial stability and economic growth are not ends in themselves, but rather means to, and necessary but insufficient conditions for, sustained human developmental progress. This seems to be a generalized argument from Asian experience, as well as from experience within Africa, the validity of which persists despite the recent setbacks in "emerging" economies. A further lesson, the basis for which may be found in earlier analysis, such as the studies of "Adjustment With a Human Face" (UNICEF, 1988), is that financial stabilization policies run the risk of being counter-productive, if their short-run implications for the health, growth, learning and earning of people have the effect of undermining their longer-term capacity to contribute to societies and economies as producers, parents and citizens. Not only must these costs be contained, they should also be minimal. To draw upon Henk-Jan Brinkman's analogy: a school is neither a shop nor even a bank—and its clients and sponsors commonly have other, more far-reaching objectives in mind.

TEMITOPE W. OSHIKOYA*

Introduction

Henk-Jan Brinkman's very informative paper interweaves three themes that certainly interest some of us who are working on Africa. The first is that financial sector reform is approaching the top of the reform agenda in Africa and policy makers can probably learn from what went wrong in East Asia. The second is that total external private finance might be small compared to other regions, but it is increasingly important and certainly large enough to trigger a financial crisis in some countries; third, although the financial sector in Africa is relatively underdeveloped, Africa gets only a fraction of the international capital flowing to emerging markets and even though Africa has hardly been affected by the contagion of the financial crisis in East Asia, there are still some lessons to be learned from that crisis.

I agree with the main lessons drawn from the paper which are as follows:

- Create macroeconomic stability (sustainable fiscal and current-account deficits, manageable inflation);
- Create capacity for prudential supervision and regulations, accounting

* Manager, Research Division, African Development Bank. The views expressed herein are those of the author and should not be attributed to the African Development Bank.

and legal systems and for risk management; establish regulation that encourages sound and prudential behaviour and competition among financial institutions;

- Institute structural reforms to improve soundness of the domestic financial sector (recapitalization, liquidation);
- Implement gradual liberalization of domestic financial sector (e.g. interest rates); caution is necessary because in thin markets volatility is usually high; sequencing of liberalization of interest rates: (a) wholesale (interbank) interest rate; (b) lending interest rate; and (c) deposit interest rate.
- Promote gradual but limited external financial liberalization.

Although I agree with many of these conclusions, I would have slightly shifted emphasis and draw attention to three issues as follows:

- the peculiar nature of the moral hazard in Africa's financial system characterized more by insider trading. This is illustrated by examples from Nigeria, Kenya, Uganda and Zambia. It is also important to outline the lessons of successful bank restructuring in some African countries which embarked on financial liberalization long before the crisis in East Asia. I would illustrate the case of Côte d'Ivoire.
- the peculiar nature of reverse private capital flows from Africa, that is, African's private capital flight. While African countries face the policy problem of how to attract their own capital back into the region, East Asian countries face the problem of how to retain their wealth within the region.
- the possible effect of global deflation resulting from the Asian crisis on Africa's fragile economic recovery and restructured financial systems.

Financial distress and reforms in Africa

Moral hazard and insider lending in selected African countries

In a study of banking reforms in Kenya, Nigeria, Uganda and Zambia, Brownbridge (1998) finds that the single largest contributor to the bad debts of many of the failed local banks was insider lending. Among the four local banks liquidated in Nigeria in 1995, insider loans accounted for two-thirds of the total loans, while 50 per cent of the loan portfolio of one of the Ugandan local banks taken over by the Bank of Uganda in 1995 was made to insiders. Extensive insider loans were also prevalent among most of the larger local bank failures in Kenya. In some of these countries, the soundness of the banks was challenged as many of the insider loans breached the large loan exposure limits and were invested in speculative projects that resulted in the mismatch in the maturities of the assets and liabilities. In Nigeria, many local banks survived mainly on the highly profitable arbitrage opportunities created by the dual foreign exchange markets.

The regulatory barriers to entry were low such that the minimum capital requirements to set up a bank in Uganda and Zambia were the equivalent in local currency of less than $50,000. Prudential criteria in the granting of licences were subverted by political interference. This was further compounded by weak banking supervision as the central banks lack the manpower and legal framework for oversight. The high incidence of insider lending among failed banks suggests that problems of moral hazard were especially acute in these banks.

Côte d'Ivoire: success through comprehensiveness

Let me now turn to the case of the successful financial restructuring programme in Côte d'Ivoire which illustrates the importance of a comprehensive approach to banking reforms. By the mid-1980s, the effects of deteriorating terms of trade on the economy began to take their toll on the country's fragile banking system. As a result, by the late 1980s, liquidation was started for four of the five state development banks. By 1990, the 14 commercial banks were experiencing a sharp drop in deposits and credits from foreign banks.

In 1991, the Financial Sector Adjustment Programme (FISAP), which was supported by the African Development Bank and other multilateral institutions, included such components as the improvement of the policy and regulatory environment; the restructuring of financial institutions; and capital market development. The implementation of the FISAP made it possible to reinforce the institutional framework of the financial sector and improved operational performance of the banking institutions. In accordance with prudential regulations, the four major banks were recapitalized. Other banks were restructured, with general expenses reduced and the staff downsized. These banks have strengthened services dealing with the recovery of frozen credits. The restructuring of Insurance Companies' balance sheet was initiated and 13 insurance companies were liquidated. By 1994, the banks' return on capital rose to almost 10 per cent, and most banks had returned to compliance with the newly toughened prudential rules. In 1995, following the revival of activities within the sector, three new insurance companies were established.

Private capital flows

While the Asian financial and economic crisis spotlights the consequences of triggering massive private capital outflow, it is by no means new to Africa. Over the past two decades more private capital relative to wealth has flown from Africa than from any other continent. According to Collier (1997), almost 40 per cent of African-owned private wealth was held outside the continent by 1990 compared to only 6 per cent for East Asia. Thus, whereas African policy makers face the problem of how to attract their own capital back into the region, East Asian policy makers face the policy problem of how to retain their wealth within the region.

The major factors underlying capital flight from Africa are the capital stock per worker, the Institutional Investor risk rating and macroeconomic distortions. Capital stock per worker in Africa is only one seventh that of East Asia. The risk ratings for African countries are important mostly because they capture the widely held perceptions of the investment community about the continent. The impact of macroeconomic distortions is well known. Capital flight is the greater, where there are pervasive macroeconomic distortions, proxied by overvalued real exchange rate caused either by misalignment or through trade restrictions.

There has been considerable debate about the efficacy of permitting unrestricted capital movements. The experience of African countries with massive capital flight demonstrates that in most situations capital controls have been ineffective. The key policy question for Africa is no longer how to keep capital in, but how to get it back, and flight capital is not likely to return with extensive restrictions on its movements.

Many of the recommendations outlined in Mr. Brinkman's paper as lessons of Asia's crisis for Africa are important not only for attracting African capital flight back into the continent, but also for increasing the region's share of direct and portfolio investment.

In recent years African countries have made considerable improvement with respect to reducing macroeconomic distortions. Excessive budget deficits and rapid expansion in money supply, high inflation and misaligned exchange rates are increasingly becoming the exception rather than the rule in Africa. Fiscal deficits as a proportion of GDP were 1.9 per cent in 1997, half of the out turn in 1995 and about one third of that in 1994. Fiscal and monetary restraints have resulted in reducing the average regional inflation rate to 17.6 per cent in 1997, representing a drop of almost half from that prevailing in 1994. No fewer than 33 sub-Saharan countries reported annual inflation of less than 10 per cent compared with just 12 in 1994. The median inflation rate fell to 5.7 per cent as the majority of African countries reported single-digit inflation rates. And the continent's growth rate increased to an average of 4.4 per cent in 1996-1997 compared with an average of 1.9 per cent for the 1990-1995 period.

To attract back private capital and foreign direct investment to the region, there is a need to sustain and deepen reforms in the following areas:

- enhancing human capital development through increased provisions of education, training, health and other social services;
- fostering social and political stability;
- building an efficient infrastructure;
- revising existing laws to remove or reduce foreign ownership limitations, often as part of broader structural adjustment packages; and
- establishing payment mechanisms to facilitate trade and cross-border investments.

Global deflation and Africa's growth prospects

The indirect effects of the Asian crisis are of great concern to African economies and their fragile financial system. The prices of commodities that are of interest to Africa are likely to be depressed as world trade volume is expected to slacken owing in part to the impact of the current economic and financial crises in Asia. The downturn in commodity prices, oil in particular, is likely to affect African growth rates in 1998. There are 10 main oil-exporting countries in Africa, namely: Algeria, Angola, Cameroon, Congo, Egypt, Gabon, Equatorial Guinea, Libyan Arab Jamahiriya, Nigeria and Tunisia. In April, petroleum prices fell to their lowest point since the early 1970s. As energy accounts for more than half of Africa's exports, a 25 per cent fall in oil prices will lower total export earnings by some $14 billion (Economist Intelligence Unit, 1998). Although the continent's many oil importers will benefit from lower prices, the effect of falling export revenues will be compounded by the decline in other commodity prices. The prices of beverage such as cocoa, coffee and tea are down 20 per cent since mid-1997. Metal prices are at a five-year low. Both copper and nickel have fallen by about 25 per cent, while gold prices are currently almost 10 per cent lower than in 1997. The last three years of export expansion, culminating in $115 billion in 1997, may be interrupted with exports falling to below $100 billion in 1998. Furthermore, the loss of export revenues will have a direct impact on the debt servicing capacity of several of these countries, which are most dependent on oil exports and have a heavy debt burden.

One of the main factors that fueled the growth of stock markets in Africa and global mutual funds investing in them was the rising global demand for commodities — the basis of the region's exports in the mid-1990s. The fall in these commodity prices is likely to reduce the attractiveness of Africa's stock markets. Another direct effect of the crisis is the likelihood of a slowdown in Asia's flows of direct investments to Africa. It is feared that the economic crisis and the consequent banking stress might cause Asia's major investors in Africa to look inward in an attempt to consolidate their financial position and, hence reduce their interest in doing business with Africa. Historically, such flows had been very small compared with those from other regions. In recent years, however, a growing number of Asian countries have taken steps to invest in Africa's telecommunication, mining and energy sectors. For instance, in Ghana, the government sold 30 per cent of its stake in Ghana Telephone Company to Malaysia Telkom for $38 million. South Africa sold a 30 per cent stake in the state-owned Telkom for $1.3 billion to Thintana Communications — a joint venture between SBC Communications of the United States, and Telekom Malaysia BHD of Malaysia.

Conclusions

I share Mr. Brinkman's main lessons to be drawn from financial sector reforms, private capital flows and the Asian crisis. In my discussion I have tried to outline issues relating to insider lending, African capital flight, and the likely impacts of commodity price deflation induced partly by the Asian crisis on Africa's fragile economic recovery and financial system.

References

African Development Bank (1997). *African Development Report: Fostering Private Sector Development in Africa.* Oxford: Oxford University Press.

______ (1998). *African Development Report: Human Capital Development.* Oxford: Oxford University Press.

Brownbridge, M. (1998). *Financial Distress in Local Banks in Kenya, Nigeria, Uganda and Zambia: Causes and Implications for Regulatory Policy.* ODI, United Kingdom: Blackwell Publishers.

Collier, P. (1997) *Globalisation: What Should be the African Policy Response?*, CSAE, Oxford:University of Oxford.

Dziobek, C. and C. Pazarbasioglu (1998)."Lessons from systemic bank restructuring, economics issues". Washington, D.C.: International Monetary Fund.

The Economist Intelligence Unit (1998). *Business Africa* (1-15 June).

Mehrotra, S. and R. Jolly, eds. (1997). *Development With a Human Face: Experiences in Social Achievement and Economic Growth*, Oxford, United Kingdom: Clarendon Press.

UNICEF (1998). *Adjustment with a Human Face: Country Case Studies*, vol. 2, G. A. Cornia, R. Jolly and F. Stewart, eds., New York: Clarendon Press.

Part Five

ECONOMIES IN TRANSITION

Edited by

Simon Cunningham

17

Introduction – Economies in Transition

SIMON CUNNINGHAM*
United Nations Department of Economic and Social Affairs

The United Nations Expert Group Meeting took place one month before the financial meltdown in the Russian Federation. On 17 August, the Russian Federation devalued the rouble, and declared a 90 day moritorium on foreign debt servicing by Russian private firms, affecting Russian banks and their foreign creditors most of all, and announced that it would restructure rouble-denominated government debt. It had been hoped that an adjustment programme agreed with the International Monetary Fund (IMF) on 13 July would prevent such a collapse. The papers presented by Mr. Joseph Smolik of the Economic Commission for Europe (ECE) and Mr. Gerard Belanger of the IMF had drawn attention to many of the weaknesses in the Russian economic and financial situation. Neither author offered probabilities that the adjustment would succeed or fail. But a week after the Fund programme was signed, the possibility of an imminent collapse seemed real and gave rise to a vigorous exchange of views during the meeting.

One of the discussants, Professor Ilene Grabel, felt that the papers had not drawn sufficient attention to the problems that the Russian economy, which she described as a house of cards, was facing . She felt that there was "simply no

* Chief, Developed and Transition Economies Section. The views expressed herein are those of the author and not necessarily the views of the United Nations.

convincing evidence presented in support of ECE's predictions for the Russian Federation and Belanger's hope (disguised as confidence) in the IMF's ability to manage crisis in the Russian Federation."

The presenters thought that she had not done justice to their papers and interventions. Mr. Smolik noted that, since the beginning of the transition, ECE had often been accused of being unduly pessimistic, and that the ECE papers had drawn attention to the adverse effects of higher interest rates and lower commodity prices on the Russian Federation. He described how increases in interest rates in the Russian Federation were an element of financial instability and how the short term prospects of the Russian economy had deteriorated since the beginning of 1998. He further explained how ECE's call for a "coherent and comprehensive programme of institutional reform" had been a consistent ECE message since early 1990, as set out in ECE (1990). He noted that some observers and institutions had, incorrectly, thought until recently that this reform was a largely accomplished task. He also felt that the ECE's papers had distinguished between the impact of the Asian crises on the Russian Federation and Ukraine, where there were serious macroeconomic repercussions, and the other European transition economies where the effects were limited mainly to the domestic stock and international debt markets.

Indeed, one of the very strong points of agreement among the discussants was that the transition economies were not a homogeneous group and were affected differently by the Asian crisis. The reader might, after studying their papers, feel that some of the differences between Professor Grabel and Messrs. Belanger and Smolik were less matters of fact than of emphasis and perspective—whereas their papers had shown that the countries most adversely affected were already weak and that their difficulties could not be solely, or perhaps even mainly, attributed to the Asian crisis, she saw the effects of the crisis as pushing them over the brink. For the countries with stronger fundamentals in Central and Eastern Europe, the impact of the Asian crisis was less severe, and, as the second discussant, Professor Paul Wachtel, noted, where domestic savings were effectively mobilized for productive investment, the chances of long-term growth were greater.

Mr. Belanger pointed out that the transition economies were in fact being treated differently by investors, as shown by their yield differentials and in the varying performance of their stock markets. Several of them, such as Poland and Hungary, had good banking systems, a fact of which investors were aware.

ECE and IMF argued that they were hoping, almost against hope and with very serious reservations, that the Russian Federation would be able to make the policy changes that they had advocated over a long period, but which it had not thus far been able to implement. Professor Wachtel questioned how IMF and the United States (perhaps as a political rather than an economic decision) were apparently willing and eager to support the Russian Federation, even though it was apparent that the country's fundamental problems were not being solved.

Mr Belanger pointed out that the first disbursement from the new IMF Russian programme in July 1998 was $4.8 billion, $1 billion less than planned. This was meant as a signal from IMF to the Russian Federation of concern about whether it would be able to deliver on its undertakings. He was also aware of the risks that the Fund was taking. Owing to the harmful effects of the high rates of interest prevailing in the Russian Federation, IMF sought to assist the Russian Government in replacing the rouble-denominated treasury bills (known by their initials as GKOs) with new dollar denominated bonds. These were to carry a lower rate of interest—4 per cent in dollars instead of 50 per cent in roubles—and to have a longer maturity of 7 and 20 years. In the event, the Government could not implement the policy changes required and the refinancing plan became moot.

Clearly, as the papers and subsequent interventions indicated, there are many lessons to be drawn from IMF's experience in the Russian Federation. The Russian Federation has been described as a "virtual economy" (Gaddy and Ickes, 1998) with half its firms operating at a loss, subtracting from rather than adding to value added, with the share of barter in payments among industrial enterprises more than 50 per cent and with 40 per cent of all taxes being paid in non-monetary form. The wisdom and feasibility of drawing up a formal IMF programme with a country in so many difficulties and which was nowhere near functioning as a modern market economy will be a subject of continuing debate for a long period to come, not just in academic circles, but also within IMF itself and among its stakeholders.

Yet, in spite of sharply different viewpoints as to whether the gravity of the situation in the Russian Federation had been adequately reflected in the main papers, the session produced a measure of agreement over many substantive lessons.

Contagion through trade

Participants drew a distinction between the direct and indirect effects of the Asian crisis on the trading sector of the transition economies. The volume of merchandise trade between South-East Asia and the transition economies was fairly small and so the direct trade effects could be expected to be small. However, Mr. Belanger did not wish to minimize the importance of trade effects: many of the transition economies produced such standardized products as steel, timber and chemicals in which they were competing with Asian producers who had gained a competitive edge through devaluation. Furthermore, the Russian Federation is a large trading partner of Ukraine and Belarus and so the poor performance of its economy would seriously affect these countries too. Mr. Smolik noted that the indirect effects of the Asian crisis could be significant if economic growth in Western Europe, the major market for the Central and East European countries, were to slow. More seriously, as Professor Grabel emphasized, the fall in the prices of oil and other commodities cut the export revenues of the Russian Federation, thus contributing to the first current-account deficit (in early 1998) in many years, and also producing a sharp fall in government revenues.

Contagion through international financial linkages

The contagion from the Asian crisis had mainly spread through international financial linkages. For example, most transition economy stock markets shared in the global sell off at the end of October 1997. There was another drop in prices again in May 1998, when world markets reacted to political events in Indonesia. However, not all financial shocks could be attributed to the Asian crisis: domestic factors in some transition economies tended to depress their stock markets as well. The Russian stock market performed much worse than the Hungarian and Polish stock markets.

The domestic debt markets have also been susceptible to shifts in investor sentiment. The most serious cases were the Russian Federation and Ukraine. Mr. Smolik outlined how they had both become vulnerable because budget deficits were financed in large part by foreign purchases of treasury bills. The prime reason for the Russian Federation's reliance on foreign holdings of GKOs, then, was its inability to raise sufficient taxes or to borrow the required amounts from domestic savers. The situation, as Professor Grabel expressed it, was that the Russian economy was highly vulnerable to a reversal of capital flows and hence a further fiscal crisis and a currency collapse.

Mr. Smolik argued that, although attention had been focused on the long-standing budgetary problems of the Russian Federation and Ukraine and their reliance on foreign funding to cover budget deficits and the vulnerability that this has engendered, tax collection systems have been inadequate in some other transition economies as well. Low revenues had translated into pressure on budgets, the inability of the state to provide necessary services and, in the international sphere, failure to gain the confidence of investors.

Exchange rates, interest rates and economic crises

Professor Wachtel thought that policy makers still had not worked out how and when to let go of a fixed exchange rate. It has advantages in controlling high inflation and stabilizing the economy, but at a cost of building up a real appreciation that could become unsustainable. The Czech authorities should have reversed the over-appreciation of the currency before the May 1997 crisis in that country. However, more had been gained by not trying to save the fixed exchange rate at that point than could have been gained by high interest rates to further maintain the exchange rate. Mr. Smolik noted that flexible exchange rate systems—crawling (depreciating) bands in Hungary and Poland and the managed float in the Czech Republic after the koruna crisis in May 1997—had helped these countries weather the storm after the Asian crisis erupted.

Similarly, Mr. Belanger pointed to the dilemmas facing policy makers in an exchange rate crisis. In the Czech case, interest rates rose during the attack and then fell back after the currency had depreciated. However, an interest rate increase could do serious damage to a banking system burdened with substantial non-performing loans. On the other hand, a devaluation could result in bankruptcies throughout the economy if banks had undertaken large scale foreign borrowing to support domestic lending.

Professor Grabel showed how rates of interest in the Russian Federation were at such high levels that not only did economic activity slow down, but, to the extent that investment took place, it tended to be only of the most speculative variety.

Finally, the *Economic Survey of Europe* noted that, while fixed exchange rates helped to control inflation and stabilize the economy, it was "highly uncertain whether such policy interventions (in foreign exchange markets and raising interest rates) will in fact be successful in moderating pressures on the financial markets or in arresting a crisis". If that was the case, Professor Wachtel asked, why were such policies followed?

Capital controls

Professor Grabel had argued that *the* lesson of the Asian crisis for the transition economies was that they should implement capital controls: policy makers could ill afford not to control international private capital flows as long as they had inadequate official reserves. She described the capital controls in force in Chile and Columbia and how controls had helped countries such as Chile, China, Columbia, India, Malaysia, Singapore, and Taiwan Province of China weather the storm better than those countries that had been "good students of neoliberalism".

Other participants also thought that a case could be made for capital controls in transition economies. Mr. Smolik noted how Slovenia, which had capital controls, was hardly affected by the turbulence from Asia. Professor Wachtel agreed that the liberal orthodoxy would be questioned in future. The implications of the different forms of capital controls should be examined more carefully.

Mr. Smolik stressed that it was essential for a country to develop its financial infrastructure before opening up to the full range of capital flows. Professor Wachtel agreed that the sequencing of liberalization was vital and that controls should be lifted and markets opened as the institutions to absorb shocks were developed. The reform of the banking sector should precede the development of equity markets. Those countries which had institutions pre-dating the Communist system had made considerable progress in reforming their banking sectors; Poland will have a more modern and privatized banking sector than other Western European countries.

Mr. Ricardo Ffrench-Davis, drawing on his study of capital controls in Latin America, described how they should complement other policies and not be a substitute for them. However, a surge in capital flows could worsen the situation when the fundamentals were otherwise sound. Capital controls could lead to a change in the composition of flows, which in turn could affect their overall volume.

Mr. Belanger considered that IMF's approach to capital controls was pragmatic. He argued that the freeing of capital flows had greatly benefited the international economy. To reap the benefits, however, required that the inflows be allocated efficiently. Where this was not assured, because of weak domestic financial sectors, large capital inflows could wreak havoc, with unsustainable asset price bubbles during the inflow period and crashes when capital rushes for the exit. With limits to the pace at which financial sectors can be strengthened, avoiding such accidents required an orderly opening of domestic financial systems. In this context, controls can buy time to correct some of the underlying weaknesses, although their effectiveness will likely erode over time. He felt that it was overly simplistic, however, to think that controls are the answer. The answer must be in correcting the fundamentals, which will make it possible for emerging markets to benefit from the availability of foreign capital to increase investment and accelerate their transformation.[1]

1 For a more detailed presentation, see IMF (1998).

Anticipating a crisis: the need to look at "new fundamentals"

Mr. Belanger noted that the failure to anticipate the Asian crisis had shown that although the macroeconomic fundamentals appeared sound, analysts had failed to notice or to pay sufficient attention to the serious deterioration in the balance sheets of the private sector—both the corporate and banking sectors—that provoked the crisis. Professor Wachtel thought that a lesson of the crisis was, then, that the traditional fundamentals, such as the ratio of the current- account deficits to GDP, the external debt of the country and its ability to service it and the real exchange rate, were very important, but account now needed to be paid to a set of new fundamentals such as the soundness of domestic bank portfolios, the strength of the banking system, the rate of return on investment, and the build-up of asset price bubbles.

Lessons for crisis management

In his intervention, Mr. Belanger drew some of the lessons for crisis management in general. One was that there was a definite need for a mechanism to "bail in" private creditors at an early stage of the crisis. The London Club could act to reschedule commercial bank debt, but there was no such mechanism for securities and bonds. Indeed, there was no mechanism for working out a rescheduling or bankruptcy at an international level. To set up such a mechanism presented complicated legal and political problems. That did not make it less necessary.

He also drew attention to the need for transparency and disclosure. IMF had not been aware of the true situation in Indonesia and the Republic of Korea before their crises erupted, in particular how much of reserves could actually be used. While agreeing with the desirability of transparency, he noted that, if IMF publicized its dissatisfaction with the policies being pursued by a government, this could itself trigger a crisis. There was a need for a system akin to yellow and red warning cards used in soccer for warning and expelling players.

It was recognized that IMF was not the only institution not to have anticipated fully the Asian crisis: before it occurred, there had been fairly universal praise for the fast growth and macroeconomic stability of these economies. Similarly, IMF and other institutions had underestimated the virulence of the contagion effects of the Asian crisis. One lesson is surely that the exact timing, depth and ramifications of a crash can never be accurately forecast. Even though many private investors had seen that there were problems in several countries, they continued placing their funds in them in pursuit of high returns and in the expectation that they would be able to pull out before the downturn occurred. In many cases, they waited too long.

References

Economic Commission for Europe (1990). "Economic reform in the East: a framework for Western support", *Economic Survey of Europe in 1989-1990.* (United Nations publication, Sales No. E.90.II.E.1), pp. 5-26.

Gaddy, Clifford and Barry Ickes (1998). "Russia's virtual economies", *Foreign Affairs,* vol. 77, No. 5 (September-October), pp. 53-67.

International Monetary Fund (1998). *International Capital Markets: Developments. Prospects and Key Policy Issues.* Washington, D.C.: IMF.

18

Impact of the East Asian Crisis on the Transition Economies and Financial Distress in the Russian Federation

UNITED NATIONS ECONOMIC COMMISSION FOR EUROPE*

The financial crisis in South-East Asia—one of the most serious challenges to the stability of the global financial system in the 1990s—is also a serious challenge to economists and policy makers in national and international bodies. It sent shock waves through the world economy and thus affected—both directly and indirectly—economic performance and economic developments in the member countries of the Economic Commission for Europe (ECE) that are in transition from central planning to the market. A few transition economies have had serious repercussions from external financial shocks, while others have experienced home-grown financial crises.

The crises in the transition economies preceded or evolved in parallel with those in Asia. This timing raises questions as to whether the causes of the crises were similar or different and in what respect? Was there a direct or indirect contagion effect? Are there new risks of crisis in other transition economies? Is it possible to identify any warning signs that might signal an increased risk of a future crisis in the transition countries? What can be learned from the experience of the countries that experienced crises?

---

* Presented by Mr. Joseph Smolik, Economic Analysis Division. This chapter comprises edited and abbreviated sections of ECE's *Economic Survey of Europe 1998*, Nos. 1 (section 3.2) and 2 (section 1.2(ii)), which were available at the July workshop. For additional details, including complete references, please see UN/ECE 1998 and 1998a — *Editors' note.*

The run-up to crisis in the Russian Federation

At the beginning of 1998, the outlook was relatively promising for the Russian economy. More than two years of slowing inflation and successful exchange rate management (providing a much needed predictability of the exchange rate) set the stage for a relatively stable macroeconomic environment. And, probably most important, after seven years of transitional depression, the economy appeared to be turning the corner: a small but still positive rate of growth of gross domestic product (GDP) was reported for 1997.[1] Russian financial markets had been hit by fallout from the Asian crisis in November-December 1997, but at that time the negative impact was relatively limited. The optimistic view of the Government at the start of 1998 was reflected in the growth targets for 1998, which were initially set in the range of 2-4 per cent. In turn, between mid-February and mid-March, the Central Bank of the Russian Federation cut its refinancing rate in three steps from 42 per cent to 30 per cent.

However, bad economic news started to accumulate in the second quarter, beginning with the publication of zero economic growth for the first quarter (implying falling output in March). The April figures did not show any improvement and confirmed that GDP had remained flat in the first four months of the year. At the same time, wage arrears—a recurrent problem for the Russian economy—started to worsen. In the final months of 1997, thanks to a concerted effort and partly using the proceeds from foreign borrowing, the Russian Government reduced its stock of outstanding wage arrears. However, wage arrears began to increase rapidly again in January 1998 and by the end of March the combined stock of public and private sector arrears had reached a record level. Discontent about unpaid wages was behind the wave of coal miners' strikes, which escalated in May with the blockade of railroads throughout the Russian Federation, including the vital Trans-Siberian route.

The deterioration of the economic situation in 1998 was at least partly due to the sharp fall of commodity prices which brought about a substantial

1 It should be noted that the accuracy of Russian statistical data has often been questioned by experts both in and outside the Russian Federation. In 1995, a comprehensive study under the leadership of the World Bank produced a major upward revision of estimates of output in the Russian Federation during the first phase of the transition—and thus a smaller decline in output from pre-transition years (World Bank-Goskomstat, 1995). Subsequently, some observers have argued that the frequent revisions of statistical data by the Russian State Statistics Committee (Goskomstat) are sometimes made in a rather arbitrary and ad hoc manner. The June 1998 corruption scandal at the Goskomstat involving a group of high-ranking statistical officers (who were alleged to have deliberately distorted statistical data) casts further doubts on the reliability of Russian statistics.

fall in export revenues. The negative impact of this fall was not confined to the corporate sector, but also affected the external balance and the public finances. It highlighted a major vulnerability of the Russian economy, i.e., that its high degree of dependence on a narrow range of primary commodity exports made it prone to shocks from fluctuations in world market prices and demand.

As a result of the deterioration in external economic conditions, but also because of chronic deficiencies in the fiscal system (see below), budget revenues in the first few months of 1998 were well below target, thus generating an excessive fiscal gap. Tensions mounted in relations with the International Monetary Fund (IMF), owing to the lack of progress in coping with the budget deficit, and the release of IMF funds under a three-year Extended Fund Facility (EFF) was de facto suspended. However, the Government was able to partly cover the soaring fiscal deficit with a new DM 1.25 billion Eurobond issue in mid-March and the authorities also announced plans to speed up some large privatization deals to attract foreign investors.

Nevertheless, the accumulation of bad economic news increased the pressure on Russian financial markets, where investors were already anxious in the aftermath of the Asian crisis. A totally unexpected change of government at the end of March added further uncertainty to an already deteriorating situation. The manner in which the change was made fostered a perception in the markets of low predictability of the political process in the Russian Federation.

The increased borrowing requirements of the Government started to raise the yield on GKOs (Government treasury bills), and in mid-May the Central Bank of the Russian Federation also raised its "Lombard rate" from 30 to 50 per cent. Another setback was the failure of Tokobank, one of the largest Russian banks, which was placed under conservatorship by the Central Bank on 7 May after facing grave liquidity problems. Excessive borrowing in 1997 had increased considerably the exposure of Russian financial institutions to foreign credit and demand for foreign exchange was rising on the Russian currency market.[2] Weary foreign investors then started to pull out of the GKO market and out of the rouble.[3] Probably the last straw was the failure of the auction of a

2 According to estimates of Capital Data Loanware, syndicated loans to Russian entities in 1997 amounted to over $7.5 billion, with Russian banks receiving more than $2.3 billion. Over $565 million of syndicated loans to Russian banks were due to be repaid in July and August 1998.

3 According to a statement by the First Deputy Chairman of the Central Bank of the Russian Federation, foreigners withdrew between $500 million and $700 million from the Russian Government securities market during the second half of May.

75 per cent stake in the oil giant Rosneft: by the deadline of 26 May, the auction had failed to attract a single bid at the initial offer price of $2.1 billion which, if successful, would have provided much needed funds for financing the budget deficit and replenishing foreign reserves.

The financial turmoil kept worsening until the last week of May. The continuing rise in the yield on GKOs was followed by a large fall in stock market prices.[4] The rouble came under growing pressure and the monetary authorities intervened heavily on the foreign exchange market. On 27 May, the Central Bank of the Russian Federation raised its refinancing rate to 150 per cent as a last resort to defend the currency. This measure, together with a concerted public campaign by top-level Russian officials proclaiming their resolve to prevent a major crisis and avoid a devaluation of the national currency, managed to calm the financial turmoil. The IMF resumed funding under the EFF, thereby signalling support for the main lines of the reform process, while at the same time the IMF reiterated the need to deepen Russian reforms.

Subsequently, interest rates began to fall and the pressure on the rouble weakened. On 3 June, the Russian Federation successfully placed a $1.25 billion issue of Eurobonds, although at a punitive interest rate premium. On 4 June, the Russian central bank reduced its refinancing rate to 60 per cent. Later in the month, the Russian authorities announced a comprehensive anti-crisis programme focusing, on the one hand, on a drastic reduction and restructuring of public spending and, on the other, on boosting public revenue. The draft envisaged, *inter alia*, cutting more than 200,000 government jobs, consolidating extrabudgetary funds, a further reduction of state orders and budget subsidies, and reform of the system of fiscal transfers from the federal budget to the regions. On the revenue side, despite lowering the revenue projections (to make them more realistic), the programme targeted new sources of budget income through a more rapid collection of back taxes, raising the efficiency of the tax collection system, and amending a number of tax laws to allow a faster rate of tax collection. In addition, the programme envisaged speeding-up the privatization process in order to raise additional revenue. Altogether this set of measures would amount to a cut in public spending equivalent to 1 per cent of GDP and extra revenue equivalent to 0.8 per cent of GDP.

[This new programme, however, was received with some skepticism by the markets and on 29 June the central bank hiked interest rates again, to 80 per cent from 60 per cent. Then, on 13 July, the Russian Federation and IMF

4 Between 25 and 27 May alone, the GKO yield spiralled from 50-53 per cent to 70-75 per cent; on 27 May the price of the most liquid shares on the Moscow stock exchange fell by some 12-15 per cent.

announced agreement on a new international financial support package of $22.6 billion, the first tranche of which would be less than $5 billion (more had been expected) as a signal that progress in implementation of reforms was essential.] Russian financial markets continued to be volatile, and considerable uncertainties about the future remained. [Finally, on 17 August, the rouble collapsed, a 90 day moratorium was declared on private debt servicing (mainly by Russian banks), and it soon became clear that the Russian Federation had entered into a major new economic contraction].[5]

The fiscal nexus of the Russian crisis

The Russian crisis reflected a number of persistent and fundamental problems in the Russian economy and these seem to have been the main cause of the turmoil, despite the apparent contagion effect from the Asian crisis. At the core of these problems was the chronic fiscal imbalance of the Russian Government and the manner in which it was being financed.

The Government had been running large budget deficits for a number of years.[6] Consequently—and in addition to the fact that it inherited the bulk of the foreign debt of the Soviet Union—the Russian public debt grew rapidly. Total public debt in 1998 (foreign plus domestic debt, excluding public sector wage arrears and overdue payables to government suppliers) was estimated at around 50-55 per cent of GDP.

Although by international standards this ratio of debt to GDP was not very high, its impact needs to be judged in relation to other macroeconomic variables, such as that total revenue in the Russian federal budget in 1996-1997 amounted to just 11-12 per cent of GDP. Russian public debt was thus 4-5 times larger than the annual budget revenue, and domestic debt alone was some 2-2.5 times higher than the annual revenue of the federal budget. In addition, the level of Russian gross foreign debt was some 1.5 times higher than the value of annual export earnings. Obviously, the strain on the federal budget stemming from the servicing of this level of public debt

5 Editors update of text (for details, see UN/ECE 1998b).

6 Different estimates of the Russian budget deficit have circulated because the Government has only recently adopted international standards— namely, the IMF's manual on government finance statistics— in the compilation of its fiscal accounts. One major distortion before 1998 resulted from the treatment of interest on GKOs, which was paid as the difference between the discounted initial price and the full face value when redeemed. Under the Russian methodology, the implied interest was treated as financing (and thus not reflected in the deficit) and not as interest expenditure. Thus, according to the Russian definition, the deficit in the consolidated federal budget in 1997 was 3.2 per cent of GDP, whereas the IMF estimated it at 6.5 per cent of GDP.

was considerable; that is, interest expenditure in the revised 1998 budget was estimated at 4.8 per cent of GDP.[7]

The composition of the debt embodied a second major structural weakness. Due to the very low level of monetization in the Russian economy and the persistent flight of capital abroad (resulting in a low level of savings deposited in the banking system), the domestic funds available to finance the fiscal deficit were rather limited.[8] Consequently, the Russian authorities were forced to attract increasing amounts of foreign funds to finance the deficit, which they did by opening the domestic treasury bill market to foreigners and by borrowing directly from the international financial markets. This increased the exposure of the Russian economy to volatile short-term foreign capital. By 1998, the size of these inflows reached alarming proportions in terms of their potential to disrupt the domestic financial markets.[9] The vulnerability of the Russian economy to an abrupt reversal in the capital flow was heightened by the relatively low level of official reserves.[10] A sudden capital outflow would thus threaten both fiscal policy (by draining a major source of finance of the budget deficit) and monetary stability (by triggering a speculative attack on the currency). These risks became tangible [events in August].

The causes of the Russian fiscal crisis are numerous, but a few of them can be mentioned here. The tax code in the Russian Federation was notoriously complicated. Tax-related issues have been subject to tens of different pieces of legislation, often giving rise to confusing contradictions. Tax legislation allowed for numerous exemptions which led to abuse and evasion. In addition, tax collection procedures were inefficient and allowed companies to defer tax payments on a large scale (the accumulation of huge tax arrears by

7 This level of interest expenditure amounted to some 48 per cent of the total expected revenue of the federal budget and to 32 per cent of the total expenditure of the federal budget.

8 The Russian budget deficit was also very large in relation to the money supply; that is, the 1997 federal deficit was equivalent to 41 per cent of the average level of broad money during the year and to 73 per cent of M_1 (UN/ECE secretariat computations, based on data of IMF).

9 The potential monetary impact of the capital inflows may be indicated by comparing them with the Russian money stock. In particular, the net inflow of portfolio investment to the Russian Federation (the bulk of which went to the government securities market) amounted to $17.1 billion during the first three quarters of 1997. This was equivalent to 43 per cent of the average level of M_1 in the period January-September and was 1.45 times larger than the absolute increase of the broad money stock during the same period (UN/ECE computations, based on data of IMF).

10 In June 1997, reserves covered just 53 per cent of the short-term debt to foreign banks, which in itself was only a fraction of all short-term obligations (UN/ECE, *1998*, p. 59). Viewed from a different perspective, the average level of official reserves during the first three quarters of 1997 amounted to just 92 per cent of the net inflow of portfolio capital in that period (UN/ECE computations, based on data of IMF).

a few large corporate entities had an especially negative fiscal impact). According to anecdotal evidence, tax evasion by individuals and companies has been widespread since the start of economic transformation. Moreover, the Russian Duma has often voted legislative amendments that increased budgetary expenditure (especially as regards wages and pensions) which were not consistent with the budget that it had previously approved. The revenue projections incorporated in successive budgets have been persistently over optimistic and actual revenue has been chronically below expectations. In both 1997 and 1998, the shortfall forced the Government to invoke the unpopular sequestration mechanism.

All these factors have had a negative impact on tax revenues and have thereby contributed to the persistence of the fiscal deficit and, as a consequence, to the escalation of the Russian public debt. The Russian authorities thus faced the major challenge of designing and implementing a wide-ranging and comprehensive fiscal reform to restore order in the public finances and to prevent a further widening of the deficit. This seems to be the central requirement of the considerable policy effort that is needed in order to improve financial and macroeconomic stability in the country.

Closely related to this problem is the broader issue of institutional reforms, the implementation of which are fundamental for laying the foundations of a sustained economic recovery. Progress in building an appropriate institutional infrastructure for a market economy has been very slow and modest, especially in areas related to tax and corporate law, as well as bankruptcy. The rule of law is still somewhat spasmodic and is being crowded out from some important areas of social life by rules and practices dictated by the interests of the new financial oligarchy, often in conjunction with organized crime and a bureaucracy that is often highly inefficient and lacking in transparency. These obvious institutional deficiencies underline the weakness of the state in its efforts to promote economic recovery. This crucial institutional hiatus cannot be closed by simply declaring policy goals or by the provision of emergency assistance. The creation of an effective institutional framework is a long-term process, which requires a long-term policy commitment by the domestic political class to a credible programme of reform.

The exchange rate and foreign financing

The issue that worried foreign portfolio investors most of all was the exchange rate of the Russian rouble. In January 1998, the Russian central bank switched from periodic devaluations to compensate for the higher domestic than foreign inflation rate to a zero nominal depreciation target, albeit with a wider fluctuation corridor for the rouble of ±15 per cent around the newly fixed exchange rate. This was seen as raising the exchange rate risk of investing in rouble-denominated assets. The escalation of financial instability in May-June, as well as the further widening and deepening of the financial and economic crisis in Asia and the weakening of a number of Asian currencies, increased the concerns of foreign portfolio investors as to whether the Russian authorities would be able to maintain their exchange rate target.

[Viewed from before the August collapse,] a rouble devaluation (or allowing the nominal exchange rate of the rouble to depreciate by more than the pre-announced target) might have provided some temporary relief for the economy. It would have boosted the profit margins (and thus the taxable income) of commodity exporters and curbed import growth. It would have added to inflation; however, the real value of the outstanding domestic debt would be eroded by rising inflation, which would also provide the Government with some additional revenue from the "inflation tax". At the same time, a devaluation of the currency would have represented a forced offset for the lack of progress in some important reforms and an implicit recognition of the policy failure to deal with some of the fundamental problems facing the economy.

[In the event,] the Russian authorities did not have sufficient resources to cope with a major run on the currency. Technically this issue could have been overcome if the international financial institutions and Western Governments had been willing to provide the Russian Federation with sufficient resources to defend the currency. However, the implied moral hazard problem and the suggestion that such assistance might delay the implementation of much needed reforms led many commentators to question the wisdom of such a move. The situation in the Russian Federation before the crash thus presented a major policy dilemma. On the one hand, it could be argued that withholding international assistance would provide the incentive for a much stronger domestic commitment to the process of institutional and economic transformation; but, on the other hand, such a course might exacerbate the considerable economic and social problems in the Russian Federation with unpredictable consequences for the rest of Europe.

The only sustainable policy course towards financial—and thus macroeconomic and political—stabilization in the Russian Federation was to move ahead with a coherent and comprehensive programme of institutional reform in which the reorganization of the fiscal system would be the top priority. A firm and irrevocable commitment of the authorities to sound and predictable economic policies and the existence of credible and transparent institutions through which such policies could be implemented were basic requirements for economic stability and sustained growth. What was most needed to restore calm and stability to Russian financial markets was for such a programme to be seen to be put in place and for the authorities to be seen to be carrying it out.

Experiences in other transition economies

Well before the Russian situation erupted, the Asian crisis had raised widespread concerns about financial stability in all emerging markets. These concerns had been rooted in the apprehension that the underlying factors (or at least some of them) that gave birth to the Asian crisis might also exist in other emerging markets. In the European transition economies, the prevalence of large current-account deficits, often accompanied by sizeable inflows of short-term capital, raised questions about their financial stability (Indeed banking crises had already visited Bulgaria, the Czech Republic, Estonia, Latvia, Lithuania and the Russian Federation). In May 1997, the Czech koruna came under attack (as did also the Slovak and Polish currencies), resulting in the abandonment of the fluctuation band and the depreciation of the currency. Subsequently, the general loss of confidence in emerging markets in the autumn of 1997 necessitated heavy intervention by Ukraine and the Russian Federation, resulting in large losses of official reserves. However, the exchange rate regimes of both countries held up, in part because of steep increases in domestic interest rates. In the other European transition economies foreign exchange markets mostly remained calm and official interventions were limited.

In general, the immediate impact of other repercussions of the Asian crisis on the real economies of the European transition economies (other than the Russian Federation and Ukraine) appears to have been limited.[11] As in other emerging market economies, stock market prices fell sharply, although there was some recovery in the Hungarian and Polish markets in early 1998. Similarly, premia on external debt rose considerably (see figure 1), leading most transition economies to postpone or cancel planned bond issues and equity offerings. Fresh bank lending continued, but at a slower pace. Although terms on new debt improved during the first quarter of 1998, borrowing costs remained above pre-crises levels. The Russian Federation and the Czech Republic were downgraded by one credit-rating agency, but six countries were upgraded or awarded first-time ratings. The most important indirect impacts of the Asian crisis on the transition thus economies appear to be the following:

---

11 The fairly weak commercial links between the transition economies and East Asia meant it was unlikely that their international trade would be directly affected.

Figure 1: Interest premia on sovereign bond issues of selected emerging market economies, 1997-1998
(Percentage points above United States treasury bonds)

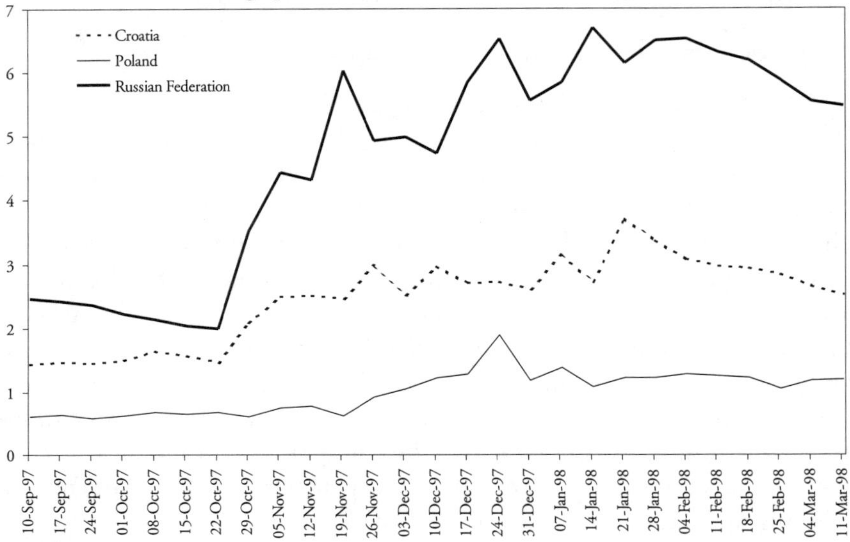

Source: The Financial Times.

- Increased costs of debt servicing, owing to larger margins on any new external debt incurred,
- Delayed restructuring and capacity expansion because of the postponement or outright cancellation of planned borrowing or equity emissions,
- Loss of official reserves and higher external debt owing to the replenishment of foreign reserves,
- Adverse repercussions on the macroeconomy of increases in domestic interest rates which were implemented by some countries to protect their exchange rates,
- Setbacks to the development of a financial market culture.

The ultimate impact of these effects will, of course, depend on how long the disruptions continue.

Are transition economies prone to financial instability?

Even given this range of experiences, some transition economies seemed to have been hit hard by the crisis and even those that made out relatively well might still have been quite vulnerable. Their degree of vulnerability depends on a number of macro and microeconomic factors. Among the most often cited—the list being far from exhaustive—are such factors as the macroeconomic policy mix and its consistency; the exchange rate regime and the strength of the commitment of the monetary authorities to stick to it; the degree of openness of the economy to capital flows; the level of monetization of the economy and of its overall credit exposure; the stability of the banking system and especially the quality of banks' asset portfolios; the state of banking supervision and regulations and their degree of enforcement; and the transparency of domestic financial markets and their regulation. The recent experience both in Asia and in the European transition economies suggests that each of these factors—and all of them in their interaction—may play a role in instigating or escalating a crisis, all the more so given the globalization of financial markets and the growing volatility of capital flows. Moreover, multiple systemic, regulatory and/or institutional weaknesses in the economy may result in a chain reaction, amplifying the depth of a crisis. Below, an assessment of the vulnerability of the European transition economies is attempted, examining, in turn external and internal factors.

External financial positions

It may be useful to compare key financial indicators for the transition economies with those for East Asian crisis economies (see table 1).[12] Prior to the crisis, the foreign bank debt of these Asian countries had grown rapidly and the maturity structure was unfavourable. For several years, over 60 per cent of their total bank debt was maturing in less than one year (hereafter referred to as short-term debt),[13] and various liquidity indicators were also unsatisfactory. On average, international reserves covered only 32 per cent of short-term bank debt (Taiwan Province of China is the exception) and 18 per cent of the domestic money stock.[14] Moreover, loans immediately available to most of these

12 While these indicators give some insights into the vulnerability to financial crisis, they do not explain its timing—many key indicators had been unfavourable for some years—or why some countries were not affected (see Sachs, Tornell and Velasco, 1996). Indeed, no single indicator provides a reliable guide to the imminence of a crisis.

13 The Bank for International Settlements (BIS) provides data on the value of bank loans maturing in less than one year. For convenience, these liabilities are referred to here as short-term debt, but it should be borne in mind that they also include medium-term obligations maturing within one year. Also, the BIS data cover only the lending of banks in the reporting area (largely the developed market economies) and thus do not give a complete picture of the total bank debt of borrowers.

14 It should be noted that official reserves as currently measured generally include foreign currency that is committed to covering forward contracts and to this extent overstate the resources available for defending the currency.

Table 1. Financial indicators for the transition economies and selected East Asian countries, end-June 1997
(Billion dollars, per cent and ratios)

	Bank debt			Credit	Official	Reserves/	Reserves/	Reserves/
	Total[a]	*Short-term*[a]	*Share*[b]	*commitments*[c]	*reserves*[a]	M_1 [d]	*DM* [e]	*ST debt* [f]
Transition economies								
Eastern Europe	46.9	20.1	42.8	23.1	50.9	1.45[g]	0.67[g]	2.73
Baltic States	0.7	0.4	47.6	8.2	2.4	0.80[g]	0.73[g]	6.74
Russian Federation	69.1	38.3	55.4	10.2	20.4	0.47	0.32	0.53
Other CIS countries[h]	3.3	1.8	54.8	36.0	3.2	0.51[g]	..	1.78
East Asian economies								
Indonesia	58.7	34.7	59.0	27.3	14.7	0.58	0.13	0.25
Malaysia	28.8	16.3	56.4	13.0	19.2	0.65	0.24	0.67
Philippines	14.1	8.3	58.8	21.4	7.0	0.78	0.24	0.50
Republic of Korea	103.4	70.2	67.9	9.9	24.5	0.60	0.15	0.24
Thailand	69.4	45.6	65.7	7.6	22.6	1.37	0.23	0.33
Total Asia above	274.4	175.1	63.8	..	88.0	0.73	0.18	0.32
Taiwan Province of China	25.2	22.0	87.3	31.4	64.9	..	..	2.58

Source: BIS, *The Maturity, Sectoral and Nationality Distribution of International Bank Lending,* First Half 1997 (Basle), January 1998; IMF, *International Financial Statistics,* December 1997; national statistics; UN/ECE secretariat calculations.

Note: Short-term bank debt includes all liabilities maturing within one year.

a. Liabilities vis-à-vis international banks, billion dollars.
b. Short-term debt/total bank debt (per cent).
c. Undisbursed credit commitments/total bank debt (per cent).
d. Official foreign currency reserves/money stock (M_1) (ratio).
e. Official reserves/domestic money stock (ratio); domestic money: M_2 less foreign currency deposits.
f. Official reserves/short-term bank debt (ratio).
g. Unweighted averages.
h. Belarus, Republic of Moldova and Ukraine.

countries from international banks (undisbursed credit commitments) have been relatively low.

Comparable indicators for the transition economies show a generally more favourable picture. In Eastern Europe, short-term debt amounted to some 43 per cent of total bank debt in June 1997, while credit commitments were relatively high (although not in the Baltic States and the Russian Federation). Liquidity indicators based on official reserves also tend to be better for the transition economies. External reserves in Eastern Europe exceeded short-term debt in mid-1997 by significant margins, and on average covered about two thirds of domestic money.[15] However, according to these ratios, the position of the Russian economy was weaker. On the whole, the East Asian economies had run smaller current-account deficits than the transition economies.

Several standard financial indicators for the European transition economies are given in table 2. First, the current-account deficits of many of the transition economies had attracted attention already in 1996, and concern grew in early 1997 when it appeared that they would widen further (the exception was the Russian Federation, which was in surplus). Second, in general these countries could be considered to be among the "less indebted",[16] although the debt burden varied considerably.

Third is liquidity. Of the three indicators presented in table 2, the ratio of official reserves to imports is the most widely used. The rule of thumb is that reserves should cover at least three months of a country's imports of goods and services (including factor income payments). By this measure, the liquidity of the Czech Republic has been more than adequate, while Slovakia has been on the borderline. However, the reserves of Ukraine and the Russian Federation have been below the recommended level (even when they peaked in the Russia Federation in mid-1997), as has also been the case in Belarus, the Baltic states and Croatia. The ratio of reserves to short-term debt of the Czech Republic, Slovakia and, especially, Ukraine, was greater than one at end-January 1997, indicating that official reserves were more than enough to cover bank debt coming due within one year. The liquidity positions of the other countries except the Russian Federation were also favourable. Perhaps the most relevant liquidity indicator in

15 Defined as M_2 less deposits in foreign currencies.

16 Based on the World Bank classification of indebted countries. In comparison, Indonesia was considered moderately indebted and the Republic of Korea, Malaysia, and Thailand less indebted by the World Bank criteria. In the wake of the Asian crisis, the external debt, particularly the short-term liabilities, of a number of the countries turned out to be larger than the officially published figure.

Table 2. Financial indicators for transition economies, 1996-1997
(Billion dollars, per cent and ratios)

	Current account (Per cent of GDP[c])		*Debt indicators, end June 1997[a]*					*Reserves-liquidity ratios[b]*			*Credit commit-ments ratio[f]*
						Short-term					
	1996	*1997*	*Gross/ exports*	*Net/ exports*	*Gross/ GDP*	*Total[d]*	*Banks[e]*	*Imports*	*Short-term debt*	*Domestic money*	
Transition economies	-3.8	-4.9	91	51	36	..	42.8	4.0	2.5	0.67	23.1
Albania	-5.3	-7.8	266	157	37	..	33.3	5.2	6.6	..	0.8
Bosnia and Herzegovina	-	-	-	-	-	..	67.9	-	-	..	1.2
Bulgaria	0.2	4.5	157	124	98	13.5	30.5	4.3	1.9	1.44	3.9
Croatia	-4.5	-14.3	63	36	32	7.1	48.6	2.5	2.3	0.94	19.4
Czech Republic	-7.6	-6.8	69	38	40	25.0	53.4	3.3	1.8	0.35	34.0
Hungary	-3.7	-3.2	99	63	51	14.1	37.0	3.9	2.1	0.68	20.6
Poland	-1.0	-3.6	119	55	28	..	46.2	5.4	4.5	0.50	21.8
Romania	-7.2	-5.3	90	54	27	12.2	38.6	3.4	2.4	0.64	28.9
Slovakia	-11.1	-10.2	88	60	51	..	46.8	2.8	1.7	0.27	27.3
Slovenia	0.2	-0.9	40	9	24	1.9	23.9	3.6	5.5	0.53	15.4
The former Yugoslav Republic of Macedonia	-7.3	-11.0	84	67	28	..	69.2	1.5	1.6	..	0.9
Baltic States	-8.3	-9.1	18	-3	11	..	47.6	2.1	6.1	0.73	8.2
Estonia	-9.7	-10.3	9	-13	7	..	39.5	2.2	4.9	0.57	6.9
Latvia	-5.6	-7.4	14	-11	7	..	40.7	2.4	15.2	0.78	5.6
Lithuania	-9.2	-9.6	27	8	16	..	48.1	1.8	5.8	0.83	10.5

(Table 2, cont'd.)

	Current account (Per cent of GDP [c])		*Debt indicators, end June 1997 [a]*					*Reserves-liquidity ratios [b]*			*Credit commit-ments ratio [f]*
						Short-term					
	1996	*1997*	*Gross/ exports*	*Net/ exports*	*Gross/ GDP*	*Total [d]*	*Banks [e]*	*Imports*	*Short-term debt*	*Domestic money*	
Commonwealth of Independent States	1.9	0.9	102	90	26	..	55.4	1.4	0.6	0.38	10.9
Belarus	-3.7	-7.9	17	12	10	..	42.3	0.5	2.2	..	45.5
Republic of Moldova	-12.9	-20.9	125	91	71	..	30.6	3.0	22.4	..	28.6
Russian Federation	2.6	1.7	119	107	27	..	55.4	1.6	0.5	0.32	10.2
Ukraine	-2.7	-3.6	45	34	18	..	42.4	1.2	4.2	0.45	37.6
Total	-0.6	-1.5	-	-	-	..	41.6	2.8	1.3	0.64	12.9

Source: National balance of payments statistics; BIS, *The Maturity, Sectoral and Nationality Distribution of International Bank Lending*, First Half 1997 (Basle), January 1998; UN/ECE secretariat estimates.

a. Ratios of gross and net debt to exports of goods, services and income; gross debt/GDP (x100).
b. Ratios of official reserves to imports of goods and services, short-term debt and the domestic money stock, respectively.
c. Per cent, 1997 estimates are for January-June only.
d. Short-term debt as a percentage of total external debt.
e. Bank debt maturing within one year/total bank debt (per cent).
f. Ratio of undisbursed credit commitments to total bank debt (per cent).

a period of shifting investor confidence, however, is the ratio of reserves to the domestic money stock (Sachs, Tornell and Velasco, 1996a).[17] In mid-June 1997, official reserves covered only 27 per cent of the money stock in Slovakia, 32 per cent in the Russian Federation and 35 per cent in the Czech Republic. In Ukraine, the ratio was 45 per cent, although still below the average for the transition economies. However, in all cases these liquidity positions were stronger than those of the East Asian economies.

Vulnerability to external shocks, including changes in investor confidence, may also be gauged by the structure of capital inflows. On the one hand, foreign direct investment (FDI), long-term foreign currency bonds, and medium and longer-term bank loans are often considered to be relatively stable sources of finance. On the other hand, foreign portfolio investment in domestic securities and various short-term capital inflows are deemed risky since they are subject to rapid withdrawal. As has been observed in various ECE *Surveys* and *Bulletins*, these latter flows have often played a major role in the capital accounts of the transition economies.[18] Moreover, they seem to be more volatile—reversals of direction have been common—compared to FDI and other long-term funds. Partly because of this, the composition of capital flows into the individual transition economies has not been very stable.

In the Russian Federation and Ukraine, portfolio flows, chiefly foreign investment in short-term treasury bills, dominated inflows for much of 1997 (although FDI also increased rapidly in the Russian Federation). In Ukraine, this type of portfolio investment and short-term funds accounted for about 80 per cent of net inflows in the first half of the year. Slovakia has been heavily dependent on short-term and various unrecorded flows, although the share of medium and long-term loans has increased; FDI has been negligible. In the Czech Republic, in contrast, the bulk of capital inflows has been in the form of medium and long-term loans and FDI. Dependence on short-term funds decreased owing to the outflow of such funds after the widening of the currency band in February 1996.

---

17 The ratio bears on the hypothetical question, if there were a complete loss of confidence in the domestic currency and money holders sought to exchange all their money for foreign exchange at the going exchange rate, how much of the demand could be met out of official stocks of foreign exchange reserves? Answering the question is tricky, as there seems to be little agreement on the appropriate measure of the domestic money stock in this context (that is, M_1, broad or domestic money).

18 In the first three quarters of 1997, in particular, such potentially volatile funds accounted for at least 40 per cent and as much as one half of net inflows into Eastern Europe.

The degree of foreign participation in local financial markets in the transition economies varies from country to country,[19] but it seems to be high by world standards. This has exposed them to abrupt reversals in flows, as, for example, when international investors (especially international fund managers) sought to cover losses in one part of the world (raise liquidity) by selling securities in other markets[20]

Four European transition economies—the Czech Republic, Slovakia, Ukraine, and the Russian Federation—had to intervene heavily to support their exchange rates at various times in 1997 (the latter two also in early 1998), although in the end the Czech Republic was not able to hold the line. Their common economic features include, first of all, exports, which had been sluggish (although they improved later in the year in the Czech Republic and Slovakia). Liquidity may also have been a problem, although as indicated above, the indicators were sometimes ambiguous. These countries have also experienced at least some periods of political uncertainty which affected confidence. Moreover, in the Czech Republic doubts arose about the ability of the Government to act decisively to stem the growth in the current-account deficit early in 1997. To various degrees, there were also concerns about the willingness of the Governments to undertake essential reforms. However, there are considerable economic differences between these four countries as well (see table 2). The scale and even the sign of current-account balances and debt burdens have been very different. Moreover, aside from the Czech Republic, FDI flows have been comparatively small and capital flows have been skewed toward the short term.

There seem to be a variety of reasons why contagion from the Asian crisis was not so pronounced in the other transition economies. Hungary, for example, had entered a virtuous circle of accelerating economic growth with a strengthening external position. In Slovenia, the external indicators had been broadly favourable for some time, and the inflow of funds has been used to further boost official reserves. Various restrictions on capital may also have limited its vulnerability to financial shocks. In Poland the current account developed

19 According to Chairman Dubinin of the Russian central bank, in 1997 non-residents accounted for 16 per cent of the $55 billion GKO market, while in Ukraine, 48 per cent of the treasury bills sold in auction during one week were bought by non-residents. In Poland, however, foreign bids were estimated at 45-75 per cent of the total bid volume in the treasury bill auction in the first week of March, 1998 (*Source:* Credit Suisse/First Boston, *Emerging Europe: Weekly Update,* 15 October 1997 and 4 March 1998).

20 According to various reports, investors in the Republic of Korea, for example, sold Russian securities when they incurred losses on the Korean market, thereby helping to drive down prices in Moscow.

much more favourably than had been expected. Moreover, output and export growth was strong, the debt burden diminished, and reserves (already adequate) increased further thanks to growing inflows of capital.

In Bulgaria, whose crisis was deepest in 1996, key external indicators showed a marked improvement in 1997. Already in 1996, the current account had moved into surplus, the funds so generated helping to create the conditions for the establishment of a currency board on 1 July 1997. The very commitment by the Government to its creation and to a policy of structural reform and full servicing of (restructured) external debt instilled confidence which stimulated various capital inflows. In consequence, official reserves rose to record levels and the country's liquidity ratio (measured as reserves to domestic money) became the highest in the region. The Baltic States ran among the largest current-account deficits in the region. However, external debt was very low (Estonia and Latvia are creditors on a net basis) and relatively large direct investment flows seem to have helped to stimulate merchandise exports. Official liquidity has been comparatively high (as would be expected given that currency boards operate in Estonia and Lithuania).

In sum, the number of transition economies seriously affected by the Asian crisis was actually small despite widespread fears about possible contagion via the financial markets. Explanations for this include increasing confidence among informed investors in the basic soundness of the external financial positions. In a number of cases, economic performance improved in the second half of 1997—faster export and economic growth, lower than expected current-account deficits, increases in foreign exchange reserves, and so on. In part these developments were the result of policy measures which, although primarily intended to curb inflation and current-account imbalances, directly supported exchange rates. In particular tight monetary policies kept domestic interest rates high and fostered inflows of funds (or at least discouraged outflows).

Internal factors

Besides the external exposure, financial vulnerability depends on the size and depth of the domestic financial sector relative to the size of the economy. The larger and deeper the domestic financial markets, the greater their potential impact on macroeconomic performance even in the case of a minor financial disturbance. Conversely, if the volume of financial transactions is small relative to the size of the economy, the overall impact of a financial shock may be less pronounced.

In this regard, the relative underdevelopment of the financial sector may be an advantage in resisting contamination by an external financial crisis. A financial crisis is very often accompanied by an economic downturn and recession which, in turn, may lead to widespread bankruptcies and defaults on bank loans. Moreover, the macroeconomic stabilization or adjustment policies which are usually pursued in response to a financial crisis often entail monetary and fiscal austerity which are likely to reinforce the depressive effect on the economy. Hence the scope of these negative repercussions within the economy is likely to be related to the size of the overall stock of credit.

Two of the composite indicators which may be used to measure the level of domestic financial exposure—the degree of monetization of the economy and the extent of credit exposure—are illustrated for some of the transition economies in table 3. On average, the ECE transition economies were relatively less monetized than mature market economies.[21] For that matter, they were less monetized than the emerging market economies in South-East Asia, especially as regards broad money and credit expansion.[22] Of course, the relatively low levels of monetization and credit expansion reflect the underdeveloped state of the financial systems in the transition economies.

Among the transition economies themselves, financial problems emerged in the countries that had relatively higher levels of monetization and credit expansion. Before its financial crisis, the relative levels of broad money and total credit in Bulgaria were among the highest in the region (probably abnormally high in relation to the state of institutional reforms and of the regulatory environment) and one of the rehabilitating effects of the crisis was to lower these ratios via inflation to more manageable levels (see table 3). The Czech Republic, which also experienced a financial disturbance in 1997, had the highest level of monetization among the transition countries.

The composition of the monetary aggregates in some of the transition countries displays another characteristic which is not very common in mature markets, namely, a relatively thin layer of quasi-money denominated in local currency.[23] This was especially pronounced in all the Baltic States, but also in

21 For example, the unweighted average monetization ratios for the member states of the European Union (except Luxembourg) in 1995 were 24.3 per cent for M_1, 69.9 per cent for broad money, and 71.4 per cent for total credit (UN/ECE, 1997, p. 75 and UN/ECE computations, based on data of IMF).

22 At the end of 1996, the ratio of broad money to GDP in Indonesia, Republic of Korea, Malaysia, the Philippines and Thailand ranged between 45.7 per cent in the Republic of Korea and 89.3 per cent in Thailand, the unweighted average for the five countries being 64.0 per cent. The ratio of total credit to GDP ranged from 52.3 per cent in the Philippines to 122.1 per cent in Thailand. The unweighted average of the latter ratio was 76.3 per cent or higher than the average for the European Union in 1995 (UN/ECE computations, based on data of IMF).

23 In the definition used here, quasi-money includes time and savings deposits in local currency.

Table 3. Monetary aggregates in selected transition countries, 1996-1997[a]
(Per cent of GDP)

	M_1[b]		*Total broad money*[c]		*Total credit*[d]	
	1996	*1997*[e]	*1996*	*1997*[e]	*1996*	*1997*[e]
Albania	34.7	..	62.6	..	6.4	..
Bulgaria	7.8	5.5	46.8	23.5	37.5	17.0
Croatia	9.0	10.9	28.6	39.0	33.5	35.9
Czech Republic	29.3	25.2	70.2	67.8	63.8	63.5
Hungary	15.3	14.9	36.6	35.2	19.2	21.2
Poland	11.5	12.5	35.6	41.4	18.3	21.6
Romania	7.3	4.8	20.7	17.9	19.1	14.7
Slovakia	25.6	23.5	64.0	63.7	58.4	56.0
Slovenia	7.8	8.4	40.6	43.4	26.9	26.6
Yugoslavia	5.3	6.9	36.6	34.1	..	..
Estonia	17.9	19.5	23.3	27.0	16.6	25.2
Latvia	12.7	14.0	20.1	22.4	6.3	8.9
Lithuania	10.6	11.3	16.6	17.2	12.4	11.0
Russian Federation	7.6	8.9	14.4	16.1	10.0	10.7

Source: National statistics and direct communications from national statistical offices to UN/ECE secretariat; IMF *International Financial Statistics,* various issues.

a. Averages of monthly or quarterly figures.
b. Currency in circulation plus demand deposits.
c. M_1 plus time deposits in domestic currency and foreign currency deposits.
d. Total outstanding claims to legal entities and households (except claims on government).
e. For 1997 the monetary aggregates refer to January-September for the Czech Republic; January-October for Bulgaria; January-November for Romania and the Russian Federation; the full year for Croatia, Estonia, Hungary, Latvia, Lithuania, Poland, Slovakia, Slovenia and Yugoslavia. GDP data for 1997 are estimates.

some other transition economies (Croatia, Ukraine). On the one hand, such a composition of broad money—which reflects the structure of money demand[24]—is partly a legacy of the past. At the same time it is at least partly an indication of continuing low levels of confidence—both of investors and of the public at large—in the local currency as a store of value. In all those countries, the share of national wealth which is kept in the form of foreign currency deposits is much higher than that stored in the form of time and savings deposits in local currency. But, paradoxically, as far as the overall financial vulnerability of the economy is concerned, such a structure of the monetary aggregates increases the resilience of the financial system.

24 Technically, it also reflects low values of the money multipliers.

Besides these quantitative aspects of the domestic financial sector, institutional aspects of the banking system plays a key role in the overall financial stability of a country. In practically all the recent crises, the poor performance of the banking sector had a negative effect, adding to the financial pressures or was even the main determinant of the crisis. Although there are important differences between the role of the banks in the financial turmoil in East Asia and in the several crises in the transition economies, the core of the problem was basically the same: imperfect intermediation and a misallocation of financial resources. This experience underlines how vital it is for macroeconomic stability in emerging markets that banks perform all of their multiple functions efficiently and prudently and that not only the operations of the banks per se but also their environment, including financial markets, be regulated and supervised properly.

Indeed, the state of the banking systems has been an issue of concern to policy makers since the start of economic transformation. Financial systems in the centrally planned economies only existed in a rudimentary form and most of the transition countries had to start building modern banking systems practically from scratch. Financial reforms, especially during the first phase of transition, turned out to be notoriously difficult and encountered numerous problems.

At different stages of the transformation process, banking crises occurred in Bulgaria, the Czech Republic, Estonia, Latvia, Lithuania and the Russian Federation. Actually, it was the start of economic recovery, based on a coherent set of market-oriented reforms, that turned out to be most beneficial for strengthening the banking systems as well, at least in some of the more advanced transition countries. The better performance of enterprises improved their financial position and this in turn contributed to an easing of the pressure on the banks.

In the Russian Federation, as well as in some other CIS countries, non-performing bank credits do not appear to have been a major problem for the economy, owing in part to the relatively low level of monetization. However, a much more important and still unresolved issue is that of other forms of non-payment: inter-enterprise arrears and non-payment of wages and taxes, the latter also provoking a chain reaction in the form of deferred payment of different types of transfers by the fiscal authorities.[25] It was thus indicative that despite some recovery in Russian output in 1997, most types of arrears continued to

25 Although non-bank arrears do not affect the stability of the banking system directly, the chain of non-payments that they provoke may (and probably does) ultimately affect the banking system (for example, when enterprises do not service their bank credits because they are not being paid by their clients).

grow in the course of the year. Although the Russian Government made some progress in 1997 in clearing its own backlog of wage arrears, as noted previously, total enterprise wage arrears continued to increase.

The official statistics on the current state of the banks' asset portfolios in the transition countries are still rather incomplete and patchy. However, the available statistical and anecdotal evidence, as well as some recent studies, indicate that even at the current stage of transformation, banks in many transition economies remain burdened with considerable amounts of substandard and non-performing loans.

Some transition countries, however, have made notable progress in strengthening their banking systems. After the successful implementation of a debt restructuring programme—which coincided with a period of strong recovery of the Polish economy—the level of bad loans held by Polish banks was reduced drastically (Belka and Krajewska, 1997 and Sota, 1996). After three waves of debt consolidation and recapitalization, Hungarian banks have also considerably improved their financial position.[26] The quality of the asset portfolios of banks has also greatly improved during the later stages of transition in Slovenia. There the share of classified assets in the total credit exposure of the banks decreased from 19 per cent in 1993 to 11 per cent in 1995 (Stiblar, 1996).

One of the negative side effects of the bad loans problem was the emergence of excessively high interest rate spreads. Faced with cash-flow losses due to the non-performing loans, banks tend to pass some of the recovery costs onto their good clients by charging an extra premium on their lending rates and levying an extra discount on their deposit rates. This increases the cost of finance to enterprises and thus has a depressing effect on their activity, while depositors forego interest income on their savings. Excessively high interest spreads could be observed in practically all the transition economies during the initial phase of reforms. They are still a feature of bank performance in a number of these countries, but the general trend in recent years has been for the spread between lending and deposit rates to shrink.

Given the discussion above on the state of the banks' assets in the different countries, it would be reasonable to expect that the reduction in interest spreads would be more pronounced in countries where relatively more progress has been made in improving the quality of credit portfolios. This is indeed what can be observed in the data. Thus the average spread between short-term

26 While in December 1994 27.2 per cent of the total stock of outstanding loans were classified as "problematic" and 8.9 per cent of the total stock as "bad", by December 1996 these proportions had fallen to 11 per cent and 2.9 per cent, respectively (Hungary, 1994, p. 121 and 1996, p. 124).

lending and deposit rates in Hungary declined from 9.8 percentage points in 1993 to 3.2 percentage points in 1997.[27] Over the same period, the spread in Slovenia fell from 15.9 per cent to 6.9 per cent.[28] Similar improvements occurred in the Baltic States. The interest rate spread in the Russian Federation also declined dramatically between 1995 and 1997, a positive outcome of the process of macroeconomic stabilization; in absolute terms, however, it still remained very high (around 31 percentage points in 1997).

Obviously, this brief overview of some of the internal factors that may affect financial stability in the transition economies is not exhaustive and there are numerous other elements to be taken into account in a financial stability package. In general, the degree of monetization of an economy undergoing a major transformation needs to proceed in parallel with the development of the proper institutional and regulatory environment and with the maturing of its markets. Thus, caution is needed in managing the process of remonetization and the deepening of financial markets that lies ahead for the transition economies. This notwithstanding, the transition economies (and especially the most advanced among them) have made considerable progress across a broad spectrum of reforms that have boosted their macroeconomic and financial stability. At the same time, a number of important problems remain and great care will be needed to minimize the risks of financial turmoil during the next phases of the transition process.

Policy implications for the transition economies

In the aftermath of the Asian crisis, there is a growing awareness of the range of financial risks in emerging markets and there is an ongoing debate about the appropriate policy mix required to reduce these risks, as well as to find ways out of a financial crisis of the Asian type. In addition, as financial markets in some transition economies were affected by contagion, which caused turbulence and agitation among investors, there is also uncertainty regarding the relevant policy reaction to this type of disturbance.

As regards the policy issues related to financial stability and crises, it is useful to distinguish short-term policy responses in a state of financial turmoil from the medium-term and long-term policies which aim to establish and preserve stability on the financial markets and to minimize the risks of financial crisis. When financial markets are shaken by a disturbance (whether internally generated or exogenous), policy makers have a very limited assortment of tools at their disposal. On the one hand, the authorities may attempt to intervene on

27 Weighted average of the bank rates on loans and deposits with a maturity of less than one year (UN/ECE computations, based on data of IMF).

28 Short-term working capital loans and 31-90 day deposits (UN/ECE computations based on data from the National Bank of Slovenia and IMF).

the markets directly, either by creating a buffer which absorbs some of the power of the attack (for example, by selling foreign exchange reserves during a run on the currency or providing lender-of-last-resort facilities during a banking crisis) or by changing policy variables that may be under their control (such as the exchange rate or refinancing rates). On the other hand, policy makers may amend market regulations with a view to isolating (or restricting the access of) actual or potential market participants to the affected market.

Responding to crises by raising the central bank refinancing rate is often seen as a means of boosting confidence in the local currency, especially when the latter is the target of speculative attack. By intervening in the money market in this way, the authorities increase the return on financial assets denominated in domestic currency. The goal is to affect the composition of money demand: given relative stability in the money demand elasticities, this should result in greater demand for monetary assets in local currency at the expense of foreign currency denominated assets.

The monetary authorities in the transition countries resorted to this type of intervention during recent periods of financial turmoil. Interest rates rose considerably in Bulgaria during the peak of the 1996-1997 crisis; a similar, though not so pronounced increase was also observed in the Czech Republic and Romania. Towards the end of 1997 and in the first months of 1998, financial markets in some of the transition economies were also affected by the Asian crisis (most notably the Russian Federation, but also Ukraine and some of the Baltic States). This again led to the raising of interest rates in these countries, especially in the Russian Federation, where the central bank raised its refinancing rate in several steps to defend the rouble.

It is highly uncertain, however, whether such policy interventions will in fact be successful in moderating the pressures on the financial markets or in arresting a looming crisis. First, a financial crisis usually breaks unexpectedly and develops more quickly than the responses of the authorities. Secondly, the authorities may lack the capacity to exert a significant impact on the markets (for example, when foreign exchange reserves are low). Thirdly, the degrees of freedom of the authorities may be limited by the possible adverse side effects or costs of the intervention.[29] Last but not least, the success of any intervention crucially

29 When considering the justification of this type of policy intervention, it is important to take into account the possible (direct and indirect) adverse effects. Thus, raising interest rates in support of the currency may induce inflows of short-term speculative capital that are attracted by the interest rate differential. However, this may increase the vulnerability of the economy to external disturbances should these flows reverse direction. Intervening on the foreign exchange market in defence of the exchange rate is also costly, as the central bank loses reserves. For example, in November 1997 alone, the Russian central bank sold more than $6 billion (or one third of its reserves) in accommodating the outflow of short-term capital and defending the rouble (data of IMF).

depends on the credibility of the authority that implements it. If a government does not have sufficient credibility (which, *inter alia*, depends heavily on its past record), markets may remain unaffected by such intervention, regardless of the magnitude of the effort. Conversely, a credible authority may induce the required change in the market with a relatively limited intervention.

Credibility affects investors' behaviour through the elasticities of demand for financial assets: high credibility is usually reflected in a relative stability of these elasticities and vice versa. Thus, if the authorities do not enjoy sufficient confidence among investors (for example investors may doubt the resolution of the authorities to deliver on their pre-announced commitments such as the maintenance of a fixed exchange rate), then in a state of financial disturbance, money demand elasticities may become highly unstable. This instability may add a self-fulfilling element in a financial crisis: the crisis occurs because most investors believe that it is going to occur. For example, if a large majority of investors expect that the fixed exchange rate will be abandoned, raising interest rates may do nothing to arrest a speculative attack on the currency. This is what happened in April-May 1997 in the Czech Republic when interventions through higher interest rates were unable to stop the speculative attack on the koruna. Similar interventions also failed to prevent the collapse of the exchange rate regimes in South-East Asia.

However, experience in some of the transition economies also provides examples of successful intervention in arresting a potential crisis. In the aftermath of the Mexican crisis, there was growing tension on the Hungarian financial markets due to widening "twin deficits" and some observers were worried that a similar crisis might occur in Hungary. However, the authorities announced a comprehensive adjustment programme and demonstrated a strong commitment to implementing it. This intervention sent sufficiently strong signals to the markets and, as shown by subsequent developments, Hungary not only managed to circumvent a crisis but after the adjustment, which was long and painful, embarked on a stable growth path.

One of the important policy lessons of the recent crises, which is especially relevant for policy makers in the transition economies, is that while it is next to impossible to arrest a crisis once it occurs, the authorities can do a great deal to prevent one emerging in the first place. Actually, the very set of external and internal factors that can lead to financial instability point to the elements which can provide strong support for financial stability, if they are targeted by adequate, timely and consistent policies. This requires that the authorities set, on the one hand, long-term goals as to the desired level of these—in very broad terms—"parameters of financial stability" and, on the other, that they closely and continuously monitor the state of these factors and keep them within certain targeted zones of stability.

It follows from the previous discussion, that such policy targets would need to include macroeconomic variables per se as well as the state of the institutional and regulatory environment. Within the set of sensitive macroeconomic variables, it appears that apart from the magnitude of the current-account deficit, the authorities should also pay close attention to the specific manner of its financing and, especially to the absolute and relative level of short-term capital flows.[30] The level of official foreign exchange reserves—as a factor of stability—needs to be compared both to the exposure to short-term capital flows (externally) and to the level of domestic monetary and credit expansion (internally).

Among the institutional factors, the development and reform of the banking systems should have a high priority on the agenda for policy makers in the transition countries. The efficient allocation of financial resources throughout the economy and sound banking performance are just two sides of the same coin. They can only be achieved if enterprise-bank relations are based on economic efficiency and market principles. Apart from adequate training, this requires proper governance and accountability of bankers. Shortcomings in this respect can lead to serious distortions in financial intermediation and to market failures. Hence appropriate regulation is needed to ensure that enterprise-bank relations meet the highest standards of efficient and prudential banking.

Another institutional and regulatory issue that has come to the forefront of recent policy debate concerns the speed of opening up the transition economies and, especially, of the liberalization of capital account transactions. The degree of openness of an economy together with its degree of exposure to foreign capital flows are two factors that directly affect its vulnerability to external shocks. One lesson of the recent crises is that a rush to liberalize emerging markets, without at the same time ensuring that they will function efficiently and that they can be properly regulated, may create excessive risks of instability. This lesson is especially relevant for the transition economies which are preparing for EU accession and which will have to harmonize their regulatory environment with that in the EU, including the liberalization of financial markets.

The main issue in the current debate is not whether to liberalize but when. Considering the embryonic state of many markets in the transition economies and the immaturity of their institutional environment, an untimely opening of the economy can expose it to a high risk of importing instability from abroad. Thus, much caution is needed in managing this process: there will be a need for

30 See also the discussion on this issue in UN/ECE, 1997a, pp. 35-36.

synchronization and coherence between the institutional build-up and the development of market infrastructure, on the one hand, and the process of financial liberalization and integration, on the other, in order to preserve stability and ensure the smooth implementation of the policy. The creation of an institutional and market infrastructure that is sufficiently strong to face volatile capital movements, which are typical of today's "global" economy, must be regarded as a prerequisite for successful liberalization of domestic financial markets.

Finally, it is of the utmost importance that the authorities in the transition countries build up a reputation for a long-term commitment to financial stability. This requires not only a long-term policy agenda but also the consistent day-to-day policy commitment to meeting these targets. This is the only way to establish a sufficient level of credibility, which would underpin the whole range of policy efforts and measures and integrate them into a coherent policy framework.

References

Belka, M. and A. Krajewska (1997). "The Polish bank and enterprise restructuring programme: debt/equity swaps. Survey results". Paper presented at the Workshop on Bank and Enterprise Restructuring in Central and Eastern Europe, Edinburgh, 2-3 May.

Hungary, National Bank of (1994). *Annual Report 1994.* Budapest.

______ (1996). *Annual Report 1996.* Budapest.

Sachs, J., A. Tornell and A. Velasco (1996). "Financial crises in emerging markets: the lessons from 1995". *Brookings Papers on Economic Activity*, 1:1996 (pp. 147-215).Washington, D.C.

______ (1996a). "The collapse of the Mexican peso: what have we learned?" *Economic Policy* (April), pp. 15-62.

Sota, P (1996). "Institutional framework for bank restructuring and the role of the authorities." Background paper presented at the joint OECD/WIIW Seminar, The Progress of Bank Restructuring in Bulgaria, Romania, Slovakia and Slovenia, Vienna, 9-10 December.

Stiblar, F. (1996). "Slovenia: restructuring of the banking sector". Paper presented at the joint OECD/WIIW Seminar, op. cit.

UN/ECE (1997). *Economic Survey of Europe in 1996-1997.* United Nations publication, Sales No. E.97.II.E.1.

______ (1997a). *Economic Bulletin for Europe*, Vol. 49. United Nations publication, Sales No. E.97.II.E.23.

______ (1998). *Economic Survey of Europe, 1998*, No. 1. United Nations publication, Sales No. E.98.II.E.1.

__________ (1998a). *Economic Survey of Europe, 1998*, No. 2. United Nations publication, Sales No. E.98.II.E.18.

__________ (1998b). *Economic Survey of Europe, 1998*, No. 3. United Nations publication, Sales No. E.98.II.E.25.

World Bank-Goskomstat (1995). *Russian Federation: Report on the National Accounts.* Washington, D.C.: World Bank. (October).

19

Economies in Transition

GERARD BELANGER AND
BASIL ZAVOICO*
International Monetary Fund

The Asian crisis started in mid-1997 and by the end of the year had started to affect the economic and financial environment of most emerging market economies, including the Central and Eastern European transition economies (CEETEs) and the Baltic States and the countries of the Commonwealth of Independent States, including the Russian Federation (B&CIS). The Asian crisis is not over. Financial markets and output in East Asia have yet to recover—although most countries have implemented strong stabilization and structural reform programmes—most with financial and policy assistance from IMF.

Capital inflows to the emerging markets continued at a high level through much of 1997, before collapsing towards the end of the year. For the year as a whole, private capital flows to the transition economies rose robustly (62 per cent) to US$35 billion, reflecting strong increases in all categories of inflows (see figure 1). The largest recipient of flows within the region was the Russian Federation, where flows increased fourfold to US$10.5 billion.

For the CEETE and B&CIS countries, the impact of the Asian crisis, so far, has been widespread but, with a few notable exceptions, relatively modest. The extent of spillover has reflected existing macroeconomic imbalances and policy weaknesses, the state of domestic financial markets, the level of

---

* Deputy Director and Personal Assistant to the Deputy Director, respectively, European II Department, International Monetary Fund. The views presented in the paper are those of the authors and are not to be interpreted as necessarily indicating the position of the Fund.

Figure 1: Net private capital flows to emerging markets, 1990-1997
(Billions of US dollars)

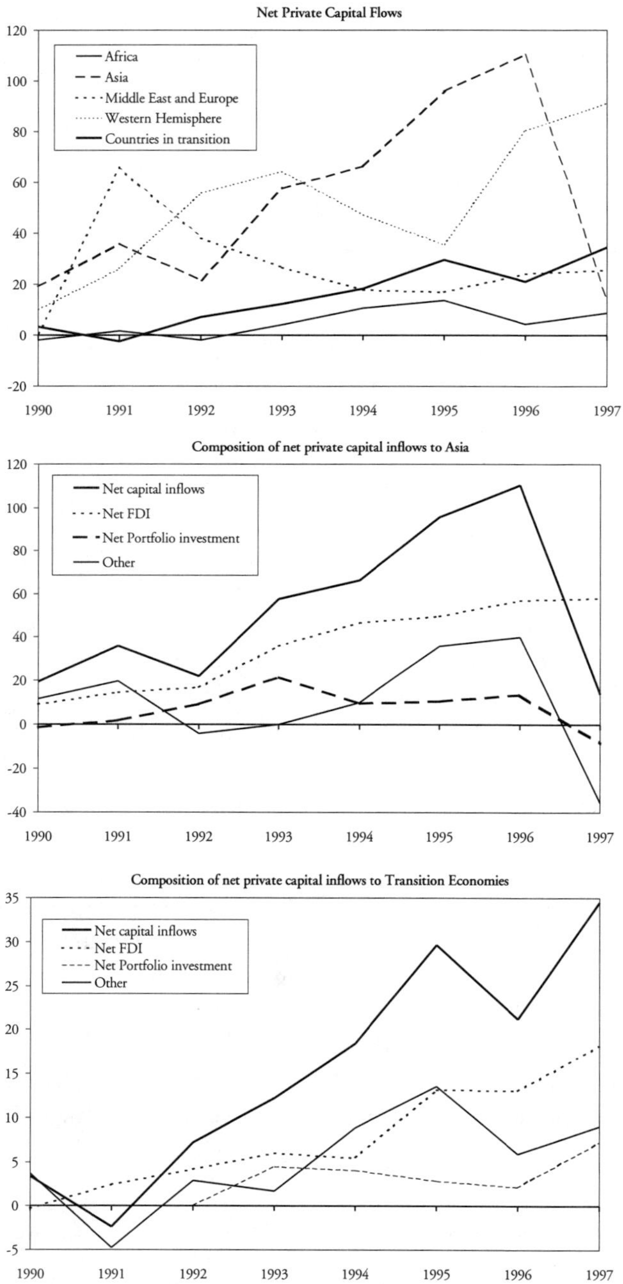

Source: IMF: *International Financial Statistics* and *World Economic Outlook.*

Table 1. Current-account balances of transition economies as percentage of GDP, 1994-1997

	1994	*1995*	*1996*	*1997*
Albania	-14.3	-7.5	-9.2	-12.1
Armenia	-35.6	-37.6	-26.7	-27.1
Azerbaijan	-6.6	-11.4	-23.6	-21.7
Belarus	-13.1	-2.4	-6.8	-7.5
Bulgaria	-2.1	-0.3	0.9	1.8
Croatia	0.7	-9.5	-7.6	-12.5
Czech Republic	-1.9	-2.7	-7.6	-6.3
Estonia	-7.4	-5.1	-9.7	-12.2
Georgia	-35.9	-14.1	-9.1	-10.2
Hungary	-9.7	-5.7	-3.8	-2.2
Kazakhstan	-11.6	-4.5	-3.9	-5.4
Kyrgyzstan	-11.2	-16.2	-24.0	-11.4
Latvia	-0.2	-3.4	-4.1	-6.9
Lithuania	-2.2	-10.3	-9.3	-9.2
Macedonia, FYR	-6.3	-6.2	-7.4	-8.5
Moldova	6.9	-8.7	-12.9	-13.3
Poland	2.3	3.3	-1.0	-3.2
Romania	-1.7	-4.9	-7.3	-5.1
The Russian Federation	3.8	1.3	0.5	-0.3
Slovak Republic	4.8	2.3	-11.1	-8.4
Slovania	4.2	-0.1	0.2	0.0
Tajikistan	-21.7	0.2	-14.2	-1.4
Turkmenistan	11.9	22.8	1.7	-32.0
Ukraine	-5.8	-4.1	-2.7	-2.8
Uzbekistan	2.1	-0.5	-6.3	-4.3
Average	-6.6	-5.0	-8.2	-8.9

Source: IMF, *World Economic Outlook.*

integration into international markets and the extent of foreign participation in local equity and bond markets. Large macroeconomic imbalances making various countries potentially vulnerable are apparent in large external current deficits for a wide range of countries of the CEETE and B&CIS (see table 1). Less than one third of the countries had current-account deficits lower than the 6-8 per cent of GDP—or even lower in cases of contagion—which has been the trigger zone for the financial crises of the 1990s.

1. The channels of transmission of the crisis

The effects of the crisis are being transmitted through two channels.

The financial channel

The initial financial impact of the Asian crisis was mainly confined to a re-evaluation of the risks associated with lending to emerging markets. This was reflected in a sharp rise in the premiums placed on Eurobond issues by countries characterized as emerging. The increase in costs made the issuance of such paper by sovereign borrowers problematic as the fiscal consequences of the higher interest rates were in many cases unsupportable, with the result that some borrowers withdrew from the market completely.

A secondary channel was the sale of domestic treasury paper in the CEETE and B&CIS countries by emerging market financial institutions in distress. Towards late 1997, for example, banks in Brazil and the Republic of Korea that had invested heavily in high-yielding Russian Treasury bills (GKOs), were forced to liquidate a substantial part of their holdings to shore up their own failing liquidity; out of the US$20 billion or so of domestic Russian GKOs held by non-residents at end-1997, about US$6 billion were held by entities in the Republic of Korea and Brazil that proceeded to sell their holdings in the early days of the crisis. While the significance of this secondary financial channel is difficult to assess, it is clear that these sales undermined market confidence at a difficult moment.

The strength of the impact through the financial channel has depended crucially on whether domestic policies—including the condition of the banking sector—were appropriate. In countries where they were sound (for example, Hungary, Poland and Estonia) the initial financial impact was relatively modest and short-lived. However, where policies were inappropriate, for example in the Russian Federation and Ukraine, the impact was much more pronounced and required quick and credible corrective action on the part of the authorities—which was not always forthcoming. The markets have, thus, been discriminating. This is apparent from the evolution of domestic stock markets, which after a brief dip recovered in several countries but plunged in the Russian Federation (see figure 2); and also from the behaviour of spreads on sovereign bonds traded in international markets (see figure 3).

The impact has also reflected the degree of integration into international financial markets. For most B&CIS countries, disturbances through capital markets were muted because, as a group, B&CIS countries have accumulated relatively little foreign commercial debt (with most borrowing contracted by

Figure 2: Stock market indices for selected countries
(September 1997 = 100)

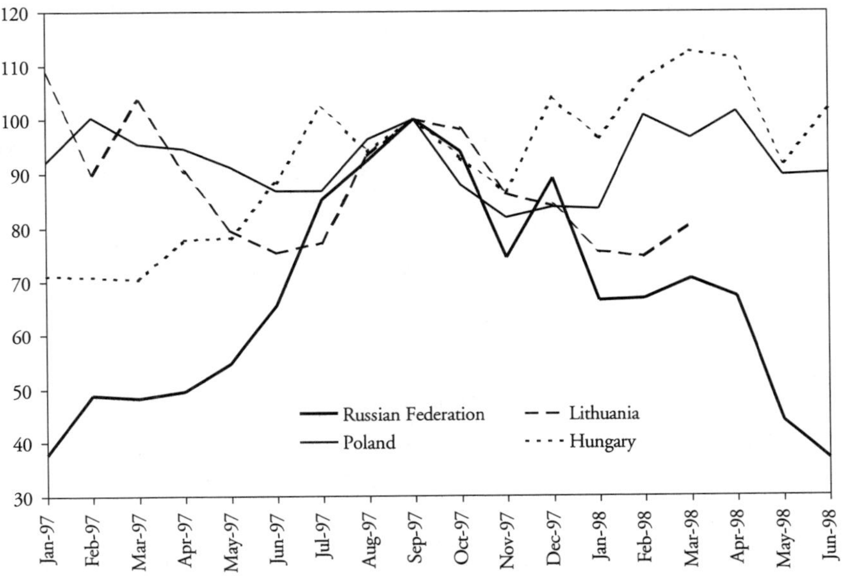

Source: International Financial Corporation of the World Bank.

the government) and because domestic capital markets are relatively small with only modest linkages to international markets. Their banking systems are, in most cases, still in their early stages of development and hence do not have substantial access to international capital markets. Since they do not depend on foreign capital, the crisis of confidence in emerging markets did not materially affect their funding operations. For countries isolated through undeveloped financial linkages or by regulation and control—such as Belarus—the effects of the Asian crisis were, to a good first approximation, zero.

This is not the case, however, for the Russian Federation and Ukraine, both of which have been actively borrowing on international capital markets, nor for the leading Central and East European economies, namely, the Czech Republic, Hungary and Poland. In the latter cases, the banking systems are more developed and also more fully integrated in international markets. Market assessments are that Hungary and Poland have probably the healthiest banking systems in the region. In the Czech Republic, the strengthening of bank balance sheets has been slower, but a programme is now under way to privatize and strengthen major state banks through involvement of strategic foreign partners.

Figure 3: Yield spreads for Brady Bonds and Eurobonds
(Basic points)

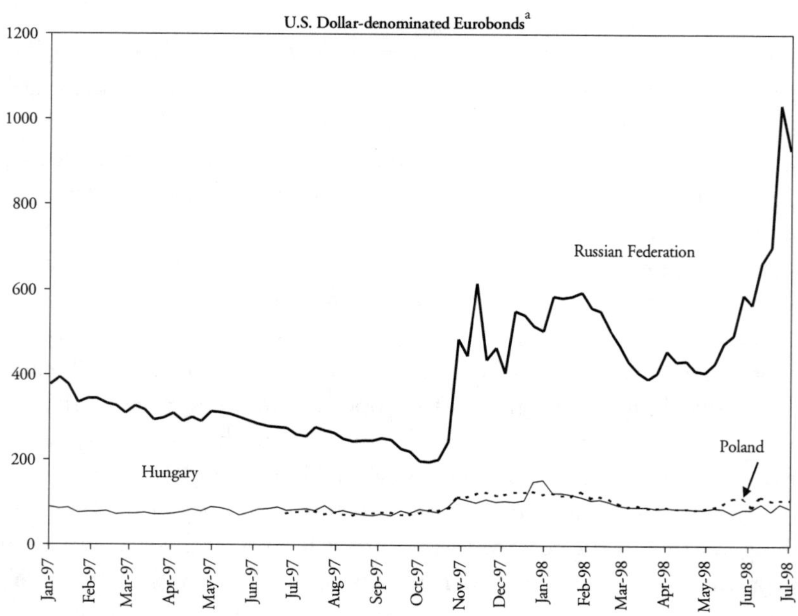

Source: International Financial Corporation of the World Bank.

a. Yield spreads on Brady bonds are "stripped" yields.

b. The Russian Federation: bond due 1 November; Hungary: bond due 3 November; Poland: bond due 4 July.

The real channel

The initial impact of the Asian crisis through the "real" channel has taken two forms: (a) a fall in demand for exports (including tourism services) resulting from demand compression in Asia as well as some increased competition on export markets; and (b) a fall in selected commodity prices, especially oil prices, which has positive effects for importers but negative effects for exporters—notably the Russian Federation—with a substantial effect on revenues. With exports of oil and gas accounting for over 40 per cent of the Russian Federation's exports, weak prices are projected to lower Russian export revenues by US $8½ billion in 1998.

The real impact of the Asian crisis is unavoidable, irrespective of domestic policies, and will certainly imply some slowdown in overall economic growth. The several financial crises of the last year are an important factor behind the slowdown in world growth from 4.1 per cent in 1997 to probably less than 3 per cent in 1998, notwithstanding robust growth in the United States and Europe. Most of the growth slowdown and contraction will be in Asia and, because direct trade between European transition countries and Asia is very small (see table 2), any decline in transition economy exports from this source is likely to be minimal.

This is not, however, the end of the story as, after domestic and export credit difficulties are resolved in the affected Asian countries, losses of export markets both to competitors redirecting exports from Asia and to Asian countries enjoying substantially devalued currencies will be felt. It is in fact already being felt, especially by those countries producing less differentiated commodities (such as steel in the case of Bulgaria, Romania and Slovakia; and also, in some cases, chemicals and timber). While this effect will be significant, it will also be manageable. For example, with Asian currencies now about 40 per cent depreciated compared to their pre-crisis levels and with reasonable estimates for the elasticity of export supply, the increase in their share of world exports to non-Asian markets can be roughly estimated at about 2 percentage points (from about 6 ½ percentage points in 1996). This will clearly dent the export growth possibilities of transition economies, especially as they are striving to expand their own market shares, but should not prevent exports from continuing to register healthy positive growth rates.

An intensification of the crisis in the Russian Federation, however, could lead to a significant expansion of contagion to neighbouring countries through the trade channel because of the importance of the Russian Federation in the exports of other CIS countries (see table 3). The Russian Federation's share in exports ranged up to close to 60 per cent in 1997 for Belarus and Moldova, and

Table 2. Share of exports to Asian countries in crisis in the total exports of transition economies, 1997[a]

	Asian countries in crisis	*Asian countries in crisis plus Japan*
Albania	0.0	0.1
Armenia	0.0	0.0
Azerbaijan	0.0	0.0
Belarus	0.1	0.3
Bulgaria	1.8	2.7
Croatia	0.2	0.3
Czech Republic	0.2	0.7
Estonia	0.3	0.1
Georgia	0.1	0.1
Hungary	0.3	0.9
Kazakhstan	1.8	4.5
Kyrgyzstan	0.8	1.0
Latvia	0.6	0.8
Lithuania	0.9	1.4
Macedonia, FYR	3.0	3.9
Moldova	0.1	0.1
Poland	1.4	1.8
Romania	2.7	3.1
Russian Federation	1.5	5.0
Slovak Republic	0.5	0.7
Slovania	0.3	0.5
Tajikistan	3.9	4.0
Turkmenistan	0.0	0.1
Ukraine	1.4	2.2
Uzbekistan	0.7	1.8
Average	0.9	1.5

Source: IMF.

a. These countries comprise: Indonesia, Malaysia, the Philippines, the Republic of Korea and Thailand.

for most other B&CIS countries was in the 20-30 per cent range. The effect could also be significant for some of the CEETEs which have been rapidly increasing exports to these markets in recent years. For example, B&CIS markets accounted for 17 per cent of Polish exports in 1997, compared to only 3 per cent for Asian countries. In addition, countries with close financial linkages with the Russian Federation, such as Belarus and Ukraine, would feel contagion through this channel as well.

Table 3. Share of exports to the Russian Federation in total exports to transition economies, 1995-1997

	1995	*1996*	*1997*
Armenia	25.4	33.1	18.0
Azerbaijan	18.2	17.6	23.1
Belarus	44.4	50.4	59.7
Estonia	17.6	16.4	6.1
Georgia	31.0	28.5	29.8
Kazakhstan	60.1	44.5	38.6
Kyrgyzstan	23.7	26.5	20.5
Latvia	24.9	23.1	20.9
Lithuania	20.4	23.8	8.7
Moldova	48.3	54.0	58.1
Tajikistan	12.7	10.3	8.3
Turkmenistan	3.6	2.0	5.3
Ukraine	39.9	35.2	22.2
Uzbekistan	32.8	22.0	30.5
Average	28.8	27.7	25.0

Source: IMF, *Direction of Trade Statistics.*

2. The impact of the crisis on the European Transition Economies

The Russian Federation and Ukraine were particularly vulnerable to contagion because short-term borrowing has been the main source of financing for their Governments. Weak follow-through in the implementation of structural and financial reforms, substantial dependence on short-term government borrowing and, in the Russian Federation, a large fiscal deficit caused by chronically weak fiscal revenues, largely explain the intensity of the impact of the Asian crisis on these two countries. In both cases, the defence of the exchange rate in late 1997 took the form of raising both interest rates and reserve requirements, and widening the exchange rate band to allow wider fluctuations of the exchange rate so as to reduce the risk of speculative attacks. After the Russian authorities demonstrated their willingness to raise interest rates to defend the rouble, pressures eased materially, allowing rates to move to more sustainable levels.

However, Russian and Ukrainian financial markets again came under renewed intense pressures from the middle of May 1998. This most recent, and most severe bout of turbulence started in the Russian Federation and reflected growing market concerns that the Russian Federation's fiscal and external positions were unsustainable. The pressures quickly spilled over to Ukraine, which has similar problems and has close financial ties to the Russian Federation.

When a combination of intervention in foreign exchange markets, hikes in official interest rate—to up to 150 per cent at the end of May—and a tightening of the budget failed to stabilize markets, the Russian Government unveiled a wide-ranging anti-crisis programme in late June. Domestic borrowing to finance the federal budget came to a virtual halt, with large net redemption of GKOs in June and the first two weeks of July. The intensity of market pressures is evident from the increase of interest rates on GKOs, which rose from about 30 per cent in May to above 170 per cent in mid-July (see figure 4). Following the announcement of the agreement with IMF—based on a programme which extends and strengthens the anti-crisis policy package—yields on GKOs fell to about 50 per cent.

Ukraine's pressing need for external financing led to the issuance of a DM Eurobond in the first quarter of 1998 (postponed from the fourth quarter of 1997) with an unprecedented spread of 1,275 basis points above domestic German rates (Bunds). Efforts to raise additional resources in international capital markets have failed. Pressures remain intense, with the National Bank of Ukraine forced to raise its refinance rate from 51 per cent to 82 per cent on

Figure 4: The Russian Federation: Average treasury bill yields[a]
(Percentage)

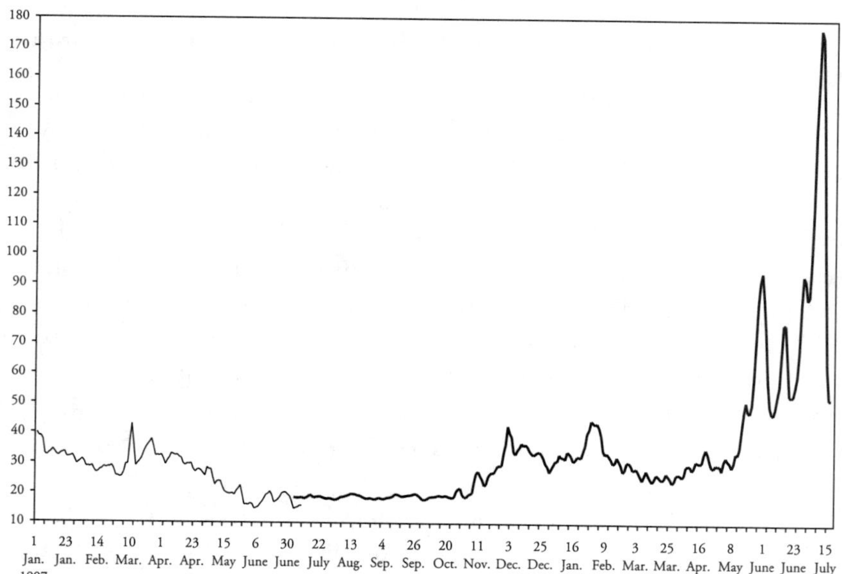

Source: Reuters.

a. Data presented as three-day centred moving average; data for January-June 1997 relate to tax-free bills while data for July onwards relate to taxable bills.

Figure 5: Czech Republic: PRIBOR and the exchange rate of the Koruna against the DM (1997-1998)

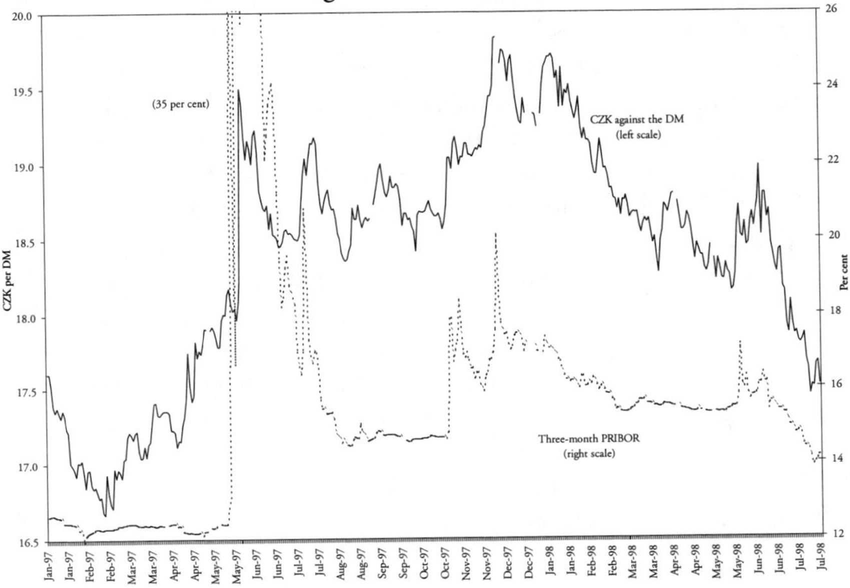

Source: International Monetary Fund.

7 July; though pressures on the exchange rate eased somewhat in the immediate aftermath of the announcement of a new Fund loan to the Russian Federation.

The Czech Republic's currency crisis of May 1997 preceded the Asian crisis. The policy response is a textbook case of how—in a context of generally good policies—an increase in interest rates quickly stabilized the exchange rate at a new, moderately lower level, which set the stage for a fairly rapid return to more sustainable interest rates thereafter (see figure 5). The latter was important because the Czech financial system is much more developed, with a much higher share of credit to enterprises relative to GDP, than other transition economies. The strategy worked because the shock of higher interest rates to the finances of enterprises was so short-lived.[1] Pressures on the exchange rate resumed in late 1997, from contagion as well as political uncertainty, but market sentiment has since improved as the external current-account position continued to strengthen.

Other countries have been little affected. For both Poland and Hungary, the periods of highest turbulence overall for emerging markets led to an easing

1 For other CEETE and B&CIS countries, which are much less intermediated, the impact of interest rate hikes would be reasonably contained even if they had to be kept high for a longer period.

of appreciation pressures on their currencies, which were, however, subsequently reversed. For example, following the Thai devaluation, the Polish zloty depreciated sharply for a short period to near the bottom of its trading band—from 2 per cent below parity to about 6 per cent below parity (see figure 6). During 1998, however, the zloty has strengthened considerably and traded at 8 per cent above parity. Periodic bad news from Asia and the Russian Federation typically have caused the zloty to depreciate by 2-3 per cent, but continued strong foreign investor interest in Poland has caused the zloty to rebound quickly each time.

For other countries, beyond the increased competition in export markets for certain products mentioned earlier, there have also been effects in the form of increased spreads (for example, Bulgaria, Croatia, Estonia, Kazakhstan and Slovakia) for new borrowing which have, in some cases, led to postponements in planned bond issues and in the form of lower foreign direct investment (for example, Bulgaria and FYR Macedonia). For heavily indebted countries, especially those with a large commercial debt component, the widening of spreads will increase debt-servicing costs (see table 4).

Figure 6: Poland: Exchange rate developments, 1996-1998

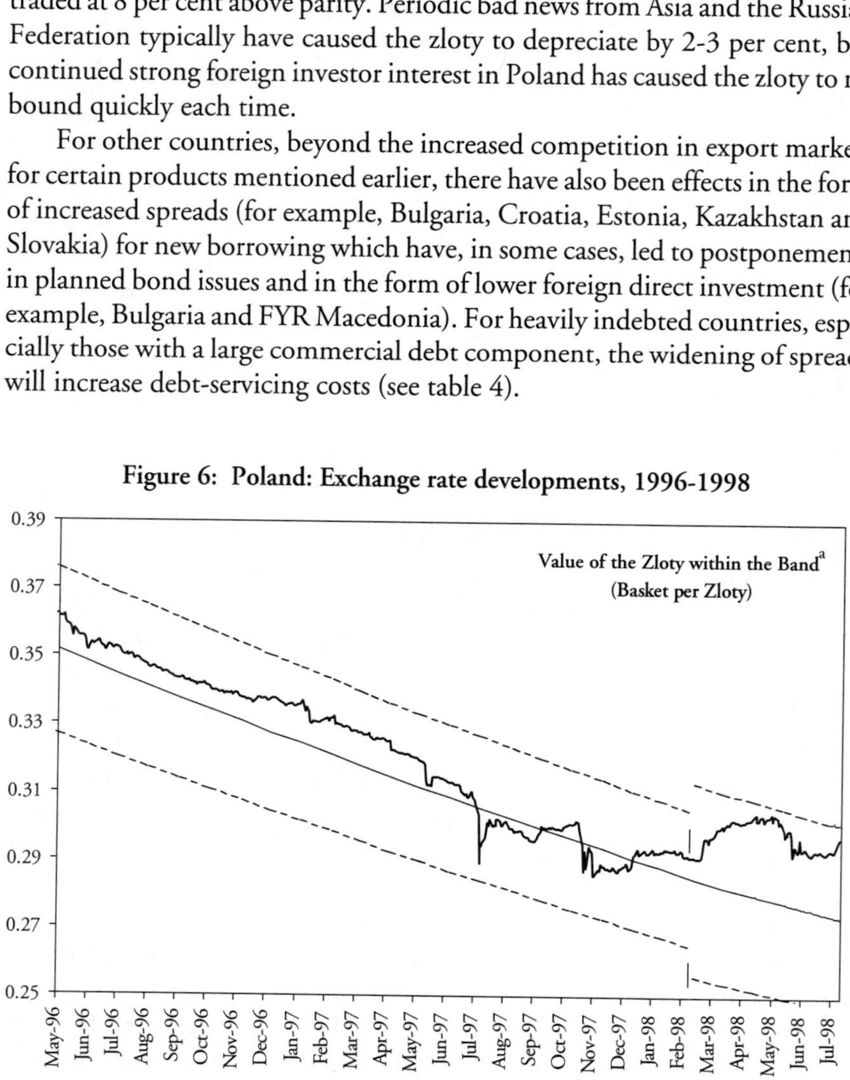

Source: Polish authorities.

a. On 26 February 1998, the band was widened from ± 7 per cent to ± 10 per cent.

3. The lessons from the crisis

While the crisis is not yet over and the financial and real repercussions are still working their way through the global economy, the key lessons are becoming increasingly clear.

A main lesson is that, as the world economy grows ever more integrated and as capital flows are liberalized, the basis for making judgements on the quality of economic management in all countries is growing much broader to encompass both stabilization and structural features.

Table 4. External debt of transition economies as per cent of GDP, 1997

	1997
Albania	34.8
Armenia	50.4
Azerbaijan	13.2
Belarus	6.9
Bulgaria	94.0
Croatia	28.1
Czech Republic	43.3
Estonia	5.6
Georgia	29.1
Hungary	52.7
Kazakhstan	21.4
Kyrgyzstan	56.6
Latvia	8.2
Lithuania	19.3
Macedonia, FYR	34.6
Moldova	46.3
Poland	28.4
Romania	25.3
Russian Federation	27.0
Slovak Republic	58.5
Slovania	21.2
Tajikistan	82.7
Turkmenistan	64.1
Ukraine	23.8
Uzbekistan	18.0
Average	36.7

Source: National authorities; and IMF staff estimates.

In a globalized economy, a few macroeconomic virtues are not enough. In the past, the "quality" of economic performance was judged largely on the basis of growth and inflation performance and the concurrent size and evolution of the current account and fiscal positions. Generally speaking, high growth and low inflation combined with low current-account deficits and modest fiscal deficits were regarded as representing strong economic fundamentals and, thus, reduced to essentially zero the probability of major economic or financial crises. Large current-account deficits were also regarded as acceptable, if financed largely by foreign direct investment and accompanied by robust fiscal positions.

It is now clear that these traditional assessments are not enough. Indeed, the traditional macro fundamentals for the five Asian countries first hit in mid-1997 were not such as to give grounds for serious worry. Growth was robust and inflation was modest (all in the single digits). Any concerns on the external side were soothed by the fiscal positions, which were in surplus in four countries or showed only a negligible deficit (Malaysia). What the macro fundamentals masked was a sustained deterioration in the balance sheets of the private sector—including both the corporate and banking sectors—that created the basis for the sudden and explosive emergence of the crisis.

The required policy framework is clear.

- Macroeconomic policy needs to be put on a sound footing with limited fiscal deficits, and a coherent approach to monetary policy and exchange rate management. Policy makers have to pay attention to current-account deficits, their financing and external debt, especially its short-term component.
- There is also a growing recognition of the fact that some flexibility of the exchange rate is useful to deter one-way bets. As was mentioned earlier, wider bands were adopted by the Russian Federation and Ukraine as part of the defence of their exchange rates. This was also done by the Czech Republic, before it let the rate float, and by Poland. It is a change in exchange rate arrangement that we are recommending to many countries.
- The issue of proper sequencing of the strengthening of domestic financial systems and capital-account liberalization is also gaining increasing acceptance.
- Strengthening and consolidating banking systems continues to be a top priority in CEETE and B&CIS countries. Also high on the reform agenda is the improvement of accounting and regulatory standards to weed out weak or insolvent institutions before they create systemic problems.

This latter point is important for a number of reasons. Most important is that whenever a currency comes under attack—as in the case of the Russian ruble over the past month—the main initial line of defence must be an increase in interest rates to help stabilize the exchange rate. Oftentimes, this increase must be very substantial to mount a successful defence.

If bank balance sheets are burdened by substantial non-performing loans, these high interest rates can quickly turn a small liquidity problem within the banking system into a big solvency problem, as weak borrowers are likely to stop servicing their bank loans as economic conditions deteriorate. Moreover, if banks (and corporations) have undertaken large-scale foreign borrowing to support domestic lending, any devaluation could quickly result in widespread bankruptcies throughout the economy. This, in turn, may make the authorities reluctant to take measures, either increases in interest rates or changes in exchange rates, that they would otherwise regard as desirable or necessary.

In conclusion, a strong banking system is the first line of defence that allows policy makers adequate scope to take necessary stabilization measures in the new environment of global capital markets.

20

Discussion – Economies in Transition

ILENE GRABEL
PAUL WACHTEL

ILENE GRABEL*

My comments focus on the three themes that are raised in the papers presented by Gerard Belanger of the International Monetary Fund (IMF) and Joseph Smolik of the Economic Commission for Europe (ECE, referred to hereafter as the ECE paper). I conclude my remarks by arguing that both papers fail to acknowledge the real policy lesson of the Asian crisis for transition economies. That lesson, in brief, is that capital controls must be implemented in transition economies lest they confront the fates of South-East Asian countries, Brazil and Mexico.

First theme: Has the Asian financial crisis had a direct spillover effect on the transition economies?

Both papers argue that the financial crisis in Asia has had little direct effect on the transition economies. What is surprising about this conclusion is that it

* Associate Professor of International Finance, Graduate School of International Studies, University of Denver.

does not follow from the very evidence of spillovers presented in the papers themselves.

Indeed, one key spillover of the Asian crisis that both papers (and especially that of Belanger) make clear is the effect of sluggish growth in much of the world on commodity prices. Both papers show that falling export revenues from oil and natural gas (for example) are particularly problematic for the Russian economy. In view of the dangerous couplet of the Russian Federation's substantial external obligations and persistent problems with tax collection, it is surprising that the ramifications of the Asian difficulties on world demand and commodity prices are so lightly treated.

Another key spillover—again one that both authors provide evidence of—but then dismiss, is that interest rates in transition economies have risen to very high levels in order to protect the value of currencies and to maintain the attractiveness of government bonds on world markets. In countries like the Russian Federation, the additional burden on the fiscal deficit that stems from the high rates being paid on bonds (42 per cent as of this writing) is not a trivial matter. Looking at the region more generally, I am not convinced that the real sector can withstand these high interest rates. And even if these high rates do not trigger a serious recession (although it is hard to believe that they will not), they are nevertheless damaging to real-sector activity insofar as they affect both the volume and "quality" of overall economic activity. Certainly, we only have to look to present-day Brazil or even Hong Kong (China), to see that when interest rates become excessively high, the real economy grinds to a halt. Moreover, when interest rates rise to the high levels we are observing today in transition economies, not only does overall economic activity slow, but to the extent that investment does take place it tends to be of only the most speculative variety (see discussion in Grabel, 1995). Perhaps 1998 have exacerbated (with merit) the exit of domestic and foreign investors from Russian markets. Surprisingly, both papers are silent as concerns the macroeconomic effects of the increase in investor flight from the Russian Federation and other transition economies. It should be noted here that this flight is made possible by the mistaken policies of unrestrained financial openness in these economies.

Second theme: What role will the Russian Federation play in the region's stability?

The evidence presented in both papers, especially that of the ECE, suggests strongly that the Russian Federation plays a central role in the economic health of the countries of Central and Eastern Europe and the Baltic States. If the Russian economy continues to deteriorate (and we have good reason to believe that the current difficulties are not close to resolution), then the region's economies are likely to experience serious difficulties, too. And the papers, in their very interesting presentations of the "facts" of the Russian Federation's macro- and microeconomic and political fundamentals, do nothing if not convince me of the likelihood of continued Russian failure. If this failure does in fact continue, then the Russian Federation may play the role of Thailand in July of 1997. Under this scenario, the Russian Federation might still touch off a regional contagion, as investors exit what they view (mistakenly) as homogenous transition economies.

All one has to do to see that the Russian Federation was a house of cards is restate what the ECE paper terms its "persistent and fundamental problems".[1] These problems are its lack of export diversification, large external obligations, a large budget deficit financed by volatile short-term capital flows, low domestic savings, low level of official reserves, and persistent problems with the tax system. All of these problems rendered the Russian Federation's economy highly vulnerable to a reversal of capital flows and hence a further fiscal crisis and a currency collapse. Given the scope of these problems, and the likelihood that they would not be solved by the fractious Government, the ECE paper's sanguine predictions about Russian reform seem more like wishful thinking than realistic analysis. There was simply no convincing evidence presented in support of ECE's predictions for the Russian Federation or Belanger's hope (disguised as confidence) in the IMF's ability to manage crisis in the Russian Federation.

Third theme: What are the policy lessons of the Asian crisis for the transition economies and especially for the Russian Federation?

It is in the realm of lessons that both of the papers offer the greatest disappointment. The ECE paper tells us that the lessons for the Russian Federation of the Asian crisis are that the authorities need to have "a firm and irrevocable commitment" to "sound and predictable economic policies" and "create credible and transparent institutions of policy-making". These points are of course correct, but they are not new lessons stemming from recent events. These very points constitute the same wish list that has been drawn up for the Russian Federation ever since the Soviet State first collapsed.

Belanger's prescriptions, too, offer little help. In the tradition of the "Special Data Dissemination Standard" drawn up by IMF following the Mexican financial crisis of 1994-1995, Belanger calls for an examination of the "microfundamentals" in transition economies. However, as was patently clear

1 It should be noted that the ECE paper was written prior to the political crisis of fall 1998.

in the Mexican and even in the Asian cases, when investors are earning high returns, both IMF and market participants simply do not care about micro- or macrofundamentals. The argument that the IMF and investors were fooled by microfundamentals and bad information is simply a red herring. If the best lesson that we can draw from the Asian crisis is that investors in transition economies better look more closely at the microfundamentals, then IMF should brace itself for another crisis.

Some concluding thoughts on policy lessons

The real policy lesson of the Asian crisis for the transition economies is that policy makers can ill afford not to control international private capital flows as long as they have inadequate official reserves and convertible currencies. Simply put: the neoliberal model of financial openness is inappropriate for transition economies (as it is for countries in South-East Asia). Unrestrained policies of financial openness render already struggling economies more vulnerable to future financial crises precisely by encouraging a greater volume of short-term, highly liquid private capital inflows. These inflows, while initially beneficial to the economy, can be highly destabilizing once they exit the country. Thus, the lesson of the Asian crisis for the transition economies is not that they should pay more attention to their fundamentals and to their institutions (though of course these should also be attended to). Rather, the lesson is that they should implement capital controls.

Measures currently in place in Chile and Colombia (often referred to as the "Chilean model") represent an extremely promising direction for protective capital controls in the transition economies. The measures balance the need for capital with the need to protect the economy from instability. In Colombia, foreign investors are free to engage in (less liquid) direct investment, but are precluded from purchasing debt instruments and corporate equity. As a consequence, foreign capital is much less able to flee Colombia en masse. In Chile, foreign investors may engage in portfolio investment, but they must keep their cash in the country for at least one year. Investors are therefore much more apt to base their investment decisions on a company's long-term economic prospects than on the opportunity for short-term speculative gain. To the surprise of many neoliberal economists, this model has been performing well. Indeed, Chile has not only succeeded in securing large portfolio investment inflows, but has also remained largely unaffected by the "Asian flu."

In the immediate aftermath of the Asian crisis, the Chilean measures received a surprising amount of attention by prominent neoliberal economists, including even Stanley Fischer, First Deputy Managing Director of IMF. At the time, Fischer made a number of well-publicized speeches in which he expressed support for the temporary imposition of Chilean-type capital controls in economies where the macroeconomic framework and the financial sector were weak (for example, Fischer 1997 and IMF, 1998). More recently, however, the issue of capital controls seems to have dropped from the IMF's radar screen even as those countries with some form of controls in place (for example, Chile, China, Colombia, India, Malaysia, Singapore and Taiwan Province of China) have all weathered the Asian storm far better than have those countries that have been good students of neoliberalism.

It must be acknowledged that contrary to the prevailing neoliberal conventional wisdom, the capital controls currently in place in many countries around the world are both desirable and viable. Capital controls of various types have played a key role in the successful development of most wealthy countries. The most powerful obstacles to capital controls today are political and ideological rather than technical as is often claimed by opponents of such policies. If the United Nations could play a role in creating intellectual and political support for capital controls, it would be doing a great deal to promote financial stability in transition economies (with the side benefit of saving IMF's fast dwindling resources).

PAUL WACHTEL*

The Asian financial crisis of 1997 provides a very clear lesson about the causes of exchange rate crises that has clear implications for emerging market economies, as well as many developing and developed economies around the world. The events in the Russian Federation in the weeks surrounding the

---

* Research Professor of Economics, Stern School of Business, New York University.

1 For a survey of the causes of exchange rate crises in the transition economies which considers both traditional and new fundamental causes, see Roubini and Wachtel (1997).

2 It is a shame that the *Economic Survey of Europe* does not get as broad distribution as other similar analyses (for example, the European Bank of Reconstruction and Development's *Transition Report* and the IMF's *World Economic Outlook*). It deserves to be widely read.

United Nations Expert Group Meeting in July 1998 provide further evidence of the importance of this lesson. The lesson is that traditional macroeconomic analysis of external sector fundamentals is not an adequate indicator of vulnerability to exchange rate crises. In addition to the *traditional macro fundamentals*—inflation, growth, external debt, current account, exchange rate—we have to monitor the *new fundamentals*: asset prices, domestic bank portfolios, corporate sector exchange rate exposure and the quality of investment projects.[1]

Events in Asia in 1997 and more recently in some of the transition economies demonstrate the significance of the new fundamentals. The two papers presented in this chapter help us sort through an avalanche of information and show the connections between the 1997 Asian melt down and economic and financial conditions in the transition economies. The paper by Belanger and Zavoico is an excellent synthesis and the excerpt from the *Economic Survey of Europe* by Smolik is a clear summary of events.[2] Both of these papers address two questions which I will discuss here in order:

1. What are the implications for the transition economies of the Asian crisis?
2. What are the lessons from the Asian crisis that are relevant to the transition economies?

Implications for the transition economies. The implications of the Asian melt down for the economies in transition (EITs) are rather straightforward. We can start with the real side of the economy. Although, worldwide recession will make it more difficult for the transition economies to grow, I would not overemphasize the effect of the Asian crisis on Central and Eastern Europe. To begin, the EITs export relatively little to Asia. More importantly, the EITs stand to benefit from low prices on their imports from Asia. It is also true that many EITs (particularly some of the former Soviet Union countries) are affected by declining commodity prices, but this precedes the Asian financial crisis. Generally, the health of the United States and Western European economies is far more important for the EITs than the health of the Asian economies.

Turn now to the financial side of the economy where international linkages may be increasingly problematic. For example, in late 1997, weakened fi-

---

1 For a survey of the causes of exchange rate crises in the transition economies which considers both traditional and new fundamental causes, see Roubini, Nouriel and Paul Wachtel (1997).

2 It is a shame that the *Economic Survey of Europe* does not get as broad distribution as other similar analyses (for example, the European Bank of Reconstruction and Development's *Transition Report* and the IMF's *World Economic Outlook*). It deserves to be widely read.

nancial institutions in Brazil and the Republic of Korea sold holdings of GKOs (Russian Treasury bills), providing a dramatic illustration of the extent to which international integration of financial institutions has taken place. It has been suggested that the Asian crisis spilled over to the Russian Federation—a contagion effect—when the banks thus dumped their holdings of GKOs. There are large international holdings of financial assets like GKOs that are incorrectly viewed by assets holders as being both liquid (short-term bills) and secure (sovereign liabilities). However, the markets for such assets often do not have sufficient depth to absorb significant changes in preferences. In that case, the Russian financial markets weathered the storm from Asia rather well. The 1998 Russian financial crisis is not due to a contagion effect but the fundamentals in the Russian Federation itself, both old ones and new ones.

All in all, the direct implications for the EITs of the Asian turmoil are few. More importantly, the real lesson of the Asian crisis is that it helps us define the new fundamentals. The Asian crisis will have a lasting effect on macroeconomic thinking because it provides us with an expanded list of fundamental issues to monitor and a whole set of new policy problems. This lesson has already been shown to be important because the new fundamentals (as well as some traditional ones) are responsible for the Russian crisis of 1998. However, it is not a lesson that has been learned very quickly by the international community. IMF and the United States (perhaps as a political rather than an economic decision) were willing and eager to support the Russian Federation earlier this year even though it was apparent that the fundamental problems with the Russian economy—some of the new fundamentals—were not being solved.

Lessons from Asia. The lessons for the EITs and the world at large from the Asian crisis is that the world needs to pay close attention to a broad set of fundamental issues. What are these *new fundamental* indicators of financial crisis?

- *Strength of the banking system.* Bad lending practices will catch up with the most robust economy and threaten the viability of banking institutions and the currency. This is equally true in developed economies (for example, Japan) and emerging market economies (for example, the Russian Federation). Good banking practices and adequate capitalization of domestic banks are important indicators of the vulnerability of the exchange rate.
- *Quality of bank supervision.* Related to the strength of the banking system is the adequacy of prudential supervision of banking. A country with competent and trusted bank examiners and a tradition of fair enforcement will be better able to withstand financial crisis.
- *Asset price bubbles.* Rapid increases in equity or property prices can have a destabilizing effect particularly if there is substantial foreign participa-

tion in asset markets. The foreign exchange markets might not have the ability to withstand small changes in asset preferences. Such concerns suggest that monetary policy ought to be tightened well before the bubble becomes apparent. However, such a policy might just attract larger financial inflows and exacerbate the problem. This conundrum is the source of increasing discussion among policy makers about the efficacy of capital controls.

- *Exchange rate exposure.* The exchange rate exposure of the financial sector, the non-financial business sector and the government should be monitored; it is a relevant risk indicator even when exchange rates are fixed. Exchange rates may not be fixed forever and such risks should not be ignored.
- *Distortions in the economy.* Robust economic growth might mask distortions in the allocation process that lead to inefficiencies. The Asian crisis shows that bad investment decisions matter.
- *Adequacy of the legal and financial infrastructure.* A lack of transparency in business activity hides problems and inadequate legal institutions make recourse to legal remedies difficult.
- *The use of financial inflows.* The size of short-term financial inflows as opposed to longer-term inflows and foreign direct investment is really a traditional fundamental indicator. The new twist that we learn from the Asian crisis is that a good analysis needs to also look at how the financial inflows are being used. Are they creating dangerous levels of foreign currency liabilities? Are they financing inefficient investments, consumption, government deficits or capital flight by the domestic savers?

These new fundamental issues need to be monitored to determine when a country might be exposed to currency crises. It is not good enough to focus only on traditional fundamentals, such as the size of the current-account deficit, the external debt of the country and the ability to service it, or the real exchange rate.

I do not mean to diminish the importance of the traditional fundamental indicators of exchange rate crisis. A large current-account deficit will sooner or later become unsustainable. A fixed nominal exchange rate that leads to a real appreciation will sooner or later collapse. However, the ability of a country to have the time to adjust a current-account imbalance or live with some real appreciation will depend on the new fundamentals and the quality of its economic institutions.

In addition, the Asian crisis has ignited important policy debates that will go on for a long time in the EITs:

- The liberal orthodoxy of the last quarter of the twentieth century will be questioned. Specifically, policy makers will debate whether capital controls should always be avoided. If the new fundamentals indicate that financial institutions are wanting in some ways, it might be appropriate to insulate the economy from international markets at least temporarily. The *Economic Survey of Europe* notes that countries with "financial systems ...relatively undeveloped with few linkages to the global system" will be less harmed by contagion effects. The implication here is that capital controls have a role to play.
- Fixed exchange rate regimes that enable a country to control inflation and stabilize the economy are attractive. But fixed exchange rates frequently lead to an unsustainable real appreciation. Policy makers have not figured out how and when to let go of a fixed rate regime.
- The efficacy of high interest rates as a response to crisis has been brought into question. Tight monetary policy might simply not be worth the damage it does in many instances. Generally, there is increasing concern that policy interventions do not work. The *Economic Survey of Europe* says: "It is highly uncertain whether such policy interventions [in foreign exchange markets and raising rates] will in fact be successful in moderating pressures on the financial markets or in arresting a looming crisis." If that is so, why do we continue to follow such policies?
- If financial market liberalization is going to remain a goal, more attention needs to be paid to the sequencing of reforms. In both Asia and the EITs, there has been little or no consideration by policy makers of the importance of sequencing. Controls should be lifted and markets opened as the institutions to absorb shocks are developed.

Finally, when comparing the transition economies to the Asian crisis it is important to make a distinction among the different crisis countries. The *Economic Survey of Europe* does not lump all EITs into one basket but it does lump all of Asia into one crisis. There are significant differences among the Asian countries. In some, the exchange rate depreciation since the start of 1997 has been in the range of 20 per cent, about the extent to which the currencies were overvalued at the time. The larger currency collapses—the real crises—are in those countries where the new fundamentals were bad for a long time and the international community eagerly overlooked the problems. These are countries where domestic financial intermediaries simply did not work any better than Soviet-type state-owned banks and where domestic savers were taking their money elsewhere. In the EITs, in developing countries and elsewhere, observers in the post-Asian crisis world will in the future be looking much more carefully at the new fundamentals.

References

Crotty, J. and G. Epstein (1996). "In defence of capital controls". In L. Panitch, ed., *Are There Alternatives?* Socialist Register 1996. London: Merlin Press, pp. 118-149.

Fischer, Stanley (1997). "Capital account liberalization and the role of the IMF". Transcript of speech delivered at the seminar "Asia and the IMF". Hong Kong (China), 19 September 1997, and summarized in *IMF Survey 1997*, vol. 26, No. 19 (20 October 1997), pp. 321-324. The full text of the paper is available on IMF's website (www.imf.org/external/np/apd/asia/FISCHER.htm).

Grabel, Ilene (1995). "Speculation-led economic development: a Post-Keynesian interpretation of financial liberalization in the Third World". *International Review of Applied Economics*, vol. 9, No. 2, pp. 127-149.

______ (1999). "Rejecting exceptionalism: reinterpreting the Asian financial crises". In J. Michie and J. Grieve Smith, eds., *Global Instability and World Economic Governance*. London: Routledge Press (forthcoming).

IMF (1998). "Seminar discusses the orderly path to capital account liberalization". *IMF Survey 1998*, vol. 27, No.6 (23 March), pp. 81-84.

Roubini, Nouriel and Paul Wachtel (1997).*Current Account Sustainability in Transition Economies.* National Bureau of Economic Research Working Paper No. 6468 (March 1998); presented at the Third Dubrovnik Conference on Transition Economies (June).

Part Six

DIRECT INVESTMENT

Edited by

Leonides Buencamino

21

Introduction – Direct Investment

LEONIDES BUENCAMINO*
United Nations Department of Economic and Social Affairs

Is foreign direct investment (FDI), unlike portfolio equity investment and bank lending, relatively immune to the adverse effects of financial crises? So it seems, according to the results of the survey conducted by UNCTAD and the International Chamber of Commerce. They found that despite the Asian financial crisis, FDI flows in Asia, as a whole, managed to increase slightly in 1997, compared to those in 1996; meanwhile, portfolio equity investment and foreign bank lending dropped sharply during the same period. FDI inflows to the five countries most affected by the crisis (Indonesia, Malaysia, Philippines, Republic of Korea, and Thailand), as a group, came out relatively unscathed, remaining near the level of the previous year. Moreover, the prospects look promising for FDI inflows to this group since approved projects for 1998 show an increase, albeit small, over those in 1997.

UNCTAD says it is not surprised by the findings of the survey because FDI embodies a longer-term horizon and involves, not only financial flows, but the capitalization of productive assets, such as technology, knowledge and skills. FDI is also driven by the strategic interests of transnational corporations (TNCs) as they seek access to new and bigger markets, resources and lower labour costs to enhance their competitiveness in the global business arena. To

---

* Economic Affairs Officer, Developing Economies Section. The views expressed herein are those of the author and not necessarily the views of the United Nations.

achieve these objectives, TNCs have to enter into long-term relationships with the appropriate institutions in the host country. In contrast, most portfolio investment is associated with the search for short-term financial gains, and bank lending decisions are also made in a short-term horizon.

Transnational corporations, the UNCTAD report continues, consider economic factors (for example, the size and growth of host country markets, availability of human resources, and access to regional or international markets, among others) as key determinants for the location of FDI. In this respect, many Asian countries, including those most affected by the financial crisis, ranked high among developing host countries in the attractiveness of the factors mentioned above. FDI also plays a crucial role in the economic growth of the Asian economies most affected by the crisis, augmenting domestic investment and accounting for significant export shares in some industries. Due to these reasons, companies from both within and outside the region hold a very positive view of the long-term prospects for FDI in Asia.

This does not mean, however, that FDI flows are not affected, in one way or another, by the financial turmoil in Asia. Indeed, some characteristics of the crisis, such as sharp currency devaluations, reduced property values, and lower valuations for many Asian firms have favourably influenced the flow of FDI by providing lucrative opportunities in terms of lower costs for TNCs wanting to establish a presence or expand existing operations on the basis of the positive prospects for the future of the region. For domestic firms undergoing restructuring due to, for instance, heavy debt-service levels, and needing an urgent infusion of funds, the financial crisis offers opportunites for direct investment through mergers and acquisitions. These factors, combined with the high propensity to export, which is a common feature of TNCs in the region, make clear why FDI levels in Asia remained relatively stable in the face of the financial turmoil.

While the discussants acknowledge the economic advantages of sustained FDI flows into Asia, they present certain related issues which they consider equally important as the trend in investment. For instance, Rippe warns that the urge to put controls on short-term capital flows as one of the ways to avert future crises could lead to overreliance on FDI (in addition to creating distortions and incentives for cheating). He argues that when economic conditions deteriorate in the parent TNC or in the country of its location, corporate earnings could slide and result in the reduction of foreign investment. Lee points to the need to make a more systematic distinction between types of FDI, such as those which are motivated by the search for market access and those spurred by the desire for cheaper production costs. The latter, she contends, needs more regulatory oversight than the former. Noting that the UNCTAD report shows that market access-motivated FDI has been dampened by the crisis while FDI motivated by lower production cost has risen. She states that whichever type of investment dominates during the Asian crisis will determine whether the trend in FDI found by the survey will continue or reverse. Tan's paper presents a micro-view of the effects of the Asian crisis, as felt at the level of the firm or industry. He says that the Asian crisis has made banks very hesitant to extend new financing to firms, leading to an acute liquidity problem and blames partly the exchange rate policies of the countries for it. Tan , however, sees a silver lining: first, he claims that the firms which chose to stay in Asia (as opposed to those that withdrew their operations from the region) will reap the benefits of increased market share, an "economic rent" originating from an oligopolistic situation. Another opportunity, he says, comes from the chance to acquire assets of firms in the crisis-affected countries at "fire sale" prices. Last, but certainly not least, he states, is the reward that Asians bestow on those companies that "stuck" with the affected country in its darkest moment, staying loyal and true until economic conditions began to improve.

To Rippe and Lee, the opportunity to acquire domestic assets in the crisis-affected economy is not an unalloyed benefit. Rippe points to a time in the 1960s when United States companies were accused of trying to dominate Europe's economies and markets, and to the 1980s, when there was some resentment in the United States to Japanese acquisitions of large tracts of real estate. Lee warns that one cannot predict how a country will react to hostile takeovers as some of these acquisitions can turn out to be. The economist, Paul Krugman argues, however, that from an economic point of view, the sale of domestic corporate assets at reduced prices in the crisis-affected economies may not be such a bad thing after all because the asset could end up in the hands of more competent foreign management; even if that were not the case, the existence of a buyer for the assets (a demand for the product) prevents the price of the asset from collapsing any further than it already has.

22

The Financial Crisis in Asia and Foreign Direct Investment

UNITED NATIONS CONFERENCE ON TRADE AND DEVELOPMENT*

While portfolio equity investment and bank lending to affected countries have fallen sharply since the onset of the crisis in Asia, foreign direct investment (FDI) flows have remained close to pre-crisis levels and are expected to remain high in the long term. However, in the short and medium terms, the crisis will have both positive and negative effects on FDI flows in Asia—as well as FDI from Asia.

Some types of inward FDI can be expected to increase in the short and medium terms due to lower costs for transnational corporations (TNCs) to establish, expand and operate affiliates and increased competitiveness of exports from Asian countries due to devaluations, and helped by more liberal attitudes and policies towards FDI. Some types of domestic market-oriented FDI can be expected to decrease in the short and medium terms due to contraction in domestic demand. The bulk of firms responding to an UNCTAD survey, however, expected to maintain the level of their FDI in the short and medium terms. Outward FDI from Asia will also be affected in the short and medium terms by the crisis, while competition for FDI between Asia and other emerging market regions is increasing.

---

* Presented by Mrs. Padma Mallampally, Transnational Corporations Affairs Officer, UNCTAD. The paper was prepared by Padma Mallampally, Karl P. Sauvant and James Zhan, in cooperation with Tom Brewer and Masataka Fujita. Research assistance was provided by Chiraz Baly. The paper benefited from comments by John H. Dunning, Andrew Cornford, Persa Economou, Lynn K. Mytelka, Terutomo Ozawa, Eric D. Ramstetter, Anh Nga Tran-Nguyen and Zbigniew Zimny.

In conclusion, there are good reasons to believe that long-term prospects for FDI in Asia remain excellent which could be helped further by policy efforts to mitigate short- and medium-term negative effects of the crisis on FDI flows and to help restore growth.

* * *

The financial crisis in East and South-East Asia has involved a sharp decrease in private external capital flows to some developing countries in the region. Net private foreign bank lending and foreign portfolio equity investment are estimated to have turned negative for the group of countries most affected by the crisis (Indonesia, the Republic of Korea, Malaysia, the Philippines and Thailand) taken together (figure 1).

FDI inflows in 1997 to the five most affected Asian countries as a group, however, are estimated to have remained close to the level attained in 1996 (figure 1 and table 1). For developing East, South-East and South Asia as a

Figure 1: FDI flows, total foreign portfolio investment flows, foreign portfolio equity flows and foreign bank lending to the Asian countries most affected by the financial crisis,[a] 1994-1997

(Billions of US dollars)

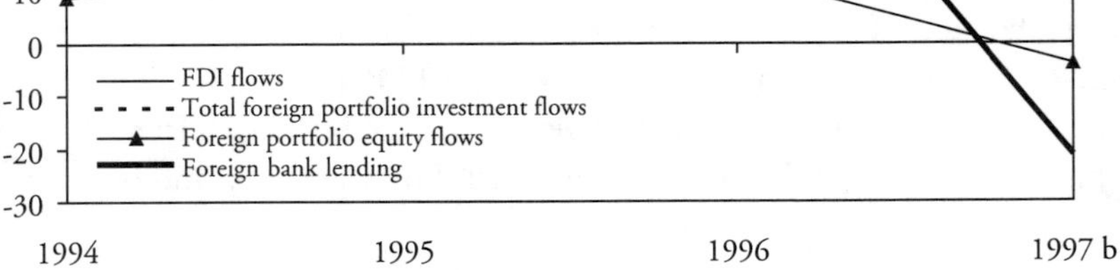

Sources: UNCTAD, based on UNCTAD's FDI/TNC database, data provided by the World Bank (portfolio flows data for 1994-1996) and the Institute of International Finance (bank lending data, as reported in IMF, *IMF Survey*, 9 February 1998).

a. Indonesia, Republic of Korea, Malaysia, Philippines and Thailand.

b. Estimates.

Table 1. FDI inflows into the Asian countries most affected by the financial crisis, 1990-1997
(Billions of US dollars)

									1997 Quarters			
Country	*1990*	*1991*	*1992*	*1993*	*1994*	*1995*	*1996*	*1997*	*I*	*II*	*III*	*IV*
Actual FDI (balance-of-payments data)												
Indonesia	1.1	1.5	1.8	2.0	2.1	4.3	6.2	4.1[a]	1.3	1.4	-0.3	1.7[a]
Korea, Republic of	0.8	1.2	0.7	0.6	0.8	1.8	2.3	3.1	0.6	0.6	0.6	0.5[b]
Malaysia	2.3	4.0	5.2	5.0	4.3	4.1	4.7[b]	3.8[b]	..	..	..	..
Philippines	0.5	0.5	0.2	1.2	1.6	1.5	1.4	2.9[a]	..	..	..	..
Thailand	2.4	2.0	2.1	1.8	1.3	2.0	2.3	2.5[a]	0.6	0.8	0.9	0.2[a]
Total for the above countries	7.2	9.2	10.0	10.6	10.2	13.7	16.9	16.4[a]	..	..	..	..
Memorandum:												
South, East and South-East Asia	20.1	21.2	27.7	47.4	55.4	65.5	77.0	80.8[a]	..	..	..	..
China	3.5	4.4	11.2	27.5	33.8	35.8	40.2	45.3	..	..	..	..
Share of the five most affected countries in total South, East and South-East Asia	35.8	43.4	36.2	22.5	18.4	21.0	21.9	20.3	..	..	..	..

(Table 1, cont'd)

Country	1990	1991	1992	1993	1994	1995	1996	1997	1997 Quarters I	II	III	IV
Approved FDI												
Indonesia[c]	8.8	8.8	10.3	8.1	23.7	39.9	29.9	33.8	-----16.4-----		-----17.4-----	
Korea, Republic of	0.8	1.4	0.9	1.0	1.3	1.9	3.2	7.0	2.1	2.3	1.0	1.5
Malaysia[d]	6.5	6.2	7.0	2.4	4.3	3.7	6.8	4.0	0.6	1.5	1.0	0.9
Philippines[e]	1.0	0.8	0.3	0.5	1.8	1.9	2.8	6.3	1.3	0.7	3.8	0.5
Thailand	8.0	5.0	10.0	4.3	5.9	16.5	14.0	10.6	2.5	2.1	3.2	2.7
Total for the above countries	25.1	22.2	28.5	16.3	37	63.9	56.7	61.7	-----29.5-----		-----32.1-----	

Source: UNCTAD, FDI/TNC database.

a. Estimates.
b. not including reinvested earnings.
c. not including FDI in oil and gas, insurance, banking, non-bank financial institutions and leasing.
d. manufacturing only.
e. Approved FDI by the Board of Investment only.

whole, net FDI flows are estimated to have increased from $77 billion in 1996 to $80 billion in 1997. While data on approved FDI projects (table 1) provide only a very imperfect idea of actual investments (or likely actual investments), the increase in approvals for the five most affected countries as a group in 1997 (including during the second half of 1997) looks promising for FDI inflows in 1998.

This is not surprising. After all, FDI flows are different from portfolio equity investment flows and bank lending, and they behave differently. These three types of flows should not be lumped together when seeking to understand the implications of the crisis.

FDI flows involve financial capital flows, but also involve the capitalization of technology, knowledge, skills and other resources that represent a stock of assets for production. They are motivated by the strategic interests of TNCs that invest in enterprises in host countries ("foreign affiliates") in their search for market access and access to resources, to strengthen the competitiveness of their corporate systems; this typically involves long-term relationships, at the level of production, between the investor and its foreign affiliates. Much portfolio investment, on the other hand, is associated primarily with a search for financial gains, often short-term gains; the time horizon for decisions regarding much bank lending is also short-term.

Portfolio equity investment—one component of portfolio investment—has traditionally been volatile, in normal times as well as in crises. For example, during 1986-1995, the volatility index for portfolio equity flows to emerging market economies (including developing countries and economies in transition) as a group was four times higher than that for FDI to those countries (UNCTAD, 1997).[1] The volatility index for portfolio equity flows to selected individual countries (including Malaysia and Thailand) was several times higher than that for FDI (UNCTAD, 1997). Portfolio equity investments (as well as international bond issues and short-term bank lending) are easily influenced by credit ratings (by, for example, international rating agencies). This can lead to a vicious circle once a financial crisis has begun: declines in creditworthiness, as manifested, for example, in credit ratings, tend to amplify financial instability through their effects on these flows.

The recent behaviour of FDI and portfolio equity investment flows to the Asian economies most affected by the crisis is reminiscent of their behaviour during the Mexican crisis of December 1994-1995 (figure 2): total portfolio investment flows to Mexico fell from $12 billion in 1994 to $7.5 billion, with

1 The volatility index is a statistical measure (the coefficient of variation) of the degree of variation of annual flows around an average over a certain period of time.

Figure 2: FDI flows, total foreign portfolio investment flows and foreign portfolio equity flows in Mexico, 1990-1996
(Billions of US dollars)

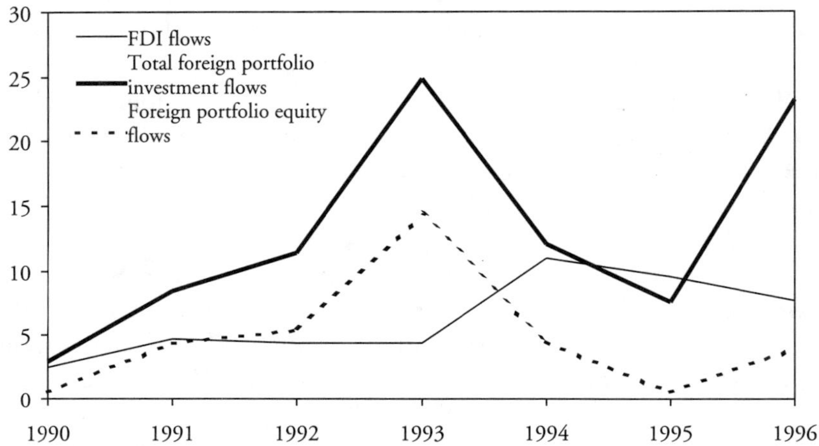

Source: UNCTAD, based on UNCTAD's FDI/TNC database (data provided by the World Bank).

portfolio equity investment flows falling from $4.5 billion to $0.5 billion in 1995. FDI inflows, in contrast, which had more than doubled in 1994, fell by only 13 per cent in 1995.

The most important locational determinants of FDI are the economic factors that influence the prospects for TNCs to engage profitably in production activities. These include the size and growth of host country markets (which depend primarily on macroeconomic performance, especially the level and growth of national and per capita real income); access to regional or international markets for exports from a host country; the availability of human resources, including relatively low-cost and, especially, efficient, flexible and skilled labour; technological and innovation capabilities; natural resource endowments; and the quality of the infrastructure. A second important set of determinants relates to the environment for conducting business and economic activity in the host country. This includes political and economic stability, and efficient and encouraging policies towards industry, trade and private enterprise activity in general, whether domestic or foreign, and institutional structures for implementing them. A third set of determinants relates to the design and implementation of policies specifically related to FDI.

Many Asian countries, including countries most affected by the crisis, have ranked high among developing host countries in the attractiveness of several of the factors mentioned above. In particular, they have built up fundamental strengths that make for high long-term growth, such as high domestic savings rates and educated, skilled and flexible human resources. These can be expected to continue to remain sound. TNCs, which typically take a long-term view, can therefore be expected to continue to take a positive view of the region's investment potential.

Expectations of continued growth of FDI flows to Asia are supported by the findings of the Secretariat of the United Nations Conference on Trade and Development (UNCTAD) and the International Chamber of Commerce (ICC) with a view towards ascertaining the nature of major companies' responses to the financial crisis (see box). The great majority of respondents reported that their confidence in the region as an investment destination has remained unchanged (figure 3). The pattern of the findings in this regard is similar across firms in major sectors (primary, manufacturing, services) and from different home regions (figures 4 and 5): over

The UNCTAD/ICC survey

The survey by the UNCTAD Secretariat and ICC, conducted in February 1998, covered 500 companies. These included the world's 100 largest TNCs (not including banking and finance companies) in terms of foreign assets, drawn from the list of such corporations prepared for UNCTAD's *World Investment Report 1997*; 200 companies that were potential candidates for inclusion in that list; the world's 50 largest TNCs (not including banking and finance companies) originating in developing countries, drawn from the list of such corporations prepared for UNCTAD's *World Investment Report 1997*; 50 companies that were potential candidates for inclusion in that list; and 100 additional firms with significant operations in Asia. A total of 198 firms responded to the survey, for a response rate of 40 per cent. The composition of the sample in terms of countries/regions in which the respondents are located ("home regions") and in terms of economic sectors is contained in the following two figures:

Breakdown of responses to the questionnaire by region

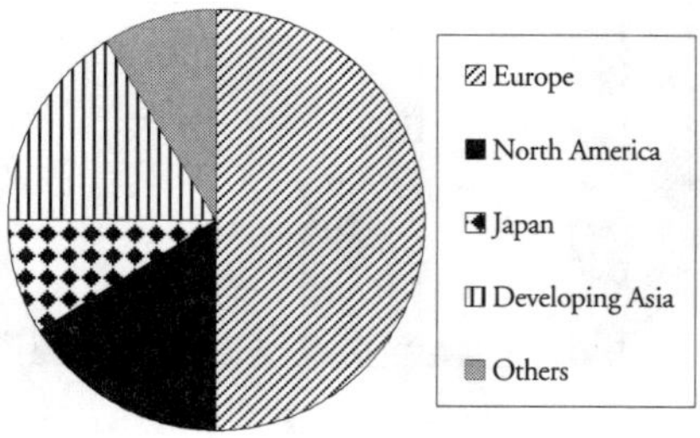

Breakdown of responses to the questionnaire by sector

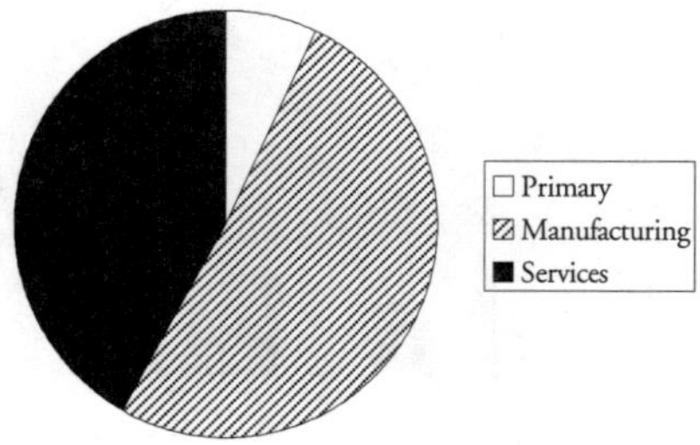

Figure 3: Long-term prospects: overall response of companies worldwide
(Percentage)

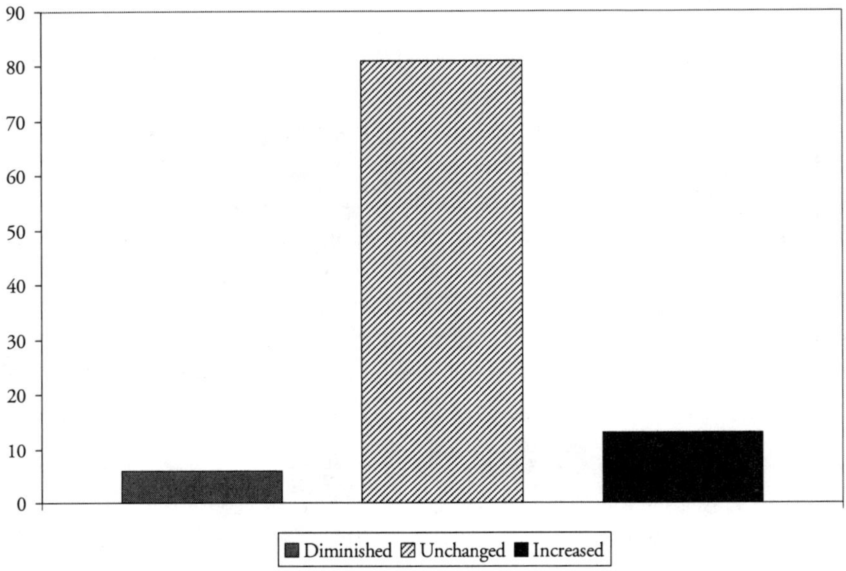

Figure 4: Long-term prospects: company intentions by home region of parent company
(Percentage)

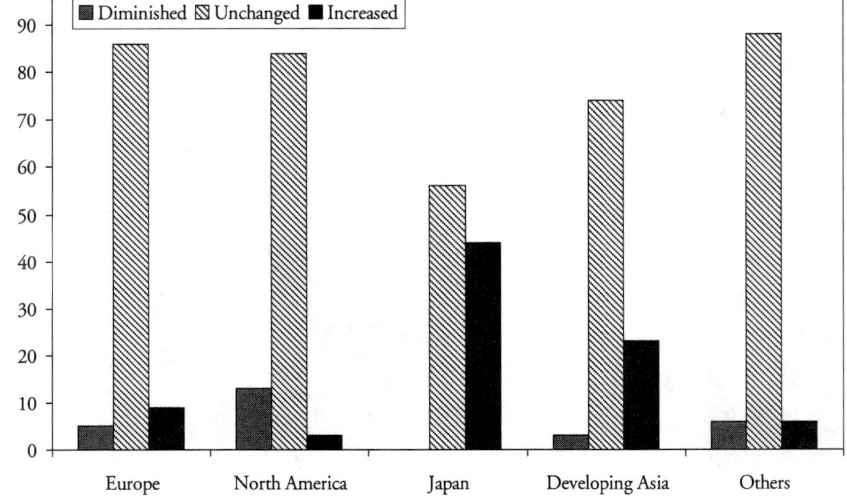

Figure 5: Long-term prospects: company intentions by sector
(Percentage)

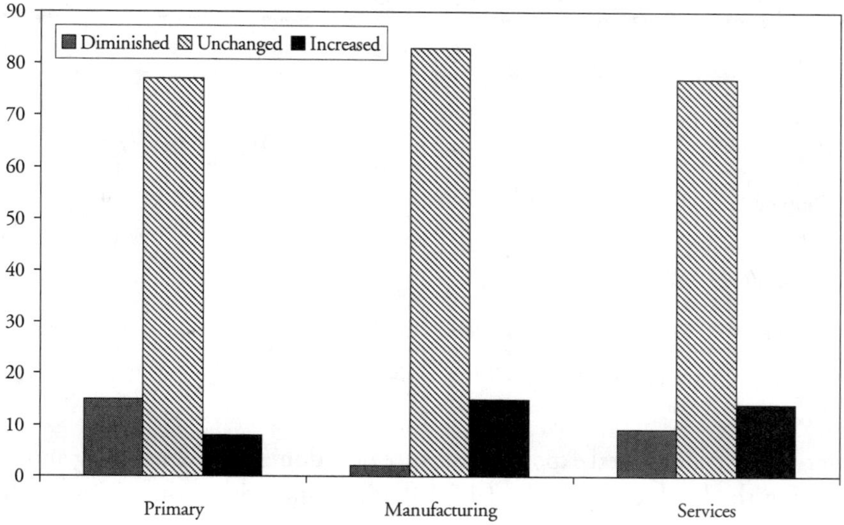

four-fifths of all respondents reported that, for them, East and South-East Asia's longer-term prospects as a destination for profitable FDI have remained unchanged. The vast majority of respondents from Europe (86 per cent) and North America (84 per cent) stated that their long-term view of the region remains unchanged. The figures were somewhat lower for Japanese respondents (56 per cent) and respondents from developing Asia (74 per cent); but this lower "no change" response was compensated by higher shares of Japanese and other Asian respondents indicating increased confidence in the region in the longer term (44 per cent of Japanese firms and 23 per cent of Asian developing country firms).

Firms from both within and outside the region thus hold a very positive view of the longer-term prospects for FDI in Asia.

As Asian countries take stock of the situation and implement measures to restore trust and confidence and increase economic activity, the question of what *immediate* implications the crisis will have for inward and outward FDI deserves attention. The reason is that FDI plays, and has the potential to continue to play, an important role in the growth of the Asian economies most affected by the crisis. In a number of them, FDI provides an important supplement for domestic investment (table 2) and accounts for significant export shares in some industries (reaching more than half of manufacturing exports and more than 40 per cent of total exports in the case of Malaysia, and

Table 2. Ratio of FDI flows to gross fixed capital formation in the Asian countries most affected by the financial crisis, 1990-1996
(Percentage)

Country	*1990*	*1991*	*1992*	*1993*	*1994*	*1995*	*1996*
Indonesia	2.8	3.6	3.9	4.3	3.8	6.7	8.5
Korea, Republic of	0.8	1.0	0.6	0.5	0.6	1.1	1.3
Malaysia	16.8	23.8	26.0	22.5	15.9	12.1	13.2
Philippines	5.2	6.0	2.1	9.6	10.5	9.0	7.3
Thailand	7.1	4.9	4.8	3.6	2.3	2.8	3.2
Memorandum:							
South, East and South-East Asia	4.0	3.9	4.5	6.5	7.3	7.3	8.2

Source: UNCTAD, FDI/TNC database.

over 40 per cent of total exports in the case of Indonesia). Maintaining and increasing the level and growth of FDI flows to and within the region could, therefore, assist in the process of economic recovery in the region.

One reason an increase of FDI flows might be expected in the near future is that companies wishing to establish a presence in the region, or seeking to increase the scale of their existing operations on the basis of favourable expectations regarding the long-term prospects of the region, find lucrative opportunities. Specifically, currency devaluations and lower property prices reduce the foreign currency costs of acquiring fixed assets such as land, buildings and capital goods manufactured locally. In addition, lower valuations of many Asian firms in the aftermath of the financial crisis reduce the costs of acquiring firms. As a result, firms from developed countries and other unaffected countries require much lower amounts, in terms of home country currencies, to establish (or add to) a given production capacity. (Levels of FDI inflows to the most affected countries similar to those in the past in terms of dollars would therefore signal increased interest by TNCs in Asia.) Indeed, for firms already planning to invest or expand their investments in Asia—whether large or small (see following quote)—the current situation presents a unique opportunity to do so at lower than anticipated costs.

Moreover, the restructuring of firms faced with large debt repayments and interest-rate hikes, and their urgent need for funds, combined with lower stock prices, provides opportunities for TNCs to undertake direct investments in the region through mergers and acquisitions (M&As) involving host country firms, including firms that otherwise might go bankrupt. Interestingly, however, the value of M&As in the five countries most affected by the crisis taken as a whole decreased (by 13 per cent) during the second half of 1997 as compared with the first half of the year (figure 6). This was largely a result of a decline in M&As in the Philippines (the country that was the least affected by the crisis among the five). The Republic of Korea and Malaysia, on the other hand, saw significant increases of the value of M&As in the second half of 1997, while the value of M&As in Indonesia remained at the same high level as in the first half of the year. TNCs from the United States and Singapore led the field in acquiring firms in the five countries, followed by firms from Germany (figure 7). Other firms from the region (especially from Hong Kong (China), Taiwan Province of China and China) are beginning to use this opportunity as well.

Currency devaluations also increase the attractiveness of Asian economies to foreign investors due to lower costs of production in terms of home country currencies. As wages and other operating costs decrease, efficiency-seeking, mobile foreign investors might find it advantageous to invest in the affected economies to take advantage of cost differentials, even if they are small, and inflation, if it occurs, could reduce their impact.

Costs of production are particularly important for export-oriented activities. Devaluations, too, make it easier for firms, foreign as well as domestic, to export from the countries concerned.

Figure 6: Cross-border M&A sales in the five Asian countries most affected by the financial crisis,[a] by host country, first and second half of 1997
(Millions of US dollars)

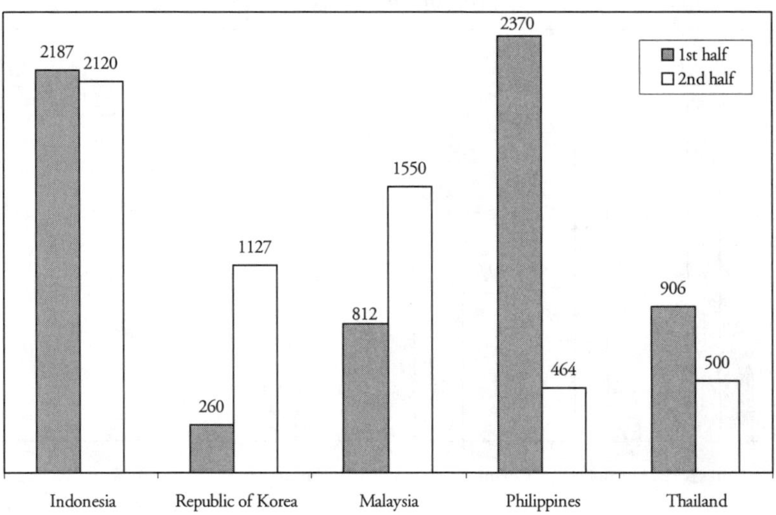

Source: Data provided by KPMG Corporate Finance.

a. Indonesia, Republic of Korea, Malaysia, Philippines and Thailand.

Foreign affiliates in Asia have high export propensities (table 3). TNCs can build on this, both in terms of increasing exports and using their existing networks to reach markets. Indeed, as the experience of the automobile industry in Mexico in the 1990s suggests, exports by foreign affiliates could increase dramatically following a currency crisis (table 4).

For TNCs, a fair amount of exporting takes place within the context of integrated international production networks established with a view to strengthening competitiveness by distributing value-added activities among locations in such a way as to maximize global corporate profits. In these networks, intermediate goods or tradable services produced by an affiliate in one country are exported to the parent firm, or to affiliates of the same parent in another country or countries; indeed, about one third of world trade consists of such "intra-firm" trade. "Privileged" access by affiliates to the TNC system—a market in itself—and advantageous access to national firms linked to TNC systems through subcontracting or other arrangements—facilitates exporting, making it easier for firms that are part of TNC networks to take advantage of the lower costs (of exported items) due to devaluation (UNCTAD, 1996).

Being part of—or linked to—TNC networks also makes it easier for firms—foreign affiliates or domestic enterprises—to switch from domestic

Figure 7: Cross-border M&A purchases in the five Asian countries most affected by the financial crisis,[a] by host country, first and second half of 1997
(Millions of US dollars)

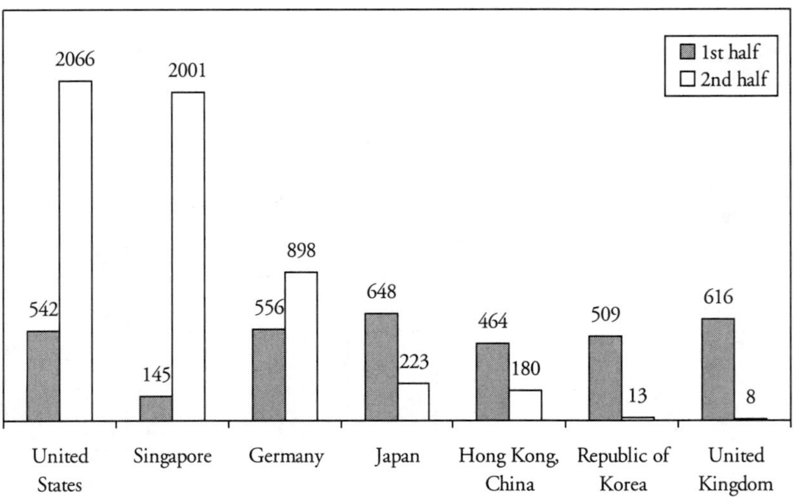

Source: Data provided by KPMG Corporate Finance.

a. Indonesia, Republic of Korea, Malaysia, Philippines and Thailand.

Table 3. Export propensity of Japanese and United States affiliates in the Asian countries most affected by the financial crisis, 1994[a]
(Percentage)

	Japanese affiliates	*United States affiliates* [b]					
Industry	*Indonesia, Malaysia, Philippines and Thailand, combined* [c]	*Indonesia*	*Republic of Korea*	*Malaysia*	*Philippines*	*Thailand*	*Total for the five countries*
Primary	86.6	77.9[d]	..	..	..	..	..
Manufacturing:	42.8	..	15.4	62.1	37.3	62.0	..
Chemicals	11.3	..	3.9	11.2	1.8	3.8	..
Electrical machinery	74.0	..	30.2	..	..	..	..
Transport equipment	9.7	..	..	e	e	e	..
Services	18.8	..	..	..	..	..	..
All industries	38.3	64.2	13.1	42.1	26.0	27.1	62.9

Sources: UNCTAD, based on Japan, Ministry of International Trade and Industry, *Dai-25 Kai Wagakuni Kigyo no Kaigai Jigyo Katsudo* (Tokyo: Ministry of Finance Printing Bureau, 1997) and United States Department of Commerce, U.S. Direct Investment Abroad: 1994 Benchmark Survey, Preliminary Results (Washington, D.C.: Superintendent of Documents 1997).

a. Exports as a percentage of total sales.
b. Majority-owned foreign affiliates only.
c. Data for the Republic of Korea are not available.
d. Petroleum only.
e. Insignificant.

Table 4. Mexico's automobile production and exports, 1993-1997[a]
(Percentage)

Year	*Total production*	*Exports*	*Exports as percentage of total production*
1993	823.2	424.5	51.6
1994	855.3	497.1	58.1
1995	699.3	598.8	85.6
1996	795.0	635.9	80.0
1997[b]	790.9	557.4	70.5

Source: Data provided by Michael Mortimore, Unit on Investment and Corporate Strategies, ECLAC, Santiago, February 1998.

a. Passenger vehicles only. Includes production by BMW, Chrysler, Ford, General Motors, Honda, Mercedes Benz, Nissan and Volkswagen.

b. Through November 1997.

sales to exports. This was demonstrated, for example, during the Mexican crisis of December 1994-1995. In the case of the Mexican automobile industry, a number of foreign affiliates reacted to the slump in domestic demand by switching—sometimes within a few months—a part of their production to foreign markets: exports increased both in absolute terms and as a percentage of total production, from 58 per cent in 1994 to 86 per cent in 1995 (table 4). Naturally, market access for exports to the large North American market in the context of North American Free Trade Agreement (NAFTA) and buoyant demand conditions in that market also helped, as did the fact that foreign automobile affiliates in Mexico were already producing at internationally competitive quality standards.

Many corporate networks of integrated international production exist in Asia. This should facilitate the process of coping with the crisis for the firms involved. Japanese TNCs, in particular, have the opportunity to use their regional and global corporate networks in this respect. Increasingly, these include also small- and medium-sized firms which, in the case of Japan, account for a substantial share of the country's outward FDI. As in the case of Mexico, the result may well be that, in the end, the export orientation of foreign affiliates in Asia may reach new record highs.

The impact of the current crisis could therefore be mitigated somewhat for a number of the most affected Asian countries because international integration at the level of production allows TNCs (and firms linked to them), to compensate for declining domestic sales through increased exports spurred by devaluation. As the experience of foreign firms in the Mexican automobile industry during the 1994-1995 crisis shows, if major international markets are open to exports, and production by affiliates is of world standards, restructuring sales towards exports can potentially help sustain FDI operations in the face of decreasing domestic demand—to the benefit, too, of the host countries involved. Whether and to what extent this potential is realized depends, of course, upon the strategies of firms.

The extent of the cost advantages enjoyed by export-oriented firms varies, of course, among industries and firms, depending upon the extent to which foreign affiliate activities in the region depend upon imports (the foreign currency prices of which will not be directly affected by devaluations). This underlines further the importance of integrating foreign affiliates into their host economies: such integration not only contributes to the building up of local capacities; but the more foreign affiliates can draw on backward linkages with local enterprises, the less import-dependent they are.

There are, however, important preconditions that need to be fulfilled if increased export competitiveness is to be effectively exploited, be it by export-oriented foreign affiliates or by domestic firms: the principal export markets in other parts of the world need to remain open to exports from Asia, and, equally important, demand in those export markets needs to remain strong enough to absorb additional imports from Asia. This is particularly important since demand in the Asian regional market, which has been absorbing increasing shares of exports from within the region, is likely to be affected adversely by the crisis and its immediate impact on incomes and growth, as well as by the current economic slowdown in Japan. It would be in the interest of all involved—host, home and third countries and firms—that these conditions are fulfilled to the maximum extent possible.

The shortage of capital for enterprises in the region, combined with a recognition of the role that FDI can play in maintaining growth and development, is leading to a more flexible attitude towards FDI. As a result, some countries in the region have, in recent months, further lowered barriers to FDI (table 5).

There are, however, concerns regarding loss of control over national firms, as governments weigh the costs and benefits of tackling potential bankruptcies by allowing a sharing of control of increasing numbers of domestic enterprises with TNCs. Foreign control of large portions of any industry—or even small portions of key industries—can of course become a sensitive domestic issue (in developed as well as developing countries). This is particularly the case if "fire sales" are seen to occur during a period of national economic stress at relatively low prices. Restrictions on hostile takeovers in some countries are in place partly for these reasons.

Table 5. FDI measures adopted since mid-1997 in the Asian countries most affected by the financial crisis

Indonesia:

- Eliminated foreign shareholding limit of 49 per cent in firms other than financial firms in September 1997.
- Approved full ownership of non-bank financial firms, including insurance companies.
- Guaranteed existing foreign ownership in financial institutions.
- Approved wholesaling of their products by foreign manufacturing affiliates or through other foreign firms in November 1997. Retailing through other foreign firms will be allowed in 2003.

Republic of Korea

- Approved hostile takeovers which will allow foreign investors to purchase up to a third of the shares of companies of the Republic of Korea without approval of the companies' boards. (The Government revised the law in February 1998, and will amend the Presidential Decree by April 1998.)
- Eliminated the requirement of government approval for takeovers of companies of the Republic of Korea with assets of 2 trillion won or more, with the exception of defence and key industries. (The Government revised the law in February 1998, and will amend the Presidential Decree by April 1998.)
- Approved the establishment of subsidiaries of foreign banks and foreign securities firms in March 1998.

Malaysia:

- Relaxed the level of foreign shareholding limits. Currently, there is a 30 per cent foreign equity limit in principle, except for export-oriented industries, high-technology industries and multimedia companies with multimedia super corridor (MSC) status. Foreign equity participation in telecommunications allowed up to 49 per cent.
- Guaranteed up to 51 per cent foreign equity participation in existing insurance companies by current holders.
- Fully/majority foreign-owned fund-management companies will be allowed.
- Relaxed Bumiputra policy. Relaxation of regulations on the release of a 30 per cent share of listed firms owned by Bumiputra to non-Bumiputra. Approval on a case-by-case basis of acquisitions of Bumiputra firms by non-Bumiputra.

Philippines:

- Raised the permitted level of foreign ownership in existing banks or banking subsidiaries as well as investment firms to 51 per cent. Existing foreign stakes, if higher, will be protected.

/.....

(Table 5, cont'd)

Philippines:

- Raised the permitted level of foreign ownership in existing banks or banking subsidiaries as well as investment firms to 51 per cent. Existing foreign stakes, if higher, will be protected.

Thailand:

- Foreign shareholding was limited to not more than 49 per cent except for export-oriented projects with at least 80 per cent export share located in Zone 3, where foreign ownership was allowed to be 100 per cent. The Board of Investment relaxed this regulation in 1997 for companies with financial difficulties so that they could have foreign ownership of more than 51 per cent on the condition that Thai shareholders of that company agree to this change and send a letter confirming their decision to change the foreign ownership share to the Board of Investment.
- The Minister of Finance, upon the recommendation of the Bank of Thailand, may release the 25 per cent cap for foreign stakes in locally-incorporated banks and finance and credit companies for 10 years. The absolute amount of equity holding up to 100 per cent will be protected after that if acquired during this period.
- Guaranteed existing shareholding structure of foreign bank branches.
- Announced that majority foreign ownership of existing promoted firms in certain industrial zones would be permitted if agreed by existing Thai shareholders.

Source: UNCTAD.

* * *

The findings of the UNCTAD/ICC survey show that more than one quarter of the responding firms expect to increase their FDI in East and South-East Asia as a whole in the short-to-medium term (figure 8). North American and Japanese firms are close to this average (19 per cent each), while firms from Europe are distinctly above it (34 per cent) and those from developing Asia distinctly below it (10 per cent) (figure 9). In the case of European firms, this may well reflect that, after having largely neglected Asia until recently (UNCTAD and European Commission, 1996), they are now taking an active interest in this region. In the case of the TNCs from developing Asia, the low proportion may reflect the impaired capacity of some TNCs to undertake outward FDI (most of which has traditionally gone to other Asian developing countries); however, they remain committed to the region, as 69 per cent expect to maintain their investment at the pre-crisis level. Predictably, firms in manufacturing (from all regions) have the highest proportion of responses that

Figure 8: Short- and medium-term prospects: overall response of companies worldwide
(Percentage)

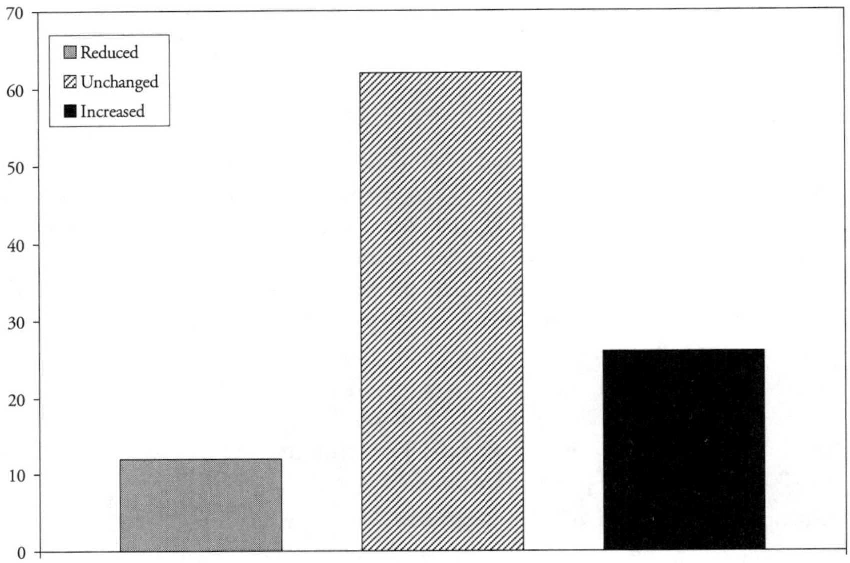

Figure 9: Short- and medium-term prospects: company intentions by home region of parent company
(Percentage)

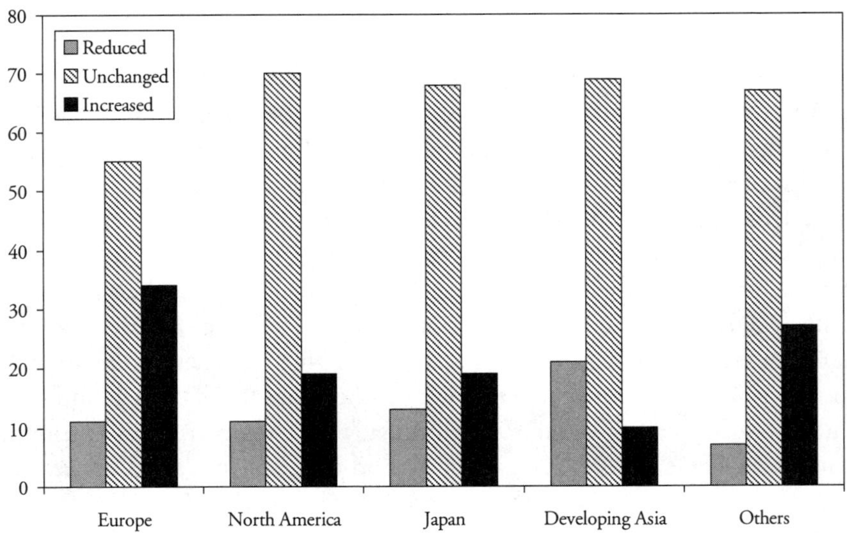

indicated they expected expansion of their FDI in Asia, with over one-third of them providing this response, as compared with one-fifth of service firms and less than one-tenth of primary sector firms (figure 10).

In the short and medium term, the Asian crisis will affect adversely some foreign affiliates producing for sale in local markets. Several Asian countries have revised downwards their forecasts of economic growth in 1998. A contraction in growth will reduce demand in domestic markets for certain goods and services, and this is likely to lead to some cancelling, scaling down or postponement of investment in the most affected countries in some industries, particularly those that already have excess capacity due to substantial investments in the recent past. Loss of asset values (in terms of foreign currency) on investments already established may also diminish TNCs' desire to expand production facilities in some industries. Not only affiliates geared to local markets, but also parent firms exporting to Asian markets may see their earnings shrink, dampening plans for expansion in the region.

In addition, reduced earnings affect the financial position of host-country market-seeking affiliates and might induce them to put on hold plans for reinvestment. In Mexico, for example, income on United States FDI fell by 45 per

Figure 10: Short- and medium-term prospects: company intentions by sector
(Percentage)

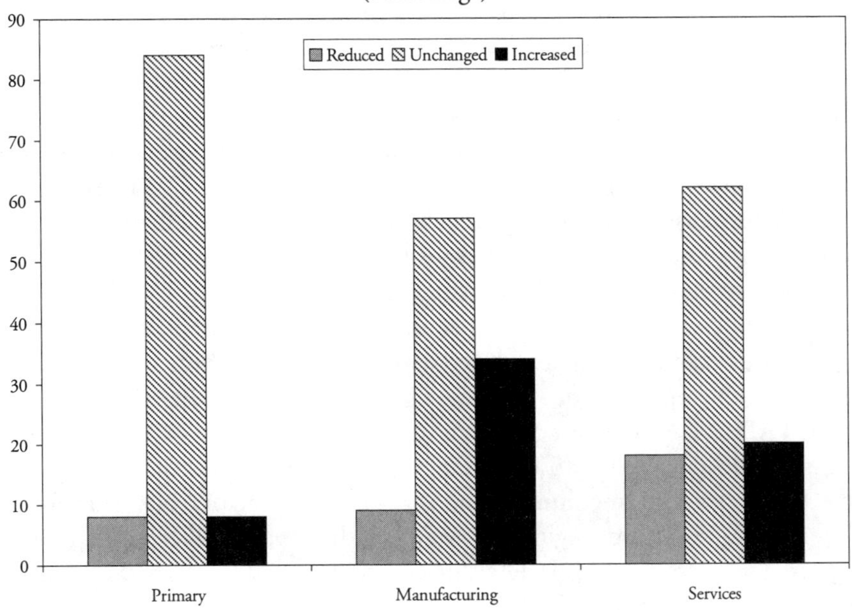

cent in 1995 (though it rose again in 1996 to a level higher than in 1994); in some industries (such as transport equipment), affiliate income turned negative in 1995.

This being said, foreign affiliates, being able to draw on their parent systems for financing, are often in a better position than domestic firms to have continuous financing (including for importing necessary inputs and providing export finance). More generally, they are in principle in a better position than domestic firms to weather difficulties—another example of the protective influence that belonging to transnational corporate systems can have. On the other hand, the likelihood of financial difficulties arising from reduced earnings is greater for affiliates of smaller TNCs with limited financial capacities to withstand low earnings or losses.

Indeed, a number of the respondent TNCs in the UNCTAD/ICC survey (12 per cent) indicated that they expect to reduce their investment in East and South-East Asia in the short and medium term (figure 8). This is most evident for TNCs based in Asian developing countries (21 per cent) and, to a lesser extent, for Japanese (13 per cent), European and North American TNCs (11 per cent each) (figure 9). As foreign affiliates in the services sector are particularly susceptible to local demand conditions, due to the non-tradability of most services, it is not surprising that such negative expectations were reported most frequently among them (18 per cent) (figure 10). Of course, even in normal times, some firms are contracting, even as others are expanding their facilities.

It is also revealing to compare the percentages of firms expecting, in the short and medium term, increases in FDI with those of firms expecting decreases. The percentage of firms in both manufacturing and services reporting an expected increase in their investments in Asia is higher than the percentage reporting an expected reduction in their investments (figure 10). The predominance of expansion plans over retrenchment plans was evident among TNCs from Europe and North America as well as Japan. Only among TNCs originating in developing countries in Asia did the number of firms expecting retrenchment exceed the number expecting expansion (figure 9).

While it is difficult to assess on balance the effects of the diverse factors exerting an upward or downward influence on FDI flows, the UNCTAD/ICC survey suggests strongly that the majority of TNCs operating in the region are likely not to change their planned investments even during the short and medium term, regardless of sector, but with some differences across home regions. However, if the number of respondents who expected an increase of FDI in Asia in the short to medium term are added to the number of respondents indicating "no change", the response rate is about four fifths or more for all home regions (figure 9).

Much will depend, of course, upon whether efforts to stabilize the financial markets and external financing positions of the crisis-affected Asian economies are broadly successful, and how soon the rates of growth of these economies are restored to satisfactory levels.

The Asian crisis most likely will seriously affect the financial capabilities of TNCs originating in the affected countries to invest abroad. Furthermore, devaluations make it more expensive for TNCs from these countries to finance their operations abroad. At the same time, their foreign affiliates may confront difficulties in raising funds in their host markets (or other foreign markets), due to the fact that foreign banks are reluctant to lend to them. Thus, it may become difficult for the Asian TNCs concerned not only to make additional greenfield investments, but also to continue some ongoing projects or to expand existing ones. Shortage of cash may also induce Asian firms to sell their assets in Europe and the United States for funds in strong currencies because that might be preferable to selling domestic assets at cheap rates. There are signs that such sales of assets are being made, particularly by TNCs from the Republic of Korea in the United States.

However, once again, a distinction needs to be made between FDI in production for export and FDI for servicing foreign markets directly, in order to understand the effects of the crisis on outward FDI from the region. To the extent that currency devaluations make exports from some Asian home countries more competitive internationally than before, some TNCs originating within the region would not be expected to increase their outward FDI. This could be the case, for instance, in some manufacturing industries in which firms from countries such as the Republic of Korea and Thailand had expanded labour-intensive activities abroad following the so-called "flying geese pattern" of restructuring, by shifting those activities to other Asian countries at a lower level of development and lower labour-costs (UNCTAD, 1995).

In any event, the consequences for outward FDI in the region as a whole may not be that significant. Although 37 per cent of FDI stock in developing Asia as a whole is from other Asian developing economies (as compared to 21 per cent from Japan, 14 per cent from the United States and 13 per cent from the European Union) (UNCTAD and European Commission, 1996), the five most affected countries account for less than one-fifth of FDI outflows from Asian developing countries (table 6). The major FDI sources within the region—Hong Kong (China), Singapore, Taiwan Province of China and China—have not been severely affected by the crisis. The consequences for intraregional FDI as a whole may therefore not be too severe. At the same time, some firms from the region may draw the lesson that they should, in the longer term, look for investment opportunities outside the region, in order to diversify risk.

Among the second tier of Asian economies most likely to be affected by a fall in intraregional FDI are Viet Nam and the least developed Asian countries (such as Cambodia, the Lao People's Democratic Republic and Myanmar) that rely more heavily on some of the most affected countries for such investment. This would set back some of the progress being made by these least developed countries to put their economies on a growth track.

One could expect that, in light of the crisis, TNCs may find other sites more attractive for new investment projects in the short to medium term. Indeed, some of the firms surveyed by UNCTAD/ICC are looking, in the short

Table 6. Top 10 FDI outward investors from South, East and South-East Asia, 1994-1996
(Billions of US dollars)

Economy [a]	*1994*	*1995*	*1996*	*Average 1994-1996*
Hong Kong (China),	21.4[b]	25.0[b]	26.8[c]	24.4
Singapore	3.7	4.0	4.8	4.2
Korea, Republic of	2.5	3.5	4.4	3.5
Taiwan Province of China	2.5	2.7	3.1	2.7
China	2.0	2.0	2.1	2.0
Malaysia	1.8	2.6	1.9[d]	2.1
Thailand	0.5	0.9	0.9	0.8
Indonesia	0.6	0.6	0.5[d]	0.6
Philippines	0.3	0.4	0.2	0.3
India	0.1	0.1	0.1[d]	0.1
Memorandum:				
Total for the five most affected Asian countries[e]	5.7	8.0	8.0	7.2
Total for South, East and South-East Asia	35.5	41.8	44.9	40.7
Share of the five most affected countries in total for South, East and South-East Asia	16.2	19.1	17.8	17.8

Source: UNCTAD, FDI/TNC database.

a. Ranked according to total outward flows for 1996.
b. Estimated by using inflows to China, the European Union and the United States as a proxy.
c. Estimated by using inflows to China and the United States as a proxy.
d. UNCTAD estimate.
e. Indonesia, Republic of Korea, Malaysia, Philippines and Thailand.

to medium term, towards expansion in Latin America, Central and Eastern Europe and Africa (37 per cent, 27 per cent and 11 per cent, respectively). But this finding should not necessarily be interpreted to indicate a switch of FDI towards these regions in response to the crisis, for two reasons:

- An overwhelming majority (90 per cent) of the survey respondents who indicated that they expect to increase their investments in Latin America and the Caribbean and Central and Eastern Europe do not intend to reduce their investments in East and South-East Asia in the short-to-medium term. Furthermore, nearly 50 per cent of those who indicated that they expect to increase their investments in Latin America and the Caribbean and Central and Eastern Europe also indicated that they expect to increase their investments in East and South-East Asia. In other words, firms see profitable investment opportunities in emerging markets in general.
- FDI flows to Latin America and the Caribbean already showed a substantial upward trend before the crisis in Asia (with annual growth rates of 31 per cent during 1995-1997) (table 7). FDI has also picked up in Central and Eastern Europe, a region which, in any event, offers much potential for further increases.

Because of good prospects outside Asia, Asia's share in the total of FDI to all developing countries would decline in any case, even though the prospects for FDI in Asia remain excellent. In other words, the relative FDI position of Asia attained during the past two decades or so is being readjusted as Latin America and the Caribbean have emerged from their "lost decade" and Central

Table 7. FDI inflows into selected regions, 1986-1997
(Billions of US dollars)

Region	*1986-1991*	*1992*	*1993*	*1994*	*1995*	*1996*	*1997* [a]
Africa	2.9	3.2	3.6	5.7	5.1	4.8	4.7
Latin America and the Caribbean	9.5	17.6	17.2	28.7	31.9	43.8	56.1
South, East and South-East Asia	15.1	27.7	47.3	58.3	66.6	77.6	82.4
Central and Eastern Europe	0.7	4.4	6.1	5.9	14.2	12.3	18.4

Source: UNCTAD, *World Investment Report, 1998* (United Nations publication, Sales No. E.98.II.D.5).

a. Estimates.

and Eastern Europe have opened themselves to FDI. This shift would occur even without any interregional diversion of FDI flows. Be that as it may, however, Asia now faces more competition in the FDI world market in general.

In spite of the variety of factors influencing FDI and the differentiated picture with respect to different kinds of investments, the most important thing to note is that most TNCs typically take a long-term view with respect to their locational decisions and, given the region's past performance and solid fundamentals in a number of respects, this leads them to remain bullish about FDI in Asia. Hence, many of the more specific factors outlined above may have only short-to-medium term implications and, in any event, are somewhat mitigated by the protective influences enjoyed by foreign affiliates through their membership in transnational corporate networks (an advantage domestic firms do not enjoy). Indeed, in the longer term, the attractiveness of the region is likely to be enhanced as Asian countries overcome their problems and reassert their economic dynamism on the basis of improved fundamental strengths.

More generally, and in comparison with other private capital flows, FDI flows have a moderating effect on the volatility of total private capital flows. This is a side effect of the deep international integration of the Asian economies at the level of production that FDI brings about. In fact, in the same way in which the debt crisis in the 1980s led governments to appreciate the non-debt creating nature of FDI, the current crisis may lead them to appreciate more the relative stability of FDI flows, apart from the other contributions such investment can make to growth sand development.

Because there are some short- and medium-term problems, and because continued FDI flows could contribute towards restoring economic growth and maintaining exports at high levels, some policy measures addressing these problems ought to be considered:

- Governments of the affected countries could make an extra effort—perhaps helped by regional and international institutions—to provide information about greenfield and joint venture investment opportunities, especially in (new) activities designated by them as priority areas. Such an effort could be of particular interest to TNCs from developing countries, as well as small- and medium-size enterprises.
- Countries might also pay greater attention to providing assistance to dynamic and innovative small- and medium-sized enterprises whose role as potential partners in international networks and technology alliances would thus be enhanced.
- In this connection, Asian countries may wish to review their regulatory

frameworks for FDI, with a view towards making them as appropriate as possible in light of their development objectives. UNCTAD's Investment Policy Reviews could be of relevance here, as would be the Investment Guides for least developed countries initiated by UNCTAD in cooperation with the ICC.

- Where appropriate, Asian TNCs could consider adopting international accounting standards as soon as possible.
- Within the framework of regional integration arrangements and other fora for cooperation—such as the Association of Southeast Asian Nations (ASEAN) Investment Area—Asian countries could formulate jointly measures that could encourage FDI and its contributions to the economies of member countries.
- Home countries that allow the use of optional reserves and grant tax deductions for the depreciated value of their firms' foreign affiliates as features of their tax policies could consider recognizing the present circumstances in Asian countries as meeting the criteria for such reserves and deductions.
- Home country political risk insurance programmes for investors could consider expanding their coverage of foreign affiliates to sudden, steep and debilitating foreign exchange devaluations.
- Countries that are host to foreign affiliates of Asia-based TNCs in financial distress could consider temporary measures of assistance to help sustain existing affiliates, where this is warranted. This would be akin to investment incentives for new inward FDI projects, but adapted to the present special circumstances in the postinvestment stage in host countries.

Naturally, such efforts would have to be embedded in more general policies aimed at restoring macroeconomic stability and economic performance, as well as strengthening institutional capabilities to advance the process of development. While specific efforts aimed at maintaining and increasing FDI flows can make a contribution to the process of overcoming the impact of the crisis, much more will, indeed, depend on the quality of those more general policies.

References

UNCTAD (1997). *World Investment Report 1997: Transnational Corporations, Market Structure and Competition Policy* (United Nations publication, Sales No. E.97.II.D.10).

______ (1996). *World Investment Report 1996: Investment, Trade and International Policy Arrangements* (United Nations publication, Sales No. E.96.II.A.14).

______ (1995). *World Investment Report 1995: Transnational Corporations and Competitiveness* (United Nations publication, Sales No. E.95.II.A.9).

UNCTAD and European Commission (1996). *Investing in Asia's Dynamism: European Union Direct Investment in Asia* (Luxembourg: Office for Official Publications of the European Commission).

23

Discussion – Direct Investment

THEA LEE
RICHARD D. RIPPE
RICHARD TAN

THEA LEE*

This is a useful, well-grounded paper. It does a good job of presenting the results of the UNCTAD survey on foreign direct investment (FDI) and raises many important topics for future research. Its main findings are that FDI is extremely stable and even growing slightly in East and South-East Asia overall in the wake of the financial crisis, with good prospect for continuing to grow. This is in sharp contrast to portfolio capital, which is about four times more volatile.

In my remarks, I hope to stimulate discussion on some of the underlying questions that I think are important.

First, will this trend in FDI last, given the political crises in Indonesia and the Republic of Korea? It is one thing for FDI to remain steady with devaluation and recession, but riots and strikes are entirely different. Already, we have noted a dramatic drop in mergers and acquisitions in the Philippines.

* Assistant Director, International Economics, Public Policy Department, American Federation of Labour-Congress of Industrial Organizations, Washington, D.C.

Second, what is or should be the role of FDI in development strategy? Should attracting FDI be an unqualified goal? Is all FDI created equal? While it is true that FDI is less volatile than portfolio flows and that this is an advantage, it should not be the only concern for developing countries. We could draw some interesting conclusions from the differences among countries, both in policies towards FDI, and in overall development strategy. As the UNCTAD paper notes, the ratio of FDI to gross fixed capital formation in the region more than doubled from 4 per cent to 8.2 per cent during the period 1990 to 1996. This ratio is especially high in Indonesia and Malaysia, and especially low in the Republic of Korea.

Finally, how do we calculate the impact of outward FDI from the originating country? Is it always beneficial, as the UNCTAD paper argues?

In order to address these questions, we need to make a more systematic distinction between different kinds of FDI. I would argue that there is an important difference in the impact on both the recipient and the host country between FDI motivated by market access and FDI motivated by the desire for cheaper production costs—labour, resources, climate etc.[1] While the paper does note this distinction, it fails to follow through to the relevant conclusions.

I do not mean to say that one type of FDI is bad and the other is good, but the FDI in search of cheap labour or lax regulatory climate needs more oversight than FDI motivated solely by the desire to improve market access. It is crucial to establish minimum international ground rules to ensure that international competition for capital does not lead Governments to weaken labour or environmental standards or ignore their enforcement to attract investment. Other issues for developing countries include the following: rules under which Governments compete to attract FDI of the type motivated mainly by the search for cheap production costs have an enormous impact on development strategy, and, whether or not developing countries should restrict hostile takeovers, or have restrictions on "fire-sale" of local firms.

The paper does note that the Asian crisis has had the opposite impact on the two kinds of FDI—FDI motivated by market access is dampened by the crisis, while the cost-cutting incentives to shift production grow. Currency devaluation combined with recession leads to bargains in the local prices of labour, land, and other assets. So long as companies are not trying to sell much to the countries where they have located production facilities, the economic crisis can lead to a windfall bonanza. Whichever of these opposing factors dominates in the Asian case will determine whether the trends noted in the paper continue or reverse.

1 Of course, in many cases, FDI is motivated by a combination of market access and cheaper inputs, but often one or the other dominates.

It is worth noting that the crisis can also convert FDI motivated by market access into FDI that stays to take advantage of cheap production costs. In the case of Mexican auto production, for example, the export propensity of the auto sector (which is dominated by foreign investment) grew from 52 per cent before the peso crisis of 1994-1995 to 86 per cent after it. After the crisis, according to the UNCTAD paper, FDI in manufacturing in Asia expanded more than FDI in services (which tends to be less export-oriented than manufacturing).

Comparing the export propensity of FDI originating in different countries gives a rough idea of the market-access versus production-cost motivations for FDI, with lower export propensity corresponding roughly to greater interest in market access. United States FDI into Asia, for example, has an export propensity of 62.9 per cent, compared with that from Japan, which has an export propensity of 38.3 per cent.

For the originating countries, different kinds of outward FDI have different consequences for jobs and wages at home. FDI motivated by market access will tend to have a more positive impact on home jobs and wages than FDI motivated by the search for lower labour costs or less regulation. However, even in the case of FDI that serves an expanded foreign market, it is still important to know why these markets cannot be served by exports. Sometimes, the reason is simply to be closer to the customer base, while in other cases, it is that tariff and non-tariff barriers make it cheaper to shift production than to export.

Some countries also differ in their propensity to serve a given foreign market through export or FDI. United States firms are three times more likely to serve foreign markets by FDI than by exports, as compared to firms from other countries.

Certainly, companies aggressively moving production out of a country (sometimes called "footloose capital") and explicitly avoiding unionized workforces in the process have a dampening effect on jobs and wages at many levels. The first impact is the direct loss of jobs. The second is the "threat effect" and is felt in other factories or industries. In this situation, workers are faced with a choice between accepting deep wage cuts or seeing their factories flee as well. The third is the threat of capital flight, which is often used to deter efforts to organize workers into unions. To the extent that this threat succeeds, overall lower levels of unionization will also tend to lead to lower wage levels.

The paper predicts that export orientation may reach record highs after the crisis, as in Mexico in the wake of the 1994-1995 turmoil. In my view, the UNCTAD paper is too sanguine about the political impact of the increased levels of outward FDI that would be involved in such a scenario.

One further problem once the additional production moves offshore is the willingness or ability of target markets to absorb additional imports indefinitely. The United States trade deficit is already showing signs of dramatic growth. United States export markets are shrinking, and import competition is growing, as is third-country competition in other markets. The European Union and Japan have shown little indication that they are ready or willing to absorb large amounts of new imports in the wake of the crisis. The United States could not be a consuming engine for the entire developing world, even if it had the will to do so. Therefore, the strategy of encouraging more export-oriented FDI may be flawed. The level of optimism may be too high.

In conclusion, it is important to keep in mind that the overall policy goal should not be simply to keep the flow of FDI high at all cost, but rather to ensure that it is contributing to social goals. Governments must make sure that their policies should not encourage and reward greenfield investments haphazardly. Greenfield investments should be closely scrutinized to ensure that they do not contribute to global over-capacity. Further, the rules embodied in international agreements (like the North American Free Trade Agreement, the World Trade Organization, and the proposed Multilateral Agreement on Investment) should aim at balancing the "rights" of corporations to invest against their "responsibilities" to the host communities and Governments. International ground rules, such as those outlined in the UNCTAD investment guidelines and the OECD Guidelines for Multinational Enterprises, must be established, circulated widely, and observed by all players.

RICHARD D. RIPPE*

The search for greater understanding of the causes of Asia's economic crisis continues, and it has taken on greater urgency in light of the difficulties recently encountered by the Russian Federation and threatened in Latin America. It is to be hoped that useful prescriptions—both for current economic policy and for the structure of the international financial system—will come out of such analysis. But an important outgrowth of this assessment will be to

* Senior Vice President and Chief Economist, Prudential Securities Inc., New York.

leave intact those features of the current system that are working well. I submit that one of those is the flow of foreign direct investment (FDI)—both the inflows to and the outflows from Asia's developing countries. The UNCTAD paper provides some useful information on the role of FDI, its determinants, and its prospects in the period immediately ahead.

Encouraging signs about foreign direct investment

As the paper notes, there was a massive surge of private capital into Asia's developing economies during the 1990s. This came in the form of portfolio investments, bank loans, and FDI. Once the crisis hit, these inflows in total receded to a trickle, and there was a net outflow of equity portfolio investment and foreign bank lending. One of the keys in ending the crisis and restoring economic growth in the countries will be to re-establish capital inflows. Since foreign banks will likely be reluctant to extend loans and since portfolio investors will have vivid memories of losses sustained on equities, bonds, and currencies, this will be a daunting task.

Fortunately, there are a number of reasons FDI should play a constructive role in the process. First, data show that FDI was being better maintained in late 1997 and early 1998 than other private capital flows. Second, as the paper documents, the historical record shows that FDI is more stable than other types of capital. Third, the survey results reported in the paper show that many transnational corporations are either maintaining previous plans or actually stepping up their investments in Asia. Such investors generally take a longer-term view of the outlook, and many of them remain positive on the region. Devalued currencies and lower asset valuations in local currencies provide an incentive to act now. Fourth, several Asian countries have changed their rules and regulations in ways that will encourage the inflow of more direct investment.

If FDI to Asia is maintained at high levels, that will help sustain domestic demand and also modernize the capital stock, thereby bolstering competitiveness of these countries. Such a pattern will also be beneficial to developed nations, limiting the extent to which Asia's current account has to move into surplus and thus the extent to which industrial countries must move into deficit.

Potential problems of relying too heavily on FDI

While it is encouraging to see favourable prospects for the continued flow of FDI into Asia, there are several cautionary notes which should be sounded. The temptation in some countries to put controls on short-term capital flows (portfolio investment and bank lending), in addition to creating distortions and incentives for cheating, could lead to over-reliance on FDI. A number of risks should be noted.

When conditions in the economies of multinational corporate parents turn sour, some will cut back on their foreign investments, too.

Some United States companies are blaming poor earnings results in recent quarters on their foreign subsidiaries. In response, managements and directors will be inclined to reduce spending abroad.

Moreover, there have been occasions in which FDI has been accompanied by many resentments from the host country. For example, in the 1960s United States companies were accused of trying to dominate Europe's economies and markets. In the 1980s, there was some resentment in the United States when Japanese investors acquired major tracts of commercial real estate, golf courses, ski resorts, and whole corporations.

At present, there is potential for a similar backlash against overseas investors in Asia. They may be viewed as buying assets at "fire sale" prices, and in the process obtaining too much influence upon those economies and their markets.

Thus it is dangerous to emphasize FDI at the expense of other types of capital flows. Today, some countries are taking actions to discourage short-term portfolio investments. But if in the process countries become overly dependent upon FDI, the potential problems enumerated above are likely to resurface in one form or another.

RICHARD TAN*

From a businessman's point of view, Asia's economic crisis has created both problems to be solved and opportunities to be seized. The difficulties have included declining sales, an overall lack of liquidity throughout the market place, and increased uncertainty associated with any foreign exchange transactions. However, for those who have confidence in Asia's medium- and long-term prospects, the current downturn represents the opportunity of a lifetime.

---

* Chief Executive Officer and President, Pacific Millenium Co., San Diego.

My company's primary business is to export to Asia. So no one should be surprised to learn that sales have been negatively impacted by the economic situation in Asia. We have seen declines in terms of both volume and price. But these drops have not been across the board. For example, the China market has clearly not been as severely affected as have the nations of South-East Asia. Also, even within South-East Asia, it seems as though the large transnational corporations really are in better shape than are the local companies.

But the defining characteristic of the economic crisis is the pervasive lack of liquidity. This isn't the first time that we have seen a sales decline; occasional sales declines are something that any business has to deal with. It is the liquidity issue which is making the situation especially unique and difficult. Whether one is talking about domestic currencies or foreign exchange transactions, companies which are based in Asian countries are finding that it is very difficult to maintain their working capital financing; and finding new sources of financing is nearly impossible. As this illiquidity works its way through the economy, the tragedy is that otherwise healthy companies are finding it difficult to manage their day-to-day cash flow.

The banks' caution takes many forms. First, since most Asian banks primarily offer credit that is collateralized by real estate, the downturn in the property markets has brought about downward revisions in the credit lines available to individual companies. But even beyond that, banks on all sides of transactions now question the security of items which until recently were considered beyond reproach. For example, letters of credit, which historically are the absolute last item that a bank would default on, are nonetheless being examined very closely, and certain issuers are suspect. The business environment offers plenty of challenges without having to worry about whether or not a letter of credit is going to be accepted. While we in the United States talk about the possibility of a credit crunch, Asia is offering us an example of just how painful that can be.

Overall, the Republic of Korea has been the hardest hit by illiquidity. Because of the intertwining *chaebol* system, businesses and their banks were simultaneously struck by the outside world's loss of confidence in a way that none of the other Asian nations has had to face. Individual companies actually had to resort to countertrade, with all of its inefficiencies, in order to continue conducting business.

Foreign currency and exchange rate policies have contributed to Asia's illiquidity. Most obviously, companies operating within those countries whose currencies have been devalued are now finding it very difficult to obtain sufficient United States dollars to pay for commodities which are typically invoiced in that currency. More subtle is the case of China, which still maintains the yuan at an officially established exchange rate. Officials in that country have taken several steps to help protect the yuan from domestic or international speculation. Taken together, they have made it much more difficult to exchange yuan for United States dollars. These conversions have always had to be accompanied by appropriate documentation, but the hurdle of what is acceptable has in practice been raised. Therefore, even companies which have plenty of yuan are finding it more difficult to make timely payment on their United States dollar-denominated payables.

Thankfully, it really is true that difficulties usually create opportunities. The severity of the Asian downturn is due in large part to the way the international community ran away *en masse* within a very short period of time. In this situation, those who don't run away from Asia are presented with both marketing and investment opportunities. Another thing to consider is that Asians will remember who left and who stayed during this difficult time.

From a marketing perspective, those who stay in Asia are in a position to increase their market share dramatically. This is simply the result of having the competition leave town. Of course, this potential increase in market share shouldn't be pursued haphazardly. The risk versus reward calculus must be closely examined. Companies need proactively to mitigate the risks through their specific business arrangements. On the rewards side, the long-term prospects must be considered as well as the short term. Asia has always rewarded those who think long-term; that is true now more than ever.

Investment opportunities abound. Asian asset prices in United States dollar terms only make sense if the investor either truly believes that Asia will lie in ruins for the foreseeable future or has an excruciatingly short time-horizon. A favourite example is that of the airline of the Republic of Korea which at one point had a total market capitalization that was less than the market value of the airplanes it owned. For those who wish to avoid non-specific risk, one strategy would be to purchase Asian currencies, put them in a safe deposit box and go play golf. Anyone who chose to do this with the Indonesian *rupiah* in June 1998 more than doubled his/her money by November.

That's not to say that I believe Asia's road to recovery will be easy or smooth. There are serious difficulties to be overcome. There are also structural changes which must be made in order to avoid any repeats of this episode in the future. Perhaps the most serious threat to Asia's future lies in the seemingly attractive alternative which Malaysia chose to pursue in September 1998. While I do not believe that the adjustment programmes which have been designed and imposed by the International Monetary Fund and others are 100 per cent correct, I can say unequivocally that Dr. Mahathir's path is bad for business.

I would therefore have to say that it is bad for Malaysia, and that it would be bad for Asia if other countries were to follow Malaysia's lead and turn inward. Nonetheless, the risk of that happening should not be underestimated. The Asian nations and their individual citizens are being asked to absorb a tremendous amount of pain. Alternatives which promise quick relief will naturally be very enticing.

On balance, I believe that Asia's future looks bright. I'll go further than that: Those who do opt to abandon Asia are fools. This region of the world will continue to account for a disproportionately large share of global economic growth for at least the next fifty years. More than any other region of the world, this is where new wealth will be created.

Part Seven

FINANCIAL MARKETS

Edited by

Krishnan Sharma and Judith Romera

24

Introduction – Financial Markets

KRISHNAN SHARMA AND
JUDITH ROMERA*
United Nations Department of Economic and Social Affairs

The preceding parts of this book looked at the surge in commercial bank and portfolio capital to East Asia and other emerging market economies. The poor institutional configuration in countries like Thailand—mainly weak financial systems and poor corporate governance—meant that many of them were not in a position to efficiently absorb and channel this capital. This surge in inflows exacerbated the overinvestment and the asset bubbles that were building up in these economies and increased the vulnerabilities within their financial sectors. This contributed to a weakening in the fundamentals of a number of emerging market countries that, in turn, triggered a massive exit of capital, plunging the countries into an economic crisis.

The analysis thus far pertains to the capital-importing countries. But a number of questions need to be explored on the side of the suppliers of funds. What were the factors behind the flow of short-term capital to these countries? Why did international banks and investors not pick up the weakening fundamentals of the East Asian and other countries earlier and, indeed, make matters worse by continuing to place large amounts of money in them until the last

---

* The authors are economists in the Developing Economies Section and Developed and Transition Economies Section, respectively. The views expressed herein are those of the authors and not necessarily the views of the United Nations.

minute? Why did inflows suddenly reverse in a manner that destabilized the currencies, financial systems and real economies? What are the factors that have made the crisis so protracted and why has it been so difficult for the Governments in the region and International Monetary Fund (IMF) to restore market confidence? What are the policy implications on the side of suppliers of finance raised by this whole episode?

These are some of the issues that the papers by Christopher Rude and Krishnan Sharma and the comments by Edward Nell, Isabelle Grunberg, Charles Lucas and Jorge Braga de Macedo attempt to throw light on.

One can envisage a framework determining the flow of bank and portfolio capital between the United States, Europe and Japan, on the one hand, and East Asia, on the other hand, based on the work of Nell and others. This can be explained in terms of the configuration of economic growth rates, real interest rates, and other macroeconomic fundamentals. Prior to the mid-1990s, these favoured the flow of capital from the industrialized world to East Asia. Higher growth rates and interest rates in East Asia, as well as improved macroeconomic fundamentals, provided attractive lending and investment opportunities.

However, during the mid-1990s, the relative attractiveness of lending and investing in East Asia was reduced by two factors in particular. First, there was a strengthening in growth and in macroeconomic fundamentals in the United States (namely the elimination of the fiscal deficit and sustained reduction in inflation). United States financial markets consequently boomed and domestic lending opportunities for banks also increased. Second, at the same time, East Asia's fundamentals weakened, as economies like Thailand and Malaysia began to register large current-account deficits and as symptoms of overheating and overinvestment began to emerge.

This set the scene for a slow down, if not a reversal, of private capital flows to East Asia during the mid-1990s. This much is not surprising. What is surprising though is the exact timing and size of the reversal in capital flows that did take place. Given that the strengthening in the United States and the weakening in East Asia was already in place by about 1995, we need to look deeper to explain why bank and portfolio flows accelerated into East Asia well into 1997. A frequently provided explanation is that market participants were not fully aware of the extent to which the region's fundamentals had weakened. Thus the relative attractiveness of lending and investing in East Asia remained high. As pointed out by Sharma, this lack of awareness was partly owing to a shortage of transparent information and to market participants' limited understanding of the structural and institutional underpinnings of the East Asian economies. This led to an unduly optimistic view of the region that interacted with internal characteristics of the fund management and banking industry to generate a bullish herd mentality. Consequently, an upward spiral of rising capital inflows was generated that became increasingly out of sync with the fundamentals of the region.

Clearly, such a situation was unsustainable and this partly explains why the reversal of capital flows was so dramatic and so huge. Yet there was another critical factor that is pointed out by Rude. This related to the nature of the exposures that both international and local market participants had built up in East Asia. Rude points out that at one time the investments by foreigners in East Asia were highly profitable but, as the aggregate investment exposures grew, their quality declined and they became increasingly speculative and risky. These exposures were highly leveraged and, to a significant degree, not hedged for currency risk. The rush to cover these unhedged exposures led to successive runs on the East Asian currencies and explains the extent of the financial panic.

The papers by Rude and Sharma also deal with the protracted nature of the crisis, the manner in which it has spread and the difficulties involved in restoring confidence. The explanations for these are best read in the context of the papers themselves. However, it would be interesting to touch on a point, made by Rude, that the IMF began to lose credibility with some market participants. This links with Rude's other point, that investors appeared to have lost confidence in the very viability and stability of globalized financial markets. Such significant changes in the attitudes of market participants may explain what otherwise seems to have been an excessive flight from financial markets all over the world during the autumn of 1998. Moreover, the serious damage that had been done to the credibility in crisis management of the Fund is widely believed to be a factor that compounded the loss of market confidence in the Russian Federation.

Moving on to policy implications, an important issue coming out of the analysis in this section concerns the need to find ways of limiting market overexuberance during booms. While improving transparency and information will help, it is unlikely to sufficiently reduce the volatile tendencies of short-term capital flows. To minimize the harmful effects of this, a number of additional measures need to be undertaken. Most obvious is the need for efficient macroeconomic and monetary management by the domestic authorities. Indeed, there may also be a need for some developing countries to have a flexible system of controls, like in Chile, that limit excessive inflows of capital.

However, these policies are not as straightforward as they appear. Lucas argues that there may not be the political will to implement corrective measures during times of excessive capital inflows. He claims that in both East Asia and in Mexico it was clear to policy advisers that there were vulnerabilities that were likely to lead to a financial crisis. Yet the difficulty is to persuade governments that are experiencing the benefits of increasing capital inflows to take corrective action before the bubble bursts. Moreover, the effectiveness of capital controls is also uncertain. They can be evaded and can damage a country's access to supplies of foreign capital. Macedo argues that, to be effective, capital controls may need to be coordinated at a regional or global level. But, in spite of the uncertainty regarding capital controls, a lesson from the developments in East Asia is that developing countries that have not already fully liberalized their capital accounts should adequately strengthen their financial sectors before doing so.

Another policy question that the East Asian crisis has forced countries to rethink concerns exchange rates. By reducing the currency risk faced by investors, lenders and borrowers, the informal pegged exchange rates that existed in a number of East Asian economies excessively attracted short-term capital inflows. While many economists argue in favour of a flexible exchange rate regime, this can lead to increased exchange rate volatility. At the same time, a fully fixed currency board regime can involve intense policy discipline that not all governments may be able to abide by. It appears therefore that some form of loosely managed exchange rate represents the most viable currency regime for most developing countries.

In addition to assessing the policy implications of financial market volatility for governments of capital-receiving countries, the papers and discussion pieces in this section go further and examine possible measures that could be implemented at an international level. Especially important among these is the need for better regulation and supervision of financial institutions in source countries and at a global level. To some extent, this would be facilitated by cooperation of the internationally active banks and other financial institutions. Such measures could be more easily implemented if, as argued by Grunberg, market institutions accept that the sum total of their behaviour damages their interests (indeed, many financial institutions have made losses from the Asian crisis). It may therefore be in market institutions' interests to accept regulation since, even if these are seen to have firm-level costs, they would also have benefits from addressing the externalities. This realisation ultimately needs to come from within the financial community.

Moreover, governments and international bodies need to rethink—and are in fact rethinking—a new international financial architecture that can enhance the stability of global financial flows. Sharma speaks of the need to better co-ordinate the functions of existing multilateral organizations and proposals have also come from many circles for a reform of the Bretton Woods institutions. Any changes made to the international financial system should ensure that the issue of moral hazard is adequately dealt with—that is, a penalty should be attached for bad lending decisions, so that lenders are encouraged to rigorously assess the creditworthiness of their borrowers.

In conclusion, a consideration of the role of commercial bank and portfolio flows, in the context of the East Asian crisis, has stimulated a fertile intellectual discussion. In a manner that is not dissimilar from what went on in the 1930s, the past year has seen a questioning by some individuals of beliefs hitherto regarded as fundamental—arguments put forward for capital controls would, until recently, have been regarded as ludicrous by most economists. Regardless of what one's views are on contentious issues like this, it is clear that addressing them is extremely important and interesting.

25

The 1997–1998 East Asian Financial Crisis: A New York Market-informed View

CHRISTOPHER RUDE*
United Nations Department of Economic and Social Affairs

"The market is a beast. When you open your economy to the international financial markets, you should know that you are inviting a beast into your house. Once he is in, he will do what he pleases."

– A New York market participant, March 1998

1. Introduction

This paper differs from other recent literature on the 1997-98 East Asian financial crisis in that it assumes that one cannot understand the origins, magnitude, effects or policy implications of the episode without taking market participants' views on the crisis into account. It will not report the results of a formal survey of New York-based market participants. Nor will it, accepting market participants' statements at their face value, reproduce uncritically a Wall Street "consensus" view on the matter. Nor, finally, will market participants' perceptions of the crisis be the only factors that it takes into consideration. This work does suggest, however, that market participants' understandings of and insights

* This paper was prepared while the author, currently at the New School for Social Research, was in residence as a consultant to the International Economic Relations Branch. The views expressed herein are those of the author and not necessarily the views of the United Nations.

into the causes, spread, consequences and policy significance of the contagion provide us with a useful point of departure for a more comprehensive, rigorous analysis of the episode. In the least, market participants can give us access to certain essential data that we simply must not ignore if we are even to begin to reach an understanding of the events.[1]

In its examination of the causes of the crisis and the extent of the contagion, therefore, the research presented here has profited from market participants' assessments of the shifts in market psychology that took place as the episode unfolded, their knowledge of the positions that international and local market participants had taken prior to the crisis, their insights into why in mid-1997 these investments proved to be so vulnerable to a sell-off of the local currencies, and their accounts of how traders and investors responded to the crisis once it had been precipitated. Similarly, in its exploration of the likely consequences of the financial disruption for both East Asia and the world economy at large, this paper has learned a great deal from what economists at major banks have been saying in their written, public statements, as well as from in-depth private discussions with many of the same forecasters about the reasons for their forecasts and, even more significantly, about the confidence that they have in their forecasts. Finally, in its examination of the policy implications of the crisis, this paper has benefited from frank discussion with market participants about the policies that need to be put in place to make certain that the present crisis remains contained and possibly to prevent a similar crisis from occurring.

Market participants' comments on and insights into the origins and extent of the contagion allow us to reconstruct how the crisis occurred and why. Several themes in their commentary are particularly useful for this purpose. First,

---

1 To be precise, the raw material on which this paper is based includes (a) written commentary and analysis produced by large multinational banks on the East Asian, United States, European and Latin American economies and on the foreign exchange, fixed-income and equity markets; (b) interviews with some of the major decision makers at these and other private sector financial institutions, including economists, investment strategists, credit analysts and traders; (c) newspaper articles from *The New York Times*, *Wall Street Journal* and *Financial Times*; (d) data and commentary taken from the International Monetary Fund, Bank for International Settlements, World Bank and Federal Reserve; and (e) the academic and other literature on the crisis and the economics of foreign exchange and banking crises listed in the bibliography. Goldman Sachs, Merrill Lynch, Morgan Stanley, Solomon Brothers, Bear Stearns, Citicorp, Chase Manhattan Bank, Swiss Bank, Deutsche Bank, Dresdner Bank, HSBC, Fuji Bank, Dai-Ichi Banks, Prudential Securities, AIG and several other institutions provided the written commentary and/or granted interviews. Most of the interviews were conducted in February and early March 1998, shortly after the immediate crisis had subsided and when market participants involved first had a chance to reflect on what had just happened. The views on the crisis expressed in this paper, however, do not necessarily reflect the views of any of the above institutions.

most market participants stress that they did not see the crisis coming until it was already upon them and that their views on the region took an abrupt about-face as the crisis unfolded—from a very positive "Asian miracle" view prior to the crisis to a very negative "crony capitalism" view that has prevailed since. Given the forward-looking nature of financial markets, this suggests, among other things, that we must be wary of explaining the crisis solely in terms of the latter point of view, as it has a clear *ex-ante*, post-crisis, revisionist stance. Second, according to many market participants, the origins of the crisis lie in over-investment in the region and over-investment not only by local investors, but also by the international creditors of local investors as well. These market participants would not necessarily disagree with the accounts of mainstream professional economists, for whom the financial collapse is understandable in terms of the region's deteriorating macroeconomic conditions, the fixed exchange rate regimes that prevailed there prior to the crisis and the weakness of the local financial systems. For the market participant, however, the modest decay in the region's macroeconomic performance that took place in 1996 and early 1997 was important because it exposed the extent of the over-investment that had taken place; exchange rate issues came to the foreground only when investors began searching for a way to reduce their exposures once these excesses became apparent, and since the excesses of the international as well as the local investor played a role in the resultant contagion, the crisis exposed serious weaknesses in the global as well as the local financial systems. Therefore, as far as most market participants are concerned, the issue of whether there was a panic or whether economic conditions had deteriorated is a false one, the unhedged exchange rate exposures are important because they acted as the trigger that would bring an already precarious financial structure down, and once the financial crisis began to unfold, it took on a dynamic of its own that no policy maker (including the International Monetary Fund (IMF)) could resist until it had run its course.

Market participants' views on the likely effects of the crisis and its policy implications are useful in a different way. Besides giving us invaluable insights into the crisis' prognosis and meanings, they show just how very troubling market participants have found the episode to be. At the onset of the crisis and at least in their written work, most private sector forecasters were initially very cautious in their assessments of the crisis' likely effects, lest they be accused of being alarmist. Privately, however, many of the same economists sensed early on that something potentially very disturbing was taking place, namely, that the crisis may have unleashed a set of contractionary forces with the strength to threaten growth not just in South-East Asia but also in the world economy at large. Almost from the very start, therefore, the crisis in East Asia forced market participants to wonder whether the world economy might slip into recession or worse.

Market participants' worries do not stop here, however. The severity of the financial implosion that took place in East Asia has prompted many market participants to question the stability of today's globalized financial system. Market participants have not only lost faith in the prospect of continued robust growth, therefore, but in the merits of financial market liberalization and globalization, indeed, in the viability of free, unregulated international capital markets as well. They worry, in particular, that financial market liberalization and globalization might have unleashed the very contractionary forces that seem now at play. On the one hand, this questioning has led to a heated debate over the future course of the international financial system that is truly remarkable for its freshness and depth. On the other hand, when faced with the choices about which policies should be adopted to avoid a global downturn or prevent a similar financial crisis from happening again, many market participants find that they do not know what to recommend.

2. What we have learned from market participants

For the sake of clarity and simplicity, we have organized what we learned about the crisis from New York market participants in terms of eight propositions. The first four propositions deal with the crisis' origins and its spread; the next two propositions focus on its effects; the final two propositions pertain to policy.

a) Up to the very eve of the crisis, most market participants thought that the investment prospects in South-East Asia and the Republic of Korea were good

Prior to the crisis, most foreign market participants—including short-term equity, bond and foreign-exchange traders, long-term investment strategists, merchant bankers, economists, credit analysts and credit rating agencies—were aware that not everything was right in the Pacific Basin emerging markets. As even the most casual reading of the market commentary will show, prior to the crisis, market participants were aware, in particular, of all of the problems that now loom so large in today's revisionist, post-crisis account of these countries. They knew that some of the domestic financial systems in the region were not well developed or well regulated and that cronyism and corruption were a normal part of business practices in several countries. They were aware that, in many instances, the local current account deficits were sizeable and external debt burdens were large and growing. Market participants also knew that the macroeconomic conditions in and export performance of the region were not as positive as they had been in the past. They were aware that the speculative activities within and short-term capital inflows coming into the region were becoming more pronounced. Market participants also saw that signs of excess capacity and financial stress were emerging, particularly in Thailand and the Republic of Korea. In addition, just prior to the crisis, they saw that the local fixed exchange rates were probably over-valued.

Prior to the crisis, however, market participants chose to ignore, or at least downplay, these considerations to focus instead on the positive aspects of the region. Indeed, up to the very eve of the crisis, the bottom line for most private sector commentary was not just that the investment prospects in the Asian emerging markets were good, but that the rates of return that an investor could expect to make in the region were higher than one could make elsewhere. To make their case, analysts stressed the openness of the region's markets and the free-market, laissez-faire attitude of its businessmen, the positive savings and investment balances (lack of significant budget deficits, high domestic savings and investment rates), the region's high growth and comparatively low inflation rates, and the more than ample rates of return that their past investments in the region had yielded. Investors' praise for the emerging market economies in East Asia became especially great in the wake of the collapse of Soviet communism in the early 1990s, when "the Asian economic miracle" was seen as embodying all that was right about unregulated, free-market global capitalism.[2] As a former hedge fund manager put it:

> "From the early 1980s on, it was an article of faith that Asia was a miracle. Savings, investment, education–all of the right ingredients for economic success were present. For years, strong economic performance and rising asset prices inspired investors, commentators and economists to uncover more evidence of good news about Asia wherever they looked. This process of mutual reinforcement continued into 1997 (Johnson, 1997)."

The private sector's favourable assessment of the region prior to the crisis was almost universal. Most private-sector banks were forecasting low inflation, strong growth, and stable exchange rates; the major credit rating agencies did not see any problems with the credit risks of the region; *Euromoney*'s Country Risk Assessments were generally positive as well.[3] As a study sponsored by the

---

2 Several market participants commented that it was ironic that world capitalism would suffer a major financial crisis only a few years after the collapse of the Soviet Union.

3 See Sachs and Radelet (1998) and Dornbush (1998) for the details.

Institute for International Finance shows, interest spreads on emerging market debt, including the debt of the ASEAN-5 countries (Thailand, Malaysia, the Philippines, Indonesia and the Republic of Korea) fell steadily between mid-1995 and until the crisis erupted in mid-1997 (Cline and Barnes 1997). Asian emerging market loan spreads were also low and falling. Finally, and most significantly, as the Bank for International Settlements (BIS) quarterly reports on the international capital markets so clearly show, capital inflows into the Pacific Basin emerging markets were massive and indeed accelerating until the autumn of 1997—when this capital was suddenly withdrawn (BIS 1997a, 1997b, 1998a). *Ex ante*, moral hazard did not induce the then-pending financial crisis. If foreign traders and investors underestimated the actual risks, it was their own mistake: capital continued to flow into the region because investors genuinely felt that the outlook for the region was quite good, not because they thought that their investments would be guaranteed.[4]

b) When the crisis erupted first in Thailand in the spring and summer of 1997 and spread to the rest of South-East Asia and to the Republic of Korea by the autumn, most international and local market participants were caught off guard; as the investment outlook for the region took an abrupt about-face, foreign investors and lenders rushed to cut their exposures to the region, and the previous capital inflow became a massive capital outflow

By the spring of 1997, a few market participants were indeed shrewd enough to see that the financial situation, particularly in Thailand, had become potentially unstable, and these market participants reportedly were quick to put on forward foreign exchange positions that would profit from any impending sell-off, at least of the Thai baht.[5] Market sources indicate, however, that most investors remained insensitive to these instabilities, and no one can claim with any credibility to have anticipated the extent of the contagion that would soon engulf the region. When the currencies in the region came under speculative attack and the contagion began to rapidly spread out from Thailand, therefore, the majority of market participants in the region were not

4 To be sure, the Governments of Thailand, the Republic of Korea and elsewhere did make certain assurances about bailouts when the crisis was already at hand, but these came very late in the game and lacked credibility.

5 Certain hedge funds were reportedly on this short list of market participants, but other types of financial institutions and a few non-financial institutions were also reportedly involved. One must stress in any case, however, that these speculative activities did not cause the sell-off of the baht, much less the general crisis. These investors had merely put on positions that would become profitable should the baht decline.

only genuinely surprised but were compelled as well to undertake a complete re-evaluation of their outlook for the countries involved. At first, only the specialists in the East Asian emerging markets were involved in the re-evaluation. But as the contagion continued to spread, market participants who did not have a direct interest in the Asian emerging markets began paying attention to the developments there. Soon even the senior management of the major financial institutions began to focus on the region. To be sure, whereas the East Asian specialists remained sensitive to the subtleties of the developments and to the differences between the countries involved, the non-specialists and senior managers were able to formulate often only very crude opinions about the region as a whole. Still, as the specialists scrambled to protect what was left of their reputations, the non-specialists struggled to make a quick study of the region so that they could advise their clients about the opportunities elsewhere, and the senior managers began to wonder how much of their capital was at risk in the Asian emerging markets, the changes in the specialists', non-specialists', and senior managers' outlooks for the region were as dramatic as the declines in the local currencies. Earlier, they all once saw free market liberalization, fiscal balances, strong savings and investment rates, solid growth, low inflation, and most importantly, very positive future rates of return. Now, often expressing a sense of mistrust and betrayal,[6] the same market participants saw only weak and poorly regulated financial systems, corruption and cronyism, current account deficits and external debts, excess capacity and declining domestic and export growth rates, looming bankruptcies, bursting real estate and other asset bubbles, and, of course, unsustainable fixed exchange rates—in short, a system of "crony capitalism" which soon became a code word for the actual and pending losses on their or their companies' investments in East Asia.

On the one hand, market views on the region were just catching up with the new, and deteriorating, economic and financial conditions. On the other hand, the new market expectations were self-fulfilling, for the sudden reversal of the capital inflows into the region that was taking place *pari passu* with the change in market perceptions was bringing about the very economic and financial conditions that market participants now feared. At the same time, local and foreign market participants were becoming aware that the spreading financial crisis was in many ways unprecedented, in that what was involved was the breakdown of private-to-private capital flows, and despite certain promises to the contrary, they were becoming cognizant as well that credible public assistance to the

6 When talking to market participants about what they felt about the region in early 1998, one could not help but notice their anger.

private sector would not be forthcoming, at least not in amounts sufficient to contain the mounting private-sector financial stress. Thus, market participants quickly saw that the likelihood of an orderly workout of the mounting private sector debt problems was small, and they knew, now that they saw the need for it, that little insurance would be coming from the public authorities.

The amount of capital withdrawn from the ASEAN-5 countries in the latter half of 1997 is remarkable for its size. According to estimates provided by the Institute for International Finance, following a net private inflow of $93 billion in 1996, the net private outflow from the ASEAN-5 economies in 1997 was $12.1 billion, a swing of $105 billion. Sachs and Radelet (1998) calculate that the swing was equal to 11 per cent of the combined GDPs of the countries involved. The BIS data tell a similar story. International bank lending to the Asian emerging market economies rose by $79.8 billion in 1996, but only $6.1 billion in 1997 (BIS 1998a). Following increases of $21.4 and $15 billion in the first two quarters of 1997, respectively, BIS-reporting banks reduced their lending to the Asian emerging markets by $3 billion and a remarkable $27.3 billion, respectively, in the third and fourth quarters.

c) *The financial panic that ensued was not willful or arbitrary, but stemmed instead from the very nature of the investment and trading exposures that international and local market participants had taken on in East Asia*

When asked to explain the origins of the East Asian financial crisis, most market participants indicate that they thought that the crisis was the result of over-investment, and over-investment not only on the part of the bankers and businessmen within the region, but over-investment by international bankers and businessmen as well. The way that market participants usually made this point was to say that "there was too much money chasing too small an investment outlet", or "too much money was flowing into the Republic of Korea and South-East Asia to be profitably placed". Often their language is more colorful, as when several market participants stated that you could see the excess capacity in Bangkok, especially in its real estate market, from your airport taxi.

Based on these considerations, when we analyse the origins of the crisis, we must be very careful to distinguish between long-term secular developments, the medium-term economic conjuncture and any immediate (efficient) cause. Discussions with market participants suggest, in particular, that the relevant long-term developments were a decline in the profitability and a rise in the riskiness of the underlying investment projects, a deterioration of local balance sheets, and a rise in the magnitude of the foreign exposures, and that these trends created a financial structure that made a financial crisis in East Asia both possible and inevitable. Changes in the economic conjuncture in 1996 and early 1997 pushed what was both possible and inevitable towards becoming a reality. The exchange rate attacks that began mid-1997 were the immediate trigger.

From this perspective, the debate over whether a deterioration of the underlying economic fundamentals caused the crisis or whether there was a financial panic is not particularly interesting, for both occurred.[7] On the one hand, the low-wage, export-oriented, foreign-financed growth strategy that the countries in South-East Asia and the Republic of Korea were following prior to the crisis became the victim of its own success. At one time, the underlying investment projects that both local and foreign capital were financing in the region were profitable and productive. But as additional productive capacity was created in one country after another in the same or similar industries, and as wages began to rise, profit margins in the export industries began to decline, and funds began to be directed towards the non-traded goods sector and into more speculative activities in the local real estate and equity markets. On the other hand, even as the relevant cash flows were becoming increasingly problematic, the balance sheets of local financial and non-financial institutions were slowly deteriorating: liabilities to foreign and local creditors were increasing, asset quality was decreasing, leverage ratios were rising, and, due to an increase in the maturity mismatch of assets and liabilities, gap- and duration-related interest rate exposures were mounting.

Meanwhile, foreign capital continued to flow into South-East Asia and the Republic of Korea from Europe, the United States and Japan. Supported by an accommodating monetary stance and low inflation, interest rates remained low in the major industrialized countries, more so in Japan, in comparison to those that prevailed in the region. As equity prices in the United States and Europe continued to reach new highs, moreover, investors in these markets found that they had sizeable exposures in highly-valued, if not over-valued, securities in companies in the industrialized nations whose earnings potential may have fallen below those available in the Pacific Basin emerging markets. Compelled by a competitive search for higher yields to take on the Republic of Korea's and South-East Asia's greater credit and country risks, international

7 Some have argued that this is the most important issue that needs to be resolved about the origins of the crisis (Corsetti, Pesenti and Roubini, 1998) and that this is what the ongoing debate that the crisis has touched off between Jeffrey Sachs (Sachs and Radelet, ibid) and Paul Krugman (1998a, 1998b, 1998c, 1998d) is all about. Not only are the origins of the crisis more complex than this, Sachs' and Krugman's disagreements are much broader.

creditors increased their exposures to local banks and corporations, both directly through loans and indirectly through local and international bond markets. Owing to the poor investment prospects at home, Japanese lenders were particularly eager to extend credits to the region, especially to the foreign branches and subsidiaries of Japanese corporations. Equity investors in the US and Europe were also driven to increase their exposure to the region's greater market risks, both for diversification purposes and to search for even higher capital gains than those that could be achieved in the West.

At one time, these foreign investments, like domestic ones, were profitable and productive. As foreign capital continued to move into the region and the resulting aggregate investment exposures became progressively larger, however, these international investments, like the domestic ones, took on an increasingly speculative tone, their asset quality declined, the associated leverage ratios and interest rate risks increased, and the maturities were shortened. Moreover, as the use of derivatives and other off-balance sheet instruments became more extensive, the aggregate market exposures became increasingly complex and opaque as well.

Two notorious off-balance sheet/derivative strategies used in East Asia illustrate this clearly.[8] Several major US banks reportedly set up "special purpose vehicles" (SPVs) to channel funds into the region, into the Republic of Korea, in particular. Under these arrangements, banks transferred some of their stock to the SPVs, the SPVs issued short-term paper in the international capital markets using the banks' stock as collateral, and then the SPVs used the foreign funds so obtained to make investments that the banks deemed worthwhile. In reality, the banks had assumed a foreign exposure, but it never showed up on their balance sheets. The second strategy employed was a "total return swap" (TRS). These were a series of triangular transactions between international investment banks, Korean banks, and Indonesian companies. Double swaps were set up between the Indonesian companies and the investment banks, on the one hand, and between these banks and the Korean banks, on the other. The Indonesian companies reportedly paid 340 basis points (bps) over LIBOR to the international banks; the investment banks in turn swapped the underlying paper to the Koreans at 280 bps over LIBOR. The counter swap took the form of Korean liabilities at LIBOR+75 bps. Under these arrangements, the Indonesians, who did not have the Korean's high credit ratings, were able to borrow, and the Korean and investment bankers made a high rate of return. The problem was that the Korean

8 Many market participants were aware of the widespread use of these two vehicles. However, the descriptions given here are taken entirely from Taylor (1998).

banks had to compensate the investment banks for any losses if the Indonesian companies went bankrupt, which they did.

The underlying investment projects that local and foreign capital were funding had already become less profitable and more risky, the local financial structures were already fragile, and the aggregate international investment exposure to the region was already excessive, therefore, when three major changes in the economic conjuncture took place in 1996 and early 1997. First, due to developments in the general international economic environment and other factors (a loss of competitiveness as a consequence of the US dollar's rise since 1995, increased competition from China, weaker growth in Japan, a slowdown in the global computer industry), export growth rates, and hence, domestic growth rates in the region began to slip. Second, the investment outlook in the US and Europe began to improve. Official interest rate increases in the US (March 1997) and Germany (October 1997) suggested that interest rates in the US and Europe would soon rise and hence that lending in the less risky Western industrialized countries would become more profitable. As the equity markets in Europe, but most especially in the United States, continued to rise to still more new highs, investors in these markets abandoned their earlier concerns about over-valuation and, amid growing talk not only that inflation had been banished but that the business cycle was a thing of the past as well, became euphoric about even further capital gains instead. And when it became clear that European Monetary Union would actually take place as planned, market participants knew that they should focus attention on how to take advantage of the opportunities in what would soon be the world's largest single pool of inevitable funds. Third, the economic and financial situation in Japan took a turn for the worse, when, following signs early in the year that economic activity was possibly strengthening, output contracted sharply in the second quarter. After an abrupt, but temporary, surge in Japanese bond yields and the yen in the spring, as Japan's banking problems began to intensify, Japanese bankers and institutional investors began to consolidate their exposures not only at home, but in the Republic of Korea and South-East Asia as well.[9]

As local economic activity began to slow and signs of local financial stress began to increase, as the outlook for investments in Europe and the United States improved, and as the financial problems in Japan grew worse, local and

9 As a working hypothesis, it is useful to think of the financial disruptions that we have witnessed in the Republic of Korea and South-East Asia as being simply an extension of Japan's domestic financial problems. To be sure, the financial contagion had up to mid-1998 caught fire in Japan's periphery, but this only suggests that what we saw through early 1998 might have been the prelude to the deeper domestic Japanese crisis that evolved through the year.

foreign investors in the East Asian emerging markets not only became increasingly reluctant to extend further credits and other moneys, but soon began searching for ways to actually reduce their exposures. When they did so, local and foreign market participants found that they now had a foreign exchange exposure that had apparently not existed before. *Ex ante,* when the investment prospects in the region seemed viable and the capital inflows were strong, the possibility that the local currencies might decline had simply not been an issue. Indeed, as the reserves of all of the local monetary authorities were increasing, in their efforts to maintain the pegs of their currencies against the US dollar, these authorities had been acting to resist upward, not downward, pressures on the local currencies.[10] So, the local private sector institutions that had borrowed extensively in the major foreign currencies and the foreign market participants that had directly or indirectly taken long positions in local currencies did not see the need to hedge against a local currency sell-off. Now, suddenly that the outlook had changed and a rush for the exit had ensued, the pressure on the local currencies was only downward. Local and foreign market participants accordingly found that they now had a large open long position in the local currencies, and an open position, moreover, that would be very difficult, if not impossible, to cover. Given the magnitude of the exposures and the urgency to close them, the relevant forward markets simply did not have the required depth and liquidity. To make matters worse, in many instances, speculators had reportedly already taken up the long-foreign currency/short-local currency forward positions that local and foreign investors now needed, thereby drying up the liquidity in the forward markets even more. Thus, while it is simplistic to say that the fixed exchange rate regimes were to blame for the crisis, investors' unhedged foreign exchange exposures had become the weakest link in the entire investment chain, and successive runs on the local currencies would be the mechanisms that would finally bring the whole, already precarious, financial structure down.[11]

10 As long as foreign capital was flowing into the Republic of Korea and South-East Asia, there was a tendency for the local currencies to rise and not fall. So had the local currencies not been tied to the dollar, they may have appreciated even more. The threat of possible exchange rate losses only became an issue when the strength of the capital inflows became problematic. This raises the larger issue of when a current account deficit is sustainable. The obvious answer is that it is sustainable as long as the capital inflow is robust. What then, determines the sustainability of the capital inflow?

11 Note that the problem here is not just the lack of the proper financial market instrument, such as an inconvertible forward rate contract. The liquidity can vanish in even normally very deep markets if market participants are trying to move in the same direction at the same time, as was the case here.

d) *Once the contagion began to spread, it followed an intrinsic logic of its own, which no private sector market participant or policy maker could resist until it had run its course*

To many outside observers, financial markets seem inherently irrational. Given the apparent randomness of the trading and the price fluctuations, market participants are either just "noise traders" or herd followers. As even the novice investor knows, however, this is not the case. Profits can be made in apparently directionless markets, for example, by following countertrend technical signals (stochastics, relative strength indicators) to find out when the market is overbought or oversold. The last ones to see an investment opportunity will not make a gain, as anyone who understands what arbitrage is surely knows. Far from being chaotic and random, financial markets have a complex and intricate structure, an inherently dynamic logic, which the shrewdest of investors understand and use to their own advantage. This does not mean that financial markets are stable, for violent changes in the structure of the market can and do take place. When these happen and we have a financial panic, the abrupt change from one financial structure to another, the very panic itself, has its own clear dynamic and inherent logic, however, as the investors in the Asian emerging markets surely came to know.

The speculative attacks mounted first against the Thai baht in the early spring of 1997 and then against all of the local currencies throughout the summer and autumn, had two immediate effects.[12] On the one hand, market participants' concerns about their exchange-rate exposures intensified; on the other hand, in keeping with interest-rate parity conditions, short-term local interest rates moved abruptly higher. As local and foreign market participants now moved aggressively to reduce their exchange rate exposures, the downward pressure on the local currencies intensified. As short-term interest rates moved higher and local yield curves first flattened and then inverted, the stress on local financial and non-financial institutions' profit margins and balance sheets grew worse. The local monetary authorities, meanwhile, found that they could do little to contain the mounting pressures. If they acted to resist the downward pressure on their currencies by ratifying the rise in short-term interest rates, they would aggravate the mounting pressures on the domestic financial structures. If they did not take credible measures to prevent their currencies from falling, their inaction would aggravate the mounting private sector foreign exchange losses. Since unsterilized intervention just gave speculators the long US dollar/short-local currency positions that they were looking for, at

12 We can thank Wyplosz (1998) for making this point.

some point the local authorities had no choice but to let their currencies fall. The crisis was on.

Soon a number of self-ratifying, mutually reinforcing vicious circles appeared.[13] With the local currencies in a free fall, local firms found that they could not meet their rising foreign currency debt obligations, pushing them into bankruptcy. Finding, consequently, that their non-performing loans were rising, foreign creditors rushed to cut their exposures to the region, increasing both the downward pressure on the local currencies and local debtors' difficulties even more. Local asset prices in both the real estate and equity markets, if they were not already falling, collapsed as concerns over rising vacancy rates, falling rental incomes, poor earnings and bankruptcies mounted. The fall in asset prices grew worse due to declining collateral values and margins calls. The capital of local financial institutions disappeared owing to the need to provision against the rise in non-performing loans, exchange rates losses on their foreign borrowings and panic deposit withdrawals, prompting further rounds of credit reductions. As local firms found that they could not obtain working capital or maintain their profit margins amid the rise in interest rates, concern that there would be no orderly workouts of the rising private sector debt problems prompted local and foreign creditors to cut their lending even further as the rush for liquidity became more intense. Finally, as the local currencies continued to fall, something that looked like successive rounds of competitive devaluations took place throughout East Asia. Far from being policy-induced means of regaining competitiveness, however, the fact that exchange rate changes were now spreading the contagion back and forth from one country to the next only shows that the vicious circles were now complete.[14] As the local currencies continued to fall, the stress on the local financial systems continued to grow, local capital struggled to meet its international obligations, foreign capital continued to flee, and the exchange rates losses became only greater. IMF's injections of liquidity notwithstanding, nowhere was there a credible lender in the last resort who appeared to be willing to lend unconditional funds in sufficient amounts to restore confidence.[15]

---

13 Sachs and Radelet (op. cit.) provide an excellent description of the various kinds of vicious circles that take place during a financial crisis.

14 As the currency of each nation declined vis-à-vis its competitors, its competitors surely suffered a loss in competitiveness. But if the currencies of the first country's competitors subsequently came under attack, it was because private speculators, and not policy makers, thought that their lack of competitiveness had made their economies and financial systems weaker, and so more vulnerable to an attack.

15 All of IMF's loans were conditional, of course.

The contagion did not abate until mid-January 1998, when, apart from Indonesia which remained subject from time to time to further dramatic sell-offs, most local currencies and equity markets first stabilized and then began to drift slowly higher. In retrospect, political uncertainty in Thailand, the Republic of Korea, and most especially Indonesia no doubt had added to the contagion. And it may not have been a coincidence that the generalized selling pressures began to recede just when Korean banks had come to an agreement with a consortium of their foreign creditors about extending the maturity of the more than $100 billion in short-term debts, and Indonesia announced its debt moratorium. Still, the speed, depth and intensity of the sell-off that took place cannot be explained by anything other than economic and financial factors, and it is hard to make the case that the Korean short-term debt agreement and Indonesian debt moratorium ended the contagion when every other policy action seemed to fail. The varying degrees to which the crisis had affected the financial systems of each country involved depended quite clearly, on a case-by-case basis, on the strengths of each country's financial system and economy prior to the crisis. Thus, Hong Kong (China), Singapore, Taiwan Province of China and the Philippines ended the episode relatively unscathed, as their financial systems and underlying economies were relatively healthy beforehand. Simply put, the crisis had to run its course until certain exposures were finally cut, and certain losses fully taken accordingly.

Because the immediate contagion has subsided, we should not be lulled into thinking that foreign capital flows into East Asia have resumed, however. Based on anecdotal evidence, direct investment into the region has probably increased owing to bargain hunting on the part of multinational corporations and international banks. Banking and portfolio reflows, on the other hand, appear to have been minimal: the immediate crisis began to abate in January 1998 amid a round of short-covering and not outright buying, and though local currencies and equity prices have continued to move higher, this has occurred on reportedly very thin volumes. Moreover, the fact that a consortium of foreign banks has allowed banks in the Republic of Korea to extend the maturity of their short-term debts to them does not necessarily mean that new lending to the Republic of Korea is taking place, much less that there is any new lending to the other countries in the region. Instead, it is probably safe to assume that foreign credit rationing is the norm. There is no point, finally, in arguing that the financial meltdown was excessive.[16] For better or worse, the

16 This is one of the major points that Sachs and Radelet (ibid.) make. However, it is very difficult to find what the proper baseline for a judgment like this might be. What, in other words, does a non-excessive financial crisis look like?

economies within the region are stuck with the capital-starved financial systems that they now have. They have, in fact, different financial systems. For when the crisis finally abated, the movement was not just from one of a multiple of equilibriums to another, as if the overall financial structure had remained the same. The change instead was from an old, inherently unstable structure to a new, if largely dysfunctional but at least stable, one.

e) Market participants worry that the East Asian financial crisis has sent a large contractionary/deflationary shock not only into the region but also into the world economy at large

During the summer and early autumn of 1997, the financial contagion in East Asia had from time to time spread to other emerging market economies, with the financial systems of Brazil, Russia and the Czech Republic, in particular, coming under pressures to varying degrees. Signs of economic and financial weakness continued to appear in Japan as well. The extent of the crisis did not become apparent, however, until late October when, immediately following the devaluation of the Taiwan dollar, Hong Kong (China), South-East Asia's financial center, became the focus of the contagion. Then, when the financial system of Hong Kong (China) became severely stressed: (a) a shudder went through world equity markets; (b) uncertainty and credit concerns increased the risk premiums on emerging market and banking debt instruments worldwide; and (c) anticipating a slowdown in economic activity, long-term interest rates began to move sharply lower in the major fixed-income markets. It became at once clear that a financial crisis of global proportions was under way and that it was sending a large contractionary impulse through the world economy.

Not wishing to exaggerate the magnitude of this impulse, the initial assessments of the likely effects of the crisis were cautious. Private sector forecasters came to a general agreement, first, that economic activity in the countries at the epicenter of the crisis would slow sharply due to the loss of foreign capital and higher interest rates, that inflation would soar as the declines in the currencies worked their way into higher domestic prices, but that recovery would come fairly soon as these countries took advantage of their increased competitiveness to export their way out of their difficulties. Second, forecasters generally agreed that the contractionary impulse coming from East Asia would be transmitted to the rest of the world mainly through current account and/or trade adjustments. Based on these two assumptions, forecasters came to the mostly reassuring conclusion that, while the immediate effects of the crisis on the countries would be large, the consequences for the world economy would not be catastrophic. As an economist at a major US investment bank put it, as terrible as the damage to the local economies might be, a global recession would be avoided "because the countries at the center of the crisis do not represent much more than 6-7 per cent of world GDP or trade, on the one hand, and because the US domestic economy is so strong, on the other".

According to what we might call the 1998 spring consensus forecast, therefore, the Republic of Korea, Thailand and Indonesia would experience a period of economic contraction, and the growth rates of the other developing nations in the area would be significantly reduced, though they would avoid recession. As a result of its close trading ties with the region, Japan would be the most seriously affected industrial country and experience a period of stagnation as well. The US trade deficit would expand rapidly, but because of the strength of its domestic economy, the crisis would reduce US GDP growth by at most ½ percentage point in 1998, with the effects diminishing rapidly in 1999. Because its trade relations with East Asia are comparatively small, Europe's growth rates would be affected least of all. World output growth would be cut by at most 1 percentage point in 1998 and by much less in 1999.

Almost from the very start, however, the specter of global recession, or worse, became a common part of market talk about what the crisis might bring. Even if their published baseline forecasts did not stray very far from the initial reassuring consensus, many private-sector forecasters were often quick to admit that the outlook was particularly uncertain and that the risks for any forecast were all on the downside.[17] As one market participant stated the issue in late 1997:

> "Do conditions today resemble the 20 year plus downturn from 1873 to 1886 following the collapse of the railroad boom which had run since 1843? Or rather, are we looking at circumstances somewhat similar to those preceding the Great Depression? Or perhaps, things are not so bad after all and we will get away with merely a 1980s Latin American-style debt crisis. And finally, this is all a bad dream. . . . . So will this be the 1930s, the 1870s, the 1980s or something new?. . . . We suspect that Bangkok 1997 will go down as Vienna 1873 in the history books. . . . . **We should stress that these are personal views and do not reflect SBC Warburg Dillon Read's core household forecasts. However what we are seeking is to raise the level of debate and the awareness of what is a rising risk profile." (SBC, 1997 (bold in original))**

17 It is important to realize just how little confidence most forecasters placed in their baseline forecasts. Indeed, the refrain that the outlook is uncertain and that all of the risks are on the downside was almost universal.

Subsequent developments would seem to confirm at least some of market participants' initial concerns about the strength of the contractionary forces, thereby reinforcing their other worries. First, market participants initially suspected and as of mid-1998 firmly believed that the crisis shattered the financial systems in Thailand, Indonesia, the Republic of Korea and, to some extent, Malaysia. While official trade credits might succeed in keeping the region on life support, with the local financial institutions de-capitalized and new foreign lending to the region apparently not taking place, they worried consequently that the necessary working capital and trade credits were not available in sufficient amounts to finance the export growth needed to jump-start the local economies. Accordingly, most private sector forecasts for the Republic of Korea and South-East Asia were very pessimistic. Negative 20 per cent growth rates for Indonesia in 1998 were common, for example.

Second, although the immediate financial contagion coming from East Asia has long passed, market participants expressed concern that the crisis left the global financial system in a weakened state. They suspected that other emerging market economies had become more vulnerable to a similar financial contagion, placing Brazil and the Russian Federation high on the list for possible attack. They also worried that the credit rationing that had been limited to the East Asian emerging markets might become more widespread. Market participants also wondered whether the collapse of asset prices in East Asia might presage similar declines elsewhere, particularly in the United States, where, feeding on its own manic logic, the already clearly over-valued US stock market has continued to rise. Were the US stock market to fall, it would bring European stock prices down in its wake. Most worrisome, many market participants expressed alarm that, because of Japan's financial exposure to the region, the financial difficulties in South-East Asia and the Republic of Korea left Japan's already fragile financial system in an even more precarious state. The likelihood that Japan's recession would deepen suggested to many not just that Japan would be unable to absorb exports coming from its depressed neighbors. It suggested as well that Japan's financial system would weaken even further, possibly becoming at some time so fragile as to implode. Should this happen, market participants could not rule out a world financial collapse of Great Depression proportions.

Third, private sector forecasters admitted that their initial cautious, more optimistic, baseline forecasts assumed not only that the financial contagion remained fully contained, but that certain other contingencies did not take place as well. Their initial baseline scenarios assumed, in particular, that China would not devalue its currency and that the major industrialized countries would not adopt protectionist measures, or let their own currencies fall, to prevent the necessary current account and trade adjustments from taking place. Should China decide to devalue to regain competitiveness, market participants fear that another round of exchange rate declines in the region would surely take place. Should the major industrialized countries raise their trade barriers and/or resort to competitive devaluations, 1929-like scenarios would again be on the horizon. Meanwhile, signs of economic weakness in China appeared, and the US trade deficit continues to break record levels.

Many forecasters acknowledge, finally, that their assumptions about the ongoing strength of the US domestic economy may not be valid for much longer. Despite signs that the US economy remains strong, the US recovery is very old and, all the talk to the contrary, very few private-sector market participants believe that the normal business cycle has been abolished.[18]

f) The financial crisis in East Asia has damaged investor confidence in complex and subtle ways: investors have lost confidence not just in the prospects in East Asia, but even more significantly, in financial market liberalization and globalization, indeed, in the very viability and stability of today's unregulated globalized financial markets

According to many market participants, the East Asian financial crisis has disturbed investor psychology much more deeply than the European currency crisis of 1992 or the Mexican crisis of 1994-95. Market participants perceived the former as needed to rebalance the European Monetary System in the wake of German unification. To attract the foreign capital necessary to finance unification, German interest rates were raised beyond levels consistent with the pre-devaluation EMS parities, so German domestic interests prevailed over those of the exchange rate mechanism. Market participants perceived the Mexican crisis as a largely isolated event, blamed the Mexican government, and knew that a tightening of US monetary policy lay in the background. Sophisticated investors, moreover, anticipated both events well in advance, and so made money in the process. Finally, both episodes were forgotten quickly, as in neither case did investors worry about the crisis' impact on the strength of the world economy.

The Asian crisis is different. Although questions have been raised about the fixed-exchange rate regimes, as we have seen, most market participants recognize

18 We should note, however, that so far the data continue to point to real strength in the domestic US economy. In fact, based on what they saw as a better-than-expected domestic economy, a number of forecasters raised their US GDP forecasts in the wake of the crisis' eruption, increasing the domestic components of their forecasts while simultaneously lowering net exports. On the other hand, very few business economists give much credence to the view that the business cycle has been abolished.

that the policies in place as well as the general macroeconomic conditions in the Asian emerging markets were generally favourable prior to the crisis and accordingly believe that the crisis had its origins in the private sector banking and financial systems. The crisis in East Asia was not anticipated, and if market reports are to be believed, international investors lost money during the contagion. The Asian crisis has shaken investors' confidence in continued robust growth for the world economy at large. For these reasons and more, the Asian financial crisis has had a profoundly disturbing effect on investor psychology.

To see exactly how and why market participants have been so severely affected, we must take note of four matters: first, what the emerging market economies in the Pacific Basin had come to represent to many market participants by the mid-1990s and thus what it meant to become disillusioned with the "Asian economic miracle"; second, certain problems stemming from the large aggregate market exposure that foreign investors had taken in East Asia prior to the crisis; third, concerns expressed by many market participants that investors were compelled to take on these exposures owing to normal competitive pressures; and fourth, the ease with which the contagion spread rapidly from one country to the next.

Prior to the crisis, the emerging market economies in East Asia, as a number of market participants stated it, seemed to be "doing everything right". Indeed, in terms of what most Western investors meant by the "Asian economic miracle", the Asian emerging market economies seemed to be the very embodiment of late twentieth century free-market, laissez-faire, entrepreneurial capitalism. When these countries collapsed into financial chaos in 1997, therefore, market participants were compelled not just to reappraise the realities in certain actually existing capitalisms, but to question as well the validity of what had become nothing less than the latest idealized model of what Third World capitalism should be. If the emerging market economies that were "doing everything right" could go wrong, investors thus were left wondering, what really was the right thing to do?

One response that market participants made to this disillusionment was to face it squarely. This meant that they would have to come to terms with the troubling question as to why, in the very emerging markets that "were doing everything right", could unregulated free market capitalism bring about such a disastrous result? Alternatively, the same disillusionment with the Asian economic model led many market participants to doubt that the "Asian economic miracle" had ever existed at all. This, indeed, is just what we find in today's consensus view on the region, according to which markets were never allowed to flourish in these countries because of "crony capitalism", moral hazard and the like.

When the crisis erupted almost without warning in the summer of 1997, international investors suddenly discovered at least four very serious problems with their strategies in the East Asian emerging markets. First, not only had they not seen that the Asian economic model was in trouble, they continued to increase their exposure to the region until the crisis was upon them. Second, they had completely underestimated the size and the riskiness of the aggregate market exposures that they all now had in the Pacific Basin. Third, as the relevant interest-rate risk premiums were low and had been falling, the financial markets themselves had not given them any warning signs about the dangers inherent in these exposures. Fourth, now that they were looking to reduce their positions in the region, they could do so only by realizing sizeable losses, because the requisite liquidity needed for an easy exit was simply lacking. Why did they not see that the crisis was coming until it was too late? Why had they been so inattentive, not just to the now obvious foreign exchange risks, but also to the much more troublesome, if less obvious, aggregate market risks that were now pulling them all down? Why had even the supposedly rational and efficient markets not priced in the true risks? Why, precisely during a period of systemic failure, does liquidity vanish just when most needed?

If they chose to do so, market participants could come to terms with these questions in such a way as to keep their faith in the markets intact. Informational asymmetries may have prevented market participants from keeping up with the true developments in East Asia. Fallacy-of-composition mistakes, even when made by prudent investors, can produce aggregate market exposures of unreasonable sizes. Market failure can account for the decline in interest risk premiums prior to the contagion. Liquidity is always a problem in one-way markets. Moral hazard as well as the illusion of certainty associated with a fixed exchange rate regime may have played crucial roles.

Defending the rationality of the market by pointing to situations when this rationality breaks down must have its limits, however. Given the magnitude of the mistakes that had been made, surely the information asymmetry, fallacies of composition, market failure, moral hazard, adverse selection and other similar problems would have had to be so great as to make them not the exception to the rule, but the rule itself. Many market participants have concluded, therefore, that a simpler explanation might be more appropriate, namely, that the markets are not always efficient or rational. To state one aspect of the issue bluntly, many market participants are now asking when does a market failure become so extensive that what has failed are the markets themselves. Making reference to the extensive use of derivatives that had taken place, a risk manager put the issue this way:

> "When the Mexican crisis was erupting in 1994, we were all thankful that swaps had not been involved to any degree. Now, since swaps were used in South-East Asia extensively, it is a mess, a total, complete mess. It is a disaster, a complete failure. The markets broke down completely."

Global investors took on the greater credit and country risks in the East Asian emerging market because of the greater expected returns that the region seemed to offer in comparison with those that could be obtained elsewhere. Initially sound and prudent, these investments grew progressively larger over time and as they did so, these investments, as we have seen, reportedly became not only excessive, but increasingly complex and risky as well. The defender of market rationality assumes that as investors know the true risk-reward structures of their exposures, investors normally do not act in this way. In this case, if indeed these exposures were truly excessive, then what took place in East Asia was an aberration. According to a number of market participants, alternatively, the normal competitive pressures found in any financial institution compel investors to take on these and similar exposures over time. In this case, the speculative excesses of the international investors in Asian financial crisis were not an exception to the rule, but instead the result of normal business practices and thus to a certain degree inevitable.

The speed at which the financial contagion spread from Thailand to the rest of East Asia and the global capital markets at large was remarkable. The international financial markets were not working as a means for allocating capital efficiently across countries but instead had become a mechanism for spreading financial panic from one nation to the next, and the cause was simply a change in the investment outlook for East Asia. One way market participants can look at the matter is to defend the viability of free markets by holding the fixed exchange rate regimes responsible for the spread of the contagion. By fixing the exchange rates, policy makers had allowed a set of market forces to build up, and now these market forces were simply exerting themselves. Alternatively, market participants could assume that the markets had become flawed in an essential way, in which case, two questions came to the forefront. Why, at certain times, do the international markets succeed in spreading only panic? Why under conditions of a globalized financial system can changes in market sentiment lead to an international financial panic of such terrifying proportions?

With the immediacy of the crisis now a receding memory, market participants can avoid the questions that the financial crisis in East Asia has raised. Indeed, the euphoria that seems to have gripped the US financial markets, especially the US stock market, on a number of occasions since then has a strong element of this very denial at its base.[19] Still, there can be no doubt that the events in East Asia have forced many market participants to face a number of very troubling questions. Market participants do not know if the failure of the "Asian economic miracle" was a failure of a "crony capitalism" or a variety of free-market entrepreneurial capitalism that had somehow gone very wrong. They do not know why they had taken on such excessive and risky positions in East Asia, whether it was an example of market failure, or whether the markets had failed. Market participants do not know whether these speculative excesses were an exception or the product of normal competitive pressures. Market participants do not know if flexible exchange rates would have prevented the crisis from engulfing the region, or whether this was due to free capital mobility.

One thing is certain, however. The East Asian financial crisis has forced many market participants to question not just the wisdom of further financial market liberalization and globalization, but even more significantly, the very viability and stability of today's globalized and largely unregulated financial markets themselves. This means that market participants are now forced to confront a very troubling dilemma. On the one hand, the questioning has prompted many to wonder not only about the merits of increased financial market liberalization and globalization, but to wonder whether these should be reversed. If, indeed, liberalization and globalization are the very problems that need a solution, an entirely new set of largely non-market rules to regulate the international financial system needs to be developed. On the other hand, since belief in globalization and free markets is deeply held, the same questioning is often accompanied by an equally steadfast denial that anything is wrong. This denial, in turn, pushes even the same market participant often to the opposite conclusion, namely, that the crisis in East Asia occurred because international financial market liberalization and integration have not gone far enough.

g) The crisis has consequently left many market participants confused about what the appropriate policy responses should be

As should be obvious from the number and variety of articles, editorials and op-ed pieces that have appeared in the business press on the Asian crisis, investor opinion on the policy implications of the East Asian financial crisis is so confused and highly divided that a market consensus view of the issues simply does not exist. In addition, many market participants simply do not have

19 Keynes (1930), in the *Treatise on Money*, argues that financial markets can be bullish and bearish at the same time, and that the stock market can rise even if the bears outnumber the bulls. He suggests, in particular, that the bears actually outnumbered the bulls in 1927-1928 in the United States well before the 1929 crash.

opinions about the relevant policy matters; and for those that do, the quality of their opinions depends largely upon their expertise. What is striking, however, is the change in the climate of opinion that has taken place. Recommendations that a private sector market participant would have dismissed out of hand only a year ago (Tobin taxes, for example) are given serious consideration. Market participants know that the situation is serious and that far-reaching reform proposals are on the agenda. The problem is that most market participants really do not know what to do.

One way of thinking about the quandary in which the crisis has left many market participants, however, is to assume, as a simple fiction, that market participants typically move back and forth between two different roles when they engage in policy discussions: that of the businessman and that of the market professional. As businessmen, market participants will resist reforms that might restrict their own room for manoeuvre, but push for reforms that advance their own interests, especially vis-a-vis their competitors. As market professionals, on the other hand, market participants will act responsibly to improve general market conditions and practices, often working quite closely with their competitors and the relevant authorities to make certain that everyone, including themselves, act with sobriety and care. Normally, market participants would appeal to a shared belief that market solutions are always preferable to resolve any disputes that might arise between what they say as businessmen, on the one hand, or as market professionals, on the other.

However, these are not normal times. For all of the reasons that we have just given, the consensus that market solutions are universally right has been broken, with the consequence that the gap between the kind of reforms that market participants are proposing as market practitioners and the reforms that they will accept as businessmen has become in many cases insurmountable. As market practitioners they are willing to entertain the idea that the market is not always right and, indeed, that proper solutions might involve increased state intervention and regulation. As businessmen, market participants have retained their faith in free markets, and so believe that any reform measures should place greater rather than less reliance on market forces.

The pro-market, pro-business stance of many of the recommendations that have been put forward for East Asia itself is clear. Since, as businessmen they were hurt by the financial collapse and subsequent slowdown in East Asia, market participants are more than willing to hold the local bankers and businessmen to account for the troubles of the region. Accordingly, many US-based market participants are quick to support campaigns against local corruption and cronyism and the rapid closing of any insolvent banks and businesses, often using moral hazard as an argument against showing leniency. For reasons of pure self-interest as well, US-based market participants also advocate increased capital account liberalization and similar efforts at opening the domestic economies up to market forces, including the breaking up of local monopolies, as this will give them greater access to these markets. They support increased transparency, improvements in local accounting practices and bankruptcy laws and so forth, as these measures will make it easier for them to manage any future investments that they might make in the area. And US-based market participants support recommendations that the countries in East Asia replace their current largely bank-centered local financial systems with United States-United Kingdom style capital market-centred financial systems, because they are strongly positioned to take advantage of the result.

Alongside these are another set of recommendations for East Asia that appeal not so much to market participants' immediate short-term interests as to their interests as enlightened market professionals instead. Under these recommendations, market participants still see that there is a need to close insolvent institutions in East Asia, but now they argue that the resolutions should be done in a deliberate and orderly way. First, any rush to close as many insolvent firms as quickly as possible should be avoided, as this will only increase the difficulties of organizing an orderly workout of the region's underlying bad debt problems. Second, instead of wasting time in deciding who it is that deserves the blame for the region's difficulties, priority should be given instead to finding ways to consolidate and resolve these bad debts as quickly as possible. If this is done in a careful and thoughtful way, foreign creditors will have to book fewer losses, and as a consequence, these foreign creditors will show a greater willingness to end the credit rationing that is keeping these countries capital-starved. Consequently third, local monetary authorities, international monetary institutions, and officials from the major industrial nations must take a very active and forceful role in making certain that the bad debts are quickly resolved and that the foreign credit rationing comes to an end as soon as possible, by pressing for debt negotiations. To this end, many market participants advocate the creation and strengthening of national and perhaps even regional Resolution Trust-like institutions, because if left to itself the private sector cannot be relied upon to take the initiative to deal with these matters.

Similarly, as market professionals, market participants still see the need to get rid of cronyism and corruption in East Asia, but the emphasis is no longer on punishing past wrongdoing, but shifts instead towards using the authority of the state to organize improvements in local business practices—even if the stricter banking regulations and greater oversight over non-financial institutions that this will entail might limit the manoeuvring room of foreign investors in the region. First, the emerging market economies in East Asia need to adopt all of the measures that the Basle Committee has laid out in its Compendium of supervisory documents, including, in particular, those spelled out in the Core Principles for Effective Banking Supervision of 1997, which argues that the local authorities must have the necessary autonomy and resources to carry out their responsibilities as a basic prerequisite for the creation of a well regulated and supervised financial system. Second, the governments in the emerging markets in East Asia need to have the power and authority to fully regulate and supervise all of the local non-financial corporations to make certain that they follow sound business practices as well. Third, supervisory and regulatory improvements have clear priority over any measures to further liberalize the capital account and/or the domestic economy, implying in the first instance, that any liberalization efforts must be properly coordinated and sequenced with developments on the supervisory and regulatory front. Fourth, there is no real need for these nations to adopt capital market-centred financial systems. As long as their financial systems are well regulated, it does not matter how they are organized, provided, on a case-by-case basis, they serve local business interests well.

Acting as self-interested businessmen, US-based market participants have very little to say, of course, about what roles they may have played in the origins of the East Asian financial crisis, as it is not in their interest to admit that they were accountable in any way. As enlightened market professionals, on the other hand, market participants have acknowledged that their own speculative excesses may have played an essential role in both the origins and the spread of the contagion, and thus that there is a need to find the proper regulatory systems and early warning mechanisms that will prevent them from taking on such risky aggregate market exposures again in the future and/or which will force them to cut their exposures well before another full-fledged crisis begins to take place.

Since the market and other informational failures that lay at the heart of the crisis in East Asia were truly massive, market participants familiar with the issues realize that the required regulatory changes would have to be far reaching and the early warning systems elaborate. First, the BIS's capital standards must be reviewed to see if stricter limits should be placed on market participants' credit and market exposures. Second, private sector financial institutions must strengthen their own internal risk measurement and control systems. Enhanced systems must be in place that allow them to measure not just their aggregate credit exposures, but to measure, on a day-to-day basis, their aggregate price and interest rate risks across financial markets as well. In particular, value-at-risk and Monte Carlo procedures must be used routinely to see if there are any particular blind spots in their investment strategies. Should the measured risks become excessive, risk managers must have the clear authority to cut the exposures and to override senior management if necessary to do so. Third, the monetary authorities of the major industrialized nations must establish procedures allowing them to monitor the total aggregate market risks that the financial institutions under their jurisdiction have collectively taken on and, hence, to warn their institutions when these positions have become excessive. Fourth, international efforts must be taken, under the auspices of the BIS, the International Monetary Fund, or perhaps a new institution, to measure and regulate the aggregate market exposures that all of the major multinational financial institutions have taken on within particular areas of the globe. Fifth, central bankers and international monetary authorities must work closely with private sector financial institutions to establish an early warning system that will alert market participants to pending economic and financial difficulties in individual countries and regions.

As businessmen, however, market participants would object to these proposals vehemently, and so much so that few businessmen would find them acceptable. The regulatory burden of the BIS capital rules, they would argue, is already great. In keeping with the new BIS rules about market risk, they are already developing their own sophisticated internal risk measurement and management systems, and the information costs and regulatory burdens of implementing the third and fourth of these suggestions would be even greater. The fifth proposal about establishing an international early warning system may be simply too elaborate. However desirable these and similar mechanisms might be from the pure policy point of view, they are too burdensome, costly and elaborate—in short, simply not realistic.[20]

Turning to the international dimensions of the contagion, the gap between what market participants will accept as market professionals and what they will accept as businessmen is even greater. Since they know that international financial markets can at times become dysfunctional, as market professionals they are willing to entertain the use of a variety of non-market solutions, including Tobin taxes and capital controls, temporary or otherwise. Since the jurisdiction of any national authority is limited to its own borders, market participants may also see a need to create regional or international supervisory

20 It is interesting to note that the BIS was holding a conference on how to measure aggregate market risk in the spring of 1997, just when the East Asian crisis was beginning to unfold and that the conference seems to have come to the same conclusion that these and similar schemes were just not feasible. See, "The Measurement of Aggregate Market Risk", BIS (1997), for a summary of the conference's major findings.

structures to enforce the taxes and capital controls and to otherwise regulate the international capital markets. As businessmen, on the other hand, they know that they would immediately find ways to avoid and evade any of these controls and regulations, pointing out as well that under today's political conditions, where organized political power still resides in the nation state, enforcement would be very difficult, if not impossible. Besides, they would counter as businessmen, flexible exchange rates would provide a better and simpler solution.

h) Market participants' uncertainty and confusion is seen most clearly in their contradictory attitudes about the International Monetary Fund

The attitude that market participants have towards the International Monetary Fund today is complex and contradictory. Most market participants supported the stabilization efforts that the Fund took as the crisis in East Asia was unfolding. They were clearly willing to defend the Fund, because austerity was what was needed to restore market confidence in the local exchange rates, against criticisms that the Fund's conditionality was too severe. Jeffrey Sachs' criticism of the Fund "was not helpful", for example, is how a number of market participants put it. Moreover, during the crisis, market participants were quick to show displeasure with any government in the region which seemed to deviate even in the slightest from the programme that it had signed with the Fund: if they thought that the government was not living up to the programme, market participants saw no reason to hold the country's assets and so sold them aggressively. And later in 1998, despite the well-known public declarations of a few, most market participants generally believed that IMF needed to be fully funded, noting both that it was over-extended and that it was the only institution in existence with a mandate to deal with any emerging market financial crisis that might appear in the future.

That being said, most market participants admit that the Fund's stabilization efforts in East Asia not only failed to limit the foreign exchange contagion, but may have actually made the domestic financial problems in East Asia, and in Indonesia in particular, worse. In the opinion of a number of New York-based market participants, for example, if any public authorities are to be given credit for containing the contagion it is the US Treasury and the Federal Reserve and not the Fund. As one market participant stated it, "Rubin and Greenspan drew the line at Korea, for political and security reasons". Moreover, even if they did not disagree with the Fund's goals, many market participants often disagreed with what they saw as the inappropriate or at least insensitive way in which the Fund went about implementing its programmes.

The language used to make this point was that the Fund was "running roughshod" over the countries, or that it was "applying the same old cookie cutter formula" which may not be appropriate. Criticism of the Fund along these lines usually focused on IMF's role in Indonesia.

However, the Fund's lack of credibility with some market participants went deeper. Focusing on the need to restore foreign investor confidence in the local exchange rates, these market participants note, the Fund's support for fiscal austerity, tight monetary policy, rapid bank closures, and the enforcement of capital adequacy standards aggravated any existing domestic financial difficulties that may have already been in place. And given the way in which the banking and foreign exchange crises had become intrinsically linked, by aggravating the stress on the domestic financial structures, the Fund's own programmes could, in turn, only increase the downward pressures on the local exchange rates. By attempting to stabilize the exchange rates through austerity measures, the Fund destabilized the domestic financial systems, whose instability, in turn, undermined any temporary exchange rate stability that its programme might have initially obtained. Since the exchange rates really did need to be stabilized, however, this suggests to these market participants that the Fund was trapped in the same contradictions that had rendered the local monetary authorities helpless to deal with the crisis, which means, of course, that the Fund was also powerless to deal with the contagion. If the Fund has lost credibility in the eyes of a number of market participants, therefore, it is not so much because they think that the Fund did something wrong, but because there was simply no right thing that it could have done, and hence, because it was ineffective.

For others, the Fund seems to have become trapped by its own historical legacy. After taking on such large unhedged aggregate exposure in East Asia that they could make only losses, many market participants in the major industrialized nations are looking for a set of mechanisms coming from the monetary authorities of the industrialized nations, and from the BIS, in particular, that will prevent them from taking on such exposures again in the future. And after seeing how the international financial markets can spread financial crisis so rapidly from one country to the next, many market participants, not wanting to witness any other similar episodes, know that extensive multilateral efforts may be needed to prevent a similar contagion. When the Bretton Woods fixed-exchange rate system was still intact or in the early years of the floating exchange rate period, the Fund had a clear mandate to deal with problems in the industrialized nations or to influence the architecture of the international economy. During this period, the Fund was, in fact, the forum within which discussions about the architecture of the world economy took place. However, in the 1980s, when the Fund was called upon to deal with the Latin American debt crisis, its focus became much narrower. Now the Fund has a clear mandate only to crisis-manage the emerging market economies, and in the wake of the Asian crisis, the Fund does not appear to be doing even this very well. In the minds of these market participants, therefore, the Fund now seems to be a largely irrelevant, and perhaps a historically obsolete, institution. Yet to their dismay, this leaves these market participants with nowhere to go. They talk of another Bretton Woods agreement, but for now, they know that this is not a real possibility.

3. Summary

The financial crisis in East Asia is an event of historical proportions. It has sent a profoundly contractionary shock into the world economy which may well bring recession, additional financial crises, or worse. The crisis may have brought the process of globalization and internationalization, which has been the hallmark of international economic developments since the early 1980s, to an end.

As seen from mid-1998, immediate efforts are needed to limit the crisis' contractionary effects. Until there is an orderly workout of East Asia's underlying credit losses, a local credit crunch and foreign credit rationing will depress activity in the region, so this must be given a high priority. To prevent Japan's recession from deepening and to make certain its banking problems do not grow worse, moreover, Japanese officials must announce and then quickly implement both a credible economic stimulation package and a credible plan to resolve its own non-performing loan problems. The major industrialized countries must not resist the trade and current account adjustments that we know are coming by either raising their trade barriers or encouraging devaluations. Once we are certain that the contractionary effects of the crisis have been contained, then there is an urgent need to address the question of globalization and liberalization: whether there is a need for a new architecture for the world economy, and if so, what shape it should take.

References

Akyuz, Yilmaz (1998). "The East Asian financial crisis: back to the future?". Geneva, Switzerland: UNCTAD, mimeo.

Azis, Iwan (1997). "The origins and implications of the currency crisis in South-East Asia". *Research Seminar in Quantitative Economics*. University of Michigan.

Bank for International Settlements (1997). "The measurement of aggregate market risk". Basle, Switzerland: BIS.

______ Banking Committee on Banking Supervision (1998). "Framework for the evaluation of internal control systems". Basle, Switzerland: BIS.

______ Monetary and Economics Department (1995). "The BIS statistics on international banking and financial market activity". Basle, Switzerland: BIS.

______ (1997a). "International banking and financial market developments". Basle, Switzerland: BIS. (February, May, August, November).

______ (1997b). "The maturity, sectoral and nationality distribution of international bank lending, second half of 1996". Basle, Switzerland: BIS.

______ (1998a). "International banking and financial market developments". Basle, Switzerland: BIS (February, May).

______ (1998b). "The maturity, sectoral and nationality distribution of international bank lending, first half of 1997". Basle, Switzerland: BIS (May, August, November).

Bergsten, C. Fred (1997). "The Asian monetary crisis: proposed remedies". Washington, D.C.:Institute for International Economics.

______ (1998a). "The trade implications of the Asian financial crisis".Washington, D.C.: Institute for International Economics.

______ (1998b). "The International Monetary Fund and the national interest of the United States". Washington, D.C.: Institute for International Economics.

______ (1998c). "US trade with Asia, APEC, and the financial crisis". Washington, D.C.: Institute for International Economics.

Blecker, Robert A. (1996). "NAFTA, the Peso crisis, and the contradictions of the Mexican economic growth strategy", Working Paper Series on Globalization, Labor Markets, and Social Policy, No. 3. New York, New York: Center for Economic Policy Analysis, New School for Social Research.

Board of Governors of the Federal Reserve System (1997a). "Minutes of the Federal Open Market Committee, meeting of November 12, 1997". Washington, D.C.

______ (1997b). "Minutes of the Federal Open Market Committee, meeting of December 16, 1997". Washington, D.C.

______ (1998a). "Minutes of the Federal Open Market Committee, meeting of February 3/4, 1998, Washington, D.C.

______ (1998b). "Minutes of the Federal Open Market Committee, meeting of March 31, 1998, Washington, D.C.

______ (1998c). "Monetary Policy Report to Congress". Washington, D.C. (February).

Camdessus, Michel (1998a). "The IMF and its programs in Asia". Washington, D.C.: International Monetary Fund.

______ (1998b). "Reflections on the crisis in Asia". Washington, D.C.: International Monetary Fund.

______ (1998c). "Is the Asian crisis over?". Washington, D.C.: International Monetary Fund.

______ (1998d). "Capital account liberalization and the role of the Fund". Washington, D.C.: International Monetary Fund.

Colaco, Francis (1997). "East Asian currency crises: 'Rogue' traders, fundamentals, contagion". *Economic and Political Weekly*, Vol. 32, No. 49.

Corsetti, Giancarlo, Paolo Pesenti and Nouriel Roubini (1998). "What caused the Asian currency and financial crisis?". New York: New York University, mimeo.

Dornbush, Rudi (1998). "Asian crisis themes". Cambridge, Massachusetts: Massachusetts Institute of Technology, mimeo.

Feldstein, Martin (1998). "Refocusing the IMF". *Foreign Affairs* (March/April issue).

Fischer, Stanley (1998a). "The Asian crisis: A view from the IMF". Washington, D.C.: International Monetary Fund.

______ (1998b). "Economic crisis in Asia". Washington, D.C.: International Monetary Fund.

______ (1998c). "The IMF and the Asian crisis". Washington, D.C.: International Monetary Fund.

Goldfajn, Ilan and Rodrigo Valdes (1997). "Are currency crises predictable?". IMF Working Paper, No. 97/159. Washington, D.C.: International Monetary Fund.

Goldstein, Morris (1998). "The Asian financial crisis". Washington, D.C.: Institute for International Economics.

Goldstein, Morris and Philip Tower (1996). "Banking crisis in emerging economies: Origins and policy options". BIS Economic Papers, No. 46. Basle, Switzerland: Bank for International Settlements.

Graff, James (1998). "A global warning". *Time* magazine (16 February).

Greenspan, Alan (1997). Testimony before the House Committee on Banking and Finance, 13 November. Washington, D.C.: Board of Governors of the Federal Reserve System.

______ (1998a). Testimony before the House Committee on Banking and Finance, 30 January, Washington, D.C.: Board of Governors of the Federal Reserve System.

______ (1998b). Testimony before the Senate House Committee on Foreign Relations, 12 February. Washington, D.C.: Board of Governors of the Federal Reserve System.

______ (1998c). Monetary Policy Testimony and Report to Congress, 24 February. Washington, D.C.: Board of Governors of the Federal Reserve System.

______ (1998d). Remarks before the Annual Financial Markets Conference of the Federal Reserve Bank of Atlanta, 27 February. Washington, D.C.: Board of Governors of the Federal Reserve System.

Institute of International Finance (1997a). "Private capital flows set to continue at record levels". Press release (30 January). Washington, D.C.

______ (1997b). "Improved financial supervision is proposed by financial leaders". Press release (4 April). Washington, D.C.

Institute of International Finance (1997c). "1997 private capital flows to emerging markets forecast to remain near record levels". Press release (April). Washington, D.C.

______ (1997d). "Global financial group sees continuing improvements in data release practices by leading emerging market economies". Press release (April). Washington, D.C.

______ (1997e). "ADB and IIF bring leaders together in forum on developing Asian financial markets". Press release (May). Washington, D.C.

______ (1997f). "Key lesson from Asian events can strengthen markets, say financial leaders". Press release (September). Washington, D.C.

______ (1997g). "New study underscore need for caution in assessing risks in emerging market" Press release (December). Washington, D.C.

______ (1998a). "Capital flows to emerging market economics", Press release (January). Washington, D.C.

______ (1998b). "Bankers propose review of bank risk capital framework". Press release (March). Washington, D.C.

International Monetary Fund (1997a). *Annual Report: 1997.* Washington, D.C.

______ (1997b). *International Capital Markets: Developments, Prospects, and Key Policy Issues.* Washington, D.C.

______ (1997c). "World economic outlook: interim assessment". Washington, D.C.

Johnson, Robert (1997). "What Asia's financial crisis portends". Op-ed piece, *The New York Times*, (December).

Johnston, Barry, Salim Darbar and Claudia Echeverria (1997). "Sequencing capital account liberalization: lessons from the experience of Chile, Indonesia, the Republic of Korea, and Thailand". IMF Working Paper, No. 97/157. Washington, D.C.: International Monetary Fund.

Johnston, Brian and John Sweeney (1997). "Down the drain: Why the IMF bailout in Asia is wasteful and won't work". Heritage Foundation Backgrounder, Washington, D.C.: The Heritage Foundation.

Kiel Institute of World Economics (1998). "The Asian currency crisis". Kiel, Germany: News from the Kiel Institute of World Economics.

Kaminsky, Glaciela and Carmen Reinhart (1996). "The twin crises: the causes of banking and balance-of-payments problems", International Finance Discussion Papers, No. 544. Washington, D.C.: Board of Governors of the Federal Reserve System.

______ (1998). "Financial crises in Asia and Latin America: then and now". Forthcoming in *American Economic Review: Papers and Proceedings*, Vol. 88.

Krugman, Paul (1997a). "Currency crises". Cambridge, Massachusetts: Massachusetts Institute of Technology (MIT), mimeo.

______ (1997b). "Asia's miracle is alive and well? Wrong, it never existed". *Time* magazine (29 September).

______ (1998a). "What happened to Asia?". MIT, mimeo.

______ (1998b). "Fire sale FDI", MIT, mimeo.

______ (1998c). "Asia: What went wrong". *Fortune* magazine (March).

Lali, Subir (1997). "Speculative attacks, forward market intervention, and the classic bear squeeze". IMF working Paper, 97/164. Washington, D.C.: International Monetary Fund.

Latin, Robert (1998). "A tree-step remedy for Asia's financial flu". Brookings Policy Briefing Series, No. 30. Washington, D.C.: The Brookings Institution.

Lui, Ligang, Marcus Noland, Sherman Robinson and Zhi Wang (1998). "Asian competitive devaluations". Washington, D.C.: Institute for International Economics.

McKibbon, Warwick (1998). "The crisis in Asia: An empirical assessment". Research School of Pacific and Asian Studies, Australian National University, mimeo.

Montes, Manuel, Kevin Quigley and Donald Weatherbee (1997). "Growing pains: ASEAN's economic and political challenges". New York, New York: Asian Society, mimeo.

Noland, Marcus (1996). "Restructuring Korea's financial sector for greater competitiveness". ACEC Working Paper, No. 96-14. Washington, D.C.: Institute for International Economics.

______ (1998). "The financial crisis in Asia". Washington, D.C.: Institute for International Economics.

Organization for International Economic Cooperation and Development and Bank for International Settlements (1997). "Statistics on external indebtedness", mid-1995 to end-1996. Paris, France and Basle, Switzerland.

______ (1998). "Statistics on external indebtedness", end-1995 to mid-1997. Paris, France and Basle, Switzerland.

Peiper, Ute and Lance Taylor (1996). "The revival of the creed: the IMF, the World Bank, and inequality in a globalized economy". Working Paper Series on Globalization, Labor Markets, and Social Policy, No. 4. New York, New York: Center for Economic Policy Analysis, New School for Social Research.

Reinhart, Carmen and R. Todd Smith (1997). "Temporary capital controls". University of Maryland and University of Alberta, mimeo.

Rodrick, Dani (1998). "Who needs capital-account convertibility?". Cambridge, Massachusetts: Harvard University, mimeo.

Roubini, Nouriel (1998). "Chronology of the Asian financial crisis and its global contagion". New York, New York: New York University, mimeo.

Sachs, Jeffrey and Steven Radelet (1998). "The onset of the East Asian financial crisis". Cambridge, Massachusetts: Harvard Institute for International Development.

Samuelson, Robert (1997). "The Asian connection". *Newsweek* magazine (15 December).

Sanstrom, Sven (1998). "The East Asia crisis and the role of the World Bank". Washington, D.C.: The World Bank Group.

Schultz, George, William Simon and Walter Wriston (1998). "Who needs the IMF". *The Wall Street Journal* (3 February).

Soros, George (1997). "Avoiding a breakdown". *Financial Times* (31 December).

Stiglitz, Joseph (1997). "Statement to the meeting of the finance ministers of ASEAN plus 6 with the IMF and the World Bank". Washington, D.C.: World Bank.

______ (1998a). "More instruments and broader goals: moving toward the post-Washington consensus". Helsinki, Finland: The WIDER Annual Lecture.

Stiglitz, Joseph (1998b). "Bad private-sector decisions". *The Wall Street Journal* (4 February).

______ (1998c). "The role of international financial institutions in the current global economy". Washington, D.C.: World Bank.

______ (1998d). "Sound finance and sustainable development in Asia". Washington, D.C.: World Bank.

Sumners, Lawrence (1998). "Opportunities out of crisis: lessons from Asia". *Treasury News*, Washington, D.C.: United States Department of the Treasury.

SBC Warberg Dillon Read (1997). *The Asian Advise* (December).

Taylor, Lance (1998). "Lax public sector, destabilizing private sector: Origins of capital market crises", mimeo.

Wolf, Charles (1998). "Too much government control", *The Wall Street Journal* (4 February).

World Bank (1998a). "Responding to the crisis: Backing East Asia's social and financial reforms". Press statement. Washington, D.C

______ (1998b). "Impact of the East Asian crisis on developing countries". Washington, D.C.:

PREM Briefing Notes.

______ (1998c). "What effect will East Asia's crisis have on developing countries?". Washington, D.C.: PREM Economic Policy.

______ (1998d). "Crisis offers opportunity for reform". Press release. Washington, D.C.

______ (1998e). "East Asia". Regional brief. Washington, D.C.

______ (1998f). "World bank financial support to East Asia since July 1997". Fact sheet, Washington, D.C.

Wyplosz, Charles (1998). "Globalized financial markets and financial crises". Geneva, Switzerland: Graduate Institute of International Studies, mimeo.

26

Understanding the Dynamics Behind Excess Capital Inflows and Excess Capital Outflows in East Asia

KRISHNAN SHARMA*

United Nations Department of Economic and Social Affairs

1. Introduction

While much research has been undertaken on the causes and consequences of the East Asian financial crisis, there has been insufficient analysis of it from the viewpoint of international financial markets. There is a need for policy makers to understand the dynamics behind the large inflows of private capital into East Asia prior to 1997 and their subsequent reversal. It is also important to gauge what is needed for market confidence to be restored and the difficulties involved in achieving this.

The present paper attempts to undertake such an analysis. While it does not attempt to be prescriptive, its aim is to suggest immediate and longer-term issues for consideration by policy makers at both the national and the international levels.

The research undertaken is partly based on interviews conducted during a field trip to Thailand, Malaysia, Singapore, the Philippines and Hong Kong

---

* Economist, Developing Economies Section. The views expressed herein are those of the author and do not necessarily reflect the views of the United Nations. The author wishes to thank all the people who provided him with assistance during his mission to South-East Asia and Hong Kong (China). He also wishes to express his gratitude to Barry Herman, Ann Orr and Ana Cortez for their comments and Ann D'Lima for assistance with the figures.

(China), in May/June 1998. A total of 34 professionals were interviewed—17 of whom worked for international financial institutions (commercial and investment banks and portfolio management companies) and 17 of whom were financial market experts working in central banks, international organizations, local banks and companies, think tanks and academia. The findings on this trip, backed up by other research, form the basis of the present paper.[1] Given the sensitive nature of some of the issues, most of the interviewees understandably wished to remain anonymous. Their wish is respected in this paper. However, where appropriate, quotations will be included without, of course, naming the source.

The paper will be structured as follows: we will start by considering whether international financial markets were wrong to channel such large amounts of capital to East Asia and, if so, why did this happen. We will then proceed to assess the dynamics behind the depth and spread of the crisis and analyse what is needed for confidence to be restored. Finally, we will discuss the short-term and medium-term policy implications of this analysis for national governments and the international community.

Before tackling these issues, the section below will provide some background by defining "international financial markets" in the context of this paper and describing the trends in fundamentals and private capital flows to East Asia in the 1990s.

2. Definitions and trends

The term "international financial markets" is broad but, in the context of this paper, refers largely to international commercial and investment banks and portfolio investors. At the same time, the important role of local investors in triggering and perpetuating the currency declines is not overlooked and is acknowledged.

Even the terms "commercial banks" and "portfolio investors" are broad and incorporate different players. An important distinction to be made is between short-term and longer-term players. In particular, we include under "portfolio investors" a variety of players including hedge funds, mutual funds and pension funds. These players share similarities but also have differences; for example, hedge funds have been argued to indulge in a greater degree of speculation while the investments of pension funds have been said to be more

1 The other research draws on reports produced by financial market institutions, newspaper articles, data and commentary produced by international organizations (namely, the International Monetary Fund, World Bank, Bank for International Settlements and Asian Development Bank) and academic papers.

long-term. Where relevant, the differences in the actions of these players will be pointed out.

Net private capital flows to Thailand, Malaysia, Indonesia, the Philippines and the Republic of Korea (henceforth referred to as "the affected East Asian economies") rose sharply during the early and mid-1990s. Indeed all the components of net private capital flows—bank and trade lending, foreign direct investment and portfolio investment—rose sharply. However, as table 1 shows, commercial bank and portfolio equity flows experienced huge reversals in 1997.

Prior to 1997, private capital flows were attracted to East Asia by a combination of external and domestic factors. For a start, sluggish growth in Europe, Japan and the United States in the early 1990s as well as low interest rates led to a decline in attractive lending and investment opportunities in the developed economies. At the same time, many of the affected East Asian countries maintained high interest rates that, together with their high economic growth rates, created the prospect of high returns to lending and investment in the region. Thirdly, financial liberalization in the late 1980s and early 1990s in many of the Asian countries opened up new investment opportunities for foreign investors. Finally, pegged exchange rates significantly reduced the currency risk attached to investing and lending in East Asia.

Table 1. External financing of five Asian economies[a]
(Billions of US dollars)

	1994	*1995*	*1996*	*1997*[b]
Current account balance	-24.6	-41.3	-54.9	-26.0
External financing, net	47.4	80.9	92.8	15.2
Private flows, net	40.5	77.4	93.0	-12.1
Equity investment	12.2	15.5	19.1	-4.5
Direct equity	4.7	4.9	7.0	7.2
Portfolio equity	7.6	10.6	12.1	-11.6
Private creditors	28.2	61.8	74.0	-7.6
Commercial banks	24.0	49.5	55.5	-21.3
Non-bank private creditors	4.2	12.4	18.4	13.7
Officials flows, net	7.0	3.6	-0.2	27.2
Resident lending/other, net	-17.5	-25.9	-19.6	-11.9
Reserves excluding gold (minus = increase)	-5.4	-13.7	-18.3	22.7

Source: Institute of International Finance (1998).

a Five economies are Republic of Korea, Indonesia, Malaysia, Thailand and Philippines.

b Estimate.

Of course, a major attraction of investing in the East Asian economies had been their strong macroeconomic fundamentals and performance. This is illustrated by table 2, which shows strong economic growth rates, relatively subdued inflation, budget surpluses and relatively high rates of domestic savings and investment. The growing current account deficits in the region were a worry but as long as exports were growing at a rapid rate, which they were up to 1995, most people thought the external deficits to be sustainable.

However, the surge in private capital inflows generated vulnerabilities in the financial sectors of the affected East Asian economies (Asian Development Bank, 1998). For a start, much of the capital inflow consisted of short-term deposits or loans to local banks, which thus were borrowing short to lend long. As a result, the maturity structure of domestic banks' assets and liabilities became skewed. Secondly, the foreign liabilities of domestic banks rose more sharply than their foreign assets. This led to a build-up in the net foreign debt in the banking sector—and much of this was short-term debt. Thirdly, a significant proportion of the foreign capital borrowed by domestic banks was then re-lent imprudently—they ended up financing risky projects or ventures that were not economically viable. In some countries, there was over-investment in the real estate sector. In the Republic of Korea, by contrast, the foreign capital financed excessive expansion by manufacturing sector *chaebols*. Even where most of the foreign borrowing was undertaken directly by local companies, as in Indonesia, it was short-term and not invested efficiently. Finally, a high proportion of the foreign currency exposures of East Asian companies and banks were unhedged which made them vulnerable to a depreciation in the exchange rate.

The inflow of private capital was far more than was needed to finance the current account deficits of these countries. However, the short-term nature of these inflows meant that they could be reversed quite easily. This was a significant risk since they had been invested in assets that were generating high returns in the short term but were likely to lose value in the imminent future—especially if economic growth were to slow down. In other words, the capital inflows were misallocated and channelled into the wrong areas of the economy. This should have raised serious questions about the sustainability of the current account deficits in countries like Thailand.

To summarize, the strong headline macroeconomic fundamentals of the five most affected East Asian countries disguised vulnerabilities in the domestic economies, and especially in the financial sector, that were becoming increasingly apparent by the mid-1990s. Ex post analysis suggests that there were warning signs as early as 1994 or 1995. Indeed by 1995, many fund managers were starting to get worried about Thailand where the above-mentioned vul-

Table 2. Economic fundamentals of selected Asian countries

	1992	*1993*	*1994*	*1995*	*1996*
GDP growth (percentage per annum)					
Thailand	8.1	8.7	8.6	8.8	5.5
Malaysia	7.8	8.3	9.2	9.5	8.6
Indonesia	7.2	7.3	7.5	8.2	8.0
Philippines	0.3	2.1	4.4	4.8	5.7
Republic of Korea	5.1	5.8	8.6	8.9	7.1
Inflation (percentage per annum)					
Thailand	4.1	3.3	5.2	5.8	5.9
Malaysia	4.7	3.6	3.7	3.4	3.5
Indonesia	7.6	9.6	8.5	9.5	7.9
Philippines	8.9	7.6	9.0	8.1	8.4
Republic of Korea	6.2	4.8	6.2	4.5	4.9
Gross domestic savings (percentage of GDP)					
Thailand	35.2	35.6	36.0	33.6	33.7
Malaysia	36.5	37.7	38.8	39.5	42.6
Indonesia	35.3	32.5	32.2	30.6	30.2
Philippines	17.0	15.2	17.0	16.8	18.8
Republic of Korea	35.2	35.4	36.5	36.8	35.2
Gross domestic investment (percentage of GDP)					
Thailand	40.0	39.9	40.3	41.6	41.7
Malaysia	35.1	37.8	40.4	43.5	41.5
Indonesia	32.4	29.5	32.5	31.9	30.8
Philippines	20.8	23.6	23.5	21.6	23.3
Republic of Korea	36.6	35.1	36.1	37.0	38.2
Budget balance of central government (percentage of GDP)					
Thailand	2.8	2.1	2.7	3.0	0.9
Malaysia	-0.8	0.2	2.3	0.9	0.7
Indonesia	-0.4	-0.4	1.0	0.4	0.8
Philippines	-1.2	-1.5	1.0	0.6	0.3
Republic of Korea	-0.3	0.1	0.6	0.5	0.0
Current account deficits (percentage of GDP)					
Thailand	-5.7	-5.1	-5.4	-7.9	-7.9
Malaysia	-3.7	-4.7	-6.2	-8.4	-5.0
Indonesia	-2.0	-1.2	-1.6	-3.2	-3.4
Philippines	-1.6	-5.5	-4.6	-4.4	-4.7
Republic of Korea	-1.3	0.3	-1.0	-1.8	-4.8
Merchandise exports growth (percentage per annum)					
Thailand	13.7	13.4	22.7	24.8	-1.9
Malaysia	18.1	16.1	23.1	26.6	7.3
Indonesia	14.0	8.3	9.9	18.0	5.8
Philippines	11.1	15.8	18.5	29.4	17.7
Republic of Korea	8.0	7.7	15.7	31.5	4.1

Source: Asian Development Bank (1998).

nerabilities were most apparent. The problems in the other affected countries appeared less severe by comparison, but they all shared a common pattern of vulnerabilities (Herman and Sharma, 1998).

Despite this, private capital inflows accelerated right up to 1997 and, in doing so, are likely to have further increased the vulnerabilities that were already apparent in the affected economies. Table 1 shows that the five affected East Asian countries had net private inflows of $41 billion in 1994. By 1996, this had jumped to $93 billion. Then, in 1997, the net inflow turned into an estimated outflow of $12 billion and, as mentioned earlier, the reversals came from commercial bank lending and portfolio investment. The following section attempts to explain why bank and portfolio flows into East Asia accelerated at a time when vulnerabilities were becoming more apparent.

3. The dynamics behind excessive capital inflows

Pegged exchange rates in some East Asian countries did play a significant part in attracting excessive capital inflows. However, simply placing the blame on pegged exchange rates does not explain why international financial markets trusted these pegs. An awareness of emerging vulnerabilities should have placed some question mark on the sustainability of these pegs. This did not happen, since financial markets' interpretation of the data coming out of these economies was inadequate.

Let us begin by summarizing the information that was coming out of the region around 1995. On the positive side, economic growth rates were high (and were expected to remain strong given high domestic savings and investment rates), inflation was not excessive and fiscal balances were healthy. While widening current account deficits and appreciating real exchange rates were being discussed, exports were still growing at a strong rate, suggesting that the external position was sustainable. On the negative side, there were worries over rising short-term foreign debt, the emergence of asset bubbles in many East Asian countries and the increasing vulnerability of the financial sector.

Thus, the data coming out of the region provided mixed signals to international financial markets. Yet by continuing to direct capital in large amounts to East Asia, markets chose to attach greater weight to the more optimistic headline macroeconomic data. There were a number of reasons for this.

First, there appeared to be "asymmetric transparency" of the above data. Figures were readily available on economic growth rates, inflation, fiscal balances, exports and imports—in other words, the headline macroeconomic data that tended to give positive signals about East Asia. Of course, information on current account deficits and credit/monetary growth—showing more worrying developments—were also easy to obtain. However, the data that were less transparent and a lot harder to interpret were those on the vulnerabilities that were beginning to emerge in the banking and corporate sector, on the intermediation of the capital inflows, and even on the level of foreign debt. Foreign debt data were available but difficult to interpret since most of this debt was owed by private companies. Thus the more transparent data were those indicators that tended to show East Asia in a more positive light.

According to an industry analyst in a Japanese bank in Singapore, in many countries there was:

> "little quarterly information about the performance of companies ... more specifically, the debt data was problematic and public information, especially on factors like non-performing loans, was bad".

Elaborating on this issue from the point of view of portfolio investors, the managing director of the Singapore office of a European investment bank noted that:

> "A lot of the superior returns (in South-East Asian countries) came from either asset inflation and PE (price to earnings ratio) expansion. Though PEs were well above their long run average, there was little data to enable a proper analysis and there was no way of assessing whether these returns have historically been the norm. Therefore, people looked at the 8 per cent economic growth, the region's excellent track record and assumed that this converted into high earnings growth. Well it does not!".

But this point, about the lack of transparency of micro information, should not be overdone. For a start, transparency is not necessarily the same as data availability. Plenty of data were available but it took considerable time and effort to obtain them. For a number of reasons, many lenders and investors did not seem to have sufficient incentive to undertake this rigorous exercise.

- In the case of lenders, there was complacency stemming from the implicit government guarantees provided to local banks and companies. This is the "moral hazard" argument, according to which international banks believed that they would not have to suffer the full consequences of sloppy lending decisions.
- In the case of large global investors, portfolio diversification may have reduced the incentive to gather information in detail. Only a small proportion of overall portfolios (about 2 per cent) of the major investment management companies are devoted to emerging markets. Now, the more diversified a portfolio, the less important it may be to spend time

> gathering more information on a small piece of it—especially if this information is hard to get or interpret.[2]

Secondly, an important factor that probably swayed markets towards attaching greater weight to the positive data coming out of East Asia was the credibility attached to policy makers in the region. This was primarily a function of the good track record of these countries. However, there were also many intangible factors that boosted credibility. For a start, in the early 1990s there was increasing talk of the superiority of "Asian values"; there was a well publicized report by the World Bank in 1993 on the "East Asian Miracle" (World Bank, 1993) and the credit ratings of these countries were very favourable. In addition, the Bank of Thailand enjoyed an excellent reputation for economic management, as did other central banks in the region. Of course, there were voices of dissent, most notably that of Paul Krugman, but these were more than offset by the optimistic view of the region and its policy makers.

Thirdly, this reliance on credibility and past performance was backward looking and meant that markets glossed over the developmental and institutional underpinnings of the East Asian countries. Thus, for instance, the implications of the interlocking relations between companies, banks and politicians were not properly understood. Neither was the deterioration in public governance in certain important areas of the economy (especially the decline in the quality of oversight by the Bank of Thailand that had taken place since the late 1980s). These considerations became critical with capital account liberalization and financial deregulation, since the bedrock of the efficient intermediation and investment of increasing amounts of capital inflows are effective institutional settings and relationships. As the director of a fund management company in Hong Kong (China), told the author:

> "There was an ignorance of institutional factors, especially in Indonesia. With hindsight, we can now say power here was heavily concentrated and used effectively for three decades, but perhaps not in a way that was conducive to robust growth in the future. It is therefore important to pinpoint turning points in trends of institutional configuration and their relation to economic development. Certain institutional arrangements are effective under certain conditions but later outlive their usefulness".

A fourth possible reason why market participants attached more importance to positive headline macroeconomic indicators in East Asia is that they

---

2 See World Bank (1997) for more detail on this point.

were influenced by past models of why currency crises occur. Under these models, currency crises are caused by excessive government deficits against a background of a fixed exchange rate regime. To finance these deficits, the government follows an expansionary monetary policy. This increases inflation and leads to a rise in the real exchange rate and a burgeoning trade deficit. Sooner or later the market realizes that official reserves will be insufficient to maintain the exchange rate peg and this triggers a speculative attack on the currency. There was little sign of monetary or fiscal profligacy in the affected Asian economies. Government budgets were in surplus and, while growth in monetary aggregates was high, inflation rates were relatively subdued. Given these factors, and the fact that export growth remained very strong until 1996, most market participants did not question the sustainability of the growing current account deficits in Thailand or worry about the sustainability of the currency pegs.

With hindsight, one factor that may have been ignored was the appreciation of real effective exchange rates in the countries of South-East Asia. But the question of declining competitiveness and the sustainability of the current account deficits in Thailand and Malaysia appeared to hit many people only in 1996 when exports slowed down dramatically throughout the region. Even then, there was a lagged response to the changing data and foreign lending and investment continued at high rates. As the head of research in a major US bank in Singapore told the author, "it takes time for an ocean-liner to turn around".

While financial markets' optimistic interpretation of economic fundamentals accounted for part of the excess capital inflows into the region between 1994 and 1996, this was exacerbated by the generation of a "bull herd" mentality. There are internal characteristics of the fund management and lending industry that encourage this behaviour, especially in an environment of optimism and high returns.

Starting with the fund management industry, it is necessary to point out two key facts. First, the performance of fund managers tends, to a significant extent, to be assessed relative to each other. Secondly, fund managers also tend to be assessed on a short-term (usually quarterly) basis.

Now the returns in most East Asian equity markets were high; even though the Thai stock market weakened in 1996 it had grown substantially prior to then. A fund manager who was deciding whether to invest in East Asia in the mid-1990s would have realized that many of his competitors were already in the region and have been earning high returns. He would have two options:

- Option A would be to invest in East Asia. The potential gain would be that the investment turns out to be good and he makes high returns; but the gains would be limited by the fact that the fund manager does not necessarily get ranked higher than his competitors. The potential loss would be that the investment turns out to be a bad one; however, the penalty to the fund manager would be limited by the fact that many of his competitors also make a loss.

- Option B would be to not invest in East Asia. The potential gain would be that the fund manager makes higher returns by investing elsewhere and in the process gets ranked higher than his competitors. The potential loss would be that his alternative investment turns out to not be as profitable as investing in East Asia and in the process he gets ranked lower than many of his competitors.

Which option would a fund manager choose? The potential losses are definitely greater under option B; thus the final decision would hinge on the probability that the gains under this option would be higher. Given that East Asia was a high return market about which most people were optimistic, it is unlikely that this probability would have been high enough to offset the losses that the fund manager would make by not investing in East Asia. He therefore follows the 'herd'—that is, other fund managers—and invests in the region.

Moreover, even if the fund manager was worried about East Asia's fundamentals, he may still have invested if he believed that he could make a capital gain and timely exit before fundamentals brought down the market. This is the "greater fool theory", which an economist in a European bank in Hong Kong (China), described as follows:

> "you know this is a stupid investment but you think somebody else can be even more stupid and take it off your hands at a higher price".

In summary, the way that fund managers are assessed can push them towards operating in a herd and having a short-term outlook.[3] This in turn may lead to excessive exuberance or over-reaction in financial markets.

In the commercial banking industry, too, there were internal factors that encouraged higher levels of lending—perhaps more than was justified by the high returns that were expected at the time. These included intense competition, the relatively short time period over which lending officers were assessed and the relatively high turnover of staff in overseas commercial banks. These compelled lending officers to make loans even where the viability of

3 See World Bank (1997) for more information on the herd behaviour of fund managers. In addition, Asian Development Bank (1998) and Montes (1998) touch on the relationship between the performance evaluation of fund managers and herd behaviour.

the project may have been unclear. At the same time, the high turnover of staff meant that mistakes committed by banks in the past (for example, in Latin America in the 1980s) were never fully learned. As Callum Henderson, a currency analyst at Standard and Poors, mentions in his book "Asia Falling" (Henderson, 1998, p. 94):

> "if economic history teaches us two things it is that markets never learn from their mistakes (partly because the 28 year-old who gets fired for making the mistake is replaced with a 22 year-old with no experience and more importantly no history) and also, in the passionate throes of economic excess, fundamentals are forgotten entirely".

In summary, even as vulnerabilities emerged as a result of excessive capital inflows, money continued to pour into the affected East Asian economies between 1994 and 1996. This was due to a one-sided reading of fundamentals and the herd behaviour described above. Both of these factors were interrelated. The skewed reading of fundamentals generated excessive optimism about future returns, which triggered herd behaviour. This led to a greater amount of capital flowing in that boosted economic activity and returns in asset markets and led to a further increase in optimism that in turn went on to further fuel herd behaviour. Figure 1 illustrates the dynamics behind the excessive capital flows into the affected East Asian economies.

Figure 1. Dynamics of excessive capital inflows into East Asia

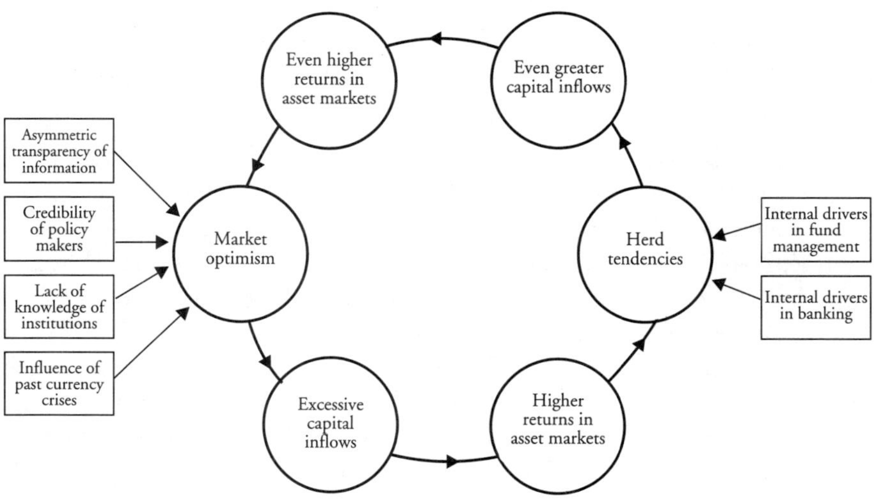

4. The reversal of attitudes in Thailand

The reversal of capital flows was triggered in Thailand and spread to other countries in the region. The initial catalyst that weakened the confidence of international financial markets was a dramatic slowdown in export growth throughout the region in 1996 (see table 2). In the early part of that year, most market analysts felt that this slowdown was temporary and, in some countries, caused by cyclical factors such as a decline in semi-conductor exports and a sharp appreciation of the US dollar to which most of the region's currencies were informally pegged. However, when this trend became sustained into the middle of the year, the markets began to focus on structural reasons—that is, the emergence of China as a major trading competitor and declining competitiveness across the region due to the growth of real wages.

The impact was most severe in Thailand where export growth became negative and made the large current account deficit look less sustainable. Moreover, since the vulnerabilities in Thailand's economy appeared more severe than in the other countries, this led to some investors and currency speculators looking closer at that country's fundamentals. More time and effort were expended in trying to obtain less transparent information: on the health of the banking sector, on foreign debt levels and foreign reserve levels and so on. Obtaining such information was far from easy but not impossible. The few investors and speculators who managed to obtain such information put together a picture that led them to believe that the current account deficit and the baht's informal peg to the US dollar were far from sustainable. As Callum Henderson says in "Asia Falling" (Henderson, 1998, p. 91):

> "Adding up the total of the current account deficit, external debt and service costs of that debt, Thailand had the heaviest external funding requirement in Asia".

This realization came to some market participants during the second half of the year. But, even then, most lenders and investors continued to retain the belief that Thailand's long-run fundamentals (that is, its high savings and investment rate and its high growth and subdued inflation rate) were healthy and would see it through its short-term weakness. As long as the economy was booming, companies would have little problem repaying their loans and their investments in the real estate market would continue to boom. This static and short-term thinking also extended to the other affected economies, where short-term capital continued to flow in at a high rate. As a market participant in Singapore commented, "nobody seemed to ask what would happen if growth slowed down".

However, a series of developments began to shift the tide of sentiment in Thailand. For a start, economic growth did slow down over 1996 to 5.5 per cent from an average of 8.8 per cent during the previous year. Just as important, property and stock markets turned down in the wake of slowing economic activity. Furthermore, in early 1997, the Thai authorities announced that a budget deficit of 1.1 per cent of GDP was registered for the last quarter of 1996. This unsettled investors, especially given the fact that earlier currency crises had all been associated with problems on the fiscal front. Finally, the closures of some financial institutions confirmed fears about the financial sector's health. None of these factors on their own carried great weight, but one by one the positive indicators that the market participants had given greater credence to were worsening while the negative features that had been downgraded in importance were increasingly coming to the fore.

By early 1997, the balance of opinion about Thailand had shifted from an emphasis on the positive to a more neutral attitude. By then, however, a critical mass of "non-believers" had built up, including hedge funds, and a tentative speculative attack on the currency had already taken place. A more major attack was launched in earnest in February 1997. While this was successfully fended off by the authorities, an increasing number of foreign and local players were beginning to bet against the baht. The balance of opinion had shifted from neutral to negative. The currency was coming under increasing pressure and by July 1997 the authorities had little option but to let the baht float and devalue.

Though commercial bank lending to Thailand had slowed during the first half of 1997, it nevertheless continued to increase in absolute terms. However, after the devaluation of the currency, there was a dramatic swing: Sachs and Radelet calculate (using Bank for International Settlements (BIS) data) that while net inflows of bank loans during the first half of 1997 were US$13 billion, net outflows during the second half of the year were approximately US$34 billion (Sachs and Radelet, 1998).

To sum up, the sharp slowdown in exports throughout the region in 1996 acted as a "wake-up call" to investors and speculators in Thailand (which had experienced a contraction in exports and also had the most apparent vulnerabilities). The increasing analysis and unearthing of information in Thailand, together with an actual worsening in macroeconomic performance, led to a shift in sentiment that led to a reversal in capital flows by investors and then by lenders.

5. The dynamics behind excessive capital outflows

5.1 The dynamics behind the spread of the crisis

The spread of contagion can be divided into three strands. The first strand was the spread of currency instability from Thailand to the Philippines, Malaysia, Indonesia and, to a lesser extent, Singapore. The second strand was the spread to North Asia and Hong Kong (China). The final strand was the effect on developing economies in South Asia, Latin America and Eastern Europe.

There have been two major forces behind the contagion (Herman and Sharma, 1998).

- While the slowdown in exports in East Asia served as a wake-up call to investors in Thailand, the Thai baht's devaluation served as a wake-up call to investors in other economies in the region and, indeed, in other emerging markets.
- At the same time, there are strong trade and investment links, both within ASEAN and, increasingly, within the global economy. This also helped to spread the crisis, sometimes to economies that did not have problematic fundamentals.

The spread of the crisis from Thailand to the Philippines, Malaysia and Indonesia was a function of both of the above factors. Strong trade and investment links led to speculative attacks on the currencies of Taiwan, Province of China, Hong Kong (China) and Singapore—economies that had superior fundamentals to the South-East Asian 4. In the case of the Republic of Korea, the wake-up call seemed to have a predominant role since the domestic economy did not have significant trade and investment links with the other countries but shared a number of similar and problematic fundamentals. Finally, the spreading of currency instability to other emerging economies in South Asia, Eastern Europe and Latin America was in some cases a function of a 'wake-up call' to investors, in other cases a function of increasing trade and investment linkages (especially through commodity prices), and often a combination of both these factors.

Now, the above analysis gives the rationale behind contagion. However, as of mid-1998, contagion has been an ongoing process whose characteristics have been changing.

- First, the "sensitivity" to contagion—that is, the speed at which problems spread from one country to another—varies at different points of time. At times of market pessimism, as was the case in 1998, this is greater. At the time of writing (mid-1998), pessimism among market participants regarding East Asia's prospects appeared to have increased significantly. The increase in pessimism occurred after the first quarter of 1998 (during the early part of 1998, portfolio capital began to flow back to some economies, but this has since been reversed).

- Secondly, while contagion initially spread from a small country, Thailand, to its neighbours and then to East Asia, today it is the large countries (Japan and Indonesia) that are generating contagion.

The first point implies that investors are likely to respond more quickly to perceived similarities in fundamentals between countries or to given trade and investment linkages than they were in the past. The second point implies that these trade and investment linkages are themselves likely to be stronger since the major problems are emanating from larger and more influential economies like Japan. This suggests that the forces driving contagion have strengthened and that international financial markets at present are potentially more volatile than they have been for a long time.

5.2 The dynamics behind the depth of the crisis

After the informal pegs were removed the currencies of the crisis countries went into free fall. The large magnitude of the currency depreciations can be explained by the actions of a number of players. First, there were the speculators, both foreign and local, who had initially attacked the currencies. Secondly, the speculative attacks and depreciating currencies led to a rush to buy dollars by local corporations in countries like Thailand and Indonesia who had a large amount of unhedged foreign currency borrowings from abroad. Thirdly, the prospect of devaluing currencies led longer-term investors (for example, pension funds) or those who had retained faith in these economies to also move out. At the same time, and very significantly, commercial banks stopped rolling over their short-term loans. All these together created a huge fall in the value of the currencies.

However, such analysis is insufficient in explaining the dynamics of the crisis. This has been a function of a vicious cycle created by two simultaneously interacting factors. For a start, there has been a steady downward reappraisal of the fundamentals of the affected East Asian countries by foreign lenders and both foreign and local investors. This, in turn, leads to downward currency expectations and, in the process, tends to trigger an element of panic in the financial markets. The outcome is an actual worsening in fundamentals, which then leads to another round of the cycle.

The downward reappraisal of fundamentals has been an ongoing process meaning that, at each stage of reappraisal, the currencies have been undergoing a bout of volatility. This downward reappraisal of fundamentals is a function of four developments.

First, as mentioned earlier, the downward reappraisal of fundamentals is to an extent triggered by an actual deterioration in fundamentals in all the affected countries, brought about by currency depreciation. These have ignited the vulnerabilities inherent in the banking system in that they sharply raised the value of debt in local currency and, moreover, the withdrawal of funds by investors and banks led to a collapse of the asset bubbles—leaving domestic banks and companies heavily exposed—and an ensuing credit crunch in the domestic economy. The effect has been most severe in Indonesia, followed by Thailand and the Republic of Korea (United Nations, 1998).

Secondly, since the breakout of the crisis, investors and lenders have increasingly been looking at a broader range of variables when assessing the East Asian countries' credit and investment worthiness. As mentioned earlier, they had previously focused primarily on macroeconomic indicators. Today they are beginning to look increasingly at not just microeconomic but also institutional variables. As a result, increasing attention is being paid to the "inefficient set up of Asian corporations", "crony capitalism", corruption, the links between politicians and businesses and so forth. At the same time, social and political tensions have increased as a result of the crisis and this has also been factored in to the markets' assessment. As the author was told by a financial markets expert in Bangkok:

> "Markets have gone way beyond what they were thinking in 1995 ... they are thinking about a full economic development scenario, not just a financial scenario".

Thirdly, given the heightened expectations of market participants, they have been disappointed by the policy response to the crisis. For instance, apart from clear cases of backtracking on reform, most notably in Indonesia, there remain a number of policy inconsistencies. In all the affected East Asian countries there are clear impediments—especially political and social—to full-scale economic reform that the authorities, in the eyes of market participants, seem either unwilling or unable to remove. Moreover, the reform programmes undertaken by Indonesia, the Philippines, Thailand and the Republic of Korea have not been entirely satisfactory from the viewpoint of market participants (this point is elaborated on in the next section). To quote a senior economist in a prominent fund management company in Hong Kong (China):

> "The whole policy process has lagged the markets. At each leg of the crisis—that is a 10 per cent or more depreciation of currencies—there were policy errors. Policy was not realigned in a credible and consistent way".

Finally, the downward reassessment of fundamentals was reinforced by bouts of contagion. For example, when Indonesia's perceived fundamentals were downgraded, markets feared that this might impact adversely on other countries in the region through trade and investment links and therefore they reassessed their fundamentals also.

As mentioned earlier, this reappraisal of fundamentals lead to a loss of confidence and downward currency expectations which, in turn, lead to financial panic. Thus, according to this model, both fundamentals and financial panic are complementary. However, the starting point is the perceived and actual deterioration of fundamentals. In a more dynamic context, every time there is a downward reappraisal of fundamentals (say, owing to contagion or some evidence of policy backtracking) capital flight occurs and the currency undergoes a bout of volatility. However, this is not the end of the story since the initial withdrawal of capital fuels further downward currency expectations and leads to more people withdrawing from local markets. In the final analysis, more capital is withdrawn than is justified by the extent to which fundamentals are downgraded.

A point to note is that financial panic would not have taken place if there were not genuine concerns about the fundamentals of the affected countries.

Figure 2. Dynamics of capital flight in East Asia

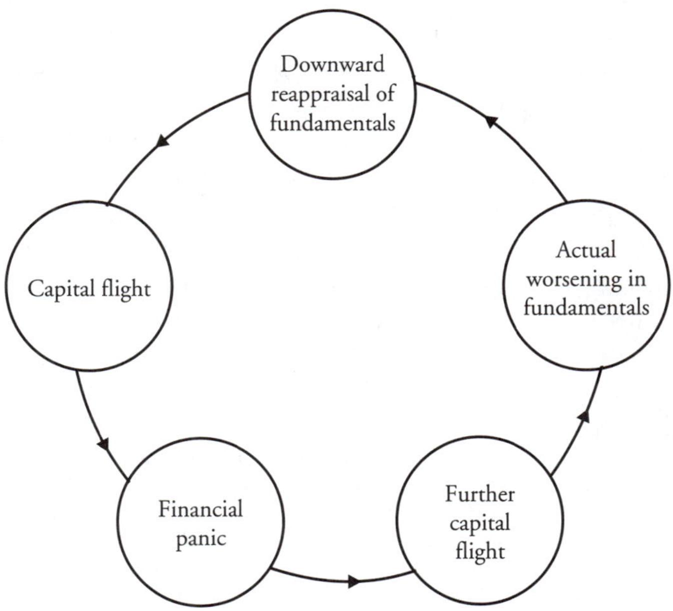

On the other hand, it is obvious that the currencies of the affected East Asian countries have fallen to levels well below those warranted by fundamentals on the eve of the crisis. This was owing to the fact that a genuine, and to an extent warranted, reassessment of fundamentals led to the financial panic.

The immediate issue facing policy makers is how to break out of the vicious cycle that has been created. To do this, policy makers need to restore the confidence of financial markets. This will, in turn, halt and eventually reverse the process of capital flight. The issues and dilemmas that need to be resolved if this is to be achieved are discussed in the next section.

6. The requirements for restoring confidence

The IMF programmes in Thailand, Indonesia, the Philippines and the Republic of Korea were introduced with the aim of restoring confidence. As of mid-1998, they did not appear to have entirely succeeded.[4] The market participants who were interviewed during the author's mission to Asia were asked to give possible reasons for this.

While most market participants appeared to feel that the framework of the IMF programmes were fundamentally sound, they also pointed to a number of shortcomings:

- IMF did not anticipate the severity of the downturn that these countries were undergoing. This initially led it to be heavy handed in its fiscal requirements. To its credit, the Fund realized this and relaxed fiscal targets in the relevant countries. But at the same time, the lack of anticipation as to the depth of the crisis led to too little money being committed.
- IMF should have been more sensitive to social conditions and feelings before implementing measures like abolishing subsidies and closing banks in Indonesia—measures that led to mayhem.
- IMF did not go far enough in its measures—in fact, it has not really resolved the key issues. The whole issue of debt workouts, which is crucial to restoring confidence, has not been addressed directly by IMF. Similarly, in the area of financial restructuring, IMF has not gone far enough in forcing national governments to undertake institutional reforms.

---

4 Admittedly, the currencies of Thailand and Republic of Korea had stabilized, and in fact strengthened. This has allowed these countries to reduce interest rates. However, Thailand and Republic of Korea cannot be said to have fully restored confidence. Much of the strengthening in their currencies was brought about by significant corrections in their current account positions (from deficits to surpluses). Yet, Thailand continued to experience periodic net outflows from the capital account in the first half of 1998 and both countries were almost entirely cut off from private sources of international finance.

At the same time, a minority of the market participants believed that the IMF approach was itself flawed and that the programmes contributed to the deepening of the crisis. In particular, the policy of higher interest rates has, according to them, been counter-productive; it has failed in most cases to halt the net outflow of capital and has intensified the economic downturn. Here IMF failed to take into account the high level of debt in the affected economies. According to these participants, IMF would have been better placed in keeping interest rates at a low enough level to allow local businesses to tick over and concentrating on resolving the foreign debt issue through promoting dialogue between foreign creditors and domestic debtors.

Despite some difference in opinion about the IMF programmes, the market participants who were interviewed shared some similar views about what needed to be done to restore confidence.

According to them, the key policy is for the national authorities to get the domestic financial sector working again. This involves a recapitalizing and restructuring of the financial sector. As part of this, market participants agree that debt needs to be both socialized and written down. Simply rescheduling debt is not felt to be sufficient in a country like Indonesia where, according to one market participant, "even if you renew lending forever you will not get your money back". Instead, a combination of nationalization and debt write-down (probably through debt-equity swaps) is suggested as the best way forward. Moreover, such a policy would also ensure that both foreign creditors and local banks pay the price for imprudent policies and thereby go some way to containing the moral hazard problem.

While such a measure may be necessary to regain confidence, this is unlikely to be sustained unless the authorities go further. The above policies solve the debt problem but further steps need to be undertaken to fully recapitalize and restructure the financial sector. Now doing this efficiently would be far from simple since it would involve a package of institutional and legal changes. To quote the director of a fund management company in Hong Kong (China):

> "Markets are looking for more than just a macroeconomic adjustment. They are looking for financial restructuring and a legal and institutional adjustment is expected for financial restructuring to be viable".

Now part of the required policies would involve legal changes. In this respect, the introduction of detailed bankruptcy codes is important as are the reform of laws to allow foreigners to own land and buy companies in countries like Thailand and the Republic of Korea. The latter measure is essential if foreigners are to be induced to buy up local banks and companies, which are now very attractively priced.

Other advocated measures include improved transparency and better accounting and information procedures. Transparency is vital for investors to be able to decide whether progress is being made on the institutional reforms. More to the point though, it is vital if they are to be able to select good investment opportunities. For instance, many Asian stocks are attractively valued today, but investors argue that without better transparency there is no acceptable way of distinguishing a good company from a bad company.

In summary, many investors and lenders are now assessing a broader range of variables and believe that a reform process will not be credible unless it involves deep-set institutional changes. As a senior economist working in fund management in Hong Kong (China), said:

> "There are a number of variables that are said to be uniquely Asian and attractive. These include high savings rates, high rates of economic growth, high productivity and small government. The financial crisis has not changed perceptions that these are high growth economies with these advantages. What has changed is perceptions about corporate governance, transparency, and about the pillars on which economies are built and capital is intermediated".

Most market participants believe that evidence of sincere efforts to undertake financial restructuring and institutional reform should be enough to restore confidence and attract capital back into the affected economies. They point out that this has not happened so far, citing evidence of backtracking and policy inconsistencies in all these countries.

However, the progress that markets expect may not be easy to achieve in the short-run owing to strong opposition in many countries to these measures. The chief economist in a major European bank in Hong Kong (China), was sceptical that the nationalization of banks and the write-down of debt would take place, as a result of opposition from both foreign creditors and local owners of banks and companies. Similarly, having better transparency sounds easy enough but may have serious consequences. Better transparency means subjecting oneself to the full glare and discipline of market forces. This, in turn, is likely to generate pressures for deeper institutional and even political change. Finally, undertaking such deep-set reforms could be difficult at a time when the affected economies are experiencing sharp downturns and unemployment is rising.

Moreover, even those countries that do succeed in pushing through financial sector and institutional reform at a pace agreeable to financial markets could see their progress undone by contagion from "less successful" countries. Thus in Thailand, where the authorities are attempting to undertake financial sector reform, with the institutional changes that this implies, there are fears that contagion from

Indonesia (which appears to have the most intractable problems in the region) could destabilize the economy and undo all efforts to initiate change.

Given these problems, it is not surprising that market participants are very bearish about the prospects for the region. Most participants expect no significant recovery in the affected economies for the next two to three years. A regional strategist in Hong Kong (China), admitted that "there is no quick fix to what is happening". Moreover, attention is increasingly focusing on the downward risks that could make conditions even worse—namely, problems emanating from Japan or a devaluation by China.

Restoring confidence in the short term therefore looks like a far from simple task, and one that could be unhinged by exogenous shocks. Some of the issues that policy makers may need to consider in the light of this situation are discussed in the next section.

7. Short-term implications for policy makers in East Asia

In the short term, the issue is how governments can restore confidence. This, in turn, means influencing and, in this case, changing the direction of market expectations. This section is not meant to be prescriptive—it simply suggests issues that need to be considered if financial markets' confidence is to be restored.

A major implication of the preceding analysis is that financial markets are looking at a broader range of variables when assessing the affected East Asian countries. In this sense, if the authorities want to regain the confidence of financial markets, it could be important to give "signals" that they are sincere in their efforts to fully implement financial sector reform, with all the institutional changes that this implies. This will in turn determine how quickly currencies are stabilized and the speed at which interest rates can be brought down.

Nevertheless, there are two dilemmas confronting policy makers.[5]

- First, the speed and distance of reform in the affected economies are likely to be limited by political and social considerations as well as by the severe macroeconomic problems that they are facing. There is really no easy way out on this front, but adequate and well-targeted financial support from outside could help. For instance, it could enable governments to provide some compensation to losers—via safety nets etc.

5 The seriousness of these dilemmas has led some economists to advocate temporary capital controls for the crisis-hit economies, to allow policy makers time to implement structural reforms against a background of lower interest rates (and relatively safe from external shocks). Paul Krugman's article in *Fortune* magazine is representative of this viewpoint (see Krugman, 1998b).

- Second, contagion could set back reform in the affected economies. Thus the reform process needs to be coordinated to some extent across the region—since if large countries like Indonesia slip behind they could hold the others back. At the same time, it is becoming imperative for the Japanese Government to address the structural problems besetting its economy.

8. Medium-term implications for developing country governments and the international community

The analysis in this paper throws up a number of issues that need to be considered by policy makers over the medium term. Once again, the aim is not to be prescriptive but to suggest areas that merit consideration.

The issue for developing country governments is how to better manage increasing amounts of private capital flows in an environment of financial globalization. An important consideration is to ensure better intermediation of these flows through improving the decision-making capacity of financial institutions and deepening financial markets, improving corporate governance and, above all, giving due thought to the speed and sequencing of financial liberalization. While these are very important issues, they have been discussed in detail elsewhere and will not be taken any further in this paper. Rather, the analysis provided here points to two other issues that also merit consideration by national policy makers.

First, there is a need for a wider provision of information—that is, better transparency. Part of the reason why banks and investors supplied excess capital to East Asia prior to 1997 was that the emerging vulnerabilities in the region were not as transparent as its macroeconomic strengths. Thus information on a wider range of variables—including microeconomic and institutional variables—needs to be made more readily available. This requires adequate investment in national statistical systems and to have better accounting and reporting standards for companies (Herman and Sharma, 1998).

However, and this is the second point, international financial markets do not always interpret information well. In East Asia, prior to the crisis, markets did not make best use of what information was available and furthermore were influenced by herd tendencies. In this sense, we can say that financial markets are not always efficient and can be volatile. National governments, therefore, need to be able to manage financial market volatility. This brings a number of issues to the fore, but there are two that are particularly relevant in the context of the preceding analysis.

The first issue concerns capital controls and capital account liberalization. While many economists see the benefit of a Chilean type system of controls on short-term capital flows, especially for a small economy, whether it is practical is open to doubt. While the Chilean method appears to have initially limited speculative inflows, it has also been increasingly evaded. Some critics also argue that the controls are damaging Chile's access to supplies of foreign capital. In the wake of these criticisms and, with Chile's currency and stock market being affected by the economic fallout of the East Asian crisis, the controls were significantly eased during the summer of 1998. The lesson here could be that controls on short-term capital inflows are unlikely to work unless all countries adopt them. Whether capital controls will be effective at a national level remains an unresolved issue.

As regards capital account liberalization, there is widespread agreement that while this may be inevitable, and ultimately beneficial, it needs to be preceded by the development of the financial sector and strong fundamentals. The chief economist (Asia) in a US investment bank in Hong Kong (China), seems to sum up this view well:

> "Countries open to global capital for a reason—it is welfare enhancing. But to open to global capital is to expose any vulnerability in your economy to the world".

The second issue is that of exchange rate policy. Pegged exchange rates played an important role in encouraging short-term capital flows to East Asia. While some economists have advocated fully floating exchange rates, there is a school of thought that has argued for fully fixed exchange rates in the form of a currency board system. However, neither system provides a guarantee against currency volatility and it appears that for most situations something in between—a form of "managed exchange rate flexibility" is appropriate.

The analysis in this paper also provides implications for policy makers at the international level. While trying to help international financial markets to work more efficiently, policy makers need to realize that they can never be totally efficient.

In terms of helping financial markets to work better, an international surveillance/early warning system could be set up to monitor the fundamentals of individual countries—especially the fundamentals of the financial sector. However, simply providing figures may not be sufficient—on countries that they know little about, markets may need to be guided. For instance, the appropriate capital adequacy ratio may vary among banks in different countries. What could be helpful in this respect is to have international standards that have countries falling into different categories and then to rate their fundamentals. For example, certain standards could be set for East Asia that are different from the standards that are set for Eastern Europe. In this way, financial markets would be provided with better information and policy makers would also have an incentive to adopt internationally acceptable standards for their financial systems.

At the same time, though, international policy makers need to consider how best to deal with inherent tendencies of financial markets to overshoot.

Renewed consideration could be given to methods of discouraging short-term speculative capital, through controls or through some variant of a Tobin tax. Such policies may be more efficient if they are passed at the international level, since unilateral measures may lead to individual countries getting penalized. How successful they would be is, however, far from clear at this stage.

Another interesting issue to consider is possible regulation, or the encouragement of self-regulation, of international financial market institutions in order to reduce the frequency and scale of booms and busts in lending and portfolio investment.[6] Market institutions may have an incentive to self-regulate since many have made losses in East Asia as a result of the present crisis. While one is not prescribing any specific measures, further research could be undertaken on several possible areas where regulation could be introduced at an international level, or self-regulation encouraged. These could include enforcing tighter regulation on the required experience and training of analysts covering emerging markets, a reassessment of the criteria by which the performance of portfolio managers are evaluated and strengthening the risk evaluation systems in commercial and investment banks. In this respect, the international community could encourage market institutions to discuss whether they have any common interest or see any scope for further self-regulation.

While the measures discussed above seek to reduce the likelihood of another crisis, they cannot eliminate this possibility. Therefore, the international community also needs to consider how to better respond to a crisis of similar magnitude in the future. This brings us to the issue of the role of IMF. The Fund has received its share of unfair criticism, since this crisis has differed from previous ones and has been a learning process for everybody. However, there are two issues that will need to be resolved in the future.

First, it is not clear as to how well equipped the Fund was to deal with the present crisis. IMF was set up to assist countries with balance of payments difficulties, and its ability to advise countries on issues as far-reaching as financial-sector restructuring and institutional reform is not clear. It appears

6 A recent paper by Stephany Griffith-Jones advances the case for regulation in source countries of portfolio flows. According to Griffith-Jones, risk-weighted cash requirements for mutual funds will both protect domestic investors in source countries and discourage excessive surges of portfolio flows to emerging markets. For more detailed information, see Griffith-Jones (1998).

that the World Bank may have more expertise on these issues. This calls for more coordination between IMF and other international organizations when dealing with similar crises.

Secondly, IMF programmes generally seek to enable full repayment of foreign creditors. While this is necessary if confidence is to be restored and new credit flows resume, it has the "moral hazard" aspect of freeing lenders from the cost of not sufficiently assessing the creditworthiness of their borrowers. Maybe the present crisis could eradicate such attitudes, if mechanisms are worked out to ensure that both creditors and borrowers suffer for bad lending and borrowing decisions.

9. Conclusion

The dynamics behind excess capital inflows to East Asia before 1997 and excess capital outflows after July 1997 provide numerous issues for consideration by policy makers.

In the short term, domestic policy makers in the region need to restore confidence. For certain reasons, this is difficult for them to achieve on their own. The policy expectations of financial market participants have grown more demanding since, unlike in the past, they are focusing increasingly on the institutional drawbacks of the region and would like to see deep-set institutional reform. At the same time, social and political considerations may limit the ability of governments to sufficiently satisfy these expectations. It is therefore necessary to have properly targeted financial support from abroad, to reduce the domestic constraints to reform. It is also important to have better coordinated policies (both across the region and in the industrialized economies) to contain contagion and to create international economic conditions that allow the affected East Asian countries to stabilize and reform more speedily.

Over the medium term, both domestic and international policy makers need to implement measures that help financial markets allocate resources more efficiently. However, they have to realize that this will not entirely eliminate the potential of short-term capital flows to destabilise recipient economies, since financial markets have inherent characteristics that cause them to overshoot. As a result, it is imperative that developing countries do not implement full capital account convertibility until they possess both sound economic fundamentals and an efficient financial sector. At the same time, the international community needs to re-assess the roles of multilateral financial institutions as part of making the architecture of international finance better suited to deterring and quelling crises.

References

Akyuz, Yilmaz (1998). "The East Asian financial crisis: back to the future?". UNCTAD, Geneva, mimeo (January).

Asian Development Bank (1998). "The financial crisis in Asia". *Asian Development Outlook 1998*. Hong Kong (China): Oxford University Press.

Bhagwati, Jagdish (1998). "The capital myth: The difference between trade in widgets and dollars". *Foreign Affairs*, vol. 77, No. 3 (May/June).

Corsetti, Giancarlo, Paolo Pesenti and Nouriel Roubini (1998). "What caused the Asian currency and financial crisis?". New York: New York University, mimeo.

Davies, Gavyn (1998). "Causes, cures and consequences of the Asian economic crisis". *Goldman Sachs Research*, New York (February).

Griffith-Jones, Stephany (1998). "How to protect developing countries from volatility of capital flows?". United Kingdom: University of Sussex, mimeo (June).

Hale, David (1997). "The Thai baht: a crisis of a different kind". *Nikko Capital Trends*. Washington, D.C.: Nikko Research Centre (August).

Henderson, Callum (1998). *Asia Falling? Making Sense of the Asian Currency Crisis and its Aftermath*. Singapore: McGraw-Hill.

Herman, Barry and Krishnan Sharma (1998). "Financial flows, financial crisis, financial policy needs" in *International Finance and Developing Countries in a Year of Crisis*, B. Herman and K. Sharma, eds. Tokyo: United Nations University Press.

Institute of International Finance (1998). "Capital flows to emerging market economies". Washington, D.C. (January).

International Monetary Fund (1997). *World Economic Outlook: Interim Assessment*. Washington, D.C. (December).

Krugman, Paul (1998a). "What happened to Asia?", Massachussets Institute of Technology, mimeo.

______ (1998b). "Saving Asia: it's time to get RADICAL". *Fortune* magazine (9 July).

Montes, Manuel (1998). *The Currency Crisis in Southeast Asia*. Singapore: Institute of Southeast Asian Studies.

Sachs, Jeffrey and Steven Radelet (1998). "The onset of the East Asian financial crisis". Harvard Institute for International Development, mimeo (March).

SBC Warburg Dillon Read (1998). *The Asian Adviser* (June).

Stiglitz, Joseph (1998). "Boats, planes and capital flows", *Financial Times* (25 March) .

United Nations (1998). *World Economic and Social Survey, 1998*. (United Nations publication, Sales No. E.98.II.C.1)

Wolf, Martin (1998). "Ins and outs of capital flows". *Financial Times* (16 June).

World Bank (1993). *The East Asian Miracle: Economic Growth and Public Policy*. New York: Oxford University Press.

______ (1997). *Private Capital Flows to Developing Countries: The Road to Financial Integration*. New York: Oxford University Press.

27

Discussion – Financial Markets

ISABELLE GRUNBERG
CHARLES LUCAS
JORGE BRAGA DE MACEDO
EDWARD J. NELL

ISABELLE GRUNBERG*

For us in the development community, the Asian crisis is a reminder of Sysiphus, who dropped the enormous rock he had so strenuously pushed up the mountain for so long. We have worked to promote sustainable livelihoods, microcredit, projects for income generation, the advancement of women, the end of child labour, etc. Now, all these small victories are set back by the enormous waves and ripples of the Asian crisis. Everything is up for reconstruction. That is why, alongside our work in the field, we are so concerned and intrigued by macro-issues.

To begin with, I will discuss a few points of detail raised by the papers, and then I will turn to major themes that are raised in the surveys: the theme of overinvestment as a cause of the crisis, raised by Krishnan Sharma; and the di-

---

* Senior Policy Analyst, Office of Development Studies, United Nations Development Programme. The opinions expressed here are personal and do not reflect the views of the United Nations Development Programme.

lemma, described in Christopher Rude's paper, between the short-term and long-term interests of financial market players.

Is the crisis different from previous ones?

This contention, by Krishnan Sharma, raises some questions. In fact, the Asian crisis of 1997-1998 is quite comparable to the Mexican crisis of 1994, at least in its causes, if not its consequences. In both cases, you had strong fundamentals, a moderately overvalued exchange rate, and large short-term, dollar-denominated debt, owed by the Central Bank (in Mexico) or private banks (in Asia). In Mexico, investor panic was triggered by the devaluation of December 1993. In Asia, it was the payments crisis in Thailand, which came to fruition and spread to other Asian emerging markets. Just as in Mexico or earlier on, in Chile in 1981 (or other Latin American crises mentioned earlier by José Antonio Ocampo), these countries had carried out extensive programmes of deregulation and privatization, reduced tariffs and stabilized inflation.

In fact, all these crises are different from the current account crises of the 1960s and 1970s: they are not spurred by governmental profligacy or loose monetary policy, but by vulnerability to volatile financial flows. Thus, there are precedents to the Asian crisis.

It is interesting to look back to the aftermath of the Mexican crisis, in particular the Halifax summit of the Group of 7 of 1995. You find the same discussions as now, of the need for a "new architecture" of the world financial system. There were even discussions of a sovereign bankruptcy court, which has also been revived in the aftermath of the Asian crisis. Yet, the Halifax summit only endorsed tougher data disclosure standards, and no new idea has emerged after the Asian crisis, either. The consequences of the inaction at Halifax are seen now. Hence, it is critical to keep this historical perspective in mind.

The end of fundamentals

There is an interesting discussion, especially in Sharma's paper, of the idea that currency crises contribute to deteriorating fundamentals (that is, external balance, budget deficits), which in turn undermine investor confidence even more, causing a vicious circle. This has interesting ramifications for theory. The author is, in fact, making the point that fundamentals are endogenous, not the independent variable upon which, traditionally, all else depends—hence the injunction to, first, "get the fundamentals right". In my own work, I have seen the demise of many established concepts such as, for example, NAIRU (the Non-Accelerating Inflation Rate of Unemployment). The same fate may await the notion of "fundamentals", which was until now a sacred cow of macroeconomic policy-making.

The need for warning systems

Some papers cite the need for advance warning systems. To some extent, the data dissemination standards were meant to facilitate that function. Yet, several difficulties should be kept in mind: First, many crises that should have happened because of shaky fundamentals did not happen. This is a well-established paradox, described in particular in the work of Ronald MacKinnon, Barry Eichengreen and Charles Wyplosz. In this situation, one has to worry about self-fulfilling predictions. Second, it may be difficult for an intergovernmental organization to act as an early warning mechanism, in particular because of this possible trigger effect, and the responsibility it entails. We need, then, to rely on the private sector. Yet, the private sector already has its early warning systems, the rating agencies—and they failed to warn anyone prior to the Asian crisis.

Overinvestment at the root of the crisis

This point is elaborated in the paper by Sharma, and it has intriguing implications. One would need to ask: overinvestment in relation to what? Probably in relation to the absorptive capacity of world markets. In other words, the other side of overinvestment may be under-consumption. Overinvestment, overcapacity and overproduction have led to falling producer prices for manufactured and primary commodities worldwide. These trends were clearly visible even back in 1996. What should have triggered alarm bells is the fact that the overcapacity was precisely in the sectors and in the areas that were supposed to act as the "locomotives" of world growth: computer microprocessors, and the successful emerging markets of South-East Asia.

We are familiar with overcapacity in sunset industries such as ship-building, or in some areas that were the cradles of the Industrial Revolution. The traditional challenge has been to adjust and reallocate resources away from traditional activities to these "locomotive" sectors. But here, even the locomotives were stalling. The world prices of microprocessors plunged by one-half in 1997.

The deterioration of world employment, whether in quantity or quality, was among the earlier symptoms of a global shortfall in world demand, which I analysed in Grunberg (1996). At the same time, shrinking opportunities for productive investment were coupled with very large amounts, an estimated $800 billion, of private capital in search of global investment opportunities. In the face of stagnating worldwide demand, non-speculative opportunities simply ran out.

Beyond efforts to regulate banks and foreign exposure, the key is, then, to restore a win-win bargain between workers, consumers and investors. No doubt, the sharp increase in income inequality in the past twenty years must have slowed down the development of mass markets. The middle-class in Africa lost much of its purchasing power through devaluation and governmental downsizing. Gross National Product contracted there throughout the 1980s, and is now contracting in Japan, South-East Asia and the Russian Federation. This stagnation of domestic markets, coupled with an unpredictable political and social environment deprives global finance of investment outlets.

Developing the potential that emerging areas have to absorb investment capital is thus an important objective. At the same time, creating a good investment environment should not come at the expense of a decent income distribution, which means sufficient tax collection and public services. All are part of a win-win bargain, and investors should do their part in helping to build the foundations of prosperous societies and expanding markets. Which leads to the second major observation.

The dilemma of collective action faced by financial markets

Christopher Rude draws an interesting distinction between the "two identities" of the financial market players that he interviewed in New York: their identities as business people, and as professional market players. In their first incarnation, the respondents are mostly concerned with their immediate, short-term interest. Yet as professionals, they also take into account the "big picture", the long term, and the shared objectives. Many have no illusion that the sum total of their behavior as rational investors produces an irrational outcome. In the financial sphere, this irrational outcome is, for example, over-shooting or unwarranted contagion. In the real economy, the irrational outcome may be, precisely, global deflation one country at a time, because the pressure of financial markets discourages growth policies.

Accepting controls, reserve requirements or velocity taxes would mean immediate costs for the individual investor, but long-term, shared benefits (less instability, more room for manoeuvre for macroeconomic policy). This dilemma of collective action presents the classical case for leadership.

Yet, it is not likely that the financial community will accept short-term sacrifices imposed from outside, whether from governments or international organizations. The leadership has to come from inside, perhaps from a major financial market player with a strong stake in the stability of the whole system. The United Nations should engage these major players in an action-oriented policy dialogue, as the stability of the world economy is also at stake.

In conclusion, the challenge of the Asian crisis, which is turning into a global crisis, should spur us to update our tools of economic analysis. From a single-minded emphasis on the "fundamentals" of a particular country, we need to turn our attention to "global fundamentals", redefined as the global balance between investment, aggregate demand and consumption. We also need to bring to some conclusion the debate on the rationality or irrationality of financial markets. It is clear that the individual conduct of financial players is rational, but the collective outcome is irrational. Solving the dilemma of collective action can help restore collective rationality to the markets.

CHARLES LUCAS*

I would like to make five brief comments on the discussion that has taken place so far.

My first point concerns Christopher Rude's suggestion of a fundamental dichotomy between the business incentives of market professionals and businessmen who run financial services enterprises. To the degree that there is a dichotomy, it arises because traders are paid large bonuses if they earn profits, but suffer no penalty if they make losses. Firm managers generally gain from firm success but suffer more than traders if the firm makes losses. At least one simple solution exists for this problem: it is creating businesses as joint ventures where the heads of the subsidiaries who are traders have an equity stake in the particular segment of the business they run. That way they personally share in the losses as well as the gains. This is a sufficient mechanism to eliminate the dichotomy. And it is the responsibility of firm management to find such mechanisms.

The second observation is that the ratings of the credit rating agencies lag the financial condition of the enterprise or country, sometimes substantially. Any credit officer of a major financial services firm knows that, and therefore performs his own analysis. It is unrealistic, as a general proposition, to expect rating agencies to play a constructive role *ex ante* in deterring the sort of finan-

---

* Vice President and Director, Market Risk Management, American International Group, Inc. The opinions expressed here are personal and do not reflect the views of American International Group.

cial crisis seen in Asia since the middle of 1997. Other deterrent mechanisms must be found, because the ratings alone will contribute little.

The third point is that markets overshoot, as they have from time to time for hundreds of years. In that sense, what happened over the past few years in Asia is an old story and should come as no surprise. When left free and open, markets tend to be characterized from time to time by virtuous cycles that take asset values far beyond what analysis suggests might be general equilibrium levels. Abruptly, and in some sense in an unanticipated way, these virtuous cycles always do end. This seems to have happened in East Asia. In American International Group, we sensed that asset values in a number of Asian economies were beyond sustainable levels, and that at some point they would necessarily reverse. We had no inkling as to when they might reverse, nor did we make specific attempts to forecast turning points.

On the other hand, it can be instructive to examine how large-scale speculative traders seem to consistently profit by huge amounts in the context of financial events such as the East Asian crises. Typically, such speculators do not attempt to anticipate the exact timing or even the immediate consequences of a crisis. Rather the speculator attempts to spot a major economic and financial vulnerability, and then anticipate a time window in which it might be exacerbated. Such large speculators typically accumulate large positions slowly over considerable time, before developing market tensions substantially raise the cost of establishing such a position. As tensions develop, the speculator will then augment his position, based on the trader's ability to see that a situation is approaching the breaking point. It is also worth pointing out that speculators sometimes get things very wrong.

The fourth comment is that the virtuous cycles in East Asia masked key vulnerabilities—in this case, balance sheet vulnerabilities. The financial panic that ended the virtuous cycle of the "Asian Miracle" not only unmasked these vulnerabilities, but attacked them directly. Much of the apparent wealth accumulated throughout the East Asian region was from unrealized gains in paper assets. This paper wealth was attacked and in many cases destroyed by the reduction in local currency values. This fundamental fact provides much of the explanation for why the crisis is so difficult to reverse—economic actors so damaged will always shift to highly risk averse behaviour, if they have any room to move at all. As is typical of financial crises historically, the risk averse behaviour following a market crash is the key factor converting a virtuous cycle into a vicious cycle. Historically, such vicious cycles have only corrected themselves with considerable passage of time, and by means of some mechanism which permits the realization and write-off of losses suffered in the crash.

My final point concerns the role of fixed exchange rates and quasi fixed exchange rates in the crisis, especially in establishing the conditions which made the East Asian economies vulnerable. The role of this particular policy has been seriously underestimated in the discussion around the table to this point. Exchange rate policy in those countries should be placed in the context of the overinvestment argument articulated by several discussants. The key point is that the fixing of exchange rates meant that investors of all types, most significantly including local investors, faced a marginal cost of capital set by US dollar short-term interest rates, rather than much higher long-term local currency rates. Investors responded in a fashion which, under the circumstances, seemed rational in the short term. But US dollar short-term rates constitute seriously incorrect pricing for local currency investments, which carry much higher risks. Thus investors undertook exposures that cumulatively were simply unsustainable.

This situation was clear to outside observers, including both officials and large speculators. Many knew that a vulnerability had been created, and expected asset values to come down at some time, through some mechanism. In other words, it was clear even before the crisis that there was bad policy by several national governments. It is clear from the record that the International Monetary Fund (IMF) saw the problem and recommended to several governments that they change policy while they had room to do so (I do not think IMF missed anything in that sense). The root problem is political; how to persuade governments who have experienced the enormous success of the sustained "Asian Miracle" virtuous cycle that their policy was flawed.

I will end by mentioning an anecdote from my time as a central banker which bears directly on my last comment. In the spring of 1981, one year before the first Mexican crisis, my boss at the New York Federal Reserve came into my office to issue the following instruction. He told me to develop an understanding of the Mexican economic situation and establish relationships with the Hacienda and the central bank. He was convinced that Mexico had overborrowed in the international capital markets, and would at some point face a financial crisis. I did as instructed and found to my surprise that the authorities at a working level in Mexico had the same opinion. A year later, after the crisis hit, I asked an official in the Hacienda why they did not change course much earlier, knowing what was likely to occur. In the meantime, Mexico had borrowed roughly $22 billion, and the interest rate spreads at which they had borrowed that money had narrowed by about 20 basis points. I asked why they had not warned their immediate boss and the President of Mexico? His answer was that such warnings had been passed on repeatedly. But it had been impossible to convince the Mexican President a problem was coming, because interest rate spreads were narrowing and the markets seemed to be thrusting money at them. It could be argued that something similar, on a much smaller scale, happened to the United States in its exchange market crisis in 1978. Then the United States Treasury and the President refused to believe that their policies were bad, even though the markets were sending them a very clear message.

Viewed in this perspective, it may be a bit unfair to place so much blame on IMF for a situation where the root problem is political within the countries in question. Where countries are riding the crest of a virtuous circle wave of massive proportions, it is not realistic to ask politicians to take corrective action well in advance, before the bubble bursts. The policy question, therefore, is how do we devise a framework that starts to produce countervailing market forces which tend to dampen the effects of the virtuous circle before it reaches the point where the collapse is so devastating. Albert Fishlow has put the problem most succinctly, saying that the old rules of the game have been taken apart by globalized financial markets, and the new rules have not yet been invented. Many observers think we need another Bretton Woods conference, and another J.M. Keynes. The nature of financial market and policy dynamics and the political realities of today's world create challenges of that magnitude.

JORGE BRAGA DE MACEDO*

In the 1990s, financial interdependence was no longer confined to mature democracies, as more and more currencies became fully convertible into each other. Interest rate spreads of emerging markets over established borrowers fell. But across the global economy, national financial policies came under increased scrutiny from international investors and rating agencies and few opportunities at testing the credibility of exchange rate parities were missed by market operators. Though not always successful in triggering a currency devaluation, these market tests called for policy responses or at least for statements about policy credibility. In short, international financial volatility and financial crises became more common.

* Professor of Economics, Nova University, Lisbon and Research Associate, National Bureau of Economic Research.

It is important to analyze financial crises in order to help national and international policy makers develop and implement appropriate responses. One source of analytical inputs into crisis management comes from economists, the other from market participants. Both can be biased.

The views of international economists might not reflect the economics profession as a whole, and the danger of bias is exaggerated when many in the group belong to the same circle of friends or colleagues.[1] Similarly, a relevant part of the world financial community resides in New York and in East Asia, but any sample of individual opinions only drawn from those two communities is likely to be an inaccurate reflection of the global market itself.[2] Nevertheless, a review of what international economists and selected market participants say can be informative.

Some background, definitions and caveats lead into a discussion of results from recent academic work. An attempt at summarizing the views of market participants and their implications for policy follows. One conclusion is that lessons from the crises in the Exchange Rate Mechanism (ERM) of the European Monetary System may be helpful in emerging markets. Containing the ERM crisis entailed more effective coordination mechanisms among monetary and fiscal authorities.[3] These may be more relevant than grandiose plans for the reform of the international monetary system.

Background, definitions and caveats

There were three waves of crises in the 1990s, the last one of which was still on in 1998. The first wave broke in September 1992 over the ERM and was solved one year later, after the fluctuation bands were widened. The second wave followed from the attack on the Mexican peso in December 1994 and had ripple effects in 1995 in both South America and Central Europe. The third began in the spring of 1997 when a minor attack on the Czech koruna resulted in its devaluation. Then the Thai baht floated in the summer of 1997, ending an implicit

1 Krugman (1998b) contrasts his views with those of other Charles River economists turned policy makers and sees evidence that these opinions are being listened to more than is typical in calm periods. A corollary of Murphy's law (called Blinder's law in Cambridge, Massachusetts) is that economists are more listened to when there is less agreement in the profession and when the issue is one where economists have less of a professional answer to provide.

2 Rude (this volume) concentrates on Wall Street, while Sharma (this volume) interviews market participants from Asia.

3 As Finance Minister of Portugal responsible for the escudo's entry into the ERM in April 1992, I followed this crisis and the responses of the European Council of Finance Ministers. The story is told in Braga de Macedo (1997), together with some tests of how the escudo fared under the attacks.

dollar peg which several of the fast growing East Asian economies also maintained. Indeed, Malaysia, Indonesia and the Philippines also experienced attacks on their currencies. Perceptions of financial crisis began to form.

Currency and banking crises spread to other Asian economies in the fall, threatening the role of Hong Kong (China), as a financial centre. The Republic of Korea, like the Czech Republic, a recent member of the Organization for Economic Cooperation and Development (OECD), suffered a combined currency, banking and debt crisis. Japan, a mature democracy and a prominent member of the Group of Seven industrialized countries (G-7), was seen as part of the problem. China was seen as capable of keeping financial stability in the region.

The prevailing perception was of an emerging markets crisis that hurt the borrowing capacity of Asian, Latin American and Central European debtors. The continued weakness of the Japanese currency exacerbated the negative impact of the financial turmoil on Asian growth throughout the spring of 1998. South Africa followed, while the Russian Federation floated the rouble and defaulted on its debt in late August.[4]

The recent turmoil in the Russian Federation has a strong domestic component and threatens to reverse the transition process. The sequels of a debt moratorium and of currency inconvertibility, let alone a bank run, will remain economically and politically hazardous for some time to come, especially due to the lack of a North Atlantic economic dialogue.

Among the large emerging markets, only Egypt seemed to have escaped a speculative attack on its currency, whereas, as of late 1998, Brazil had thus far succeeded in keeping its dollar peg. Nevertheless, the fear remained that this emerging markets crisis will spread from the Pacific to the Atlantic and hurt growth prospects in the European Union (EU) and the United States.

These, then, are the events on which we need to focus. I will now make some comments on terminology.

Since almost all but a dozen mature democracies might be classified as emerging market economies, the notion hides a lot of different national and regional circumstances.[5] However, if the notion of emerging market encompasses too many economic varieties, that of financial crisis is often misused. The term applies best to a combination of currency, banking and sovereign debt crisis having strong negative effects on the national economy.[6]

4 Brinkman (this volume) deals with the attack on the rand in the spring and summer of 1998 and compares it to the 1996 episode. Belanger and Zavoico (this volume) shows the deteriorating situation in the Russian Federation. See also Dornbusch (1998c).

5 This is the case even among Thailand, Malaysia, Indonesia and the Republic of Korea, as documented in Ito (1998). Dornbush (1998b) asks whether China is next in line for a devaluation, an option he strongly rejects.

6 This is the definition proposed in Portes (1998).

With the definitions of emerging markets and financial crisis in mind, we turn to the appropriate level of policy response, which may still be national, regional or global, depending both on the contagion mechanism and on the availability of instruments and institutions.

Contagion patterns are not well understood, but geography and hegemony seem to play a role[7]. Both are at work, for example, when it comes to the economic policy autonomy of Hong Kong (China), relative to China or to the role of Japan—not an emerging market and yet it is part of the Asian problem, rather than helping solve it.[8] In addition, given the status of the Russian Federation as former hegemon in parts of Europe, perceptions of crisis elicit strong responses by the United States and by the EU, hopefully in a coordinated fashion.

The so-called architecture debate features a reform of the system of international relations and its main institutions, which for the most part were established half a century ago. The reflection of regional cooperation arrangements such as the EU is one of the issues in the debate where the geographic/hegemonic pattern of contagion matters. The role of Japan acquires special salience because it was seen as the major player in South-East Asia, where the current crisis originated. Reforms of the international system have been resisted by the G-7 and by its members in the EU but they may now have a better chance if they are not overly grandiose. One reason is that market resistance to change is lower in times of crisis.

Economists' propositions

The main source of debate among economists hinges on the role given to fundamentals versus financial panic. Because both are probably at work, interpretations often depend on a balancing of each factor.[9]

If structural problems and policy inconsistencies make it inevitable that a combination of currency, banking and debt weakness will lead to a financial crisis with severe real consequences for the national economy, then the weaknesses must be addressed even at the risk of encouraging moral hazard behaviour.[10] But because crises are cumulative processes and have a self-fulfilling

---

7 Krugman has popularized the superstar model in connection with income distribution within professions. It may also apply to crisis contagion.

8 Krugman (1997b) emphasizes this point.

9 Krugman (1997a) describes the "canonical model" of currency crises and adds in closing, "But everyone agrees that a sufficiently credible currency will never be attacked, and a sufficiently incredible one will always come under fire." See also Krugman (1997b).

10 The interview of the United States Treasury Secretary in the *New York Times Magazine* of 19 July 1998 used the phrase "moral hazard" often.

character, their costs of correction end up being much greater than the cost of adjustments called for by disequilibria in the fundamentals. Therefore, prevention efforts almost always make sense.

One way to parse the debate between those who focus on fundamentals and those who emphasize panics is to look for areas of agreement in what are the causes of a financial crisis. Although the list of favourite causes leaves a great deal of room for interpretation, it helps focus on the disagreement.[11]

That bad shocks and policy mistakes make things worse is uncontroversial, but the practical question is rather how the severity and duration of the bad shock and the irreversibility of the policy mistake make a difference to the perception of crisis. The attack on the Czech koruna, for example, was short-lived because devaluation was coupled with a temporary import deposit scheme and measures to deal with the fragility of some of the financial institutions.[12]

Financial fragility is seen as decisive in the combination of currency, banking and debt crises. In that context, the maturity structure of capital inflows matters more than their size, because financial fragility comes from failures in the maturity transformation of short-term liabilities (deposits) into long-term assets (loans) that banks are supposed to provide.

Another uncontroversial point is that financial liberalization and banking deregulation require improved prudential supervision, the question being how to achieve this supervision in global markets. In particular, does this require a new institution? Instead, can the Bank for International Settlements (BIS) and the International Monetary Fund (IMF) substitute for the role of an international lender of last resort? The architecture debate continues on this issue.

There is again consensus on the statement that large and free foreign exchange reserves, and/or a flexible exchange regime reduce the probability of a crisis. Yet it may not be possible to agree on what finite level of free foreign exchange reserves and exchange rate flexibility averts a crisis.

The state of the architecture debate is that an international lender of last resort helps if it does not exacerbate moral hazard. For fundamentalists this is a bigger "if" than for those who hold that crises are self-fulfilling. Finally, both sides agree that a crisis always has a combination of causes.

---

11 The discussion by Perotti of Velasco (1998) included the list followed in the text.

12 Drabek and Brada (1998) claim that the Czech peg lasted too long and led to an unstable trade policy. They also point out that before the crisis most economists viewed the currency experience favourably. Another cost of this policy was that capital account liberalization was conducted to alleviate exchange rate pressure even when it aggravated problems of corporate governance. This pattern is reminiscent of the recent relaxation of the import deposits in Chile. See references in note 16 below.

A financial crisis comes in many forms—because it combines a currency collapse, with or without resort to exchange controls, a bank run or the threat thereof and a debt default or moratorium. Its anatomy often includes the expected bailout of private debts by the state, or by international institutions. Such expectations are easier to form in the presence of cronyism and with weak corporate governance.[13]

The converse of the previous point, that financial liberalization and banking deregulation require improved prudential supervision, is that capital account liberalization without improved banking supervision is also found in most crises. Overinvestment is the mechanism through which the combination results in banking and currency crises.[14]

Even in countries with high savings ratios, overinvestment generates large current account deficits and real appreciation. If these deficits are financed by short-term, unhedged liabilities in foreign currency and by the ever greening of bad loans, it is tantamount to making private debt into an implicit public debt.

Once the issue of anatomy is clarified, the geography of a crisis depends on the pattern of contagion. Suppose a financial crisis is going to occur in country X; will it spread and if so how?[15] In the emerging markets crisis, the spread is global, from Singapore to Chile to South Africa.

National policy responses to a large capital outflow may be a combination of allowing reserves to drop, increasing interest rates, and depreciating the currency. The relative importance of each one depends on the particular circumstances of each country.

Maybe depreciation is ruled out by an exchange rate arrangement, as in Brazil, or is very costly in terms of financial reputation, as was the case in Mexico and the Republic of Korea, which had just joined the OECD, and in the Russian Federation, who had just been accepted into the G-7.

There may be constraints on the rise in interest rates that is politically or socially viable, and the increase in interest rates is more costly the weaker the banking system. Allowing reserves to drop, on the other hand, is a less likely option the lower the ratio of reserves to liquid liabilities. And if reserves are low, and cannot drop further, one of the two other alternatives, no matter how unpalatable, must be contemplated.

---

13 This is emphasized in section 4 of my (1998b), drawing on work carried out at the European Bank for Reconstruction and Development (EBRD), Transparency International and elsewhere.

14 What Krugman (1997b) and (1998a) calls "Panglossian values". See also Corseti, Pesenti and Roubini (1998).

15 Tornell (1998).

The exchange rate option will be more likely to be chosen the greater the real appreciation observed. But devaluation is a beggar-thy-neighbour policy to the extent that it attempts to restore competitiveness at the expense of trading partners and may elicit retaliation. It therefore needs to be coordinated.

The same is true of exchange controls, which almost always function as a devaluation in disguise. Even when they seek to prevent excessive inflows, they are often not matched by free outflows, or even by a relaxation of existing controls. This was true in Portugal in the early 1990s, but can also be found in the Chilean experience.[16] The issue is, then, how devaluations and exchange controls can be coordinated at the regional or global level, to lessen their beggar-thy-neighbour character.

Systems like the ERM and its code of conduct come to mind, but they are difficult to adapt in the current world system.

It may be, then, that the current crisis serves as a coordinating device by allowing responses that would not happen in calm periods. Even if they serve as coordinating devices, crises should be avoided.

When crises loom, there is a great deal of interest in advance warning systems. Nevertheless there has been little progress in developing practical crisis indicators.

Foreign exchange reserves, for example, are still compared to imports with reference to the so-called "three month IMF rule", without taking into account the exchange rate regime.[17] A better candidate for a reserve indicator, especially for inconvertible currencies, would be the ratio of reserves to external debt. Under a fixed rate and free capital mobility, reserves should instead be compared to the broad money stock (M_2). While reserve adequacy depends on the exchange rate regime, none of these average measures are satisfactory under uncertainty. Reserves should ideally be related to the volatility of the current account or of short-term capital flows.

A high ratio of bad loans to total loans is another indicator, which has been used in looking for evidence of a lending boom. The increase in real lending to private sector and state-owned enterprises is in turn how a lending boom is identified. The usual criterion for internal balance, namely a sustainable fiscal position, was satisfied in the Asian economies but it remains a serious problem in transition economies and especially in the Russian crisis.[18]

16 Agosin and Ffrench-Davis (this volume). See also Dornbusch (1998a), Cordella (1998) and De Gregorio (1998) and note 12 above on the Czech experience.

17 Ghosh and others (1998).

18 Criteria for policy sustainability in the context of transition economies are described in Branson and others (1998). See also Belanger and Zavoico (this volume) and IMF (1998), chap. V.

Real appreciation in terms of effective rates is another early warning indicator. There again, care must be taken to net out the component of real appreciation, which accompanies any successful development experience.

Propositions heard on Wall Street

Opinions commonly found among market participants do not allow us to pass judgement on the different aspects of the current emerging market crisis, but they suggest some implications for policy. The following four market-informed propositions suggest that the surprise element was genuine.

First "investment prospects were good until the crisis hit". This would seem to dispute the overinvestment story and it may reflect active involvement in the financing of such investments. Second "sentiment changed abruptly and turned inflows into outflows". This also shows the surprise element but it also underscores the severity of the crisis, to the extent that such reversals would be very short-lived otherwise. Third, "exposure was complex and opaque, yet it was reduced very quickly". This proposition strengthens the previous two points, to the extent that it shows panic, also a feature of the fourth observation, that "liquidation induced herd behaviour".

Other propositions go more towards opinions on the state of the world and may therefore be more influenced by professional opinion. Thus "the crisis was like a worldwide deflationary shock" and "confidence in unregulated globalized financial markets was damaged" imply views about what to do and whether or not economists are useful in sorting out the implications for policy.[19]

In addressing this question, market participants often reflect a confusion between their opinions as businesspeople (who prefer to keep free markets and perhaps flexible exchange rates) and their views as market professionals.[20] Similarly, they may accept to strengthen regulation and supervision, including risk management techniques, before further liberalization of the capital account.[21] And the so-called Tobin tax proposal may also be acceptable on this market professionals' perspective.[22]

19 Leading columnists provide a more or less idiosyncratic combination of the two primary inputs. For example Wolf (1998) combines market sensitivities with citations from academic economists.

20 For Rude (this volume), the latter perspective might instead favour promoting orderly workouts and regional institutions like the "resolution trust".

21 Dornbusch (1998b) suggests mandatory value-at-risk reviews, as called for by the Basel Committee of the Bank for International Settlements. While developments in the technology may allow this, the concepts are still foreign to many financial institutions.

22 Dornbush (1998b) quotes the literature, including the original pieces by Jim Tobin. Krugman mentions the opinions of Larry Summers and Stan Fischer. See also Stiglitz (1998) and Radelet and Sachs (1998).

Indeed, the fact that top-rated academic economists with policy roles disagree and markets care about it would seem to confirm that "these are not normal times".

There is widespread agreement between academics and market organizations, such as the Group of Thirty, that some improvements in orderly workouts are desirable and easy to achieve.[23] Nevertheless, the traditional difference remains between national action on private debt and international action on sovereign debt. In the absence of international enforcement, the "pre-nuptial agreement problem" makes these improvements less likely to be accepted outside of a broader set of changes in the international system.

Lastly, the current crisis has uncovered an unusual amount of disagreement within the Bretton Woods institutions. And if they do even appear to agree with each other, the IMF and World Bank may not be capable of influencing the architecture of the international economy.

Pointers for policy

The immediate effect of the crisis is to underscore the problem of tariff escalation from the inter-war period, which could well spread to non-tariff barriers like exchange controls today. Liberalization and globalization must be better managed to prevent protectionist pressures from taking over. Seeking to avoid contagion by reverting to trade and financial protectionism could well prove in the late 1990s as ultimately futile a beggar-thy-neighbour policy as it was in the early 1930s.

Managing the emerging markets crisis means, therefore, avoiding a relapse of protectionism while fostering reform in the international system to allow a more effective regional and global response to threats of contagion of national crises. The issue is then how can devaluations and exchange controls be coordinated at the regional or global level in order to lessen their beggar-thy-neighbour character?

Over and above the parallels between the current emerging markets crisis and the Mexican devaluation of December 1994, the lessons from the crises in the ERM may be helpful in that they were overcome by a more effective coordination mechanism among monetary and fiscal authorities.[24]

---

23 For example, the IMF should lend into arrears and there should be sharing or majority-voting clauses in bond and bank loan contracts, allowing IMF to shelter countries from legal action (Article 8.2b of IMF Articles of Agreement). This list draws on the conclusions of the June 1998 Trans-Atlantic Economic Dialogue meeting, on Portes (1998), and on Eichengreen and Portes (1995).

24 The comparison among emerging markets is in Chinn and Dooley (1998). Krugman (1997b) includes the ERM.

In the ERM crises of 1992-1993, Portugal and Ireland suffered currency attacks based on what was happening to the Spanish and British currencies, in what was described as "geographic fundamentals". These attacks were short-lived but they nevertheless led Ireland to request a realignment in January 1993 and Portugal had to partly follow several realignments of the peseta. Given that the ERM code of conduct is based on multilateral rules for exchange rate changes, fundamentals should be less of a geographic than of a policy problem. Yet this peculiar form of neighbourhood contagion was pervasive at the time.[25]

Systems like the ERM and its code of conduct rely on shared economic and societal values. They may be difficult to adapt to the variety of emerging markets in the current world system, but they are certainly useful in both Central Europe and Latin America, where regional arrangements like the Central European Free Trade Agreement (CEFTA) and the Southern Cone Common Market (Mercosur) are spreading from trade to investment.

---

25 One possible reason is that the financial reputation of these countries was not fully established as their regime change was quite recent (1987 for Ireland, 1989 for Spain and 1992 for Portugal). A related reason is that testing the ERM parity made sense when the real appreciation was perceived as excessive by export-oriented firms and the Government may have been sensitive to their pressure. The bet proved correct for Spain, which initiated two realignments during the ERM turmoil. The Portuguese response was to follow in part, so as to reinforce its own credibility without suffering the direct consequences of a competitive depreciation. See my (1997b) for details.

EDWARD J. NELL*

The Asian crisis hit a group of economies whose fundamentals were generally sound, and in many cases, improving. Moreover, the sound condition of these economies was widely heralded. Employment was high, and growth of gross domestic product (GDP) was exceptionally high—nearly reaching double digits at times—both for a decade or more. Productivity growth was high, wages were strong and rising, poverty was declining and governments were investing in infrastructure. Saving rates were high, as was the ratio of investment to GDP. Governments and business cooperated well, especially in developing technology; governments ensured that labour markets were flexible, and that the climate for investment was good. This meant repression, but in recent years a number of countries had begun to move towards greater democracy. Under Western pressure the Asian economies removed capital controls and began to develop free capital markets; they also began to open up their trade. Even when small weaknesses in balance of payments began to emerge, they were generally ignored so long as exports were strong and growing.

When the crisis came, it struck suddenly and the impact was systemic. It affected both financial and real relationships in every country, and the impact was across the board. In financial markets it hit stocks, bonds, trade credit and banking; it affected investment, consumption and trade on the real side, leading to the virtual collapse of growth, and in some countries to contraction, while the interaction through trade and capital markets spread the contagion throughout the Asian region.

So the crisis was economy-wide. Yet, surprisingly, most studies of the Asian crisis stress micro issues and micro relationships, rather than factors that affect the economy as a whole. This is clearly the case with mainstream explanations, but it also tends to be true of alternative approaches, as can be seen from the views reported in the Rude and Sharma papers.

Drawing on those papers, we have both mainstream and alternative explanations. The mainstream explanations comprise the following:

- "Crony capitalism". Government support allowed business to overexpand and to develop inefficient, wasteful production facilities. When this was discovered, capital began to withdraw.
- Inexperienced bankers and central banks panicked after moving too far too fast, believing they would be bailed out (moral hazard).

* Malcolm B. Smith Professor of Economics, New School for Social Research, New York.

- Lack of transparency caused Western bankers to invest too much on terms that were too easy in projects that were unsound.

The alternative explanations include:

- Currency crisis. Lack of regulation and premature removal of controls, coupled with inexperience, let a normal currency fluctuation spiral out of control.
- Self-fulfilling speculation. Once speculators believed that the currencies were going to fall, their actions made it happen; in addition, reliance on derivatives that were not understood let the crisis spread.
- Minsky debt-deflation—"fear has overwhelmed greed" with the result that a run developed, leading to premature liquidations and business failures, which compounded the problem in a downward spiral.
- Overinvestment, creating excess capacity. This was owing to a belief that firms would be bailed out (moral hazard, crony capitalism).

There is some merit to all of these. But none is able to explain why the crisis struck when it did, how it worked or why it became economy-wide, in both financial and real sectors.

An important thread running through many of the alternative explanations is that deregulation, especially the removal of capital controls and the opening of stock markets, far from strengthening the Asian economies, actually contributed to their downfall. Too much short-term capital was allowed to flow in; this capital was then channelled by an inexperienced banking and financial system into speculative investments in land and construction, resulting in a term-structure mismatch, so that when it began to flow out, difficulties in liquidation emerged. The resulting collapse in market values then led to panic and a speculative run. This led to steep declines in the values of Asian currencies and so on.

One might ask, what was short-term capital needed for? The Asian economies were growing very fast without it; they did not need it for balance of payments support, since they were mostly in balance or in surplus. Short-term capital, by definition, is not direct investment—it is not new factories or technology transfer. Short-term capital refers to loans of *money*. Why did the Asian economies need money, and where did the money they borrowed come from? Did someone else have to make do with less money so that it could flow to Asia?

These issues are surely at least part of the story. But some crucial features of the crisis still lie in the dark. Why were the banks so willing to lend so much short-term capital, in the first place? And why did it flow out of Asia at the particular time that it did, and why so suddenly?

Some light can be thrown on these questions by considering the working of modern monetary systems. The capital flows in question were flows of capital in monetary form, and they were managed by banks because, at least in large part, they were *created* by banks. No one had to do with less money because of the funds that flowed to Asia. The money was created the same way banks create deposits when they make loans to domestic borrowers; a loan is made, and a deposit created simultaneously, and reserves are raised as necessary.

It is customary to think of banks as "intermediaries", lending out the sums that have been entrusted to them by depositors, subject to holding back sufficient reserves to enable them to meet anticipated withdrawals. This picture was surely correct at one time—certainly prior to the First World War , and it was at least partly correct for the inter-war years. But for the advanced, hard-currency economies of the post-war era it is highly misleading.

By now a large and complex literature exists on the endogeneity of modern money. Summarizing and oversimplifying, including leaving out qualifications in order to draw a starkly simplified picture: Banks create deposits by making loans to qualified borrowers; deposits are liabilities, loans are assets, and the two are kept equal. Banks must have adequate capital to cover the risks of non-performance on the part of their assets. The central bank operates the system to ensure that there will always be sufficient reserves to enable clearing.

Under these conditions, reserves do not constrain bank lending. Central banks act defensively, pegging interest rates and ensuring that reserve requirements are always met. (Always provided, that is, that the exchange rate is not an issue—as when it floats, or is protected by capital controls; and sometimes the exchange rate can be partly protected by the fact that, for institutional as well as economic reasons, the country may be the supplier of a major reserve currency, e.g., the dollar.) Nor do banks typically lend what has been previously deposited. On the contrary, they create money by creating deposits, and finding the reserves to back those deposits; when loans are repaid, money is cancelled. (Governments create money when they spend and cancel it when they collect taxes.) The constraint on banks—and it is a weak one—is their own capital, which has to cover risks.

So banks are constrained, not by reserves but by capital; they cannot lend more—cannot create more deposits—than their capital can cover. Note that any individual bank can easily raise more capital by selling equity or borrowing. For an individual bank the capital ratio is not a quantity constraint; it is a price constraint.

The situation is different for the system as a whole, however. Suppose the banking system *as a whole* tried to lend more (create more deposits) than its ratio of capital-to-assets justified. If the risks were quantified properly, then a certain fraction of the newly created assets will fail to perform; these assets will have to be marked down, bringing the capital-to-asset ratio back to (approximately) the correct level! (This will involve legal, insurance and bankruptcy expenses, which will come out of capital.)

So for the system as a whole, bank capital acts as a constraint, although one that individual banks may feel they can manipulate. It can be shown that bank profits tend to vary with the rate of interest, the real rate of interest, that is. Bank capital grows with the reinvestment of bank profits. In the simplest case the growth rate of bank capital equals the rate of interest. Demand for loans, on the other hand, grows with the rate of growth of GDP.

Suppose that the real rate of interest is less than the rate of growth, $i < g$. In these circumstances, bank capital will be an active constraint. Banks will tend to try to find ways to reduce risk; they will be cautious, so that credit, especially for risky projects, will be in short supply. Credit will be cheap, but not so easy to obtain. Governments will be encouraged to supply insurance, or to assume risk, or directly to augment bank capital.

Now suppose $i > g$. Bank capital permits lending to grow faster than the demand for loans; at some point there will emerge unexploited lending capacity. Banks will be willing to take risks; they have the capital to cover them and they are in search of customers. Banks will tend to push loans; credit will be plentiful, though expensive.

Notice that the incentives in this situation are such that an inequality between i and g, in either direction, will not tend to be self-correcting. If $i < g$, then capital in banking is growing too slowly, but for precisely that reason, capital will not flow from the corporate world into banking. If $i > g$, then bank profits will not flow from the financial sector into real activities.

With these points about modern banking systems in mind, consider the transactions between a government and its domestic economy. The government creates money to buy goods and services, and taxes that money back, cancelling it. The taxes have the effect of making the money generally acceptable. When the economy sells more to the government than it pays in taxes, it earns a surplus, which is to say, the government runs a deficit. Deficits are a potential addition to reserves—calling for sterilization, that is, offsetting their impact—while surpluses run reserves down. When deficits are absorbed by treasury bills, securities of the highest grade are thereby provided to portfolios. The effect is to strengthen portfolios, reducing risk, which, in turn, contributes to the ability to extend credit.

Next, consider relations with the rest of the world. When the country as a whole sells more abroad than it buys, it runs a trade surplus, which is a stimulus, and brings in potential excess reserves, which have to be sterilized. Trade surpluses and domestic deficits have exactly the same effects.

These points can now be applied to examining the Asian crisis. The basic argument is that in Asia, the rate of growth was greater than the real rate of interest for decades, creating a persistent shortage of credit. By contrast, since 1980 in the United States and other advanced Western economies, the real rate of interest has tended to lie above the rate of growth, so that banks and financial institutions have tended to have underutilized lending capacity. So when deregulation led to the opening up of Asian markets, funds were available in the West, and needed in the East.

Note that the Asian economies pegged their exchange rates; they were *not* free to set their domestic monetary policy just as they pleased. But their strong fundamentals gave them an unusual degree of freedom, or perhaps, apparent freedom. To peg the exchange rate, they had to set their nominal domestic interest rates sufficiently above dollar nominal rates to cover risk, which, however, was estimated to be low (Rude and Sharma). But given their reserves and their trade balances, they could keep their real rates low relative to their growth rates.

Consider first, the initial position where Asian growth rates lay above Asian real interest rates, which were greater than United States and European interest rates, which exceeded United States and European growth rates. (Remember, Asian *nominal* rates were higher than United States rates and exchange rates were pegged.) United States and Asian inflation rates were not so different; both government budgets and external trade were in balance in Asia, whereas the United States was in deficit on both accounts. The relative positions of the rates can be exhibited along the line below, with the Asian real interest and growth rates above and those of the United States below:

```
________________iA__________gA__________
      gUS    iUS
```

In these circumstances, there will be unexploited lending potential in the United States and a shortage of bank credit, especially for risky ventures, in Asia. Hence, banks will tend to create and direct a flow of short-term funds towards Asia. This was the situation that prevailed in the late 1980s and early 1990s when capital controls were removed and markets deregulated in Asia.

Even though exchange rates were pegged, and were considered safe (Rude and Sharma) in these conditions it might still be prudent for short-term funds supplied to Asia to be hedged, that is, to be covered by forward dollars. (A United States bank lends dollars to an Asian borrower, who buys an option to buy dollars at the time of repayment, at the price prevailing now.) This will tend to drive down Asian forward currency values. These will then have to be supported, tending to nullify the advantage of the inflow of dollars.

Now consider what happened when the United States economy improved in the mid-1990s. Asian growth rates still exceeded Asian real interest rates, but the United States growth rate rose to almost the level of United States interest rates. Asian government budgets were still in balance, but Asian trade now tended to run a deficit. The United States trade was still in deficit, (though it was debatable how serious this was) but its government budget was now in balance. And the United States inflation rate had fallen markedly as the dollar strengthened.

_______________________iA___________gA______

gUS iUS

At this point there will no longer be unutilized lending potential in the United States; g has risen and i declined. The government deficit has been eliminated, which means that the supply of new treasury bills will be reduced. Portfolios cannot add as many highest grade securities; so over time risk will increase, reducing lending potential. On the other hand, there is no longer much short term advantage in lending to Asia, since the real interest rates are the same. (Asian nominal rates are still higher, but as trade deficits have emerged, there is now risk of exchange rate changes, though market players underestimated this (Rude and Sharma)).

But United States inflation has fallen, and as the United States Government deficit was eliminated there developed a widespread expectation that United States interest rates would fall. That is, bond prices could be expected to rise on United States financial markets. Hence, there was an incentive for short-term funds to flow to the United States in expectation of capital gains.

So, short-term funds initially flowed from the United States (and Europe) to Asia because of the configuration of growth rates and real interest, and they started to flow back because of a change in that configuration. But what opened the gate for the flood was the elimination of the United States Government deficit. Once the flood started, the term structure mismatch became evident, compounding the difficulties, bringing other problems to the fore, and the outflow turned into a run on the currencies. The crisis was on, triggered by the very success of United States policies.

References

Agosin, Manuel and Ricardo Ffrench-Davis (this volume). "Managing capital flows in Chile".

Belanger, Gerard and Basil Zavoico (this volume). "Lessons from the transition economies in a year of crisis".

Brinkman, Henk-Jan (this volume). "Financial reforms in Africa and the lessons from Asia".

Branson, William, Jorge Braga de Macedo and Juergen Von Hagen (1998). "Macroeconomic policy and institutions in the transition to EU membership", NBER Working Papers num. 6653, July.

Chinn, Menzie and Michael Dooley (1998). "Latin America and East Asia in the context of an insurance model of currency crises", paper presented at the NBER Summer Institute.

Cordella, Tito (1998). "Can short term capital controls promote capital inflows?", unpublished, Washington, D.C.: International Monetary Fund (26 August).

Corsetti, Giancarlo, Paolo Pesenti and Nouriel Roubini (1998). "Paper Tigers: A preliminary assessment of the Asian crises", paper presented at the NBER Summer Institute.

De Gregorio, Jose (1998). *Chile Economic Report No.1*, unpublished, Universidad de Chile (July).

Dornbusch, Rudi (1998a). "Capital controls, an idea whose time has gone", Cambridge, Massachusetts: Massachusetts Institute of Technology (MIT), (March).

______ (1998b). "Is China next?", *Financial Times* (4 August).

______ (1998c)." Russia: Meltdown or stabilization?", MIT (August).

Drabek, Zdenek and Josef Brada (1998). "Exchange rate regimes and the stability of trade policy in transition economies". WTO, Geneva (forthcoming).

Eichengreen, Barry and Richard Portes (1995). "Crisis? What crisis? Orderly workouts for sovereign debtors", CEPR.

Ghosh, Atish, Anne-Marie Gulde and Holger Wolf (1998). "How much is enough? Foreign reserves and exchange-rate crises", paper presented at the NBER Summer Institute.

Grunberg, Isabelle (1996). "Rival firms, rival states: how do people fit in?". Office of Development Studies, United Nations Development Programme, Discussion Paper No. 4.

International Monetary Fund (1998). *World Economic Outlook.* Washington, D.C., IMF (May).

Ito, Takatoshi (1998). "Lessons from the Asian currency crises", paper presented at the NBER Summer Institute.

Krugman, Paul (1997a). "Bahtulism. Who poisoned Asia's currency markets?", *Slate (14 August).*

______ (1997b). "Currency crises", paper presented for an NBER conference (October).

______ (1998a). "What happened to Asia?", paper presented at a conference in Japan

______ (1998b). "Japan's trap" (May).

______ (1998c). "Saving Asia: It's time to get radical", *Fortune* magazine (7 September).

Macedo, Jorge Braga de (1997). "Crises? What crises? Escudo from ECU to EMU", *Nova Economics,* Working Paper No. 313 (December).

Portes, Richard (1998). "The Asian financial crisis", paper presented at the Trans-Atlantic Economic Dialogue, Brookings Institution and CEPR, Lessburg, Virginia (June).

Radelet, Steven and Jeffrey Sachs (1998). "Onset of the East Asian financial crisis", paper presented at the NBER Currency Crisis Conference and to the United States Agency for International Development (USAID) (January).

Rude, Christopher (this volume). "The 1997-1998 East Asian financial crisis: A New York market-informed view".

Sharma, Krishnan (this volume). "Understanding the dynamics behind excess capital inflows and excess capital outflows in East Asia".

Stiglitz, Joseph (1998). "Boats, planes and capital flows", *Financial Times* (25 March).

Velasco, Andrés (1998). "Financial crises in emerging markets: A canonical model", paper presented at the NBER Summer Institute.

Tornell, Aaron (1998). "Currency crises do not spread randomly", paper presented at the NBER Summer Institute.

Wolf, Martin (1998). "Threats of depression", *Financial Times* (26 August).

Notes on the Contributors

Manuel R. Agosin is a professor in the Department of Economics and Director of the Centre on International Economics and Development at the University of Chile. He has also been working as a consultant to governments and international organizations. Mr. Agosin holds a Ph.D. in economics from Columbia University.

Iwan J. Azis is a professor of economics at the University of Indonesia and currently is a visiting professor at Cornell University. He provides forecasts of the Indonesian economy for Project LINK, an international collaborative forecasting network with a headquarters at the United Nations Department of Economic and Social Affairs. His research is also on interregional capital movements and investment allocation, decision-making practices of management, decentralization, foreign investment impact assessments, and the link between macroeconomic policies and income distribution. Mr. Azis holds a Ph.D. from Cornell University.

Gerard Belanger is Deputy Director of the European II Department of the International Monetary Fund, with responsibility for the Baltic countries, the Russian Federation and other countries of the former Soviet Union. He was previously Senior Advisor in the European I Department of IMF and was closely involved with several Eastern European countries. Mr. Belanger holds a Ph.D. from the University of Western Ontario.

Michael Casey is Vice President and Portfolio Manager at Federated Investors, Inc. with responsibility for the foreign fixed-income department. He has been involved in the international bond markets either as a portfolio manager or economic forecaster for the past 12 years. Mr. Casey holds a Ph.D. from the New School for Social Research and has a Master's degree in economics from the London School of Economics.

Befekadu Degefe is Director of the Beaman Centre for Economic Studies in Addis Ababa. He was a professor of economics and Head of the Economics Studies Unit at the University of Addis Ababa from 1969 to 1993. He has also worked as a consultant for the United Nations Economic Commission for Africa and as regional advisor and country economist for the World Bank. Mr. Degefe has written widely on development issues, including works on economic integration, human capacity building and debt.

Ricardo Ffrench-Davis is Principal Regional Advisor in the United Nations Economic Commission for Latin America and the Caribbean (ECLAC). Previously, he was Postgraduate Professor of International Economics at the University of Chile. He was Director of Research at the Central Bank of Chile from 1964 to 1970 and 1990 to 1992. He was Director and Vice President of the Centre for Economic Research on Latin America (CIEPLAN) during 1976-1990. He has authored numerous professional articles and several books.

Ilene Grabel is an associate professor of international finance at the Graduate School of International Studies in the University of Denver. She has published and spoken widely on the topics of financial crises, financial regulation, portfolio investment and stock market promotion in emerging economies. She holds a Ph.D. in economics from the University of Massachusetts-Amherst.

Isabelle Grunberg is a senior policy analyst at the Office of Development Studies in the United Nations Development Programme. She has been a visiting lecturer at Yale and has written extensively on financial and political topics. Ms. Grunberg holds Master's degrees from the London School of Economics, the Sorbonne and the Institut d'Etudes Politiques de Paris.

Azizul Islam is Director of the Development Research and Policy Analysis Division of the United Nations Economic and Social Commission for Asia and the Pacific. His main professional interests are in comparative development strategies, fiscal policy issues, international trade, and the role of transnational corporations. Mr. Islam holds a Ph.D. in economics from Boston University and a Master's degree in development economics from Williams College in Massachusetts.

Daniel Lederman is an economist with the Office of the Chief Economist for Latin America and the Caribbean at the World Bank. He has written on financial vulnerability and contagion, the political economy of economic reforms, violent crime, institutional reform, economic growth and trade. Mr. Lederman is currently a Ph.D. candidate at the School of Advanced International Studies of Johns Hopkins University, from which he holds a Master's degree.

Thea Lee is Assistant Director for International Economics in the Public Policy Department of the American Federation of Labour-Congress of Industrial Organizations (AFL-CIO), where she oversees research on international trade and investment policy. Previously, she worked as an international trade economist at the Economic Policy Institute in Washington, D.C. She has testified before the House of Representatives of the United States Congress on several international trade policy matters.

Charles Lucas is Vice President and Director of Market Risk Management for the American International Group, Inc. (AIG). Mr. Lucas joined AIG in 1996 from Republic National Bank of New York, where he had been Senior Vice President and Director of Risk Assessment and Control. Earlier, he had been at the Federal Reserve Bank of New York, where he had a 25-year career, most recently as Senior Vice President in charge of the international financial markets staff.

Jorge Braga de Macedo is a professor of economics at Nova University, Lisbon and is a research associate of the National Bureau of Economic Research. He has worked at the International Monetary Fund and was the Minister of Finance for Portugal between 1991 and 1993. Mr. Macedo holds a Ph.D. in economics from Yale University.

Padma Mallampally is a transnational corporations affairs officer in the United Nations Conference on Trade and Development (UNCTAD). She has authored numerous papers on foreign direct investment and transnational corporation activities and their implications for developing countries. She has also contributed to UNCTAD's *World Investment Report*, dealing with foreign direct investment and transnational corporations. She holds a Ph.D. in economics from the University of Chicago.

Roberto Mariano is Professor of Economics and Statistics at the University of Pennsylvania. He has been a consultant to the Central Bank and the National Economic and Development Authority of the Philippines, the Asian Development Bank, and other official institutions and private companies. His current research activities concern financial markets and economic growth in Asia. Mr. Mariano holds a Ph.D. from Stanford University.

Richard Morgan is Deputy Director in the Programme Division of the United Nations Children's Fund (UNICEF). He has worked in Africa for over 20 years, mainly in rural development, district planning, emergency rehabilitation and the formulation of public policy centred on human development.

Edward J. Nell is Malcolm B. Smith Professor of Economics at the New School for Social Research in New York. A former Rhodes Scholar, Mr. Nell is the author or editor of numerous books including *The General Theory of Transformational Growth*, which was published in 1998.

Temitope W. Oshikoya is Manager of the Research Division at the African Development Bank. He has consulted for the World Bank, taught at universities in North America and Africa and published articles on finance and development issues. Mr. Oshikoya is an associate of the Chartered Institute of Bankers in London.

Cristián Ossa is currently an advisor in the Latin American Bureau of the United Nations Development Programme. He has had a long and distinguished career in the United Nations. This included being the Deputy Special Representative of the Secretary-General in Haiti and Resident Coordinator for the United Nations Development Programme during the first years of the United Nations peace-building operation in Haiti. He worked in the Government of Chile in his early years and studied at the University of California at Berkeley and in Chile.

Richard D. Rippe is Senior Vice President and Chief Economist of Prudential Securities, Inc. He joined the firm in 1991. Mr. Rippe, a 19-year veteran of Dean Witter Reynolds and its predecessors, was previously that firm's Chief Economist, Assistant Director of Research, and a member of both its Investment Policy and Stock Selection Committees. Mr. Rippe holds a Ph.D. in business economics from Harvard University.

Christopher Rude has returned to graduate studies in economics and is at the New School for Social Research, following a career as an economist at Swiss Bank Corporation and the Federal Reserve Bank of New York. He worked as consultant to the United Nations Department of Economic and Social Affairs during 1997/1998. He holds a Master's degree in Political Science from the University of Chicago and studied economics at the University of Wisconsin.

Joseph Smolik is a senior economic affairs officer in the Economic Analysis Division of the United Nations Economic Commission for Europe (ECE). Currently he specializes in the external financial relations of the transition economies and contributes on this subject to the ECE's *Economic Survey of Europe*. He holds a Ph.D. in economics from the University of Illinois, Champaign-Urbana.

Barbara Stallings is Director of the Economic Development Division of ECLAC. Before going to Santiago in 1993, she taught political economy for 15 years at the University of Wisconsin. Her research interests centre on development strategies, macroeconomics and international finance and she has authored numerous professional articles and books. Ms. Stallings has doctorates in economics (Cambridge) and political science (Stanford).

Richard Tan is the Chief Executive Officer and President of the Pacific Millennium Company (PMC), a vertically integrated forestry products company, serving Asian markets, with offices in China, Taiwan Province of China, Hong Kong (China), Malaysia and Thailand. Its Industrial Division operates a paper mill in Hong Kong (China) and corrugated box plants in China. Mr. Tan received an MBA from the University of Southern California.

Paul Wachtel is Research Professor of Economics and Vice-Dean for Program Development at the Stern School of Business, New York University. He was a research associate at the National Bureau of Economic Research and joined NYU in 1972. He is an associate editor of *Japan and the World Economy* and is a senior economic advisor to the East West Institute. Mr. Wachtel holds a Ph.D. from the University of Rochester.

Robert Wade is Professor of Political Science and International Political Economy at Brown University. He has worked as an economist at the World Bank and the Office of Technology Assessment of the United States Congress and has taught at MIT, Princeton University and Sussex University. Mr. Wade's research has focused on institutional aspects of economic development and he has authored numerous articles.

Basil Zavoico is Personal Assistant to the Director of European II Department of IMF. He was previously Resident Representative of IMF in Estonia and a senior economist in the European II Department. Mr. Zavoico has been on the staff of the International Monetary Fund since 1975. He holds a Master's degree in economics from the London School of Economics.

The following contributors are staff members of the Development Policy Analysis Division in the United Nations Department of Economic and Social Affairs:

Henk-Jan Brinkman monitors and analyses economic policy developments in Africa. He has written on such issues as economic adjustment in Africa and human stature as a measure of the standard of living. He is the author of *Explaining Prices in the Global Economy: A Post-Keynesian Model,* which will be published by Edward Elgar in 1999. Mr. Brinkman holds a Ph.D. in economics from the New School for Social Research and a Master's degree in economics from the University of Groningen in the Netherlands.

Leonides A. Buencamino monitors and analyses lending programmes and policies in multilateral development institutions, as well as economic developments in selected countries in Asia and the Caribbean. He holds an MBA from New York University and a Bachelor's degree in economics from the Ateneo de Manila University, Philippines.

Ana L. Cortez has written on issues such as social protection and social security reforms in developing countries, adjustment policies in Latin America and external debt in the developing world. Ms. Cortez holds a Master's degree in economics from Fundação Getúlio Vargas, Brazil.

Simon Cunningham is Chief of the Developed and Transition Economies Section in the International Economic Relations Branch. He has worked since 1976 as an economist in the United Nations Secretariat, contributing to the *World Economic and Social Survey,* the *Report on the World Social Situation* and many Secretariat reports. Mr. Cunningham was educated at the University of Oxford and the University of Edinburgh, from which he received his Ph.D.

Barry Herman is Chief of the International Economic Relations Branch. He joined the United Nations in 1976 and prior to that taught development and international economics at the City University of New York, Dickinson College and the University of Michigan. Mr. Herman holds a Ph.D. in economics from the University of Michigan, an MBA from the University of Chicago, and a Bachelor's degree in mathematics from Columbia University.

Soo-Won Lee was a consultant to the International Economic Relations Branch in 1997-1998, on loan from the Ministry of Finance and Economy of the Republic of Korea. He was previously a visiting researcher at the Korea Institute of Finance in the Republic of Korea. He worked at the Economic Planning Board for 14 years as a director or deputy director. Mr. Lee holds a Master's degree in policy science from the Graduate School of Saitama University in Japan and a degree in business administration from Korea University.

Ann Orr is Chief of the Developing Economies Section in the International Economic Relations Branch. She has worked in the area of structural adjustment and economic reform in the developing countries, with a focus on Asia. Prior to joining the United Nations, she worked at the United States Department of Commerce and was a consultant to the World Bank. Ms. Orr holds a Ph.D. from the University of Pennsylvania.

Alberto Padova monitors and analyses economic policy developments in Latin America and has written on external debt and other international financial issues. Mr. Padova previously worked as an economic analyst in the private sector. He graduated in economics from the University of Venice and holds a Master's degree in economic development from the University of Reading.

Judith Romera monitors and analyses economic developments in Western Europe and covers issues relating to the Economic and Monetary Union of the European Union. Prior to joining the United Nations, she taught economics at the Universitat Autònoma de Barcelona and Universitat Politècnica de Catalunya. Ms. Romera holds a Bachelor's degree in economics from Universitat Autònoma de Barcelona and a Postgraduate degree in advanced economics from Universitat Barcelona, Fundació Bosch i Gimpera.

Krishnan Sharma covers international financial issues and monitors and analyses economic developments in South and South-East Asia. Mr. Sharma previously worked for the Henley Centre for Forecasting in London, where he undertook macroeconomic and financial analysis and specialized in emerging economies. He holds a Master's degree in economics from the University of Sussex.

Wenyan Yang is responsible for monitoring and analyzsing social and economic developments and policy issues in developing and transition economies in South-East and East Asia, and international trade flows, and has contributed to numerous United Nations reports on international economic issues. Ms. Yang holds a Master's degree in economics from New York University and a Bachelor's degree in economics from Peking University.

Index